MULTICULTURAL
HAWAI'I

GARLAND REFERENCE LIBRARY OF SOCIAL SCIENCE
VOLUME 1108

MULTICULTURAL HAWAI'I

THE FABRIC OF A MULTIETHNIC SOCIETY

EDITED BY
MICHAEL HAAS

GARLAND PUBLISHING, INC.
A MEMBER OF THE TAYLOR & FRANCIS GROUP
NEW YORK AND LONDON
1998

Library of Congress Cataloging-in-Publication Data

Multicultural Hawai'i : the fabric of a multiethnic society / edited by
  Michael Haas.
        p.   cm. — (Garland reference library of social science ; v. 1108)
        Includes bibliographical references and index.
        ISBN 0-8153-2377-8 (alk. paper)
        1. Pluralism (Social sciences)—Hawaii. 2. Multiculturalism—Hawaii.
  3. Minorities—Hawaii. 4. Hawaii—Ethnic relations. 5. Hawaii—Social
  conditions.   I. Haas, Michael, 1938–   . II. Series.
  HN79.H3M85   1998
  305.8'009969—dc21   97-30365
                                                                CIP

Printed on acid-free, 250-year-life paper
Manufactured in the United States of America

Contents

Tables

Preface

Arthur Schlesinger's *Disuniting of America* (1991) identified unscholarly excesses in current efforts to reword textbooks used in public education so that certain ethnic groups would be uplifted. But his main objective, to attack multiculturalism as a basic principle, was more ideological than empirical. I found his fear of a balkanized America to be unfounded because, in more than three decades of residence in Hawai'i, I had been enriched by multiculturalism, not "disunited." Accordingly, I looked at the index to his book, only to find that Hawai'i was not cited, and indeed a similar gap appears through most current writing opposed to multiculturalism. I then wrote the venerable scholar, whose other publications are deservedly well respected, to ask why he did not have anything to say about the Aloha State. His honest answer, that he knew little about Hawai'i, prompted me to conceive this book.

If there is to be a debate about increasing or resisting multiculturalism, an obvious theoretical approach is to examine a model. Beyond models, an empirical approach is to study a multicultural society that works. In this volume the authors agree that multiculturalism exists in Hawai'i, and they seek to describe the parameters of multiculturalism within various sectors of society. This descriptive task, in turn, suggests the need for a deeper theoretical understanding of why harmonious multiculturalism exists in Hawai'i, a task in part accomplished within each chapter and in part summarized in the concluding chapter. I am grateful to Praeger Publishers for permission to rework certain portions of my *Institutional Racism: The Case of Hawai'i* (1992) into the chapters that I am contributing to this volume.

The reader will find that the past history of Hawai'i is one of ethnic conflict, with winners and losers, and the present situation in the Aloha

State also is filled with dilemmas and injustice. Hawai'i has not solved all its problems by itself, and I have encouraged the chapter writers to present these dilemmas. What is different about Hawai'i is how solutions to these problems have been and are being pursued. Each chapter weaves different threads together in creating the fabric of a multicultural society.

In addition to the subjects covered in this book, I initially sought essays on housing, interracial marriage, and public health, but not every topic could be included. In editing a multiauthored volume, there were inevitable problems of coordination, and some prospective writers were less conscientious than others, so some drafts unfortunately never made their way to print. In two cases, I regretfully substituted an essay of my own when these sorts of problems emerged. I was further embarrassed by having to refer to my topical essays in the third person in the introduction and conclusion chapters in order to provide parallelism with discussion on the contributions of the other authors.

At this time, I wish to acknowledge the kind assistance of David Estrin in encouraging me to bring this publication to the public, to the contributing authors who have responded to my invitations and challenges, to the Hawai'i Community Foundation, which secured E. B. Black Foundation financing of this book, and to Leslie Lang for professional editorial assistance. Most of all, I am indebted to the people of Hawai'i, past and present.

Michael Haas

MULTICULTURAL
HAWAI'I

CHAPTER 1

Introduction

Michael Haas

THE MONOCULTURAL-MULTICULTURAL DEBATE

First-time visitors to Hawai'i on packaged tours often arrive at Honolulu airport, are greeted with *leis* and music by dark-skinned young people, and are bused to lavish hotels for a week of fun in the sun. They learn about something called the "*aloha* spirit" while on bus tours and absorb the friendliness of the Islands by observing smiling faces and receiving courteous, seemingly deferential treatment. All too many live in this plastic tourist bubble, unaware that there is a complex society behind what may appear to be a gentle façade.

A different Hawai'i is on display a few miles from Honolulu International Airport, where a unique park, known variously as Hawai'i's Plantation Village or Waipahu Cultural Garden Park, adorns the landscape underneath an abandoned sugar mill. The park consists of reconstructed plantation houses that have been furnished by eight major ethnic groups of Hawai'i which, once upon a time, worked side by side in the sugar cane fields. Heritage associations of each group have obtained clothing, cooking implements, photographs, and the like from former plantation workers in order to portray what life was like on the plantations. Represented are exhibits from Chinese, Filipinos, Japanese, Koreans, Native Hawaiians, Okinawans, Portuguese, and Puerto Ricans. The park does not run organized tours on a regular basis from Waikiki hotels; instead, the word spreads in certain circles, and local residents of the Islands are the primary visitors. Often, grandparents tell their grandchildren about how for years they suffered in the open sun for hours without stopping in order to save enough money so that their children could go to college and become, as they have, bankers, corporation executives, teachers, and United States senators. The park provides a window into ethnic history that exists nowhere else in the United States, yet its existence is barely known. As a leaflet provided by the park proclaims, the story behind the village "is the saga of the creation of Hawai'i's unique multicultural society."

While the people of the Islands celebrate their past, a debate is occurring throughout the United States mainland today on the subject of culture, ethnicity, and race. A question in the debate, while California is on the brink of becoming the second state in the union to have a majority of non-Caucasians (Maharidge 1996), is whether the United States should maintain a dominant culture or instead allow itself to become a nation that recognizes the presence of many different cultures. The debate has arisen of late on the U.S. mainland because advocates of multiculturalism have been able to command significant political attention, thus threatening the dominance of monoculturalists and the basic precept of monoculturalism, namely, that a diverse society needs a high degree of cultural unity. In some cases, the debate is a backlash to excesses of certain multiculturalists, who often respond in the debate with various abstract propositions about the virtues of multiculturalism and inherent racism of monoculturalism.

The debate, for a resident of Hawai'i, seems rather shallow. Monoculturalists and multiculturalists argue about abstract macrosociological and normative propositions, but neither side seems willing to present evidence to support its case. Monoculturalists warn of the dangers of a loosely integrated multicultural society in Bosnia, Lebanon, and elsewhere. Multiculturalists, notably those from Asia, proclaim that they represent civilizations that have proved themselves over time and that they are not intending to give up their cultures while residing as citizens of the United States, a land that reinvents its culture every so often.

Meanwhile, the debate between monoculturalism and multiculturalism tends to exclude the one case in the world where multiculturalism has long been regarded as successful. Most monoculturalists and multiculturalists admit that they know little about Hawai'i and, implicitly, that they do not need to know about a multicultural success story to carry on the debate. Monoculturalists can easily brush the example of the fiftieth state aside as an example of exceptionalism, that is, a unique case that has no relevance for the ongoing debate on the U.S. mainland. The absence of attention to Hawai'i on the part of multiculturalists is more baffling, however.

Perhaps the paucity of scholarly analyses of the Aloha State in terms of the monocultural-multicultural debate is the main reason for the tendency for both sides to ignore facts and instead to argue in terms of morality alone.

One motivation for this volume is to provide detailed analyses of diverse sectors of the Aloha State, identifying multicultural approaches to a multiethnic reality. With knowledge of how multiculturalism has sewn together the fabric of the society of Hawai'i, the debate will be better informed about possibilities and realities.

That Hawai'i is an example of a multicultural society is not in dispute. Each author in this volume notes that ethnic groups in the Aloha State take pride in their cultural heritage, speak the language spoken by their ancestors, have developed a unique "local culture," and yet coexist with those who practice a "mainland culture" in the Islands. That Hawai'i is a case of successful multiculturalism is also evidenced by high rates of cross-ethnic intermarriage, a lack of out-group scapegoating, an absence of recent violence along ethnic lines, and a lack of cultural malaise amid diversity. That the fiftieth state has serious economic, political, and social problems is undeniable, but the manner in which they are addressed without overt racism appears exemplary when compared to other parts of the world.

What is problematic is how to characterize the nature of multicultural Hawai'i and how to explain relative success in attaining ethnic harmony. The authors in this volume seek to do both. Three approaches are evident. Some authors sing the praises of the Aloha State with little criticism. Other authors dwell on serious ethnic problems that fester and await resolution. A middle approach is to note that Hawai'i has had both successes and failures in addressing ethnic problems, but the reasons for lack of success are to be found in the nature of the world economy and polity, which limit the ability of Islanders to handle their own affairs.

How has Hawai'i solved problems of ethnic conflict? Are there any lessons or techniques to be learned that can be copied elsewhere? These are more difficult questions, left in all modesty for readers to determine, yet vital if islands in the middle of the Pacific are to play a constructive role in the ongoing monocultural-multicultural debate.

MODELS & THEORIES OF ETHNIC RELATIONS

How do ethnic groups relate to one another in Hawai'i and elsewhere? The variety of answers to this central question tends to focus on conflictual versus cooperative models of interaction. Some models are static, but most are dynamic. Thanks to William Newman (1973), several models have been developed that assign alphabetic letters to different ethnic or racial groups at two distinct time periods, but most schematic representations fail to identify dominant, subordinate, integrated, and segregated groups. Accordingly, in the discussion below, I use capital letters for dominant groups, lowercase letters for subordinate groups, and I bracket segregated groups. Arrows represent transitions between time points (Tables 1.1–1.3).

Nathan Glazer (1982) is the author of one of the most useful static models. According to his formulation, there are three basic models of ethnic and race relations in the United States (Table 1.1). The Southern model is biracial, depicting Caucasians (A) and African Americans (B). The Northern model characterizes all groups as ethnics, including European immigrant groups (A_1, A_2, A_3), African Americans (B), and Puerto Ricans (C). The Western model recognizes the separation of Caucasians (A) in the mainstream, natives of North America (B) on the reservations, and Mexicans (C) in small border towns and *barrios* of the big cities.

TABLE 1.1
Historical Models of Ethnic Diversity

Name of Model	Glazer's Model	Haas's Reformulation
Southern	$A + B$	$A + B \rightarrow -A + B + c \rightarrow [B] + [c]$
Northern	$A_1 + A_2 + A_3 + B + C$	$A + B \rightarrow -A + B_1 + B_2 + B_3 + c + d$
Western	$A + B + C$	$A + E \rightarrow [a] + [B] + [e]$

However, Glazer's models can be embellished with a historical perspective. Natives of North American (A) came first. In the South, Caucasians (B) came next and either exterminated or removed the indigenous peoples; Africans (c) were then imported and eventually segregated. In the North, the aboriginal peoples were first encountered and then liquidated, pushed back, or placed on reservations; European groups (B_1, B_2, B_3) were quickly assimilated, and Glazer believes that the African Americans (c) and Puerto Ricans (d) have faced much less segregation and thus have a chance to rise to the level of Caucasians. In the West, some native peoples (A) managed to survive the conquistadors, *mestizo* Mexicans (E) lived in peaceful coexistence awhile, but non-Hispanic Caucasians (B) arrived later to enforce an enclavization of the two earlier groups.

Newman, in contrast, seeks to characterize alternative policies of ethnic relations. He explicates several dynamic models, to be discussed next (Table 1.2).

For *assimilationists*, the ideal state of affairs is for representatives of various latecoming ethnic groups to adapt to the dominant ethnic group as the price of belonging to a single political and social system. Assimilation can proceed along attitudinal, behavioral, cultural, marital, or political dimensions (Gordon 1964). Successful assimilation occurs whenever an ethnic group voluntarily abandons its own culture to adopt another culture instead; forced assimilation tends to be resisted and is generally unsuccessful. The Han Chinese were generally successful in Sinification, but Russification failed. Assimilation presupposes that one group is superior to all others, so the model can be reformulated as a capitulation by subordinate groups.

For *amalgamationists*, a multiethnic society should encourage a new culture that incorporates the best elements of all cultures within a single country. The concept of the "smelting pot" or "melting pot" means that all ethnic groups lose their distinctiveness in order to adopt a new culture that unites diversity within a single national state (Crévecoeur 1782, quoted in Schlesinger 1991; Zangwill 1914). Thus, efforts to promote "Americanization" at the beginning of the twentieth century were viewed as more progressive than the Anglo-conformity advocated by assimilationists. The amalgamation of French culture from the separate cultures of Alsace, Bréton, Burgundy, and other provinces may be viewed as a success story. The forging of a *mestizo* society in Mexico is another example of successful amalgamation. In the United States, however, the Anglo group sought to define "American culture," thus turning the amalgamationist goal into an assimilationist reality unacceptable to latecoming ethnic groups (Novak 1971).

TABLE 1.2
Normative Models of Ethnic Diversity

Name of Model	Newman's Model	Haas's Reformulation
Assimilation	$A + B + C \rightarrow A$	$A + b + c \rightarrow A$
Amalgamation	$A + B + C \rightarrow D$	$a + b + c \rightarrow D$
Separatist pluralism	$[A] + [B] + [C] \rightarrow [A] + [B] + [C]$	$[A] + [B] + [C] \rightarrow [A] + [B] + [C]$
Segregated pluralism	$A + B + C \rightarrow [A] + [B] + [C]$	$A + b + c \rightarrow [A] + [b] + [c]$
Bifurcated pluralism	$A + B + C \rightarrow A_1 + B_1 + C_1$	$A + b + c \rightarrow A_1 + b_1 + c_1$

The main alternative to assimilationism and amalgamationism is *pluralism*, namely, a coexistence of diverse ethnic groups. Pluralism, however, has many variants. Newman (1973, 54) distinguishes between segregated and integrated forms of pluralism, but his "integrated pluralism" assumes that various ethnic groups will live in segregated enclaves within big cities and small towns. Accordingly, I have identified three types of pluralism.

Separatist pluralism describes a nation of nations, the utopia that Horace Kallen (1915, 1924) sought to promote in the United States. When ethnic groups voluntarily prefer to live rather far apart in semiautonomous regions of a country, ethnic conflict can be minimized, as in multiethnic Switzerland, but the separatist pluralism of the former Yugoslavia is a counterexample. As Newman (1973, 56) points out, the United States had a degree of separatist pluralism when Germans chose to concentrate themselves in Pennsylvania, Dutch and Swedes in the Hudson and Delaware valleys, and Norwegians in Minnesota and Wisconsin. In later years, the American population shifted, obliterating most residues of this former separatist pluralism.

Segregated pluralism exists when the separation between groups is involuntary. During the era of slavery, African Americans and Caucasians lived and worked in close juxtaposition, as did Chinese and others who built the transcontinental railroad. When slavery ended and railroads linked the Atlantic with the Pacific, Caucasians enforced separation in various ways, from establishing separate drinking fountains to restricting residence of subordinate groups to the "other side of the tracks." Much of the civil rights movement in the United States consisted of efforts to end the many forms of overt segregation, though much housing segregation remains. South Africa, which instituted apartheid in 1948, began to desegregate in the 1980s.

A *bifurcated pluralism* exists when ethnic groups adapt to a monocultural mainstream in public, yet maintain a strong ethnic identification in private life. According to the "modified pluralism" of Nathan Glazer and Daniel Moynihan (1963), immigrant groups do not retain their root cultures intact within the United States; instead, they retain some but not all traditions from the old country while developing new traditions. The invention of the "Irish-American" hyphenated culture, thus, is viewed as a way of avoiding assimilation through modest assertions of cultural pride that do not challenge mainstream politicoeconomic control. For example, bifurcated pluralism is manifest in the form of ethnic bloc voting for centrist candidates.

TABLE 1.3
Other Models of Ethnic Diversity

Name of Model	Components
Genocide	$A + B \rightarrow -B \rightarrow A$
Colonialism	$A \rightarrow A + b + c$
Independence	$A + b + c \rightarrow A$
	$\rightarrow B$
Migration	$A + b + c \rightarrow A$
	$\rightarrow B + c + D$
Ethnogenesis	$A \rightarrow A + b + c$
Tiered pluralism	$A + b + c \rightarrow A + [B] + c$
Multiculturalism	$A + b + c \rightarrow A + B + C$

Newman leaves out several models (Table 1.3). *Genocide* is the elimination of one or more ethnic groups, as in the American holocaust of Native North Americans (Stannard 1992). *Colonialism* exists when elites of a country power go overseas to dominate previously autonomous peoples. Colonial rule is overcome by reversing the process, whether by achieving *independence,* as in the breakup of empire, or by *migration,* in which various peoples leave one state to join another where they are treated with more dignity, sometimes as the new irredentist majority (B), or as a refugee minority (c) under the protection of a previously dominant group (D).

Ethnogenesis is the origin of new ethnic groups from older ones. Gregory Bateson (1936) refers to this process as "schismogenesis," which occurs when feuds within preliterate extended family groups develop into separate identities. Those who lament multiculturalism and multilingualism often argue that former social unity is being torn asunder by elitist efforts at ethnogenesis (cf. Schlesinger 1991).

When some affluent but separated groups exist between dominant and subordinate groups, *tiered pluralism* exists. The rise of East Asian ethnics from subordinate roles to economic affluence within ethnic enclaves but not on an equal basis with dominant groups has been conceptualized as possible because of a "split labor market," "middle-man minorities," "internal colonialism," and similar formulations (Bonacich 1980; Portes and Manning 1986; Carmichael and Hamilton 1967). Tiered pluralism is a more generic version of the concept of African Americans as a caste apart from Caucasians in the traditional South, where African Americans could rise no higher than to middle-class status (Dollard 1949).

The most important model left out of previous formulations is *multiculturalism*, a situation that exists when ethnic groups retain their distinctiveness culturally, even as hyphenated Americans, but are incorporated into the mainstream, socioculturally and politicoeconom-ically. In a multicultural society, various ethnic groups recognize that they are integral parts of a more encompassing whole yet insist that the contributions of their cultures to the larger society must be recognized. Successful multiculturalism exists when a dominant group accepts diversity as of positive benefit to the society, gives up total dominance, and allows formerly subordinate groups to enter the mainstream, though not all groups may achieve upward social mobility. Hawai'i, rather than serving as an exemplar of the amalgamationist melting pot, is portrayed in the following chapters as a multicultural society.

All the above taxonomies have ideological and utopian elements, but they are mere superficial descriptions of intergroup relations. What is of more interest is to determine the underlying forces that propel a society toward one model or another, toward cooperative rather than conflictual relationships. Why do some ethnic groups assimilate? Why do some dominant ethnic groups amalgamate? Why do some forms of pluralism lead toward bifurcation, separatism, or segregation? How is a truly multicultural society possible? The processes identified by the arrows in the diagrams need to be specified.

Several scholars have attempted to classify alternative theories of ethnic relations. Crawford Young (1993), in a recent review, identifies primordialism, instrumentalism, and social constructionism as basic types. Joe and Clairece Booher Feagin (1996, chap. 2) distinguish between theories of order and theories of power-conflict. In relation to Hawai'i, I have elsewhere identified several other theories (Haas 1992, chap. 3). A brief statement of the most prominent theories appears below.

One of the earliest theories of ethnic relations may be called *social distance theory* (cf. Haas 1992, chap. 3). For Robert Park (1928), ethnic relations pass through four phases—competition, conflict, cooperation, and accommodation. For Milton Gordon (1964), there are seven stages: acculturation, structural assimilation, amalgamation, identification, absence of prejudice, absence of discrimination, and absence of value and power-conflict. The starting point of these cycles is migration, and the end point is assimilation; but the social dynamic is the spread of information. Social distance theories assume that ethnic groups keep apart out of ignorance; if they would intermingle, they would abandon their prejudices and treat one another equally. Social distance theorists, thus, seek primarily to explain the existence of prejudice; they argue for social integration as a key that will unlock harmonious ethnic relations.

Another important theorist is Talcott Parsons, whose *functionalism* argued that social systems require the performance of four functions—goal attainment, adaptation, integration, and pattern maintenance. The pressure for assimilation, thus, is viewed as fulfilling the requirement of order within society, whereas pressures for multiculturalism strain the capabilities of a system for equilibrium. Since ethnic identification is ascriptive, Parsons felt that ethnic conflicts need to be managed with care in order to maintain an orderly society; although he agreed that African Americans should not be barred from voting, he feared that social order would break down if change were too rapid (Parsons 1969, chap. 11). Parsonian theory focused on the need for social equilibrium and sought to identify causes of social disorder.

Mass society theory represents the other side of the coin from functionalism, looking at the unmet needs of ordinary people more than the needs and prerogatives of those who hold power. According to the theory of mass society, as developed initially by Émile Durkheim

(1893), industrial society abolishes traditional agricultural jobs and creates factory employment, thus drawing workers to the cities for employment; due to this rapid social change, recent arrivals in the city lack family and church ties, and the newcomers engage in deviant behavior, which in turn is resisted by long-term residents and their agents, the police. A similar transition is now occurring from industrial to post-industrial society. In both cases, the assertion of ethnicity may be seen as an effort by those who are isolated from established social networks to find a form of identification that serves to link them with civil society (Greeley 1974; Geschwender 1978; Olzak 1992). For example, the exploitation of workers who lack supportive unions today stimulates ethnogenesis and ethnic struggles as available methods for combating the intolerable conditions of mass society. For mass society theory, the principal phenomenon to explain is social deviance, that is, such anomic behavior as racial violence.

Prejudice and discrimination enable privileged groups to stay on top, but what happens when prejudice fades but discrimination persists? *Racial equalitarianism* is the theory that any inequalities between ethnic groups are artificial, due to various forms of institutional discrimination (Haas 1992, 67–69). The American dream of upward mobility on the basis of merit would be realized if all ethnic groups were treated nondiscriminatorily, according to racial equalitarianists. William Ryan (1976) has definitively identified how seemingly race-neutral policies, practices, and procedures in fact discriminate against minorities. For example, test scores were first developed as an objective measure of intelligence so that college admissions officials would admit those most likely to succeed. The tests, however, were standardized on mainstream Caucasians, and applications for admission from outside the mainstream were disproportionately turned down. Unprejudiced college admission bureaucrats, powerless to change admission policies, were thus forced into making discriminatory decisions. The aim of affirmative action, accordingly, is to identify artificial barriers to nondiscriminatory treatment and thereby to determine how to dismantle institutional racism. Presumably, affirmative action advances by self-studies of unequal results, which are traced back to artificial barriers, but when institutions fail to act in a progressive manner, civil rights enforcement is necessary. Social science studies are then needed as evidence of discrimination, whether intended or inadvertent. However, affirmative action has engendered considerable controversy because advantaged groups fear that new procedures tilt the balance in the direction of minorities who are disadvantaged by institutional racism. As Milton Gordon (1981) puts it, the color-blind theory is a model of "liberal pluralism" that undertakes remedies to proven cases of discrimination, whereas race-conscious corrections in policies, practices, and procedures to avoid discrimination constitute a "corporate pluralism" that appears to be "reverse discrimination."

Racial equalitarianism was invented to account for unnecessary ethnic inequalities, but many prejudiced observers of ethnic relations believe that some ethnic and racial groups are more meritorious. Those who believe that inequality is inevitable tend to subscribe to *primordial theories*, which argue that there are biological reasons why members of ethnic groups associate with, cooperate with, or dominate members of other ethnic groups. Biological superiority in matters mental and physical is central to social Darwinism, which views the struggle between the races as vital to the otherwise precarious survival of *homo sapiens* (Hofstadter 1944). More recently, ethnicity is said to be a part of the genetic code (Shaw and Wong 1989), and the need for ethnic identity is posited as an instinctual impulse to find a sense of belonging (Van Den Berghe 1975), consciousness (Barth 1969), meaning (Geertz 1973; Keyes 1981), or simply self-interest (Gordon 1981). The primordialist perspective posits that ethnic identity cannot erode, that a color-blind post-ethnic society will never emerge. When ethnic identities are challenged, we should expect ethnic conflict more than ethnic cooperation. Insofar as it is human nature for humans to need some sort of identity in order to survive within the safety of a group, conflict is inevitable. Primordialists primarily seek to explain the persistence of ethnic identifications.

Instrumentalism (I prefer the term *pragmatism*) views ethnic identities and ethnic conflict or cooperation as a function of competition for rewards. Pierre Van Den Berghe (1967) once argued that cooperative ethnic relations are increasingly required as economies shift from plantation feudalism to industrial production to post-industrial societies, but he is now a primordialist. William Newman (1973, chap. 4) has postulated that conflict is viewed as normal because societies are so organized that there is a struggle for competing resources in which ethnic group membership provides either a privileged position to protect or a subordinate role to overcome. The extent of assimilation, amalgamation, or pluralism is thus a function of material rewards and punishments within a polity and a society. As Young (1993, 22) has noted, instrumentalists seek "to identify the political factors which might activate it, to discover the cultural entrepreneurs who supplied its doctrine, and the activists who exploited such solidarities." Instrumentalists (pragmatists) include both Marxists and rational choice theorists, as material realities are assumed to determine behavior (cf. Feagin and Feagin 1996, 44–47). From a pragmatist perspective, ethnic conflict and cooperation is primarily a matter of the pocketbook.

The final theory is known as *social constructionism*. The central thesis is that ethnicity is a fiction. The primary reason for classifying individuals by ethnicity and race, according to Michael Omi and Howard Winant (1986), is to enable Caucasians to discriminate against non-Caucasians. Thus, calculating elites invent a pseudorational discourse in order to immobilize the masses. Although social constructionists focus on strategies used by elites to disempower masses, they could just as easily focus on efforts to mobilize the masses to achieve decolonization, such as struggles of anticolonial nationalists to overthrow imperial oppressors (Fanon 1961; Marable 1986; cf. Tilly 1978). Whereas racial equalitarianists seek to undo the effects of institutional discrimination within the framework of civil rights norms, social constructionists explain ethnic tensions in terms of larger political agendas.

Although the various theories attempt to account for social processes relating to ethnic relations, none so far has a complete explanation. Nevertheless, Hawai'i has moved from a monoethnic past before intensive outside contact to the present period of multiethnic multiculturalism. How this relatively peaceful transition occurred is of considerable interest to the world. After describing past and present realities in the chapters to follow, the task of the concluding chapter will be to see which theory provides the best explanation.

CONTRIBUTIONS TO THIS VOLUME

In inviting a large number of writers to address various aspects of multicultural Hawai'i, I expected that the essays would provide different assessments, as one might expect in a multicultural society. The topics cover a broad range, involving family life, work, and recreation, all of which are interconnected, as the perspicacious reader will soon see. Since some authors pleaded for a historical exposition to avoid duplication of efforts, I was drafted into writing an introductory history (Chapter 2) that contains facts but not explanations. The invited essays, written in isolation from one another, aim to fill pieces of a jigsaw puzzle, but inevitably some pieces remain.

The center of gravity of Chapter 3, by Derek Bickerton (Language and Language Contact), is in the late nineteenth and early twentieth centuries, when the Hawaiian language fell from primacy, to be replaced not by English but by Hawaiian Creole English, which consists of an amalgam of words from several languages and thus has the necessary ingredients to be called a full-fledged language. The essay provides a fascinating discussion to inform those who fear or support multilingualism.

In Chapter 4 (The Media), Helen Geracimos Chapin covers the same historical eras to identify how newspapers, radio, and television developed in response to language pluralism. As she indicates, the media in Hawai'i are so diverse that there are more radio stations in Honolulu, a city of just less than one million, than in metropolitan Dallas, which has a population of some 3.5 million. Her discussion carries Bickerton's essay on multilingualism one step forward.

Cultural diversity is richly portrayed in Chapter 5 (Music), where Anthony Palmer notes that people in the Islands attend a wide variety of Asian, Native Hawaiian, and Western musical performances. Although music plays a central role in the lives of those who seek to preserve their cultural heritage, the focus of this chapter is on the way in which consumers of musical performances in Hawai'i are rewarded by the fact that segregated ethnic enclaves do not exist in music. Members of various ethnic groups seem so encouraged by musical diversity that they cross over to enjoy and perform the musics of cultures other than their own without being seen as "traitors" to their own culture. Meanwhile, what began as Native Hawaiian music both has been rediscovered and has syncretically been transformed into a modern idiom.

In Chapter 6 (Literature) Rodney Morales encounters a paradox. In the 1970s, young writers sought to identify a distinctly Island genre of literature that would depart from mainstream forms, and Bamboo Ridge Press was formed. Some two decades later, the movement has been attacked as a new "neocolonial" mainstream that is inattentive to politics, notably efforts of Native Hawaiians to achieve greater control over their own community concerns. The Literary ferment does much to unmask a debate now taking place in Hawai'i, where some non-Caucasians who favor the socioeconomic status quo in the 1990s also control the political establishment, while other non-Caucasians have been left behind. The essay, which may interest Islanders more than mainlanders, provides a window into how interethnic tensions are expressed and handled in the Aloha State, thereby demonstrating that multiculturalism does not entail Caucasian marginalization, as all ethnic groups have inner disagreements.

Despite some ethnic rivalry in literature, the people of the Aloha State remain culturally resilient, as indicated by Yasumasa Kuroda, who in Chapter 7 (Public Opinion and Cultural Values) seeks to identify values that distinguish local residents of Hawai'i from outsiders, especially those from the U.S. mainland. Kuroda also asks whether there is a mosaic of cultures or instead a tendency toward assimilation, based on a survey of many attitudes and values of registered voters in Honolulu. Readers who fear attitudinal balkanization in a multicultural society should pay special attention to this chapter.

In Chapter 8 (Politics), Michael Haas shows that political power, once held by Native Hawaiians, was seized by the economically dominant Caucasians until the middle of the twentieth century, when a more multiethnic politics emerged. Although Japanese gradually took control, politics in recent years has become increasingly multiethnic, even nonethnic. The analysis is particularly relevant to Caucasian mainlanders who fear the loss of political power as multiculturalism advances.

In Chapter 9 (Organized Labor), Edward Beechert also presents a broad historical sweep. He shows how subsistence agriculture, as traditionally practiced by Native Hawaiians, was converted into wage labor, but amassing profits on the sugar cane plantations required the importation of many workers from around the world. In due course these plantation workers formed a united front in a part of the United States that is more highly unionized than almost any other. Multiethnic recruitment in Hawai'i, though opposed for many years by unions on the mainland, was vital for the success of the trade-union movement in the Islands, and ultimately served as a model for the mainland.

Chapter 10 (Social Stratification), by Jonathan Okamura, presents a less sanguine view of the future of the fiftieth state. Although Chinese and Japanese rose to a position of near equality with Caucasians by the end of the twentieth century, they leapfrogged over Native Hawaiians in so doing. Filipinos and Samoans have not experienced the success of the lighter-skinned East Asians in regard to income and occupational achievements, and their educational attainments do not predict better times ahead. The chapter serves as an antidote to those infected with Pollyanna notions of the inevitability of social mobility after the waning of overt prejudice.

Explanations for social and economic pessimism often point to the school system of Hawai'i. In Chapter 11 (Elementary and Secondary Education), Michael Haas examines how Native Hawaiians were enthusiastic about Western education, and the Kingdom of Hawai'i was the first country in the world to adopt universal free public education in the nineteenth century; yet Native Hawaiians have been left behind in the twentieth century. Today, as earlier, language issues are central to an understanding of how the schools serve minorities. The chapter examines the role of bilingual education, yet another bone of contention between monoculturalists and multiculturalists.

In Chapter 12 (Higher Education), Michael Haas documents ethnic disparities and efforts by the University of Hawai'i (UH), the largest institution of higher learning in the Islands, to promote greater diversity. Staffed at the top levels primarily by mainland-born personnel, UH may be one of the least multiethnic institutions analyzed in this volume. Efforts of the multiethnic legislature and student body in seeking to localize the university without a backlash from faculty or Caucasian students plays a central role in the analysis.

We are often led to believe that those at the bottom of the social ladder tend to engage in criminal behavior. In Chapter 13 (Crime and Justice), A. Didrick Castberg computes ethnic correlates of perpetrators and victims of crimes, and thereafter tries to explain disparities by noting the ethnic composition of personnel at each stage of the criminal justice system, from arrest to sentencing and parole. Although the prisons are dominated by certain ethnic groups, Castberg searches in vain for an explanation based on racial prejudice.

Macroeconomic concerns are analyzed by Ibrahim Aoudé, who in Chapter 14 (Political Economy) links the globalization of the world economy to the failure of certain ethnic groups, notably Filipinos and

Native Hawaiians, to achieve the upward mobility attained in earlier decades by Chinese, Japanese, and Koreans. Aoudé is profoundly pessimistic about the future of Hawai'i's economy, in which the gap between rich and poor is increasing.

Where is the Aloha State headed, and how can the multiculturalism of Hawai'i be explained? Here, a diverse volume requires a summation (Chapter 15). The aim of Chapter 15 (Conclusion) is to specify the Aloha State's model of ethnic relations, based on the raw materials of the various chapters, and to ascertain which theoretical explanation best accounts for the complexity of multicultural Hawai'i.

DEFINITIONAL CLARIFICATIONS

Before examining each chapter, the reader should be aware of some ambiguities and caveats in regard to ethnic groups in Hawai'i, especially statistics for the various groups. First of all, half the population born nowadays has a mixed ethnic heritage, yet generalizations and statistics about ethnicity presuppose distinct ethnic groups. For decades, the federal census applied the "one drop of blood rule," whereby a person with any non-Caucasian blood was considered "colored" regardless of skin color; in the 1900 census conducted in the Territory of Hawai'i, for example, the "colored" population was divided into Chinese, Indians, Japanese, and Negroes. On the U.S. mainland, this rule generally enabled census workers to classify persons with one drop of African blood as "Negro" (the Spanish word for "black"), even though a person's biological ancestry might include some combination of Asian, Caucasian, and/or Native North American parentage. Where there was confusion, the census worker classified a mixed-race person according to the predominant race of the community in which the person resided; the assumption was that most individuals lived in racially segregated societies. In Territorial Hawai'i, this rule resulted in separate counts for "Asiatic Hawaiians" and "Caucasian Hawaiians," a distinction that was dropped in 1940. In 1960, the federal census for the State of Hawai'i, as elsewhere, first allowed ethnic self-identification; if a person reported several ancestries, only the first was recorded. Individuals unable to give any answer to a self-identification question were assigned the ethnic background of the person's father. From 1980, the race of the mother was taken to be definitive, in view of so many single-parent families with absent fathers.

Within Hawai'i, however, the state government's Department of Health has conducted an annual sample survey of health conditions, with a question about ethnicity. Individuals are asked to select either a single ethnic identity or to state, if they wish, that they are of mixed ancestry. Those of mixed ethnicity, in turn, are asked to provide information on all four grandparents. If one of the grandparents has part-Native Hawaiian ancestry, then the classification is "part-Hawaiian." Most researchers currently aggregate pure (*piha*) with part-Hawaiians (*hapa*) in enumerating statistics about Native Hawaiians. Differences in definitions, thus, are crucial (Table 1.4).

TABLE 1.4
Ethnic Composition of Hawai'i from Two Sources, 1990 (in percent)

Ethnic Group	U.S. Census	Hawai'i Health Survey
African American	2.4	1.5
Caucasian	31.4	24.1
Chinese	6.2	4.7
Filipino	15.2	11.4
Hawaiian	12.2	.8
Japanese	22.8	20.4
Korean	2.2	1.1
Puerto Rican	2.3	.3
Samoan	1.4	.3
Mixed	NA	35.5
part-Hawaiian	NA	18.0
other mixed	NA	17.5

Key: NA = not available
Note: Columns sum to 100 percent when all other groups are included.
The figure for "Caucasian" represents non-Hispanic Caucasians.
Source: Hawai'i (1994b, 37); U.S. Census (1993, 7).

These definitions also affect Filipinos in a peculiar way. In the federal census, those tracing their parentage to the Philippines are counted as Filipinos. In actuality, many Filipinos came to the United States with some Chinese or Spanish ancestry. In many cases, those whom the federal census counts as Filipinos will be classified as "Mixed, Other than Part-Hawaiian" in the Hawai'i sample survey because they respond "Filipino Spanish Chinese" when asked about their ethnicity. As for those of pure Chinese ancestry who move to

Hawai'i from the Philippines, they could self-identify as Filipinos, be classified in the federal census as Chinese, and yet be counted in the Hawai'i sample survey as "Mixed" if they say "Chinese Filipino." For 1990, the federal census reports that 25.5 percent of the population claims multiple ancestries (U.S. Census 1993, 27), but these include such combinations as Irish-Germans, whereas the State of Hawai'i (1994b, 37) reports that mixed persons constitute 35.5 percent of the population of the Islands.

Yet another peculiarity about ethnicity in the Islands is how to count members of the ethnic group that is dominant on the U.S. mainland, usually known as Caucasians or "whites." When the first white-faced outsiders visited the Hawaiian Islands, the term *haole* (without breath) was applied to refer to these strangers, as they could not speak the Hawaiian language. Over time, the verbal association between *haoles* and Caucasians stuck. Thus, when Chinese took up residence early in the nineteenth century, they were not called *haoles* even though they did not speak Hawaiian. However, not all Caucasians are considered *haoles*. When Portuguese plantation workers arrived, they were classified by their country of origin, Portugal; since they were laborers, Portuguese did not have the same social standing as *haoles*, who were of American or Northern European origin. Small numbers of Germans and Norwegians were also recruited as plantation workers, but they quickly left the sugar cane fields and became indistinguishable from *haoles*, unlike Portuguese who remained at work as plantation foremen. Later, Puerto Ricans and Spanish arrived in Hawai'i, and they were counted separately in statistical compilations of agencies of the territorial government, but they were considered "Caucasian" or "white" in federal statistics.

The definition of "Hawai'i resident" is also problematic. The military population accounts for as much as 9 percent of the total Island workforce today. State statistics, however, exclude all military, who usually retain residency elsewhere and thus do not vote in local elections (U.S. Census 1993, 59). Some 17.7 percent of all Caucasians at work in the fiftieth state are in the military, thereby skewing federal statistics in relation to other ethnic groups. Thus, low-paid service personnel contribute significantly to lowering the average income for Caucasians, compared to other groups. Similarly, 55.7 percent of employed African Americans in Hawai'i are in the military.

At least one more oddity remains regarding ethnicity in the Islands. Okinawans are not ethnically Japanese, yet most entered Hawai'i as plantation workers with Japanese passports. Today, many Okinawans are trying to reclaim their separate ethnic identity, and statistics may ultimately reflect a distinct group of Okinawans. However, a considerable number of Okinawans married Japanese over the years. Their children were considered Japanese, not mixed in ancestry, so it is unlikely that Okinawans will emerge as numerically significant. Still, the Okinawan Heritage Association is reviving interest in Okinawan culture, and the association has an exhibit at Waipahu Cultural Garden Park.

THE CHALLENGE

The recent reassertion of Okinawan identity suggests a major theme to be pursued in future chapters. The Hawai'i described in this volume is a complex society that is in flux. The reader will learn about the various multicultural parameters of life in Hawai'i in the various chapters, but what is elusive is the search for reasons why the Aloha State can manage ethnic tensions with more success than elsewhere. The reality of contented multiculturalism despite many socioeconomic problems beguiles many social observers, who nonetheless can readily identify common threads that bind together a complex society into a single tapestry.

CHAPTER 2

A Brief History

Michael Haas

EARLY VISITORS TO HAWAI'I

More than a thousand years ago, a hardy, seafaring Polynesian people set sail in the South Pacific for an unknown land. After arriving in the Hawaiian archipelago, they developed a unique culture and language. In due course, a class of *ali'i* (nobility) divided up the land, imposing hierarchical control over *maka'ainana* (commoners), who cultivated food and developed fishing grounds sufficient to feed a population that increased to at least 300,000 and possibly to 800,000 inhabitants by the mid-1700s (Stannard 1989).

The first Westerners to arrive were explorers on Spanish ships (Haas 1991). In 1527, one of the three vessels in an expedition by Alvaro de Saavedra was shipwrecked; two survivors made their way to Hawai'i and intermarried with the local population (Fornander 1880, ii–106). Madrid evidently saw no reason to colonize the archipelago, which lay between its larger prizes, México and the Philippines.

When England's Captain James Cook arrived at Kaua'i in 1778, more than two centuries after the Spanish first appeared, he named the archipelago the Sandwich Islands after his benefactor, the Earl of Sandwich. In 1779, on a return visit, he landed at the island of Hawai'i, but he found himself in an ongoing civil war. Cook was killed while trying to take a chief hostage in order to retrieve a small ship hijacked by several Native Hawaiian warriors.

Unlike previous visitors, the English were eager to expand their commerce. Trading ships soon began to dock in ports for rest and supplies. For the route from Canada to Australia, Hawai'i was in a strategic location. George Vancouver, who sailed to Hawai'i on several occasions in the late eighteenth century, was astonished when one of the chiefs, named Kamehameha, sought an alliance with Britain so as to prevail in a civil war with rival chiefs on the various islands. Kamehameha even offered to cede the island of Hawai'i to Britain, and although the Union Jack went up in 1794, London was more concerned with European matters, and the flag soon came down (Kuykendall 1938, 41).

KINGDOM OF HAWAI'I

By 1795, Kamehameha I unified the Hawaiian Islands under a single political regime. As contact with the artifacts of Western civilization whetted the appetite of Kamehameha to purchase fine clothing and instruments of modern technology, the *ali'i* followed suit. To obtain Western commodities of various sorts, including weapons, Kamehameha agreed to supply British merchant ships with sandalwood, in demand within China, and the Native Hawaiian people worked long and hard hours to provide the treasured resource. Foreign traders offered credit to the monarchy as an advance on the purchase of sandalwood logs. When the sandalwood forest was exhausted, the creditors called in their loans of $200,000, which resulted in onerous taxes on the people (Kuykendall 1938, 91–92). The commerce-minded *haoles* soon controlled the economy of the archipelago (Kent 1983, chap. 1). After two Russian ships visited Kaua'i in 1804, during the reign of Catherine the Great, small Russian trading posts were established on Kaua'i, but the venture was abandoned in 1817.

After sandalwood, the principal industry was to service whaling ships and their crews, who docked in port from the 1830s. As trade boomed, the *haole* population increased (Table 2.1). More Western contact meant that new diseases were introduced, but practical measures of public health to cope with various epidemics were unknown; the native population fell from 300,000 or more in 1778 to 142,050 by 1823 and 71,000 by 1853 (Nordyke 1989, 178).

Missionaries, primarily from New England, began arriving in Hawai'i during the 1820s. When Kamehameha I died in 1819, his favorite queen, Ka'ahumanu, persuaded the new king to decree an end of the *kapu* (taboo) system of religious restrictions, which had been violated with impunity by the crews of foreign ships without the dire consequences assumed by the native faith. The people were seeking a new creed when the Christians arrived, and there were mass baptisms in

TABLE 2.1
Population of Hawai'i by Ethnic Group, 1778-1990

Year	Total	Hawaiian	Caucasian	Chinese	Japanese	Black	Filipino	Korean	Puerto Rican	Samoan	Vietnamese	Guamanian
1778	300	300 (100)										
1853	73	71 (97)	2 (2)	–(–)								
1860	70	67 (96)	2 (3)	1 (1)								
1866	63	59 (93)	2 (4)	2 (2)			–(–)					
1872	57	52 (91)	3 (5)	2 (4)								
1878	58	48 (82)	4 (7)	6 (10)								
1884	81	44 (55)	17 (21)	18 (23)	–(–)							
1890	90	41 (45)	19 (21)	17 (19)	13 (14)							
1896	109	40 (36)	22 (21)	22 (20)	24 (22)							
1900	154	38 (24)	29 (19)	26 (17)	61 (40)	–(–)		–(–)				
1910	192	39 (20)	44 (23)	22 (11)	80 (42)	1 (–)	2 (1)	5 (2)	5 (3)			
1920	256	42 (16)	55 (21)	24 (9)	109 (43)	–(–)	21 (8)	5 (2)	6 (2)			
1930	368	51 (14)	80 (22)	27 (7)	140 (38)	1 (–)	63 (17)	6 (2)	7 (2)			
1940	423	64 (15)	112 (27)	29 (7)	158 (37)	–(–)	53 (12)	7 (2)	8 (2)			
1950	500	86 (17)	124 (25)	33 (7)	185 (37)	3 (1)	61 (12)	7 (1)	10 (2)			
1960	633	102 (16)	202 (32)	38 (6)	203 (32)	5 (1)	69 (11)	NA	NA			
1970	774	133 (17)	255 (33)	52 (4)	207 (27)	8 (1)	95 (12)	7 (1)	4 (1)			
1980	930	175 (19)	245 (26)	56 (5)	218 (24)	17 (1)	134 (14)	11 (2)	7 (1)	11 (1)	3 (–)	2 (–)
1990	1108	205 (19)	263 (24)	51 (5)	222 (24)	27 (2)	168 (15)	12 (1)	3 (–)	15 (1)	5 (1)	2 (–)

Key: NA = not available; – = less than 1,000; (–) = less than 1 percent.

Note: Figures are in 000s. Parenthesized figures are percentages of the civilian and military population, and add to 100 horizontally when other ethnic groups are included. For 1778, Stannard (1989) claims 800,000. Figures report U.S. Census data to 1960; because of redefinitions of ethnic categories, the years 1970-1990 are based on the State of Hawai'i Health Surveillance Survey except for blacks, Filipinos (many of whom were improperly classified as "mixed"), and Guamanians and Vietnamese (who were not counted in the Hawai'i survey). "Hawaiian" figures include persons with any Native Hawaiian ancestry. "White" figures include Portuguese, Puerto Ricans, Spanish, and other Caucasians.

Source: Lind (1967, 28); Nordyke (1989, 178-79, 183); Hawai'i (1993-94, 37); U.S. Census (1993, 7).

the 1830s (Meller 1958b, 796). The missionaries believed that Christian teaching insisted that good people wear considerable clothing to protect the modesty of their bodies, and they undertook to dismantle the Hawaiian polytheistic religion as idolatrous. Although they introduced public health services, ostensibly to save the indigenous population from extinction, the Native Hawaiian population continued to decline. When many missionaries decided to stay in Hawai'i rather than to return to the U.S. mainland, the American Board of Missions could not support the growing missionary community. By 1837, because of a recession in the United States, the Board began to cut off financial support, so the missionaries had to become more economically self-supporting. Some embarked on commercial ventures; others became government workers, but they had less influence in the political arena than the traders for most of the century (Meller 1958b).

British interests were dominant in Hawai'i up to the 1830s (Stevens 1945, 14).[1] In February 1843, the commander of a British ship forced the Hawaiian king to grant powers to a British commission, but in July, when London learned of the daring move, the effort to claim a British colony was disavowed. In 1840, the kingdom adopted a British-style constitution. References to the "Sandwich Islands" ended that year, since the constitution was proclaimed on behalf of the "Hawaiian Islands" (Clement 1980). Most outsiders concluded that there was little of economic value in Hawai'i (Bradley 1942, 39–52); the imperial powers could obtain all they wanted from Hawai'i without the inconvenience of having to govern the country. Britain and France agreed in November 1843 that Hawai'i should remain independent; their entente on this matter, formalized by a joint communiqué, was soon accepted by U.S. President John Tyler, who extended the Monroe Doctrine to the archipelago (Geschwender 1982, 195; Stevens 1945, 18–20). The ruling monarchs, who wanted to avoid being gobbled up by imperial powers, trusted the early missionaries, who did good works but initially took no plunder, asking them to serve as cabinet ministers and in other supporting roles so that the kingdom could more easily govern itself in a manner that foreigners expected. Before taking up their official posts, the Americans acquired Hawaiian citizenship.

In 1802, a Chinese merchant decided to mill sugar cane, indigenous to the Islands. The land proved eminently suitable for large-scale cultivation, and by 1836 the first major plantation opened, located at Koloa, Kaua'i. To develop a more extensive sugar cane industry, however, *haole* traders could not obtain a sizable foreign bank loan, since they lacked collateral. Land was not for sale in traditional Hawai'i; it was held in common on behalf of the people by the monarchs. An 1841 law allowed *ali'i* to lease land to foreigners for up to fifty-five years, but this did not satisfy bankers in the United States, who required transferable assets. Accordingly, *haole* advisers prevailed on the king to introduce a system of private property. Under the terms of the so-called Great *Mahele* of 1848, the land was divided as follows: 39 percent for the *ali'i*, 24 percent for the crown, 36 percent as government land, and 1 percent for the *maka'ainana* (Kent 1983, 31), but foreigners still could not own land. The *Kuleana* Act of 1850 enabled Native Hawaiians to file a claim for their own *kuleana* (land where they lived and which they put to productive use) if they paid hefty fees to survey the land and register their titles; if they failed to do so, others could file claims of adverse possession instead. Thus, Native Hawaiians suddenly were allowed their own private property, provided they followed complex legal regulations. *Haole* entrepreneurs then entreated the Native Hawaiians to sell at profits that seemed staggering. The indigenous population soon became tenants on land owned by others, and foreigners owned two-thirds of the land by 1886 (Morgan 1948, 137). *Haole* landlords were able to clear more land to grow sugar cane, whereas large numbers of displaced Native Hawaiians needed to sell their labor to feed themselves and pay rent. Since there were not enough Native Hawaiians to work the land for commercial exploitation, in part because the native population eschewed plantation work, sugar interests sought to import aliens from China and later Japan (Table 2.2). The king, concerned that the Hawaiian race was dying out, agreed; he thought that the new workers might intermarry with the Native Hawaiians to strengthen the bloodline (Geschwender 1982, 208–9). A few Germans, Norwegians, Polish, Russians, and Spanish came as contract laborers, too, but the only Caucasian immigrant group of any size was from Portugal. Portuguese, however, were not considered *haoles* because they were plantation workers (Geschwender, Carroll-Seguin, Brill 1988), although they took jobs requiring more skilled labor. Thus, Hawai'i developed into a multiethnic society, and most of the population was non-Hawaiian by 1890.

TABLE 2.2

Streams of Labor Immigration to Hawai'i by Ethnic Group, 1852–1946

Ethnic Group	Era of Arrival	Number Arriving	Percent Male	Percent Children
Chinese	1852–85	28,000	89	5
S. Pacific Islanders	1859–84	2,500	87	11
Portuguese	1878–86	10,700	57	46
	1906–13	5,500	60	43
Norwegians	1881	600	84	20
Germans	1881–88, 1897	1,300	72	36
Japanese	1868, 1885–97	45,000	82	1
	1898–1907	114,000	82	1
Galicians	1898	370	83	25
Puerto Ricans	1900–01, 1921	6,000	60	46
Blacks	1901	200	68	NA
Koreans	1903–05	7,900	90	6
Russians	1906, 1909–12	2,400	70	26
Spanish	1907–13	8,000	56	39
Filipinos	1907–32	119,000	92	5
	1946	7,300	93	12
Samoans	1919, 1952	NA	NA	NA
Vietnamese	1975–79	3,463	51	48

Key: NA = not available.

Note: "Percent male" is the ratio of male adults to all adults, children excluded.
In 1898, Galicia was a part of Poland.
Most "South Pacific Islanders" were from what is now the nation of Kiribati.

Source: Lind (1980, 37; 1982, 12); Nordyke (1989, 91, 253); U.S. Census (1902, 573; 1922, 1180; 1983, 13, 66).

In the 1840s, many Native Hawaiian plantation workers walked off the job. Accordingly, in 1850 the Masters and Servants Act legalized a system under which costs of transporting Chinese or other workers to Hawaiʻi were to be paid by means of lengthy work contracts, which could be broken only under penalty of a jail sentence, thereby creating a condition of legal peonage. The penal code of 1850, which established the principle of matching the ethnicity of the defendant with the ethnicity of members of juries (Nelligan and Ball 1992), did not apply to violations of work contracts, however. A revision of the Masters and Servants Act in 1867 reduced the penalty from a jail sentence to a fine. In 1872, workers were allowed to prepay the cost of their transportation, and the law was amended in 1882 to proscribe the practice of extending the contract as a penalty for desertion (Conan 1946, 56; Fuchs 1961, 87); but these government reforms were often mere scraps of paper to the plantation owners. Laborers from China began to leave the more undesirable agricultural jobs to engage in carpentry, cleaning businesses, and rice farming, leaving Japanese and Portuguese on the plantations. Chinese shopkeepers were segregated into a ghetto in downtown Honolulu, where they were harassed until they accumulated enough capital to set up profitable businesses (Fuchs 1961, 91–94). Back on the plantation, wages were set on the basis of race: Portuguese and *haoles* were paid the most, followed by Chinese, and Japanese were the lowest paid (Conan 1946). Chinese and Japanese workers, unhappy with this discrimination, went on strike from time to time. Hawaiʻi became a multiethnic caste society in which *haoles* and a few upper-status Native Hawaiians lived the good life, Portuguese became plantation supervisors, Asians were plantation laborers, and lower-status Native Hawaiians tried to eke out an existence through traditional subsistence agriculture or as unskilled workers in the towns.

After the death of King Lunalilo in 1872, two candidates vied for the throne. Queen Emma, who had protested injustices against her people, ran a campaign against a more moderate David Kalakaua. After *aliʻi* electors were bribed by the *haole* commercial leaders of Honolulu in early 1873, supporters of Emma stormed the building where votes were to be announced. Since Queen Emma's supporters included Native Hawaiians who defected from the police force, the *haole* foreign affairs minister then obtained 150 American and British troops from warships docked in Honolulu to put down the demonstration, and marines occupied the government building. After the *pilikia* (trouble) subsided, the marines withdrew, although gunboats thenceforth were rotated to ensure continuing *haole* control.

The new king traveled to Washington to campaign on behalf of the sugar interests for a common market between Hawai'i and the United States. In 1876, Congress ratified the Treaty of Reciprocity, removing trade barriers between the Islands and the United States for a seven-year period. In 1886, as a condition of renewing the Treaty of Reciprocity, Congress demanded that Hawai'i grant the U.S. Navy exclusive use of the estuary at the Pearl River on O'ahu, which in due course became known as Pearl Harbor. When the congressional demand led to protests from many quarters, Kalakaua demurred. In mid-1887, the heads of the largest sugar companies and their *haole* allies called upon a group known as the Hawaiian Rifles to gain control of strategic locations throughout Honolulu. The king was forced to sign the Reciprocity Treaty and adopt a new constitution, later known as the "Bayonet Constitution." Under the terms of the constitution, the king remained a constitutional monarch, but there were two qualifications for voting: (1) Those born in Hawai'i, regardless of ancestry, could vote, even if they were also Asian, European, or U.S. citizens. (2) Native Hawaiians and others had to have a yearly income of $600 or own $3,000 in property. As a result, one-third of Native Hawaiian voters were disfranchised.

The Reciprocity Treaty, which was supposed to be a treaty of perpetual peace, brought so much profit that the larger sugar corporations no longer needed foreign bank loans. With sufficient capital for further development, the largest corporations began to strangle independent businesses by dominating insurance, shipping, and wholesale trade, and they bought their own sugar refinery by 1904 (Geschwender 1982, 200–1).

In 1889, part-Hawaiian Robert Wilcox sought to put Kalakaua's sister, Lydia Lili'uokalani, on the throne; his uprising was crushed by government troops, aided by marines from an American ship in port. When Queen Lili'uokalani ascended to the throne upon the death of Kalakaua in 1891, she lamented the decline in status of her people, many of whom were so alienated that they felt driven to despair, drunkenness, and suicide. She then contemplated various measures to restore Native Hawaiians to a place of dignity in their own land.

In 1891, the McKinley Act repealed tariffs on all countries exporting sugar to the United States, but American sugar growers received subsidies, thereby making Hawaiian sugar too expensive on the mainland. Through annexation, this trade barrier could be eliminated. In January 1893, in response to a petition signed by two-thirds of the registered voters, Lili'uokalani indicated an interest in changing the constitution to reserve more powers to the crown (McGregor 1991, 14). When the *haole* cabinet protested, she renounced her intention to redistribute power, but a secret Committee of Safety formed among thirteen persons, including six *haole* citizens of Hawai'i, five American citizens, one English citizen, and one German. The U.S. minister to Hawai'i, John Stevens, then assured the conspirators that American troops in port would land to support a *coup d'état*. On January 16, Stevens ordered 162 troops to disembark from the USS *Boston*, seize the government building, and place the queen under house arrest in the palace, demanding that she relinquish sovereignty.

REPUBLIC OF HAWAI'I

Leaders of the conspiracy, responding to the military action, went to the government building to declare the monarchy dissolved. They proclaimed a provisional government under martial law, pending annexation by the United States. The American flag went up on the government building two weeks later, and President Benjamin Harrison submitted a treaty of cession to the Senate. Inasmuch as a British commander had taken the same action some fifty years earlier, Lili'uokalani (1898, chap. 40–47) awaited a similar disavowal to resume her position, as the United States had appeared to violate the Reciprocity Treaty. Newly elected President Grover Cleveland, suspicious of the legality of the *coup*, withdrew the treaty from the Senate and sent an investigator, James Blount, to Honolulu. When Blount arrived, he had the American flag lowered and ordered American troops to return to their ships. In his later report, Blount said that most people favored the queen, opposed the provisional government, and did not want to be annexed to the United States. Cleveland then refused to push annexation as an action that he reasoned would be contrary to international law (Dudley and Agard 1990, 25–46).

Accordingly, leaders of the *coup* proclaimed the Republic of Hawai'i in 1894, continuing martial law. Congress, meanwhile, repealed the McKinley tariff in 1894, so the privileged position of

Hawaiian sugar cane was restored. The Republic then declared crown lands to be government lands, much of which were later sold or leased to plantation owners. By 1895, pineapple began to emerge as the second most important cash crop, so there was a new demand for land and labor.

The constitution establishing the Republic of Hawai'i increased property qualifications for voting, thereby reducing Native Hawaiians to less than 20 percent of the registered voters.[2] Wilcox then mapped strategy to restore Lili'uokalani through a counterrevolution; when his plot was discovered in 1895, the movement was crushed. Lili'uokalani was then arrested for treason, but in 1896 she was released from confinement in the palace. She then went to Washington to press a claim for Hawaiian independence, but the planters had already been there, lobbying for their interests, and her efforts were in vain.

William McKinley was elected president in 1896, and the United States won the Spanish-American War in 1898. In the aftermath, Congress voted to annex Guam, Hawai'i, the Philippines, and Puerto Rico. The annexations were made by a joint congressional resolution, not a treaty, in 1898. There was no referendum in Hawai'i or in the other newly acquired possessions.

TERRITORY OF HAWAI'I

In 1900, Congress passed the Organic Act, which established Hawai'i as a territory of the United States. Alaska, Arizona, and New Mexico were also territories at the time, governed by presidentially appointed governors who reported to the Secretary of Interior. Laws of the previous government were still valid unless they contradicted provisions of the U.S. Constitution. Congress declared former crown lands to be government lands, some of which had already been sold or leased to private plantation owners. County governments began in 1903, and the island of O'ahu incorporated as the City and County of Honolulu in 1907.

According to the terms of the Organic Act, Hawai'i was to hold elections for local offices and to elect a nonvoting delegate to the House of Representatives from 1900. With the population predominantly Native Hawaiian, voter registration reflected that fact. Knowing that Native Hawaiians accounted for more than two-thirds of the eligible voters, Robert Wilcox emerged as the standard-bearer of the

Home Rule Party on a platform of reestablishing the monarchy; the Democrats nominated Prince David Kawananakoa, and the Republicans picked part-Hawaiian Samuel Parker. Wilcox received the most votes as delegate to Congress, and his party won elections to the territorial legislature. When the legislature convened, Native Hawaiian delegates spoke in their native language. Since this locus of political power did not suit the *haole* elites, the Democrats prevailed on Kawananakoa to drop out, and the Republicans nominated Prince Jonah Kuhio Kalaniana'ole, who won in 1902. From 1902, the Republicans attained a firm political hegemony in the territorial legislature, while electing most congressional delegates in the next half century (except in 1922, 1924, and 1932). In short, as of 1900 some 29,000 *haoles*, of whom fewer than 2,000 were registered to vote, controlled a population of 154,000 persons, some 40 percent of which were immigrant Japanese plantation workers (Hawai'i 1902a, 21). Despite a subsequent ban on speaking the Hawaiian language in the schools, Native Hawaiians maintained a voting coalition with the *haole* Republican elites until after World War II. Even governors appointed by Democrats Woodrow Wilson and Franklin Roosevelt did not challenge the power of the *haole* Republicans, who maintained political control for a half century, treating government as an extension of the plantation system of autocratic rule, with elites at the top, virtual serfs at the bottom, and a middle level of professionals and shopkeepers as a buffer between the two layers. The five largest sugar companies ("the Big Five")[3] and allied *haole* corporations assumed oligopolistic control over the territory's economy, jacking up prices whenever possible to maintain their economic dominance (Kent 1983, chap. 6).

Former crown and government lands from the days of the monarchy and the republic, nearly half the acreage of the Islands, were ceded by the Republic of Hawai'i to the Territory of Hawai'i. Since most Native Hawaiians were landless and could not live as they had for centuries, Kuhio felt obligated to do something for his people, who were still declining in population. In 1919, when nearly all the arable land had been cultivated (Shoemaker 1946, 194), the territorial legislature recommended that land be set aside for Native Hawaiians. Plantation owners, whose leases on 26,000 prime agricultural acres were about to expire, offered to donate 200,000 acres of their least desirable lands for homesteading by Native Hawaiians (Faludi 1991a). Accordingly, Congress passed the Hawaiian Homes Commission Act in

1920; when it went into effect in 1921, the act set aside some 200,000 acres of the nearly 2,000,000 acres of ceded lands for ninety-nine-year leases by those with at least half-Hawaiian ancestry at an annual rent of $.02 per acre, to be paid to the territory's Department of Hawaiian Home Lands. In order to raise funds to provide services to the homesteaders, however, the Department of Hawaiian Home Lands leased more than 60 percent of the land to corporations and wealthy individuals on a long-term basis (Faludi 1991b). The initial rent to corporations was as low as $3.33 per acre, a hefty figure in 1921 but a giveaway by the end of the century, so the Department of Hawaiian Home Lands increasingly lacked sufficient funds to offer basic services to the homesteaders. Most homestead land was unsuitable for habitation and was never distributed because no roads, power, or water were available. The effect of having many Native Hawaiians voluntarily resettled into segregated communities in rural areas was to isolate one part of the former ruling race from the mainstream of social change, creating a sharp division between rich and poor Native Hawaiians. When the part-Hawaiian population later increased, land parcels remained the same, so a decreasing percentage could take advantage of homesteading. In due course, the territorial government also leased more former crown and government lands to corporations (U.S. Commission on Civil Rights, Hawai'i Advisory Committee 1980). Increasingly, Native Hawaiians became alienated from their ancestral lands, while homestead lands were used for commercial purposes (U.S. Commission on Civil Rights, Hawai'i Advisory Committee 1991).

Hawai'i passed a Chinese Exclusion Act in 1886, but exemptions permitted further importation of 15,000 "coolies" in the 1890s (Lind 1938, 250). The Chinese Exclusion Act, first adopted by Congress in 1882, applied to the Territory of Hawai'i from 1900, and the Organic Act prohibited Chinese legally residing in the Islands from moving to the mainland. In 1907, the territorial legislature established a commission to explore various options, since there was a shortage of plantation workers. The Dillingham Commission, as the body was known, concluded that Congress should grant Hawai'i an exemption to bring in more Chinese. California members of Congress, however, wanted to maintain Chinese exclusion and to extend the ban on immigration to all Asians. Japan bowed to the inevitable in an executive agreement, known as the Gentlemen's Agreement of 1907, under which Tokyo would refuse to grant exit visas for its citizens to emigrate to the United States; an exception was the institution of picture brides for the predominantly male Japanese plantation workforce. In 1924, all Orientals, female and male, were barred as immigrants under a new congressional immigration act. According to the Naturalization Act of 1790, which applied to Hawai'i from 1900, only Caucasian immigrants were eligible for American citizenship. Although the plantation owners wanted to continue to apply the Masters and Servants Act, Congress was aware of the cruel means, including the use of a long-lash whip, to enforce discipline on the plantations, so the Organic Act was written to void the legislation. The Civil Rights Act of 1867, which prohibited peonage, was thus in principle enforceable in the territory. Accordingly, Chinese in large numbers walked off the job on the plantations in 1900 to join kinfolk who had already started businesses in the cities (Table 2.3). Most Japanese remained on the plantations, but they decided to strike at almost every plantation for better working conditions; the result was only meager concessions. Plantation interests, preferring to keep the price of sugar competitive, felt that the solution to labor unrest was to bring in more subservient workers, while using police of Native Hawaiian ancestry to break up strikes. An inflow of workers from Korea, the Philippines, and Puerto Rico soon began (Table 2.4), but strikes continued because the new laborers also wanted equal pay for equal work.

   Haole political leaders feared the future voting strength of ethnic groups from Asia. Accordingly, they sought to deny U.S. citizenship to Chinese and Japanese who had been citizens during the era of monarchy. In 1901, federal courts in Honolulu ruled that citizens of the independent State of Hawai'i automatically became citizens of the United States with the adoption of the Organic Act in *Achi v Kapi'olani Estate* (1USDistCtHaw86) and *U.S. v King Thai Shah* (1USDistCt Haw118). In 1917, the effort to deprive Puerto Ricans of voting rights in Hawai'i was challenged successfully in *Sanchez v Kalauokalani* (24Haw21), which ruled that they were American citizens. Filipinos were treated differently. In a case decided in 1916, *In re Ocampo* (4USDistCtHaw77), the federal court ruled that Filipinos were from a "possession" of the United States, so Philippine nationals could not become citizens until the Philippines became an independent country, which did not occur until 1946.

TABLE 2.3
Urban and Suburban Population in Hawai'i by Ethnic Group, 1890–1990 (in percent)

(a) Urban Population

Ethnic Group	1890	1910	1920	1930	1940	1950	1960	1970	1980	1990
Black	NA	46.2 (100)	56.9 (100)	57.2 (80)	NA	NA	26.7 (34)	31.7 (46)	24.2 (33)	18.9 (25)
Caucasian	31.9 (100)	39.9 (86)	47.4 (83)	50.0 (70)	49.0 (63)	51.0 (62)	39.7 (50)	36.9 (54)	42.2 (57)	32.1 (43)
Chinese	28.8 (90)	44.2 (96)	56.9 (100)	71.1 (100)	78.0 (100)	82.5 (100)	78.9 (100)	68.5 (100)	74.0 (100)	68.8 (91)
Filipino	NA	3.7 (8)	.9 (2)	7.6 (11)	13.1 (17)	28.4 (34)	32.0 (41)	31.4 (46)	32.2 (44)	27.8 (37)
Guamanian	NA	NA	NA	NA	NA	NA	NA	NA	40.7 (55)	28.7 (38)
Hawaiian	30.6 (96)	35.1 (76)	42.0 (74)	47.0 (66)	48.3 (62)	48.9 (59)	NA	NA	33.3 (45)	24.6 (33)
Japanese	3.1 (10)	15.2 (33)	22.4 (39)	34.0 (48)	38.4 (49)	50.1 (61)	53.5 (68)	50.4 (74)	52.8 (71)	44.7 (59)
Korean	10.1 (22)	26.6 (47)	40.3 (57)	NA	NA	NA	NA	NA	70.0 (95)	62.2 (83)
Puerto Rican	7.9 (17)	15.0 (26)	33.1 (47)	NA	NA	NA	NA	NA	27.2 (37)	17.2 (23)
Samoan	NA	NA	NA	NA	NA	NA	NA	NA	53.5 (72)	40.1 (53)
Vietnamese	NA	NA	NA	NA	NA	NA	NA	NA	68.0 (92)	75.3 (100)
Total	25.5 (80)	27.2 (59)	32.6 (57)	37.4 (53)	42.4 (54)	49.6 (60)	46.5 (59)	42.3 (62)	44.7 (60)	36.3 (48)

Key: NA = not available

Note: Figures report percentages of the Hawai'i civilian and military population living (a) in central Honolulu and (b) in the suburbs of Kailua and Kane'ohe. Parenthesized figures are normed, with 100 assigned to the ethnic group with the highest percentage of urbanization or suburbanization each year; other groups are expressed as a percentage of the top figure. "Hawaiian" figures include persons with any Native Hawaiian ancestry. "Caucasian" figures include Portuguese, Puerto Ricans from 1940, Spanish, and other Caucasians.

Source: Thrum (1893, 12); U.S. Census (1932, 48; 1943, 5; 1952, 35, 37; 1962, 17; 1972, 28, 47; 1983, 11, 13, 16; 1993, 7, 12).

TABLE 2.3 (*continued*)
Urban and Suburban Population in Hawai'i by Ethnic Group, 1890–1990 (in percent)

(b) Suburban Population

Ethnic Group	1970	1980	1990
Black	2.4 (21)	13.0 (86)	3.6 (41)
Caucasian	11.3 (100)	15.1 (100)	8.7 (100)
Chinese	8.2 (73)	10.1 (67)	6.3 (72)
Filipino	2.5 (22)	3.6 (34)	2.2 (25)
Guamanian	NA	3.3 (22)	2.3 (26)
Hawaiian	NA	14.7 (97)	7.5 (86)
Japanese	6.4 (57)	8.6 (57)	6.9 (79)
Korean	NA	6.5 (43)	3.6 (41)
Samoan	NA	3.4 (23)	2.1 (24)
Vietnamese	NA	1.6 (11)	1.7 (20)
Total	8.2 (73)	11.0 (73)	6.5 (75)

For key, note, and source, see Table 2.3a.

Plantation labor recruiters preferred employing pliable illiterates from the Philippines, though some were well educated. Unlike Chinese and Japanese, whose governments had a diplomatic presence in Hawai'i, there was no overseas representative to protect Filipinos until after 1935, when Manila sent Uncle Tomás types. The Filipinos, who were sending money to their families in the Philippines, soon claimed that they received lower disposable income than they enjoyed before coming to Hawai'i (Willis 1955, 19). Moreover, most could neither bring members of their families to the Islands nor import brides in order to start new families. Since they could speak little English at first, they were unable to communicate with workers from other countries and formed trade unions of their own to protest working conditions. Plantation owners evicted social workers who tried to teach English to the Filipinos. While conditions improved for other ethnic groups, thus, Filipinos became virtual serfs (Abbott 1967, chap. 12).

TABLE 2.4
Immigrant Population in Hawai'i by Ethnic Group, 1910–1990 (in percent)

Ethnic Group	1910	1920	1930	1940	1950	1960	1970	1980	1990
Black	13.4 (13)	10.6 (12)	6.6 (8)	NA	NA	NA	1.1 (3)	3.6 (4)	3.6 (5)
Caucasian	34.3 (34)	21.5 (24)	11.9 (14)	7.7 (11)	5.5 (10)	3.8 (9)	3.3 (9)	4.9 (6)	4.5 (6)
Chinese	66.8 (67)	47.5 (53)	27.5 (33)	16.8 (25)	11.1 (20)	9.1 (22)	11.1 (31)	22.1 (26)	2.9 (4)
Filipino	99.8 (100)	89.0 (100)	83.5 (100)	68.1 (100)	55.2 (100)	41.3 (100)	35.3 (100)	45.8 (53)	44.5 (59)
Guamanian	NA	NA	NA	NA	NA	NA	NA	2.8 (3)	3.2 (4)
Hawaiian	0.0 (0)	0.0 (0)	0.0 (0)	0.0 (0)	.2 (-)	.3 (1)	.3 (1)	.7 (1)	.3 (0)
Japanese	75.0 (75)	55.5 (62)	34.7 (42)	23.7 (35)	16.7 (30)	12.1 (29)	9.6 (27)	9.5 (11)	7.7 (10)
Korean	92.0 (92)	70.4 (79)	46.2 (55)	35.8 (53)	25.2 (46)	NA	20.6 (58)	54.0 (63)	54.9 (73)
Samoan	NA	NA	NA	NA	NA	NA	NA	28.1 (33)	18.2 (24)
Vietnamese	NA	NA	NA	NA	NA	NA	NA	86.0 (100)	75.3 (100)
Total	48.9 (48)	34.1 (38)	18.6 (22)	12.4 (18)	15.3 (28)	.10.9 (26)	8.9 (25)	14.2 (26)	14.7 (20)

Key: NA = not available.   -- = more than 0 percent but less than 1 percent

Note: Figures report percentages of the Hawai'i civilian and military population for each ethnic group born abroad. From 1974, "Chinese" figures include Koreans. "Hawaiian" figures include persons with any Native Hawaiian ancestry. "Caucasian" figures include Portuguese, Puerto Ricans from 1940, Spanish, and other Caucasians. Parenthesized figures are normed, with 100 assigned to the group with the highest percentage of foreign born; other groups are expressed as a percentage of the top figure.

Source: Lind (1980, 92); U.S. Census (1913, 572; 1922, 1173; 1932, 49; 1943, 5, 11; 1952, 35; 1962, 17, 119; 1972, 193, 195-96; 1973, 178, 180; 1983, 38, 65, 71; 1993, 58, 124-25).

In 1924, after eight months of strikes for an increase in salary of $2 per day and a reduction in working hours from ten to eight, Filipino workers protested efforts to evict them from their homes and took two strikebreakers as hostages. After sheriff's deputies arrived to quell the disturbance, sixteen strikers were shot dead and four law enforcement officers died in what became known as the Hanapepe Massacre. Some sixty Filipinos subsequently served jail sentences of four-year terms (Johannessen 1956, 70; MacDonald 1944, 130). Following a public outcry over the incident, an investigative commission, headed by a carefully chosen Philippine official from Manila, came to Hawai'i. The resulting report was a whitewash, claiming pay to be "more than sufficient wages to live on" (Ligot 1926, 20). Territorial Attorney General John Matthewman issued an opinion designed to inform Filipinos that they could claim no special rights: Filipinos, he said, were neither aliens nor citizens, but instead "subjects" without constitutional protections under American law (Wright 1972, 59), that is, a conquered people not unlike American Indians after the wars of the nineteenth century but without treaty protection. Pablo Manlapit (1933), an attorney who led the strike, was disbarred for "subornation of perjury," jailed, released with the understanding that he would move to California, and later deported to the Philippines (Kerkvliet 1991).

De facto peonage was established quickly, since the plantation owners could deport any alien who refused to accept labor conditions. Trade union organization was thereby frustrated. As recently as 1969, when most of these conditions had been ameliorated, a report funded by a major plantation corporation characterized a surviving Filipino plantation camp as remaining in a state of "feudalism" (Moore 1969, 34).

The *haole*–Native Hawaiian Republican coalition outvoted the Democrats, who were lampooned in the press as southern "Bourbons." The Republican Party, controlled by the Big Five, co-opted some support from affluent members of other ethnic groups as they emerged. There was no barrier to Portuguese becoming citizens and Republicans. Daughters and sons of plantation workers from China and Japan, whose parents were ineligible for citizenship, were escorted by plantation supervisors to the polls, where they were instructed how to vote (Fuchs 1961, 179, 321; Kent 1983, 76). The effect of the division of the electorate into two coalitions was to pit a Caucasian minority against a more numerous but largely disfranchised Asian minority, with Native

Hawaiians voting *haoles* into a dominant position in order to share such rewards of power as contracts and jobs.

Formal political power resided in the territorial governor, who by law had to be a Hawai'i resident. The governor, who could rely on armed forces at the military bases in case of trouble, was otherwise answerable to the Big Five, which could shut down all basic services at its whim. Recalcitrant members of the legislature were bullied into ratifying the will of the Big Five in the years before World War II.

One of the largest sectors of the territory consisted of the military population, which was segregated from the mainstream on military bases. One evening in 1931, Thalia Massie, wife of naval Lieutenant Thomas Massie, walked home from a nightclub in Waikiki. Arriving home with her face bruised and her lips swollen, she claimed that she had been raped (Wright 1966; Marumoto 1983). Meanwhile, police arrested five young local men who were having an altercation with a couple in another car at about the same time. Although she identified the five as her rapists after police brought them into her hospital room four or five times, the evidence was so slim that a jury of local residents refused to bring in a verdict in *Hawai'i v Ahakuelo* (1931). Incensed that justice had not prevailed, the Massies sought revenge. With the aid of two subordinate naval officers, the Massies arranged to abduct one of the defendants, who was tortured and accidentally shot. In *Hawai'i v Massie* (1932), the conspirators were convicted of murder despite an eloquent defense by their attorney, Clarence Darrow. After sentence was passed, Governor Lawrence Judd commuted the sentence to one hour of detention in the office of the governor. For Asians and Native Hawaiians, this was "*haole* justice." In 1938, in the so-called Hilo Massacre, some 500 workers suddenly found themselves used for target practice by sixty police, who were shielding a ship serviced by strikebreakers; some fifty-one strikers were wounded in the resulting gunfire (MacDonald 1944, 138).

For some, a campaign for self-rule (statehood) seemed the best strategy to prevent future Massie cases and Hilo Massacres (Wright 1966). A plebiscite in 1940 revealed that statehood enjoyed 3:1 support (Schmitt 1977, 602). Many *haoles*, however, were insensitive to this change in political climate, continuing to believe as before that they alone could hold the society together (cf. du Puy 1932).

Japan became a powerful nation as the twentieth century unfolded. When imperial Japan annexed Manchuria in 1933, however, Tokyo appeared to be a potential threat to American interests in the Pacific. Ineligible for American citizenship, many Japanese residents suffered persecution of various sorts. *Nisei* (second-generation Japanese born in the United States), for example, had to show their birth certificates when registering to vote, whereas those with white faces were accepted without question (Fuchs 1961, 177). Politically, the Japanese community was divided between separatists, who avoided the unpleasantness of discrimination by minimizing contact with *haoles*, assimilationists, who wanted to reduce discrimination by repudiating Buddhism and Japanese culture, and confrontationists, who demanded their rights (Jacobs and Landau 1971, 211–12).

After World War II broke out, the divisions among Japanese narrowed. Japanese on the West Coast of the United States were relocated to internment camps in 1942. Because Japanese comprised about one-third of the population of Hawai'i, this remedy was deemed impractical despite a plea, considered by President Franklin Roosevelt, from the head of the local telephone company and others to remove them all (Borreca 1991; Lind 1946, 62–63; Matsunaga 1987, A4). Since the military were suspicious of the local Japanese, the president ordered his appointive governor in Hawai'i, Joseph Poindexter, to suspend the writ of *habeas corpus* and to declare martial law. Lieutenant-General Walter Short, the Pacific military commander, then became military governor in accordance with a contingency plan drawn up six months earlier. The military ruled the Islands during the war, with power to try civilians in military courts. The press, subject to censure, could not report on court proceedings, in which 99 percent of the defendants were found guilty (Anthony 1955). All residents were fingerprinted, a curfew required that heavy blankets must black out all light from inside homes, and mail was subject to censure. Sugar workers were forbidden to change jobs, and all holidays were suspended. Those out of work were assigned jobs by the U.S. Employment Service. When Poindexter demanded the restoration of *habeas corpus* in 1943, he was ignored by the military governor. Thus, the military assumed powers unprecedented in American history, even exceeding those enforced against Southern states after the Civil War.

During the war, the Federal Bureau of Investigation (FBI) gathered information on individual Japanese who were suspected of conspiring with Tokyo. Despite the fact that no evidence ever emerged about any disloyal acts of Japanese in Hawai'i, some 540 were interned in small camps on Oʻahu, and 930 were transferred to mainland camps; families who lived near military bases continued farming their land but were not allowed to live in their homes (Ogawa and Fox 1986), and *Nisei* members of the territory's National Guard were dismissed. Many Japanese, living in fear that they would be rounded up, were harassed by persons of other races during the war. In October 1944, when military rule was rescinded by the president, the military maintained martial law. Some 413 internees were allowed to go home, but 50 aliens remained in internment camps; and 67 Japanese Americans were shipped to the mainland. In 1946, wartime military rule in Hawaiʻi was retroactively ruled unconstitutional in *Duncan v Kahanamoku* (66SCt606).

There was a bright spot during the war. *Nisei* students from the University of Hawaiʻi (UH), with the approval of the military governor, formed the Varsity Victory Volunteers (VVV) in February 1942. When Assistant Secretary of War John J. McCloy visited the Islands at the end of the year, he was so impressed by the VVV that in January 1943 he gave orders allowing Japanese-Americans to enlist in the armed forces to fight in the war. VVVs then served in the 100th battalion and later the 442nd regiment of the army, one of the most highly decorated units of the war in Europe.

World War II ushered in other developments. Previously segregated Christian churches, with sermons in English, Filipino, and Japanese languages, offered services in English and became multiethnic (Tangonan 1991). When some *haoles* fled to the mainland during the war, Chinese bought homes in some of the more affluent neighborhoods, thereby promoting housing desegregation. Because the federal Ramspeck Act of 1940 guaranteed nondiscrimination in U.S. government jobs, the federal civil service accommodated many of the newer middle-class Japanese Americans; similar regulations affected the territorial civil service. As a result, Japanese in increasing numbers occupied educational and civil service positions in the territorial government. Japanese increasingly moved off the plantations to Honolulu to middle-class jobs in the private sector vacated by *haoles*.

When members of the 442nd regiment returned to civilian life, they were able to take advantage of the "GI bill of rights," enabling many Japanese veterans to go to college at government expense. The newly college-educated *Nisei*, however, found that *haole* employers in the private sector undervalued their degrees, preferring to hire them at more traditional jobs.

Before the war, mainland-based trade unions tried to organize Caucasian workers, but they were unable to make headway on the plantations, where Asians formed ineffectual monoethnic labor organizations. During the war, the independent-minded International Longshoremen's and Warehousemen's Union (ILWU) gained momentum by combining Filipino and Japanese workers into a powerful bloc of workers; with only 5,000 members in 1943, they had signed up 33,000 by 1945 (Schmitt 1977, 138), building cross-ethnic solidarity through such activities as baseball and bowling leagues. In preparation for postwar strikes, the ILWU encouraged Filipino and Japanese members to vote for Democratic candidates in order to show solidarity (Daws 1968, 367). In 1946, some 28,000 workers went on strike at thirty-three of the forty-four plantations for seventy-nine days. Although Filipino immigrants were then imported as scabs, they instead joined the strikers, and the plantation owners soon granted the ILWU the right to represent the workers as the exclusive collective bargaining agent. A similar victory was repeated in 1949 after a 178-day strike involving some 2,000 dockworkers (Kent 1983, 135). The militant solidarity among Asian workers was good news for the Democratic Party. Afraid of losing power, the *haole* Republican elites brought the House Un-American Activities Committee to Hawai'i to delegitimate the ILWU, whose leaders were vulnerable to charges of sympathy with Marxism. With this faction of Democrats neutralized, power in the Democratic Party shifted to a cadre of Japanese American war heroes with recent professional degrees, who in turn mapped a strategy for political victory.

In 1952, Congress passed the McCarran-Walter Immigration Act, which permitted aliens born in Japan to become American citizens. After a flood of Japanese became American citizens in the next two years (Honolulu Star-Bulletin 1954b, A3), the Democratic Party achieved a landslide in elections for the territorial legislature in 1954, a victory sometimes known as the Democratic Revolution. Japanese-Americans constituted the largest bloc of voters, and they cast their ballots largely for the Democratic candidates (Digman and Tuttle 1961). As a result of their solidarity with Filipinos in the labor struggles involving the ILWU, the victorious Japanese Democrats might have sought to provide equal opportunity for all ethnic groups, for the 1954

Democratic platform pledged "to shift the tax burden from those least able to pay to those who are most able to pay" (Honolulu Star-Bulletin 1954a). The pledge, however, was never honored, and Filipinos were regarded as mere junior partners. In retrospect, as one-time Lieutenant Governor Thomas Gill remarked, "Making the old order over became less important than simply making it" (Wright 1972, 239). For Nadao Yoshinaga, longtime ILWU stalwart and later state senator, "Their being Democrats disgusts me. I feel that the Democrats in the legislature . . . regard the legislature as a purely political field for personal advancement" (Kent 1983, 149). With Japanese in the ascendancy, the solution of socioeconomic problems of Filipinos and Native Hawaiians seemed postponed to the day when the two groups might command a majority of votes, if ever.

The 1954 triumph occurred in part because the *haole* oligarchy refused to co-opt upwardly mobile Japanese into prominent positions in the Republican Party. Political change coincided with economic developments that further marginalized the Big Five. Henry J. Kaiser, for example, moved to Hawai'i, with more capital available than the Big Five combined (Kent 1983, 105).

From the 1950s, as unionization drove up wages on the plantations far beyond paychecks of workers in Third World countries, profitability of local agriculture was reduced. The Big Five soon began to invest in pineapple and sugar cane in Asian countries, then diversified their investments, became multinational corporations, and moved many of their headquarters in due course to the mainland. Tourism was looming as the top industry to replace agriculture, where mechanization displaced workers, but a boom in trans-Pacific travel arrived in the 1960s along with the jet plane and statehood (Table 2.5).

The campaign for statehood, which began in the period before World War II, accelerated after the war, in part spurred by the excesses of military rule during the war. Before 1941, a Hawaiian Equal Rights Commission was set up to make sure that Hawai'i received equal status with the then forty-eight states. In 1947, the Equal Rights Commission was retitled the Statehood Commission, with a mandate to explore all possible methods for becoming the forty-ninth or fiftieth state. In 1956, John Burns, a *haole* from a poor section of Honolulu, won election as the territory's nonvoting delegate to the U.S. House of Representatives. Burns, a Democrat, put together a winning strategy for statehood in

TABLE 2.5

Sources of Hawai'i Income by Industry, 1900–1990

Year	Defense	Sugar & Pineapple	Tourism	Total
1900	NA	$27 (96)	NA	$28
1910	NA	43 (93)	NA	46
1920	NA	98 (93)	NA	105
1930	NA	94 (93)	NA	101
1939	NA	89 (76)	$4 (4)	113
1950	$147 (29)	226 (44)	29 (5)	513
1955	273 (37)	261 (35)	55 (7)	747
1960	351 (19)	237 (8)	131 (7)	1,805
1965	430 (17)	293 (11)	225 (9)	2,530
1970	639 (14)	326 (7)	595 (13)	4,427
1975	1,442 (19)	503 (7)	1,360 (18)	7,411
1980	1,865 (15)	821 (7)	2,875 (24)	12,226
1985	2,810 (17)	563 (3)	5,244 (31)	16,875
1990	3,203 (12)	545 (2)	9,739 (36)	26,945

Key: NA = not available.

Note: Figures are in $000,000s; totals include all industries. Parenthesized figures are percentages of the total, and add to 100 percent horizontally when all industries are included.

Source: Hawai'i (1901, 30; 1910a, 21; 1920a, 28; 1931, 40; 1940, 4; 1970a, 65; 1986, 366–67; 1990, 344–45; 1993–94, 312–13); U.S. Census (1942, 1135; 1943, 10).

which he urged that Alaska be admitted as a stepping-stone to admission of Hawai'i. His strategy worked, and in 1959 Hawai'i became the fiftieth state, confirmed by a plebiscite in which support was 16:1 in favor of statehood (Schmitt 1977, 602). The United Nations, having monitored the Territory of Hawai'i for some fifteen years, then removed Hawai'i from its list of non-self-governing territories.

STATE OF HAWAI'I

Statehood meant that the people of the Islands could elect their own governor. Some federal regulations that prevailed in agencies of territorial government were superseded by laws passed by the new state legislature. Since most governmental functions before statehood were handled at the territorial level, Hawai'i's new state government began with more powers than any other state. For example, there is a single statewide school district and a centralized public health system. County functions are limited largely to fire fighting, police protection, waste disposal, and water distribution.

Military bases remained. Since the Defense Department paid no rent to the Department of the Interior, which officially managed the Territory of Hawai'i, the statehood act made Hawai'i the only state that charges no rent for the use of state land for military bases, many of which are on lands that had been set aside for Native Hawaiians at the time of annexation in 1900.

William Quinn, a Republican, was the last appointive governor. When he won the state's first election for governor in 1959, he was committed to what he called a "New Hawaii," promising to change the economic foundation of the Islands. The new senators were Democrat Oren Long and Republican Hiram Fong. Although Fong and Quinn urged the Republicans to give a prominent role to non-*haoles*, their views did not prevail, and the Republican Party slipped into relative insignificance. In 1962, Democrat John Burns overwhelmingly defeated Quinn to become Hawai'i's second elected governor. Reelected twice, Burns remained in power for nearly twelve years, a feat attributed to strong trade union backing, which brought overwhelming support from Filipino and Japanese voters. With voters free in primaries to choose separately for governor and lieutenant governor, Burns had a different lieutenant governor in each term of office. He appointed his first lieutenant governor, part-Hawaiian William Richardson, to be chief justice of the state's supreme court. During Burns's third election campaign in 1970 (when he was opposed by Lieutenant Governor Thomas Gill), he gave the nod to George Ariyoshi as his running mate, and the voters concurred. In 1973, Burns's health declined so rapidly that he resigned, making Ariyoshi governor. A Japanese American 442nd veteran who traced his ancestry to Okinawa, Ariyoshi won election in his own right in 1974 and then served until 1986, when he was ineligible for another term of office because of a two-term limit added to the state constitution.

Statehood also meant that businesses could relocate from the mainland to Hawai'i with confidence that they would be subject to the same federal protections and regulations as in any other state. Tourists felt free to travel to Hawai'i, and the structure of Hawai'i's economy changed (Table 2.5). In the mid-1960s, during the era of American involvement in the Vietnamese civil war, defense was the largest industry. When military spending fell after U.S. withdrawal from Vietnam, the tourist industry emerged as the top source of state income, responsible for one-third of all jobs in Hawai'i (Harpham 1983).

Because of the dependence of the economy on outsiders to buy pineapple, sugar, or to come as tourists, and the decreasing interest of the Big Five in Hawai'i, the new Democratic leaders were reluctant to rock the boat economically, so they agreed not to fight the Big Five (Kent 1983, chap. 10). Through a property tax based on potential use, vacant lots and single-family dwellings gave way to commercial investments from the U.S. mainland as well as foreign countries. Each year from 1971, investors from Japan bought more property for golf courses, while financing hotels and visitor hospitality businesses. Many Japanese American Democratic leaders, with an unparalleled opportunity to influence rezoning to upgrade land use from agriculture to residential, also cashed in on a real estate bonanza (Cooper and Daws 1985). *Haole* Republicans showed how to use the political system to enrich themselves, so the new power elites felt no embarrassment in playing by the same rules as they saw them (Honolulu Star-Bulletin 1972, v).

Many Caucasians, disenchanted with overcrowded California or drab parts of the mainland, began to migrate to Hawai'i to fill positions in the expanding economy, producing a boom in luxury housing. Statehood also came as the postwar "baby boom" took off, with an associated need for moderately priced new homes. With limited land available, the result was ultimately an upward spiral in the price of residences, beyond the reach of most local workers.

Meanwhile, the Immigration Act of 1965 addressed the need of immigrants to have members of their immediate personal families join them in Hawai'i, and Filipinos began to arrive in the fiftieth state in large numbers (Table 2.4). As immigrants, they were expected to fill the lowest-paying jobs, and the hotel boom provided plenty of opportunity to make beds, water lawns, and otherwise cater to tourists from Australia, Canada, Europe, Japan, and the U.S. mainland. Thus, the ethnic mix after statehood began to change in ways that appeared to undermine the power structure of the Democratic Party, based as it was overwhelmingly on loyal voting by Japanese Americans, whose relative share of the population declined (Table 2.1).

While Filipinos and Caucasians increased in population, filling jobs in the private sector at first, many wanted public sector jobs appropriate to their professional qualifications. Because of earlier efforts by *haole* private sector employers to hire Japanese only in subordinate roles, government jobs were already filled disproportionately by Japanese Americans, who in turn gave good services and jobs to local residents who had been victims of discrimination in the first half of the century, but new residents from the mainland and the Philippines were treated unfairly (Haas 1992, chap. 5–8).

When Hawai'i became a state, some 1.5 million acres of federal land that had been crown and government land before 1893 were ceded from the territorial government to the new state government. The Admission Act of 1959 required that the land be used for various purposes, including the benefit of Native Hawaiians and the general public. Some Native Hawaiians believed that they had a prior claim to the crown lands, whereas government land was for the general public, but neither Congress nor the new state legislature specified which lands were for which purposes. To clear land for housing and public works, such as new freeways, someone inevitably had to move. In 1971, when the pig farmers of Kalama Valley were to be evicted by Bishop Estate,[4] the largest landowner, in order to make room for houses, a protest sit-in was organized to defend the homes to be bulldozed. The bulldozers won. Subsequent evictions on O'ahu repeated the pattern, as Native Hawaiians were disproportionately displaced by these "development" projects. On Maui, as plantation agriculture shut down in view of lower profitability and higher return from the sale of prime agricultural land for golf courses and real estate developments, absentee owners began to bid for condominium units that they might occupy only a few weeks of the year, increasing property values beyond the capacity of local residents to buy their own homes, as on O'ahu, and similar plans emerged for the remaining islands (Kent 1983, 167–71).

In 1971, Congress passed the Alaska Native Claims Settlement Act. Native Hawaiians were astonished that Alaskan natives received forty million acres of land and nearly $1 billion for land that was federalized in order to build the Alaskan oil pipeline (New York Times 1971). As a result, two organizations were formed to work on the reparations issue—the Congress of the Hawaiian People in 1971 and

Aboriginal Lands of Hawaiian Ancestry (ALOHA) in 1972. In 1973, ALOHA raised $150,000, enough to hire former Secretary of the Interior Stewart Udall to lobby Congress on the issue (Dudley and Agard 1990, 109), and Hawai'i's congressional delegation introduced a bill for Native Hawaiian reparations in 1974. In 1980, Congress formed the Native Hawaiians Study Commission, which submitted a negative report (U.S. Congress 1983), and the reparations issue died.

In 1974, thanks to members of Hawai'i's congressional delegation, the Native American Programs Act was amended to add Native Hawaiians as a category of indigenous peoples of the United States, thereby enabling Native Hawaiians to qualify for federally funded programs of various sorts. A corporation named Alu Like was formed in 1975 to undertake needs assessment surveys. As an outcome of several task force studies completed in 1985, new legislation was introduced to address the various problems identified, such as the federal Native Hawaiian Health Care Act of 1988, which authorized some financing for nine community-based Native Hawaiian health centers to promote traditional Hawaiian and Western methods of healing. By 1998, Alu Like expects to operate on a budget of some $14 million, derived mostly from federal funds, for projects involving education and employment as well as health.

In 1976, nine young Native Hawaiian community leaders, taking their cue from the occupation of Alcatraz by an American Indian group, landed on the island of Kaho'olawe, which the U.S. Navy had been using for target practice from December 8, 1941. Although later carried off the island under arrest, they made the point that Native Hawaiian *'aina* (land) was being abused. The Protect Kaho'olawe 'Ohana soon filed *Protect Kaho'olawe 'Ohana v U.S. Navy* in court, charging that the navy failed to prepare an environmental impact statement and that the bombing was destroying archaeological sites. The Hawai'i state legislature, meanwhile, commissioned a report on the island (Hawai'i 1978a). In 1980, the 'Ohana and the navy reached a consent decree, placing certain portions of the island under the stewardship of the 'Ohana, and the president ordered an end to all bombing of the island from October 1990. In 1990, Congress established the Kaho'olawe Island Conveyance Commission to determine to which agency or organization the island should ultimately be returned. The recommendation of the commission (U.S. Congress 1993), to which President Bill Clinton agreed, was that from 1994 the island would come under the authority of the Kahoʻolawe Island Reserve Commission, which is now supervising the cleanup of ordinance and the transformation of the island into a Native Hawaiian cultural preserve.

In 1978, a constitutional convention recommended several important changes. By constitutional amendment, English and Hawaiian became the two official languages of the state, which pledged to promote the study of Native Hawaiian culture, including the history and language of the native people. The convention also urged the establishment of a special department of Hawaiian affairs to look after ceded lands and related matters. The state legislature obliged, and the Office of Hawaiian Affairs (OHA) was set up in 1979, with authorization to receive 20 percent of the income from ceded lands to aid Native Hawaiians (Star-Bulletin & Advertiser 1991). A nine-member Board of Trustees, elected by a roster of persons of Native Hawaiian ancestry, manages OHA. One project, the Native Hawaiian Legal Corporation, saved some 360 acres of *kuleana* lands worth $16 million from acquisition by non–Native Hawaiian corporations resulting from land title claims using the legal principle of adverse possession (Ashizawa 1990).

Several organizations emerged to promote the idea of returning land to the Native Hawaiian people. In 1984, a Native Hawaiian Land Trust Task Force explored the question of providing sovereignty to Native Hawaiians, similar to arrangements for some four hundred Native American nations. In 1987, a constitutional convention for a Native Hawaiian nation met, drafted a constitution, issued a declaration of sovereignty for *Ka Lahui Hawaiʻi* (the nation of Hawaiʻi), and elected part-Hawaiian Mililani Trask as *kiaʻaina* (governor). In 1989, the convention reconvened, amended the constitution somewhat, and the movement continued. Although a few of those seeking sovereignty favor a restoration of the monarchy, most prefer the establishment of something similar to Indian reservations, where Native Hawaiians can have a considerable degree of political autonomy, along with a return of federal land in Hawaiʻi to a Native Hawaiian trust and reparations of up to $10 billion for back rent (Glauberman 1992, A2).

In 1982, John Waiheʻe, who achieved prominence during the 1978 constitutional convention, was elected lieutenant governor. Since Governor Ariyoshi was ineligible to run in 1986, Waiheʻe then ran for governor and won. The voters also selected Benjamin Cayetano, a second-generation Filipino, as lieutenant governor. Waiheʻe and

Cayetano were reelected in 1990. When Cayetano was elected governor in 1994, the mantle was passed to a representative of yet another ethnic group.

CONCLUSION

The history of Hawai'i has many unique elements compared to the other forty-nine states. An independent kingdom, powerless to defend itself against the United States, was annexed in 1898 without a plebiscite, an action that today would occasion an outcry from the world. The injustices to Native Hawaiians associated with this act remain largely unaddressed by Washington. Chinese immigrant plantation workers, arriving with only the clothes on their bodies, were subjected to Chinese exclusion acts, were ineligible for American citizenship until 1943, yet have prospered. Japanese, after decades of intense discrimination, emerged proud and strong at the ballot box after 1954, and then appeared to be the new rulers when Ariyoshi became governor. Filipinos, who were recruited as plantation workers, some even as unwitting strikebreakers, were initially denied the opportunity to learn English and raise families; although they consistently voted for Democrats, some began to complain about discrimination under a Japanese governor as they sought in the 1970s to compete with other ethnic groups for middle-class jobs. *Haoles* have fallen from dominance to a role of accommodation to a multiethnic power structure, a role that many *malihini haoles* have found difficult to learn. Other groups, such as blacks, Guamanians, Koreans, Puerto Ricans, Samoans, and Vietnamese, have been accorded less attention because they have seldom comprised more than 1 or 2 percent of the total population.

Yet somehow the competitive coexistence of Hawai'i's ethnic groups seems to work without embittered rancor despite occasional ugly flare-ups. Institutional racism exists, but the prevailing norm is to end racism. The public often seems more adept at achieving multicultural harmony than the leaders, but problems, as everywhere, remain.

NOTES

1. A French ship commander briefly seized the kingdom in 1839.

2. Chinese born in Hawai'i were also stripped of voting rights under the constitution (Glick 1980, 224).

3. Two sugar firms were founded by sons of missionary families (Alexander & Baldwin and Castle & Cooke). The others developed from commercial houses operated from Boston (C. Brewer), Bremen (Hackfeld), and Liverpool (Theo H. Davies). Hackfeld, ordered sold under the Alien Properties Act in World War I, was bought by a new Hawai'i firm (American Factors) for a fraction of the market value (Geschwender 1982, 204).

4. In 1850, Charles Reed Bishop married Bernice Pauahi Paki, a cousin of King Kalakaua. Bishop drew up a will for Princess Ruth, under which half the crown lands (400,000 acres) would revert to Bishop's wife. When Ruth died in 1883, Bishop wrote out a will for his wife, setting up a trust to control the lands upon her death. The will provided that a school be established on half the land to provide education by Protestant teachers; this was the origin of Kamehameha Schools. In 1884, a codicil of the will provided that none of the remaining land could be sold "unless . . . a sale may be necessary for the establishment and maintenance of said schools, or for the best interests of the estate" (Sullam 1976, 4–5). In practice, the Bishop Estate trustees have leased land for a fixed period. When leases expire, rents for new leases often increase astronomically, prompting those living on the land to move. (Earlier fixed rents become bargains in the later years of tenancy). State and local governments in Hawai'i control 38.7 percent of the land, and the federal government 9.8 percent; some seventy-two private landowners (including Bishop Estate) hold more than 1,000 acres, accounting for 46.7 percent of the land, leaving 4.5 percent to smallholder private ownership (Sullam 1976, 4). Much residential housing is built on property leased by the Bishop Estate and other large private landowners.

CHAPTER 3

Language and Language Contact

Derek Bickerton

INTRODUCTION

The history of language contact in Hawai'i further illustrates several themes that run through the present volume. On the negative side, the fact that Hawai'i represents a perhaps unique success story in racial integration cannot be read to mean that Hawai'i has entirely escaped the subtler forms of racism, particularly those generally referred to as institutional racism. From a more positive viewpoint, however, the language situation in Hawai'i argues strongly against the validity of the increasingly popular "English-only" position, which holds that social and cultural integration cannot proceed unless all languages but the dominant one are ruthlessly suppressed. Indeed, efforts to impose monolingualism failed completely.

In Hawai'i, the linguistic history of contact between Native Hawaiians and Caucasians, known locally as *haoles* (*haole* being originally the Hawaiian word for "stranger"), was for almost a century primarily a story of *haole* accommodation to the Hawaiian language, rather than Hawaiian accommodation to English. When the sugar boom came and massive immigration from Portugal, China, Japan, and elsewhere took place, the integration of this diverse population proceeded apace, at first largely through the medium of a pidginized form of Hawaiian, later through a mix of English and Hawaiian with other languages, and finally through an entirely novel creole language created by the children of immigrants and former residents alike. Interested parties—educators, businessmen, government agencies—have tried repeatedly to enforce a one-language policy on the multilingual peoples of Hawai'i. But the linguistic history of Hawai'i is in large part the story of how these efforts failed. Regardless of what they were told, residents of Hawai'i, including many who paid lip service to the propaganda of their rulers, have continued in practice to do their own thing, or rather, things.

To understand this unique linguistic history, one must first rid oneself of the classic stereotype of Caucasian/non-Caucasian contact— a stereotype reinforced not merely by lay opinion but by almost all academic studies until the 1990s (cf. Reinecke 1969; Tsuzaki 1971; Carr 1972). According to that stereotype, Caucasian/non-Caucasian contacts are always carried on via the medium of some European language, no matter how badly mangled. Thus, contacts between Native Hawaiians and *haoles* must have been carried on in some form of pidgin English (perhaps with a sprinkling of Hawaiian words) that derived ultimately from some hypothesized, unattested variety of pidgin English allegedly spoken by sailors worldwide (Goodman 1985; Holm 1986). After establishing itself in Hawai'i's ports, this pidgin supposedly spread to the plantations and served as the means by which immigrant plantation workers communicated with their bosses and one another. During this time, the pidgin allegedly stabilized and expanded, developing seamlessly into the creole language—known locally as "pidgin"—which became the native tongue of most inhabitants of Hawai'i during the territorial period.

This elaborate scenario was based on a minimum of evidence but was accepted because (a) no one produced an alternative account, and (b) the scenario admirably fitted the perceptions of *haole* academia, which saw other ethnic groups as inevitably occupying a clientlike, dependent role, unable even to communicate with one another unless "Massa" furnished the means. One might more plausibly have supposed that, in a country ruled and largely populated by Native Hawaiians, some use would have been made of the indigenous language. But only when research was undertaken in the 1980s did the existence of a form of pidgin Hawaiian receive confirmation through citations in contemporary documents, through the memories of elderly Native Hawaiians, and through the discovery of perhaps its last surviving speaker (Bickerton and Odo 1976; Bickerton and Wilson 1987).

EARLY DOMINANCE OF THE HAWAIIAN LANGUAGE

Over the past several years, extensive archival research by Julian Roberts (1995a; 1995b; 1997) has produced a radically different account, based on literally thousands of documents (books, newspaper and magazine articles in several languages, letters, diaries, and, most valuable of all, court records going back to the 1850s) and covering the entire period of language contact from the 1780s to the twentieth century. We now know that, while a little pidgin English was used from the earliest period onwards, the predominant means of contact, first between Native Hawaiians and Euro-Americans, later between both of these and the several ethnic groups brought to Hawai'i to work on sugar plantations, was a pidginized variety of the Hawaiian language. Pidgin Hawaiian was acquired even by visiting sailors; Robert Jarman (1838, 124), a whaler who visited Hawai'i in the 1830s, reported that "Their [the Hawaiian] language is particularly easy to learn. During the short time we lay here, almost all acquired a smattering of it, enough to get ourselves into trouble, or conciliate, as we chose best."

Much supporting evidence reverses the received wisdom that sailors brought a pidgin English to Hawai'i. Although many Native Hawaiian sailors probably acquired some pidgin English by working on British and American ships, there is no evidence that they used this on their return home (if they did return—many did not), and nothing suggests that such a pidgin could have been transmitted to the plantations. On the contrary, such evidence as the word-lists for new plantation workers produced and distributed by the Hawai'i Sugar Planters Association until the 1960s indicates that, from its establishment in the 1830s onwards, the technical language of the sugar industry was drawn almost exclusively from Hawaiian, and from a pidginized rather than a vernacular version of that language.

Even the New England missionaries who came to Hawai'i in the 1820s began by picking up pidgin Hawaiian. Soon, some graduated to fluency in vernacular Hawaiian, and throughout the nineteenth century there was a small minority of foreigners who could hold their own linguistically with Native Hawaiians, just as there was a small minority of Native Hawaiians who acquired fluency in English. But the majority of newcomers never progressed past a pidginized version of Hawaiian, which stabilized toward the middle of the nineteenth century as that version began to be used by early Chinese immigrants, among others, for communication with both *haoles* and Native Hawaiians—and even between speakers of mutually incomprehensible Chinese dialects (Spear 1856, 58). Many newcomers mistakenly believed this pidgin to be the true Hawaiian language.

Indeed, the consequences of contact upon the Hawaiian language caused English and Hawaiian language purists alike to react with condemnation. One writer complained that the Islands would soon be "filled with a mongrel race, which shall speak like certain men of old, 'half in the speech of Ashdod,' employing a corrupted dialect of the Hawaiian language, and cursing and swearing in broken English" (Missionary Herald 1841, 149). Thirteen years later, the missionary Artemus Bishop ([1854] 1968, 3) denounced the "corrupted tongue" that had "long prevailed between natives and foreigners . . . which the former only use in speaking to the latter." A writer in a Hawaiian language newspaper distinguished no less than four varieties of the language: pure, mixed, corrupted, and altered. Use of these inferior varieties by Native Hawaiians was, according to this writer, no longer limited to contacts with foreigners, for "through associating with foreigners [some Native Hawaiians] act as though they hardly know the language" (J.N. 1873).

In part, these developments arose from the attitudes of Native Hawaiians to their own language. If there is a continuum of attitudes from those least tolerant of grammatical error (such as the French) to those most tolerant, Native Hawaiians would find themselves on the latter end. This tolerance, which allowed *haole* and other newcomers to enter (or to feel they had entered) Hawaiian society, however, was a two-edged sword, bringing about a superficially harmonious society but at the cost of diluting Hawaiian language and culture and allowing alien values and attitudes to infiltrate the community.

MASS IMMIGRATION AND DESTABILIZATION

Linguistic tolerance had further consequences after the Reciprocity Treaty of 1876, when large numbers of immigrant laborers entered the Islands, first from China and Portugal (as well as smaller numbers from other European countries), next from Japan and Korea, and later from Puerto Rico and the Philippines. By 1890, Native Hawaiians found themselves a minority in their own country, with far-reaching linguistic consequences. Hawaiian continued to supply the commonest mode of interethnic communication, especially on the plantations, where veteran Native Hawaiian workers had to explain the process of sugar cultivation to new and largely unskilled immigrants. However, the relatively stable and conventionalized pidgin Hawaiian built up over the previous century was disintegrated by this torrent of newcomers, who were obliged to communicate with one another (and with residents and previous immigrants) before they had had either time or opportunity to acquire even a pidginized version of Hawaiian.

The result, by the mid-1880s, was a *macaronic pidgin*, that is, a structureless jumble of words drawn from several languages. The Hawaiian language still predominated, but English played a gradually increasing role as more and more English-speaking supervisory staff entered the plantation system. However, many utterances contained ingredients drawn from three or four languages, such as "you *nani hanahana?*" which was composed of the following:

> you [from English]
> *nani* ["what" in Japanese]
> *hana* ["work" in Hawaiian (*hanahana* is pidgin Hawaiian for "work")].

In other words, "What work do you do?"

From contemporary documents, one can easily piece together a picture of communicative strategies during the quarter century following the Reciprocity Treaty of 1876. Immigrants used their own languages wherever they could; in consequence, older residents, particularly Native Hawaiians, would pick up small numbers of useful words from each of the major immigrant languages. William Oleson (1886, 10), principal of Kamehameha School for Boys, commented that "the native [Hawaiian] boy is a rarity who has not several phrases in Chinese and Portuguese." Oleson, who forbade the teaching and speaking of Hawaiian, observed that even recent immigrants from Japan were using English, Hawaiian, and Portuguese words. When one's own language failed, the prevailing strategy was to try to speak the other person's language; if this too failed, words from other languages were spoken until understanding was achieved. Thus, one Portuguese laborer, who wished to emphasize the date of his journey to the town of Wailuku, said "*Apopo* I go tomorrow *Wailuku manan*," using Hawaiian (*apopo*), English, and Portuguese (*manan*) words for "tomorrow."

Although English ingredients of this macaronic pidgin were gradually increasing, the Hawaiian component still outweighed all others; in verbatim quotes from defendants and witnesses in criminal trials, Hawaiian words outnumbered English until the early 1890s by a ratio of at least four to one. Contrary to received opinion, many *haoles* were still obliged to communicate preponderantly through some form of Hawaiian. For instance, on April 1, 1892, in testimony before the 5th Circuit, Criminal Court (1208, 41–42), Otto Isenberg, owner of a plantation in Kaua'i, asked *"Pehea pilikia?"* ("What's the trouble?") of a Japanese employee severely kicked by a German foreman (he subsequently died), and received the reply *"Eha 'opu!"* ("Stomach hurts!").

THE ROLE OF CHILDREN

So far, this account has confined itself to the linguistic behavior of adults. Outside of the Native Hawaiian and Portuguese communities, there were few children, and those few usually acquired a fluent command of Hawaiian. However, after the fall of the monarchy, more and more Native Hawaiians abandoned or concealed the use of their language, and control of that language no longer constituted a viable means for communicating with the greater part of the population. In the 1890s, the only linguistic medium regularly available to all was the unstructured, highly variable macaronic pidgin illustrated above. But that pidgin lacked most resources available to all natural languages, having a very limited vocabulary and a virtual absence of syntactic structure. The latter limitation made utterances more than four or five words long almost impossible to express or interpret. Accordingly, this pidgin was not viable as anyone's native language.

What happened then repeated what had previously happened in dozens of similar colonial plantation cultures worldwide (Bickerton 1983). The children, in every case, transformed a relatively undeveloped pidgin into a full human language, complete with all the grammatical apparatus that the antecedent pidgin had lacked. Eleven years after the overthrow of the monarchy, Wallace Farrington (1904, 43), an observant journalist and later governor of Hawai'i, speaking of local newsboys, noted that "however pure the English, Chinese, Portuguese or Hawaiian they may speak in the school or homes, they have a complex pidgin English that is a universal language. They all meet on the 'I-been-go' method of communication."[1] One is inevitably struck by the fact that he picked the past-tense marker "been" (characteristic of all English-influenced creole languages) as stereotypic of the language of children, for the pidgin of their parents was almost entirely devoid of tense marking.

This "universal language" was what is nowadays confusingly called by all local people, "pidgin" or "Hawai'i Pidgin." In reality, of course, this "pidgin" is a creole language, known to professionals in the field as Hawai'i Creole English (HCE). HCE shares many features with Louisiana Creole French and the Gullah of the South Carolina Sea Islands, the other two indigenous American creoles, as well as with Papiamentu in the Dutch West Indies, Jamaican Creole, Haitian, and many similar languages worldwide. As a creole, its rapid delivery and complex sentences contrast strongly with the slow, hesitant delivery and short, simple utterances of old, true pidgin-speaking immigrants, very few of whom survive today.

From a sociolinguistic viewpoint, the most salient feature of HCE is uniformity, which was not true of the macaronic pidgin to which various ethnic groups had brought some features of their ancestral languages. In many cases, anyone who had spent any time in the Islands could identify a speaker's ethnic origins simply by reading a short transcript of his or her speech—without ever having to hear a distinctive accent, simply through the speaker's choice of words and the ways in which those words were put together.[2]

In contrast, as Farrington (1904) noted, the creole was from its inception homogeneous throughout the Islands. Contemporary citations of early (1897–1917) creole show no difference whatsoever between locally born speakers, regardless of the origins of their parents. On a call-in radio talk show in which I took part during 1977, neither the studio panel nor any listener could correctly identify the ethnicity of a locally born male whose tape-recorded speech was played over the air. Everyone tried to base their identification on what he talked about, rather than the way he talked! HCE's uniformity meant that in the early 1900s, for the first time, a concrete bond of unity existed between everyone who could call the Islands home, regardless of skin color, cultural heritage, or any other determinant. Numerous factors might still stand in the way of a completely unified society, and several ethnic groups still sought to maintain their own languages, but for the first time almost everyone had access to a common way of speaking.

LANGUAGE AND OFFICIALDOM

Thus far, I have taken, so to speak, a worm's-eye view of language contact in Hawai'i—how the "language wars" actually appeared to the troops on the ground, who had to cope with and somehow survive in a rapidly changing linguistic environment. But all episodes of contact occurred within a wider context of language policy. In order to put the ground struggle into perspective, I must now look from the viewpoint of authority, where, as elsewhere, the generals had few clues about what was really happening in the trenches.

The Native Hawaiian people's unusually tolerant attitude toward the languages of others was largely shared by their ruling class. But by the mid-nineteenth century, some Native Hawaiians were concerned about the erosion of their language. In the 1860s, the Ministry of Education made determined efforts to reverse the trend by which small but increasing numbers of Native Hawaiians, particularly those in the upper class, received their education through the medium of English.

Originally, the missionaries' attitude had been one of promoting education and literacy in the Hawaiian language. They were the first to produce written versions of Hawaiian, to translate the Bible into Hawaiian, and to preach in Hawaiian. Their children, who included the founders of many of Hawai'i's larger businesses, were another matter. Already by the mid-nineteenth century there was emerging among them, and among others who sought their fortunes in the Islands, a vision of Hawai'i's future that did not include the Hawaiian language— a vision of a docile, well-educated population that could compete commercially with other English-speaking areas.

Indeed, the short-lived governmental attempt at reviving the teaching of the Hawaiian language, as mentioned above, was in large part a reaction against strong pro-English adherents. For example, the *Pacific Commercial Advertiser* (1860) editorialized: "The English schools for natives . . . should be located, too, in the English settlements at first, where native children have opportunities of exercising daily what English they learn at school. And in the vicinity of such settlements an effort should be made to *place all native children* of suitable age, say from four to ten years, in English schools *immediately*" (emphasis added).

To Americans in the golden age of imperialism, Hawai'i appeared an anomaly: an independent, indigenously governed state separated from the United States only by water. No matter that Hawai'i had electricity, streetlights, and telephones before most of the United States did; no matter that Hawai'i's literacy rate exceeded that of most European countries. Possession of these qualities, *haoles* argued, could owe nothing to the qualities of the Hawaiian nation, but must have come about solely through the actions of the *haole* advisers and experts who had managed to insinuate themselves into the self-destructively tolerant Hawaiian government. Therefore, the *haole* elite (all those who would benefit from a docile workforce well-schooled in English, as well as those who hoped to promote a tourist industry) strongly urged that the Islands be Americanized—which meant, of course, linguistically Anglicized—as rapidly as possible.

Before the Anglicization movement began, there was a current of wishful thinking about how Anglicized Hawai'i already was. One writer in *The Polynesian* (1854) claimed that "the English language is already, to a very great extent, the business language of the Islands, and a knowledge of it is becoming more and more indispensable to the native." Nearly two decades later, an acute observer, Isabella Bird Bishop (1874), commented repeatedly on the negligible or nonexistent English of the Native Hawaiians whom she met and spoke with during an extensive tour of the Islands. A writer in *The Friend* (1887, 63), frankly admitting his motivation of "gradually getting [Hawai'i] into working order as a small but somewhat effective 'Anglo-Saxonizing machine,'" claimed that "English is already settled in its place as the controlling language of the country. It is the governing language of the laws and of the courts. It is supreme in business and in journalizing [*sic*]."

Such statements were pure propaganda, designed to stimulate tourism for Hawai'i and to encourage active American support for the military coup that *haole* business leaders were already contemplating. In fact, Hawaiian continued to be used as the legal language in many court cases well into the twentieth century, while in 1887 more newspapers were published in Hawaiian than in English. Shortly after the overthrow of the monarchy, James Blount (1893, 3), sent to Hawai'i by the American government on a fact-finding mission, reported on the true situation: "I see in the newspapers that the War Department is issuing in a documentary form information in relation to the islands. In one of them it is stated that the natives generally speak the English language. This is quite contradictory to my information from intelligent persons here and my own observation. . . . The natives . . . are generally unable to converse with you in English or to understand what is said to them."

Nevertheless, from 1882 onward, children taught in schools where English was allegedly the language of instruction outnumbered those where the language of instruction was Hawaiian. However, many teachers knew little more English than their students. In 1888, a writer in the *Pacific Commercial Advertiser* noted that "English was stopped like the study of Greek when the lessons were over," and that all the children played either in their own languages or in Hawaiian. Concurring, Blount said, "They learn in the schools the English language as an American child would learn the Latin or Greek languages" (Nemo 1888).

After the fall of the monarchy, the pace of Anglicization was stepped up. In 1896, the Hawaiian language was made illegal in schools, and in a few decades the number of Hawaiian speakers had shrunk to a few thousand in isolated areas. Although no contemporary sociologist seems to have studied the question, this trend may well have been due to a feeling by Hawaiian speakers that their native language was now a language of powerlessness and that the future lay with English. But if Native Hawaiians abandoned their own language, there was no motivation for non-natives to try to acquire Hawaiian.

Moreover, none of the languages of the immigrants was equipped to take the place of Hawaiian. Although many local residents had acquired a few words of Chinese and Japanese, fluent use of these languages was restricted almost entirely to native speakers. The Chinese and, to an even greater extent, the Japanese did all in their power to maintain their languages; each group sponsored private schools, which operated after normal school hours and taught exclusively in its own language. Some Japanese even sent their children back to Japan to receive secondary or even primary education. But the local language schools had only limited effectiveness, due to antiquated teaching methods and the excessive burden they placed on students. These schools declined in numbers between the two world wars, and many were swept away in the tide of xenophobia that accompanied World War II.

The *haole* establishment hoped that English would fill the vacuum resulting from the decline of Hawaiian, but such a view was unrealistic, since native English speakers made up only 5 to 6 percent of the population. Instead, that vacuum was quickly filled by HCE, which spread quickly among locally born speakers of all ethnic groups. After 1920, HCE began to be acquired as a second language by new immigrants. Only after World War II, when creole speakers made up a large majority of the population, did such immigrants generally achieved full fluency in HCE.

HCE was soon spotted by educators and targeted for destruction. In 1921, the first shot was fired in a *Hawaii Educational Review* article listing the "incorrect functioning," "errors," and "confusions" found in the speech of students. Not until the 1970s would the educational community begin to grasp that HCE was a separate language, rather than some idiosyncratic kind of "broken English." During those fifty years, numerous articles and books appeared with similar misanalyses. The history of efforts to eradicate creole in the schools belongs more properly to the history of education in Hawaii. However, repressive language policies were carried so far that, according to the memories of some older residents, students in more than one institution were rewarded for informing on their classmates who used creole even outside the school grounds!

LANGUAGE IN HAWAI'I TODAY

As with all attempts to extirpate languages and dialects, the campaign to stamp out HCE failed completely, merely implanting the unhealthy and ambiguity-laden attitudes expressed by the local mother portrayed on the cover of a recent popular work, Douglas Simonson's *Pidgin to Da Max* (1981), who says to her children, *"How many times I tol' you . . . No talk li'dat!"* ("Don't speak that way!"). Like many stigmatized languages and dialects, HCE is at one and the same time (and often by the same people!) despised as some kind of uneducated "broken talk" and admired as a bonding mechanism among the locally born as well as a mark of working-class toughness and anti-*haole* solidarity.

Under these circumstances, code switching (changing one's variety of speech according to social context) became a *sine qua non* in the Islands. The same people who were being berated by teachers as substandard language speakers were in fact performing prodigies of linguistic virtuosity—repidginizing their creole for the benefit of immigrant grandparents, switching into standard English (or something close to it) at their white-collar jobs or in court, then returning with visible relief to their natural speech when they were with friends or younger relatives.

The main social role of HCE has been as a badge of community identity—"local" (that is, raised in Hawai'i, even if one happens to be that apparent oxymoron, a "local *haole*") as against the rest of the world. Local people traveling on the mainland United States and operating in standard English mode will immediately switch into HCE if, while in transit at some airport, they happen to bump into the merest acquaintance from the Islands.

However, there are signs that, at least among the urban middle class, "progress" is achieving what several generations of prescriptivist teachers failed to achieve. Every year, one hears less and less HCE spoken in public places. The increase in immigration from the mainland United States since statehood has given speakers of mainland English varieties a plurality, if not as yet a majority of the population. Continued pressure from corporations and government agencies, unwilling to take on employees who deal directly with the public if they have even a distinguishable local accent, has also played a part. Indeed, some unfortunate legal decisions have upheld the prerogative of employers to refuse to hire speakers with nonmainland accents. In the case of *Kahakua et al. v Friday* (876F2d698), two Hawai'i-born weather forecasters brought suit against their employers, the National Weather Bureau, because despite having the requisite qualifications they were not promoted to positions which would have required them to give recorded forecasts. The Bureau claimed that their accents would be unintelligible to nonlocals, and the forecasters lost their case in 1989.[3] As a result of these and other pressures, HCE in its original form is spoken only in predominantly agricultural areas by working-class people in their sixties or older.

Some younger working-class locals have attempted to halt the decline of HCE by accentuating whatever is left of the creole features in their speech as a boundary marker against younger mainland-born *haoles*, who increasingly compete for less-skilled jobs. Similarly, side by side with, but not necessarily as a part of, the Hawaiian sovereignty movement, the Hawaiian language has been revitalized over the last decade, in particular through a language-immersion program for students, who are by no means drawn exclusively from the Native Hawaiian community.

We have yet to see how far these trends can reverse the linguistic history of the present century. While the renaissance of the Hawaiian language seems to be widely accepted, HCE remains controversial, being regarded by many laypersons as "not a real language." Every five years or so, there is a flurry of comment in the local press, with articles pro and con, and a spate of letters to the editor. In recent years, more and more locals have been prepared to speak out in favor of "pidgin," and the State Board of Education has softened its views on the use of HCE in classroom situations, while taking care to distance itself from the minority of activists who demand that HCE be accorded equal status and perhaps even used as a language of instruction in some schools and grades.

Progressive decreolization, and the growing percentage of mainland *haoles* among Hawai'i's people, almost certainly preclude any significant use of HCE in future teaching. However, there is every likelihood that HCE will persist, albeit in a somewhat diluted form, for as long as those born and raised in Hawai'i identify with the local culture and feel the need to distinguish themselves from the rest of the American population. Other languages, too, seem likely to continue to flourish. All signs indicate that the Hawaiian language will at least maintain and possibly strengthen its position. Given the constant influx of tourists from Japan, Japanese is shifting from a maintained ethnic language to one acquired by members of any ethnic group who do business with these tourists; for the benefit of the latter, as well as for resident Japanese, two television channels broadcast exclusively or mainly in that language. The recent influx of immigrants from Central America and México has introduced yet another language, Spanish, which is now broadcast for several hours each week on the public access channel.

Recently, an unofficial language-policy organization, the Hawai'i Coordinating Council on Language Planning and Policy, was formed. Among the organization's *Statement of Goals* (c. 1996) is a "language other than English for all," meaning that all residents should speak a language in addition to English. The Council's program has no official backing, but the state of affairs envisaged has already been partially achieved *de facto*. With some 25.5 percent of the population bilinguals and multilinguals (U.S. Census 1993, 28), Hawai'i probably has the most linguistic diversity of any state in the Union, even if one does not count HCE as a separate language.

Could the fact that Hawai'i is also the most racially tolerant of those states be nothing more than mere coincidence? Hawai'i's experience might suggest that proponents of "English-only" policies need to do some serious thinking about the effect those policies may have on the already dangerously high levels of racial tension in mainland America.

NOTES

1. Depending on context, *"I been go"* might mean "I went" or "I had gone." In pidgin, either would be rendered simply as *"me go"* or *"I go."*

2. Of course, if one person were imitating the speech of a person from a different ethnic group, all bets are off. For instance, I have heard an elderly Native Hawaiian woman give a perfect imitation of the speech of a Japanese immigrant.

3. In 1989, the City and County of Honolulu won in a court case filed by a job applicant who was claimed to have a "heavy Filipino accent" (699FSupp1429; 888F2d591).

CHAPTER 4

The Media

Helen Geracimos Chapin

THE GROWTH OF MEDIA

A *medium* is a form of communication and a social process. The most basic, elemental origins of media can be traced back to when individual human beings came together to communicate and solve problems of survival (Yaple and Korzenny 1989). The media today should play a similar role in global survival.

Ethnic conflict seems to be the war of choice in the late twentieth century. When not in open warfare, groups have conflicting goals among themselves over what form to choose: acculturation, assimilation, or pluralism (Levinson 1994, 15–18). Should they partially blend folkways, mores, and laws, and thus acculturate? Should they strive for total assimilation? Or can they maintain their identity within a pluralistic system—a system in which groups differ from one another but participate simultaneously in and are members of the larger society?

In order to discuss Hawai'i's situation, I will place certain specific terms in context. By *ethnic*, I mean the tribal group identity into which people are born. By *cultural*, I mean the totality of socially transmitted behavior patterns that a group acquires. Both ethnic and cultural groups may include a combination of racial, religious, national, and other traits. Because of the particular history of Hawai'i, there is no absolute division between the ethnic and the cultural.

From a single indigenous population that lived in isolation for 1,500 years, Hawai'i has since its invasion by outsiders become perhaps the most ethnically and culturally diverse democracy on the planet, having done so in a relatively, though not entirely, peaceable manner. The media in Hawai'i have developed in a similar manner, and today may be the most diversified in the world. In this chapter, I will examine printed newspapers, broadcast radio, and television.[1]

Newspapers entered the Hawaiian kingdom in 1834, radio in 1922, and television in 1952. Print and broadcasting are different technologies, but they share in common that they are imported, intrusive forces that impact upon history even as they record it. Their separate and joint histories carry many paradoxes, which is not surprising, as they are the products of human beings who themselves, while inventing highly complex technologies, stubbornly cling to basic ethnic identification.

Harold Isaacs (1975, 38ff., 216–17) calls ethnic identification "idols of the tribe"—idols that are deep universal responses to our body type and name, kinship circle, location, our language, history, and religion, and the nation of which we are a part. With the beauty of ethnicity, observes Isaacs, may go the brutality of blood. It is my contention that in Hawai'i, over two centuries, long before the rise of electronic technology, the media have been an interactive force in achieving multiculturalism within enormous social changes covering an independent nation, a republic, a territory, and a state.

Let me review technology before turning to each medium's individual role in multiculturalism. Marshall McLuhan (1962) has stated that technology may be more revolutionary than politics and that the use of a particular tool or tools is the driving mechanism behind cultural change.

Print is relatively new to human experience. In prehistoric times, humans gained information from one another through signs and the spoken word. About 3,500 years ago, the written word became a source of knowledge. Since the invention of movable type by the machinery of a "press" in fifteenth-century Europe, literate societies have used print as the chief means of communication. After the 1600s, as a direct outgrowth of the Industrial Revolution, the newspaper became a major source of information. Print to this day, however, retains ethnic identification, such as the familiar Roman, Italic, and Gothic fonts.

Harold Innis, in *Empire and Communications* (1972), has stated that print is an imperialist force which has conquered wherever it has collided with an older, oral culture. Print assists in empire building and colonizing. A newer technology disrupts and abrades an older one (cf. Innis 1951; Jankowski and Fuchs 1995, 26). Hawai'i, an isolated, preliterate society—oral, memory based, communal, with a nature-based religion and a barter economy dependent upon food yields from the ocean and land—was washed over after contact by competition, Christianity, money, a market economy, private property, printing, and literacy.

The mobile printing press entered the Islands in 1820 with American Protestant missionaries from New England (Chapin 1996). Profoundly impacting the native culture, the missionaries tried to stamp out traditional religion and customs while introducing a writing system for the Hawaiian language. Writing was quickly applied to the production of monthly newspapers by handset type on a manually operated wood and iron press; later, weeklies emerged from steam-driven and electric presses, and then large daily editions were printed by hot lead on linotype (Chapin 1984). Newspapers incorporated such other inventions as mass advertising and the camera, the former leading to increased profits for the papers, the latter making photojournalism possible. After World War II, there were faster, more sophisticated presses, and since the early 1970s a computer technology has been established.

Radio, chronologically the next revolutionary technology, was made possible with the harnessing of electricity. The invention of the wireless in 1844 meant that, for the first time in human life, messages traveled faster than the messenger. Information was detached from any solid commodity, and space became inconsequential. In 1898, the news of U.S. annexation of Hawai'i took seven days to arrive in the Islands by steamship from California. In 1903, on New Year's Day, the Pacific Cable, containing electronic circuitry, was installed—a technologically significant act that connected the Islands in seconds to the mainland United States, Europe, and other countries and continents. The cable destroyed the ocean barrier surrounding Hawai'i and annihilated distance.

The first known radio program in the United States was a Christmas Eve broadcast in 1906 from Brant Rock, Massachusetts. In 1922, two Hawai'i radio stations joined the new mass medium, which today comprises 564 licensed stations in the United States. The Federal Communications Commission (FCC) in 1927 allocated wavelengths to broadcasters, and networks emerged (Nicol 1974).

Television, yet more revolutionary by incorporating radio waves with the transmission of images, was technically feasible by 1931, but did not broadcast until April 30, 1939, at the opening of the New York World's Fair. By mid-1940, there were twenty-three television stations in the United States. World War II brought all activity to a halt, but from 1946 on there has been phenomenal growth of television, the main goal of which was and is to entertain (Settle 1983).

NEWSPAPERS

Newspapers, the oldest and longest-running medium, have played a paramount role in promoting multiculturalism. The size and content vary, but they are recognizable by their format on newsprint and the miscellany of topical subject matter. The United States' founders considered newspapers so important as an information source that they protected a free press and free speech under the First Amendment to the Constitution.[2]

Appearing first in Hawaiian, then in English, an astonishing 1,000 separate newspaper titles have appeared in 160 years in Hawai'i. More than 100 titles have been produced in Hawaiian, plus some 270 in eleven other languages or in English for various ethnic groups. Therefore, more than one-third of all the newspapers have represented those whose ancestral tongues have not been English: African American, Chinese, Filipino, Hawaiian, Japanese, Jewish, Korean, Portuguese, Samoan, Spanish, and Vietnamese. Furthermore, fully one-third of all these publications have been bilingual and even trilingual, that is, printed in two or three different languages or dialects—Japanese and English, for example, or Tagalog, Visayan, and Ilocano. Thus, while newspapers were imported from the United States into what was first an outpost, then an integral part of America, they have encompassed diversity and multiculturalism from their earliest days.

Four categories may be used to classify newspapers: establishment, opposition (or alternative), official, and independent. These may shift and overlap as the role of newspapers change in the context of their times, contributing further to diversity.

The *establishment press*, the first category, also called the commercial or mainstream press, was instituted in the Hawaiian language by the missionaries, who soon after their arrival began their own rise to power in the kingdom. Missionary printers, from 1834, taught young Native Hawaiian male students at the Lahainaluna School on Maui to write, set type, and produce four-page papers. By 1836, the first foreign language paper appeared—an English language journal backed by American business interests, who were bent on gaining influence in the growing port town of Honolulu. Bilingualism accompanied this dual language situation. The English language *Pacific Commercial Advertiser* (1856–) and its Hawaiian language counterpart, *Nupepa Ku'oko'a (The Independent Press)* (1861–1927), were edited by missionary descendants fluent in Hawaiian and by ardent Native Hawaiian Christian news reporters fluent in English. *Nupepa Ku'oko'a*, the longest-lived Hawaiian language paper, became a rich storehouse of information on the Hawaiian language and customs. Stooping to a baser enterprise, establishment political activists who were newspaper leaders conspired to overthrow the monarchy in 1893, to defeat the Native Hawaiian nationalist counterrevolution in 1895, and to promote annexation to the United States. Nevertheless, by the early twentieth century, establishment papers appeared in other languages; for example, plantation periodicals produced by sugar and pineapple management, with columns in Filipino and Japanese, were aimed at reaching ethnic groups entering Hawai'i as plantation labor in order to propagandize them of the superiority of American values. Inadvertently, while consolidating economic, political, and social power, the establishment thereby added to multiculturalism.

Responding to economic realities, the metropolitan dailies and suburban weeklies, although predominantly in English, have come to include over the decades multicultural editorial and advertising content. To identify just a few, supermarkets and restaurants advertise specific ethnic foods; Saturday church columns promote services from Korean Christian to Samoan Mormon and Greek Orthodox. Features appear on Black History Week, St. Patrick's Day, and other ethnic holidays. Discussions cover the Native Hawaiian immersion program in the public schools as well as Native Hawaiian sovereignty issues. Increasing numbers of Asian Americans have been employed on these newspapers, but, to this day, employment of Native Hawaiians is very low, and upper-level editorial and management levels are more than 60 percent Caucasian (University of Hawai'i 1985).

Opposition newspapers, sometimes called the *alternative press*, arise to do verbal battle with and to resist the establishment. Over two centuries, indigenous and ethnic language opposition papers have been a force to be reckoned with and have contributed to the Islands' racial amalgam.

Native Hawaiians, who avidly adopted literacy, produced from 1861 a nationalist press that challenged the promotion of imperialist American interests. In Hawaiian and English, this press articulated arguments for keeping Hawai'i an independent country. Hawaiian nationalist papers reached their height of influence in the 1890s, when at least twenty newspapers spoke for 45 percent of the population of 90,000. Such journalists and political activists as Robert and Theresa Wilcox, who copublished several papers, and John Bush, editor of *Ka Leo o ka Lahui* (*The Voice of the Nation*) (1889–1896), were expertly bilingual. The presence of these papers decreased rapidly after annexation.

Print fosters independent thinking, but it also enables government to centralize and oppress dissenters (Altschull 1984, 5; Forer 1987). The most blatant example occurred after the overthrow, when the oligarchy eliminated guarantees of free speech, and arrested, fined, and jailed a dozen Native Hawaiian and allied Caucasian oppositionists for "seditious libel" and "conspiracy"—that is, for pro-Hawaiian sentiments. But attesting to their tenacity, Native Hawaiians are making a comeback. A sovereignty movement based in part on the arguments of nineteenth-century nationalist news media resurfaced in the 1970s, grew stronger in the 1980s, and became prominent in the 1990s. Such papers as the tabloid *Ka Wai Ola o OHA* (*The Living Waters of OHA*) (1980–), produced by the Office of Hawaiian Affairs, and printed in English but with columns in Hawaiian, are aiding the sovereignty movement.

At this point, the role of language should be examined. By the usual linguistic dynamics, the Hawaiian language should be disappearing. Language is, of course, intimately connected not just to the media, but to education and government. Over the nineteenth century, English rapidly moved from being a foreign language to being a dominant language. In a process identified as "linguistic genocide" (Day 1985), English replaced Hawaiian in 1854 as the language of instruction in many public schools and from 1870 was the original language on government documents (Day 1985; Kimura 1985). The Republic of Hawai'i after 1895 outlawed Hawaiian in the public schools. Yet, against all odds, the Hawaiian language is resurging in education and public discourse and is very much alive today.

Other opposition or alternative papers arose in ethnic languages. These papers, produced by educated cadres, have a dual, paradoxical role: to foster pride in the home country, thereby keeping readers in touch with their roots, and to inform readers of the new land's customs and practices, thereby helping to acculturate or assimilate. Ethnic journals were an outgrowth of the worldwide recruitment across two centuries for plantation labor and of independent chain migration. Hawai'i may claim to have one of the most numerous ethnic language presses in the world (Beechert 1985).

For example, the Chinese were initially recruited in 1851, and the first Chinese journals were issued in 1881; to date, there have been at least twenty-six Chinese or Chinese-English papers. *Chung Hua Hsin Pao* (*United Chinese Press*) (1900–) continues to publish and is a primary source of information for new immigrants.

The second ethnic press to appear held a unique position. The Portuguese, who were recruited from 1878 to 1884, and their newspapers, commencing in 1885, were used as buffers by the oligarchy between the dark-skinned laborers and their *haole* bosses. *O Luso Hawaiiana* (1895–1924) was the longest lived of some thirteen different titles. No Portuguese papers are in print today, but descendants of the Portuguese, who have tended to blend with other groups, still retain a strong awareness of their ancestry.

The third press, the Japanese, is the most remarkable in numbers and influence. By 1896, the Japanese comprised the largest immigrant group, with a literacy rate at about 50 percent in the 1900s (U.S. Census 1902, 912; 1913, 586). More than 120 papers have appeared in Japanese or Japanese and English since 1892. In their heyday, the era of the 1920s to the 1940s, the papers reached one-third of the population, reflecting the Territory's demographics.

These papers illustrate another dynamic. Ethnic or indigenous language papers usually do not speak in a single voice, for there are differences of opinion within almost any cultural group. The establishment, by contrast, will be unified in its determination to retain power. For example, the oligarchy applied a divide-and-conquer strategy by fomenting dissension among the Japanese language newspapers, accusing the "rabid Japanese press" of "trying to stir up agitation" (Pacific Commercial Advertiser 1919).

Similarly, a virulent "Americanism" campaign sought to destroy the papers and the Japanese language schools, arguing that the "Anglo-

Saxon" brought civilization to the United States and Hawai'i. In 1924, *Hawaii Hochi* (*Hawaii News Record*) (1912–) backed strikes for better pay and working conditions, while *Nippu Jiji* (*Japan-Hawaii Times*) (1906–1985) editorially counseled moderation. The 1924 strike lost. But when the territorial legislature passed a law to ban Japanese language schools, a strong-willed, highly focused editor led the fight to save them. Frederick Shinzaburo Makino, himself the offspring of a Japanese father and English mother, and *Hawaii Hochi* battled the case all the way to the U.S. Supreme Court, which, in 1927, declared the law unconstitutional.

During World War II, in an ironic reversal of fortune, Japanese language papers again prevailed. After the December 7, 1941, attack on Pearl Harbor, the military government shut down all ethnic language papers. Four were allowed to reopen (two in Japanese and one each in Chinese and Filipino) under strict censorship, when the military government realized there was no other way to inform immigrants. The Japanese-language papers have receded in influence since the war, but the principal one, the semimonthly *Hawaii Herald* (1980–), in English and occasional Japanese, reaches younger generations of Japanese Americans, and remains an important voice for ethnic pride, the transmission of cultural values, and intergenerational dialogue.

Two other prominent ethnic presses are the Korean and Filipino. The Korean, totaling about thirty papers, has been chiefly interested in politics in Korea. The Filipino, however, has had a historic role since Pablo Manlapit, a union organizer, brought out *Ang Sadata* (*The Sword*) (1913). At present, such journals as the *FIL-AM Courier* (1986–) and the *Hawaii Filipino Chronicle* (1992–) reach new immigrants from the Philippines.

In the last third of this century, such ethnic papers as the *Hawaii Herald* have become part of the establishment because of political ascendancy by non-Caucasians. There is a paradox here, too. The ethnic press reflects the continuation of immigration into Hawai'i; yet Hawai'i also has the highest ratio in the nation of mixed marriages—about 50 percent. Thus the papers are simultaneously ethnic enclaves with multicultural outreach. They are concerned with the histories of their own groups locally but report outside events; for example, *Hawaii Jewish News* (1977–) has content on Hawai'i and Israel. *Mahogany* (1988–) features Island and mainland African Americans. Still another type is the ethnic paper aimed at the visitor or tourist market, such as the Japanese language *Waikiki Bichi Purisu* (*Waikiki Beach Press*) (1971–).

Labor papers, too, have shifted roles from opposition to establishment. These journals hit their stride from the 1930s to 1950s, serving as organizing tools across racial lines for unions struggling against an exploitative management. The *Honolulu Record* (1948–1958), under Koji Ariyoshi, was especially effective. The *Record* was sponsored by the International Longshoremen's and Warehousemen's Union (ILWU), but *Nisei* (second-generation) Ariyoshi followed his own independent bent in advocating racial equality and a free press. During the anti-Communist hysteria of the McCarthy era, Ariyoshi was prosecuted and jailed as one of the "Hawai'i Seven" who were supposedly engaged in a conspiracy to overthrow the American government. Six of the Hawai'i Seven were either Japanese or married to Japanese. The witch hunt, reminiscent of the oligarchy's anti-Japanese campaigns of the 1920s, was an effort to remain dominant. Ariyoshi (1953, 60) predicted that the oligarchy would lose its power and that anti-Communism would eventually "rot in the garbage heap of history." In the 1950s and 1960s, labor papers, reflecting the increased prosperity of labor itself, moved into the mainstream.

Official papers, the third category, present an interesting dynamic. In that Hawai'i is the most militarized state in the Union, military newspapers are an active presence. The army papers in particular, representing an equal opportunity service whose enlisted personnel is one-third non-Caucasian, have promoted the combination of ethnic pride and patriotism.

Independent papers, the fourth category, are not beholden to any special interest. A nineteenth-century example set the model for racial blending. Two *haole* journalists, the Swedish Abraham Fornander and the American Henry Sheldon, who both married Native Hawaiian women, challenged rising American dominance and advocated Hawaiian independence in the *Honolulu Times* (1849–1851). The best contemporary representative is *Ka Leo o Hawaii* (1922–), the student-run University of Hawai'i at Manoa newspaper, which is overseen by a publications board but left alone editorially. Over the years, *Ka Leo* has been a model of multiculturalism in content and multiethnic staffing.

Today, all papers operate in an environment of internationalism. Reporters and editors work at video display terminals. At the center of a plant's operation is the central processing unit. Wire press material enters directly by satellite into the computer. From the 1990s, newspapers appear on home computers. The *Honolulu Star-Bulletin* beams a daily version into the World Wide Web.

RADIO: THE HOT MEDIUM

Radio reaches only one of our five senses, the aural. This hot medium or tribal drum (McLuhan 1964, 259) raises a sense of immediacy and personal association that has applications to multiculturalism (Fishman et al. 1982).

Similar to newspapers, the Islands contain a surprisingly large number of radio stations that have been multicultural from their first days (Fishman et al., 1982). On May 11, 1922, the first stations, KGU and KDYX (later, from 1930, KGMB) blurted out "Hello, hello," and "*Aloha*" (Schmitt 1978, 107). The stations were originally owned by newspapers. Radio, however, like television, fits into three broadcast categories: commercial, noncommercial and public, and professional.[3] KGU affiliated with the National Broadcasting Company (NBC) in 1931, followed by other affiliations interconnecting radio stations on mainland cities with Honolulu on Oʻahu and the main towns on the Neighbor Islands of Hawaiʻi, Maui, and Kauaʻi.

After World War II, the number of radio stations burgeoned, increasing each decade to the present size. The City and County of Honolulu, with a population of 836,231, has the same number of stations as metropolitan Dallas, Texas, with a population of 3.5 million—thirty-two stations in all, sixteen each of AM and FM (Harada 1996). In addition to commercial stations on Oʻahu, in 1996 noncommercial stations include Hawaiʻi Public Radio, with four channels, and KTUH, the radio station of the University of Hawaiʻi at Manoa.

From the beginning, radio owners perceived that, to attract advertising revenue, the appeal should be to all listeners. *Haole*-owned, pro-establishment English language stations aired Hawaiian music, Sunday sermons in Japanese, and Filipino cultural programs. The nationally popular *Hawaii Calls,* featuring Hawaiian music, beamed in the 1930s to mainland audiences, went off the air in the 1960s, but has been revived in the 1990s, and reaches national and international audiences.

Nevertheless, the 1960s were a turning point, when ethnic and indigenous stations came on the air. The rise in consciousness of "roots," the resurgence of Native Hawaiian identity in the 1970s, and continued migration into the fiftieth state have contributed to an increasing number of language and cultural programs on the English language stations, and to other stations dedicated exclusively to individual ethnic groups, principally the Japanese and Filipinos. KISA-AM is the leading Filipino radio station locally—and in the United States (Mayberry 1979).

Two especially interesting types of radio's multicultural outreach are Native Hawaiian and "local" programming. The sovereignty movement, while composed of groups with different goals, in essence wants some kind of self-determination for Native Hawaiians. "Local" is a classification of persons who are non-*haoles* and have forebears connected to the plantation experience. The informal creole tongue of locals, as described in the preceding chapter by Derek Bickerton, is an amalgam of words, phrases, and tonal pitch that pervades both Native Hawaiian and most radio stations in the Islands.

Native Hawaiian and "local" radio presently lead in the ratings. The Arbitrons, to radio what the Nielsens are to television, have since 1991 rated KCCN "Hawaiian Radio" as having the most listeners. KCCN-AM and -FM are twenty-four-hour stations that play Hawaiian music, conduct interviews, air education and informational programs, and broadcast from outside the studios on special occasions. A third station, KINE-FM, has call letters that derive from *da kine*, the all-purpose pidgin term for "this" or "that."

Local radio has attached itself to the automobile in Hawai'i, which leads the nation in car ownership per person. From 1991, KSSK-FM has been the top "Drive-Time" station during peak hours from 6 to 10 A.M. (Adams 1991). Heading up "Drive-Time" is the KSSK duo of mainland-born Michael W. Perry and Hawai'i-born Larry Price, who introduced the "phone posse," an informal but potent volunteer community assemblage of 60,000 listeners, who call to report speeding vehicles, accidents, and car thefts, which Perry and Price then relay to the police.

Attesting to the immediacy of radio and multiculturalism, KIKI-AM found itself in a major flap in 1993, when what appeared to be anti-Hawaiian remarks were broadcast. KIKI's general manager, Lee Coleman, advised a mainland advertising agency to aim its Acura ad campaign at professional, high-income, white-collar Caucasian and Japanese, and not at the Native Hawaiian population. In a singular exaggeration and simplification of sovereignty goals, Coleman described the movement as one "where Hawaiians want to retake the Islands and remove all foreigners and foreign business." Protests poured in from the general public (Fernandez 1993; Tanahara 1993). KIKI publicly apologized and agreed to help the public have a greater understanding of issues relating to sovereignty. The station subsequently for a year aired "Historic Notes," prepared by the Hawaiian Historical Society, on a wide range of cultural and historical subjects.

Radio also targets the visitor market. KORL-FM appeals to Japanese visitors in the 12- to 44-year-old bracket with music, sports, entertainment tips, and lessons in Hawaiian. Its twenty-four-hour trilingual format reaches three islands. KZOO also broadcasts in Japanese, and Island residents also tune in.

On the Neighbor Islands, where there are two dozen stations, several call themselves "Hawaiian," air Hawaiian music, and highlight news and features of interest to Native Hawaiians. In fact, most "mainstream" stations on the major islands include substantial Hawaiian, "local," and ethnic language and cultural broadcasting. Today, residents average twenty-two hours per week listening to radio (Harada 1996).

TELEVISION: A MIXED PLATE

Television, the newer mass medium, is not just the most powerful communications force in the Islands, but in the world. Totally co-opted in the globalization of the media, all Hawai'i's commercial broadcast stations are owned by mainland or international conglomerates.

In 1952, local television broadcasting, similar to newspapers and radio earlier, immediately initiated ethnic programming. In 1972, the FCC opened the skies to all. Since the advent of live news by satellite in 1976—the satellite was named "Lani Bird" in an "idols of the tribe" attempt to humanize and localize it—television has been the primary medium of information and entertainment. In 1976, KITV, after firing an all-*haole* news team, opened its evening news with four non-*haole* newscasters. Ethnic announcers subsequently appeared on all the network news shows.

There are twenty commercial, two public or noncommercial, and eight local cable stations. In fact, Hawai'i is "the most cabled state in the world" (McLaughlin 1989). Besides these stations, there are foreign broadcast companies: the Chinese Communication Broadcasting Company, Japan TV News, and the Voice of Korea. Satellite programs are beamed directly from Japan and the Philippines. Noncommercial television is thriving, too. The successful Hawai'i Public Television has four channels; and public access *'Olelo*, financed jointly by private and public funds and incorporating "narrow casting" (meeting the needs of audiences who otherwise would not have voices on television), plans to expand from four to seven channels. In total, 97 percent of Island households receive television, whereas newspapers reach roughly only 20 percent (Hawai'i 1992, 382–406).

Noncommercial television stations are the most multicultural. An overview of a typical week's programming, however, illustrates that commercial television is also multicultural. If "local" programming is identified with radio, then a "mixed plate" is the metaphor applicable to television. A *mixed plate* is a meal that contains a variety of foods: for example, Japanese rice, Chinese noodles, Hawaiian-Japanese teriyaki steak or chicken, Korean *kim chee*, and *haole* salad and bread. Talented Pamela Young, whose ancestors are Chinese, hosts a program called *Mixed Plate*, which beams events of local interest from Hawai'i, New York, Las Vegas, San Francisco, and elsewhere. Add to this the enormous popularity of food and cooking shows, such as Hari Kojima's *Let's Go Fishing*, a program that originated with the Japanese American Kojima in a secondary role to a *haole*, but now features Kojima as the premier host who fishes and then cooks his catch. Other shows star Island chefs preparing "Pacific cuisine."

Weekend commercial programs offer Japanese movies and Korean Christian shows. Noncommercial programs include *Samoan Hi Lights*, karate and sumo (these last two appear on weekdays, too), *Soul Train*, and coverage of board meetings of the Office of Hawaiian Affairs (OHA). Public access *'Olelo* on Sunday evenings runs programs produced by Chinese, Filipinos, Hispanics, Japanese, Native Hawaiians, and other ethnicities. Some individuals air their own shows, such as Native Hawaiian activist Haunani-Kay Trask and moderate OHA member Billy Beamer.

During the week, in the evenings or prime time, commercial stations air a *Philippines Today* show and subtitle movies spoken in

Cantonese, Filipino, Japanese, Korean, and Mandarin. Noncommercial stations carry one or two hours of Hawaiian language and other cultural programs on Native Hawaiian subjects, and several hours on Spanish culture and language to reach the growing Hispanic population. Hawai'i Public Television offers *Spectrum,* an award-winning program on a full range of subjects that appeal to audiences across the spectrum of island groups. One station features "Shinchan," the Japanese version of Bart Simpson. Appearing on commercial and noncommercial stations are such local comedians as Bu La'ia and Frank DeLima, who lightheartedly spoof themselves and all racial groups. Sometimes misunderstood by newcomers, ethnic humor has proven to be a very effective communications mode that defuses tensions in a pluralistic society.

Unfortunately, employment patterns in radio and television are not as mixed a plate as programming. A study of employees by ethnic categories, comparing 1975 to 1988, shows that Caucasian officials and managers dropped from 70 percent in 1975 to 61 percent in 1988. Asian employment (not separated by ethnicity) rose from 27 to 32 percent, and African Americans from 1 to 4 percent (Haas 1992, 119). Regarding professional employees, Caucasians decreased from 65 to 53 percent between 1975 and 1988; Asians increased from 29 to 38 percent; and African Americans from 3 to 5 percent (Haas 1992, 120). Consequently, there was an increase in non-Caucasian hiring, likely a response in part to affirmative action.

CONCLUSION

At all levels, communication is culture and a container of human interaction (Carey 1989, 155). Culture is a learned body of behavior; it is in a dynamic, evolving, constant state of becoming. Classification by race or ethnicity is similarly transient. One may even choose one's culture or ethnicity. Others do not choose but are chosen. Many are loyal to more than one identity (like myself, Greek American in Hawai'i).

There are competing agendas, however. One is between open and closed communication systems. On one side are those who believe that fragile ethnic cultures and emerging nations need protection; on the other side are those who support open information and cultural exchange. However, as we know all too well from the daily headlines, talk radio, and trash television, the media are all too ready to exploit and make entertainment from conflict and violence. There are enormous problems to be solved. In an economically internationalized world, the possibility of the media as the tool of the profit-driven marketplace invading the entire globe is frightening. Today, almost all the press, print and broadcast, has fallen under the control of huge absentee corporations with global economic agendas. The Federal Communications Act of 1996 allows companies to own a greater number of stations, and vast conglomerates of mergers and closures are taking place. Newspaper organizations own television and radio outlets, book and magazine publishing firms, record companies, cable television, and computer and software outfits, not to mention baseball teams and food companies (Compaine 1982). Multinational companies may eventually control the communications systems of the entire world. Centralized "news management" and control of information by huge media organizations, with direct lines into government, may make the old questions of "press freedom," not to mention democracy itself, seem quaint and antiquated.

At home, the enormous Gannett Corporation, formerly just a newspaper chain, is a total information company that owns the Hawai'i News Agency (HNA), which manages the business of both Honolulu dailies. This arrangement has led to ongoing charges of monopolistic practices, which have been denied. Additionally, Hawai'i's economy is rocky, and there are indications of a widening class gap and increased tensions between the haves and have-nots.

Nonetheless, there may be some light to shed on this dark view. A pan-Pacific community is in the making. In 1976, the year Hawai'i was propelled into the media space age, newspapers, radio, and television recorded the triumph of the older, communal Native Hawaiian culture rediscovering the ancient art and science of the Polynesian voyaging canoe. *Hokule'a* navigated, without instruments, over the open ocean between Hawai'i and Tahiti, once again linking ancient Polynesian communities by sea. In 1995, a similar voyage up the West Coast of North America was connected to the "Kid Science" education program at Honolulu's Bishop Museum and aired on three hundred mainland broadcasting stations. Meanwhile, in 1994, Hawai'i Public Radio and a "Pacific News Organization" (PNO) linked up with various Pacific Island chains, some very remote, to broadcast news and distribute regional newsletters. Pluralism connected to media is a vital force that can reach scattered communities (Omandam 1994).

The media in the Islands are proud of their multiculturalism. Hawai'i offers a model if the world wants one. Institutional and personal racism occur, but they have no legal standing and are unpopular. Class exploitation is a stubborn problem, but evokes a heightened concern (Kent 1996; Okamura 1996b). Dissenting voices are given media time.

What is the future of multiculturalism? Will we, as Joseph Hrabe (1994, 554) asks, have social pathology or ethnic communalism? Will we remain mostly peaceable, as is the Native Hawaiian sovereignty movement, or will bloody brutality kill the beauty? The question is not whether a planetary Internet will emerge, but how we will deal with problems and avert cataclysms. Interactive media promise to eliminate boundaries of oceans and skies and to restructure the pattern of personal lives and social interdependence. Worldwide, television's infinite reach may ultimately lessen ethnic conflicts and hostility. Meanwhile, we might try the Hawai'i model of a multicultural media in which power is shared and all groups have access.

NOTES

1. I am not including magazines as, in contrast to newspapers, they have had only a minor influence.

2. The first non-English press in the American colonies was in German, in 1732 (Miller 1987).

3. Radio also includes amateur or "ham."

CHAPTER 5

Music

Anthony J. Palmer

A group was gathered at one of the airport gates to say farewell to a young man departing for the U.S. mainland to attend college. What was different with this scene was that the young man was loaded with *leis* (flowered garlands) riding high on his neck, up to his chin. The group was quite diverse, representing a wide variety of ethnicity and race. Accompanied by four *'ukulele*, the group joined in singing *Aloha 'Oe*, the famous farewell song. In my many hours spent in airports across the country, never have I witnessed a musical offering of any sort. Here, this is not unusual, for Hawai'i is a musical state with perhaps as many performers per capita as any place in the world. Musical expression is as natural to Island residents as politics is to Washington, D.C. Hawai'i is significant within the fifty United States for an *aloha* spirit that is complete only with the inclusion of music and dance as preeminent means of expression.[1]

The *aloha* spirit has been an important contribution to a climate of respect for differences. Diversity in ethnic and national backgrounds has fostered an enjoyment of differences and a willingness to be open and explorative. Witness an annual community event. In the *Honolulu Weekly* of December 27, 1995, the official guide of the sixth annual First Night—the alcohol-free New Year's Eve celebration on the streets of downtown Honolulu—there appeared a listing of the various musical and dance offerings:

> Arabesque Dancers performing dances from India to Morocco
> Country Dream Dances—American country dancing
> *Na 'Ohana o ke Anuenue*—children sharing their Hawaiian dances
> Romano Kheliben performing authentic dances from Southern and
> Eastern Europe, the Middle East and Northern India

Tahitian Music and Dance, courtesy of Kawaiahaʻo Church, the first Hawaiian church
Te Haʻa o ka Lauaʻe and *Waimakane Makamae*—hula and chant
Kings Kids—*hula*, Samoan Slap Dance
52nd Street—jazz
A Renaissance First Night—in period costumes with authentic instruments
Accordion Dance Music—waltzes, tangos, other jubilant dances
Backstreet Blues and R&B Band
DHT Show Kidz & Friends—Broadway and Disney favorites
Hickam Karaoke Corner
Honolulu Community Concert Band—big-band arrangements
John McCreary-Concert Organist—classical organ music
Kim Char Meredith-Vocalist—contemporary religious music
Lila Kane's Symphony of Sounds—world-beat choral and percussive sounds
Mozart's "Coronation Mass" by the Choir of St. Andrew's Cathedral
Night Train—blues
Pamana Singers of Hawaiʻi—Filipino songs
Partners in Pan—Jamaican steel drums
Pleasant Peasant Band—music of the Balkans, Eastern Europe and the Middle East played on authentic instruments
Raymond Kane-Hawaiian Slack Key—slack key guitar
Robert Aeolus Myers—*reggae*, hip-hop, *salsa*, etc.
Rodgers and Hammerstein Sing-Along
Rodney Perez and Tropi-Jazz—*salsa*
Samoan Choir
Shakuhachi-Japanese Bamboo Flute
Sofa Kings—classical rock
Sounds of Aloha Chorus—barbershop chorus
Sun Drum Village—African drummers
Tawantinsuyo—seven musicians from various Andean nations.

The foregoing represents just a small portion of the music and dance available in the Islands. In addition, China, Korea, Pacific nations, and such groups as the Maori, Tongan, Samoan, and Indonesian are also prominently represented.

In the chapter below I provide not so much a history of Hawai'i's music—that entails volumes, although some historical references will have to be made. Rather, I attempt to show the following:

1. Native Hawaiian culture held music and dance in high esteem. Consequently, with the revival over the last two decades, there has blossomed a wide acceptance of music generally and Native Hawaiian music specifically in everyday life (at the state legislature, symphony concerts, church services, schools, etc.).

2. Vast arrays of musical multiculturalism exist side by side, occasionally interacting, yet retaining their uniqueness and individuality.

3. Music is taught and carried on by a wide array of people who are not necessarily ethnically identical to the music they represent. Likewise, their students frequently do not match ethnically the music studied. Japanese, for example, study *hula*, while Asians, Native Hawaiians, and Polynesians study Western music, and Westerners study any number of Asian and Pacific musics.

4. Musical hybrids, such as *hapa haole* and *Jawaiian*, have arisen as a consequence of the syncretic nature of Native Hawaiian culture.

5. The people of Hawai'i are not wont to be separated by ethnicity. There are simply too many mixtures and intermarriages of nationality, language, culture, and identity to challenge any ideas of purity. Recency of arrival in the Islands does to some degree help to maintain purity of culture for a short time; but, within a generation or two, the bonds begin to loosen and ethnic purity, especially for the children, becomes difficult.

6. Still, cultural identities coincide with the musical traditions for a number of reasons, not the least of which are language and knowledge of tradition.

7. Institutions unique to the Islands have fostered nonresident groups to further enhance the musical palette.

8. Tourism, a high economic priority, has broadened the entertainment venues for a variety of musics, principally Native Hawaiian.

The center of activity is Honolulu, whether talking about music or government. Two-thirds of the one-million-plus population live on Oʻahu, and, while many events take place on other parts of the Islands, Honolulu is the focus for most of the concerts and other events. Honolulu contains the primary concert house, Blaisdell Auditorium, and only recently has there arisen on Maui a fine arts center that serves as home to the Maui Symphony Orchestra, a community orchestra, and other performance groups. The auditorium at Leeward Community College in West Oʻahu hosts a wide variety of music and dance performances. Also, recently built is the Pearl City Community Cultural Center, which has a fine auditorium, although it is too small to accommodate the larger audiences necessary to sustain a professional company. Most recently, the venerable Hawaiʻi Theater—a 1,400-seat house in downtown Honolulu—has been renovated and now offers a variety of musical events. The Neighbor Islands are not devoid of artistic activity but the sheer number of audiences and appropriate venues is insufficient to compare. Thus, I must necessarily focus on Oʻahu and Honolulu.

NATIVE HAWAIIAN MUSIC

The first Polynesians to occupy Hawaiʻi arrived as early as 300 A.D. (Kirch 1985, 298). Native Hawaiians, although of East Polynesian origin, developed a unique culture by the time Captain James Cook arrived in 1778 (Kirch 1985, 285). While significant differences presently exist between Native Hawaiian music as it was encountered by Captain Cook and the subsequent missionary arrivals in the early nineteenth century and other Polynesian music, the roots are recognizably East Polynesian (Tatar 1993, 307–309).

Native Hawaiian musical culture in 1778 consisted of various drums, nonpitched idiophones, a small number of aerophones, a few chordophones, and, most prominent of all, the voice (Roberts 1926, *passim*, but see especially photoplates). The origin of the *hula*, the all-encompassing music and dance tradition of Native Hawaiians, is steeped in various legends describing its divine source (Hopkins 1982, 20–23). The development of the *hula*, which became the complete expression of Native Hawaiian spirituality, is unrecoverable. Only the chants, preserved in oral tradition, give a hint of the historicity of *hula*. That body of chant, nevertheless, is the basis for a modern reconstruction which is as vital today as at any time in Hawai'i's post-contact history.

Because of the high value that Native Hawaiians placed on music and dance, they were receptive to a variety of musical influences. The post-contact period of musical history is characterized by seven distinct periods:

1. (1820–1872): Arrival of the missionaries up to the establishment of the Royal Hawaiian Band. Two major musical genres: hymns and secular music. Brought by heavy sea traffic: accordion, bass viol (missionaries), flute, guitar, piano, and violin. Church music was of mainland origin—unadorned, soulful, sober New England harmony. Secular music from Europe and Asia: Mexican, Italian, and German instrumental and vocal ensembles to Burmese singers. Native Hawaiian traditions were discouraged (only a small revival of chant occurred under Kamehameha III in the 1830s and 1840s). In this period, the kernel of Native Hawaiian music germinated in fertile creativity.

2. (1872–c.1900): The time of Henry Berger, the Royal Hawaiian Band, and the royal music clubs. Waltz in fashion. Pianos and zithers accompanied prolific compositions of royalty. Common folk embraced guitar. Native Hawaiian music, now firmly based in hymn harmony, discovered wider possibilities in melody. *Hula ku'i* (a falsetto style of singing) appeared.

3. (c.1895–c.1915): American urban music. Ragtime. Native Hawaiian quintets, typically an ensemble of strings, in great demand as dance bands. *Hapa haole* (half Hawaiian/half English) officially launched. *'Ukulele* was discovered.

4. (c.1915–c.1930): "Jazzed-up" Tin Pan Alley versions of *hapa haole* music spread to mainland America.

5. (c.1930–1960): Considered a golden age. *Hapa haole* music became big business. Full orchestras added slick Hollywood sound to Native Hawaiian songs. Radio, movie, and television coverage at a peak. Revues with Native Hawaiian musicians

were featured performers at hotel venues across the mainland. Mainland musicians adopted Hawai'i and composed brand new big-band music.

6. (1960–1970): Lack of interest in Native Hawaiian music. Radio featured only about 5 percent Native Hawaiian music. Rock and roll dominated.

7. (1970–present): Search for ethnic identity parallel to such movements on the mainland. Energetic revival of old Native Hawaiian music (Kanahele 1979, xxv-xxvi).

The present period benefited greatly from action by the Hawai'i state legislature. The process began in the late 1960s and early 1970s, when a groundswell of support for Native Hawaiian *hula,* language, and music developed in the community, paralleling the resurgence of ethnic concerns on the mainland. There was a fear that the existing Native Hawaiian speakers would be lost before they had an opportunity to pass on their legacy. The renaissance in Native Hawaiian culture during this time resulted in to the creation of the Office of Hawaiian Affairs (OHA) after the 1978 constitutional convention, which led to an amendment to the state constitution mandating "the study of Hawaiian culture, history and language" by providing a Hawaiian education program and using community expertise "as a suitable and essential means in furtherance of this program." Although Native Hawaiian culture had been taught prior to 1980, no systematic approach incorporated studies from kindergarten through grade twelve. The next program was a guide to achieving certain qualities central to the Hawaiian's sense of life's meaning, for example:

> Elements of affective development including *aloha*, sharing, cooperation, consideration and caring for others, respect for self and others, responsibility, industriousness and other such cultural values important in our multiethnic society are an essential part of the program to be modeled by *kupuna*, teachers, community resources, parents and administrators (University of Hawai'i c.1995, ii–1).

Thus, Native Hawaiian music received critical aid at a most opportune time, and activity to recover lost repertoire—chants, dances, and related expressions—was launched.

Hula is now respected throughout the state as a true Island treasure. There are hundreds of *hula halau*, schools where *hula* is taught. According to Manu Boyd, OHA is presently compiling a directory in the hope that more will be known about teaching aspects of *hula*. According to Boyd, some 2,000 schools in Japan and some three thousand to four thousand schools in Mexico teach *hula*. It should be noted that studying *hula* usually involves chant, costume, dance, decoration, instrumental accompaniment, and setting. The University of Hawai'i at Manoa (UHM) Music Department offers both major styles in its courses: the *kahiko* (ancient style) and the *auwana* (modern style). Noenoelani Zuttermeister, who represents the *kahiko*, has roots going back to her uncle, Pua Ha'aheo, of pure Hawaiian blood, a famous chanter and teacher. Victoria Takamine, who teaches the modern *hula*, has connections with the Beamer family, whose roots can be traced back to the fifteenth century on the island of Hawai'i and to Kamehameha I (Kanahele 1979, 29). In all *hula* classes one finds a variety of ethnicities—descendants from Asia, Europe, and various Pacific Islands, etc.—because musical styles in the Islands are not split along ethnic lines. People study by interest, not nationality, a common feature throughout the state.

The Merrie Monarch Festival is an annual event honoring King David Kalakaua, who reigned from 1883 to 1891. Kalakaua, given the name "Merrie Monarch" for his lavish parties and celebrations, brought back the *hula* in glorious form. An accomplished musician, Kalakaua composed both chants in Hawaiian and songs in the Western mold with Hawaiian text. Considered quite gifted, he was especially admired for his writings in the Hawaiian language.

The festival began in 1964 as a tourist attraction, but the *hula* contest, introduced in 1971 with just nine dancers, "blossomed and became the main event" (Hopkins 1982, 125). In 1996, the festival featured eighty-six dance performances, equally divided between ancient and modern forms, with twenty-six solo and sixty group performances in all. Twenty-two different *halau* were represented and included *keiki* (children) through professional-level adults. The 5,000-seat arena where the festival is held was sold out for the three-day affair.

The Kamehameha Schools, established to benefit Native Hawaiians, initially prepared students to become successful citizens. Native Hawaiian studies were not prominent. The Annual Songfest, begun in 1921, had been operating for almost three decades when Winona (Nona) Beamer began her tenure as a teacher of Hawaiiana (her own term) in 1949. Her efforts made Hawaiian Studies a major feature of the school curriculum (Kanahele 1979, 31). On May 31, 1996, the Hawai'i Alliance for Arts in Education (affiliated with the Kennedy Center Alliance) honored Auntie Nona with the Alfred Preis Award for lifetime achievement in the arts. During the event, it was mentioned more than once that standing *hula* was not allowed before 1965 at the Kamehameha Schools, an indication that *hula* has come a long way in recent decades. With the revival of Native Hawaiian culture statewide in the late 1960s and 1970s as support for changes in curriculum, the Kamehameha Schools now have a burgeoning program in the language and culture of Hawai'i.

The Songfest follows months of preparation in rehearsals by all ninth- through twelfth-graders. The whole class is involved, both as a mixed singing group and as two separate groups of boys and girls. (However, the freshman class sings only as a mixed group.) Students are selected by their peers to lead the groups in rehearsals and performance. Based on a different theme each year, appropriate songs are selected, and musicians are carefully appointed to make fitting arrangements of the songs for the various classes. Language as well as music is a chief contest component, so the five judges consist of two for music, two for language, and one for overall effect including language and music. The event is telecast statewide, and thousands attend the performance each spring. The importance of the Kamehameha Schools Songfest and its regular academic program is the effect it has on its graduates. Native Hawaiian music is not just practiced at the school as a prominent part of the curriculum; the graduates frequently find a continued use of music in their adult careers as teachers, musicians, and in avocational pursuits.

The UHM Music Department has also supported Native Hawaiian music. A newly established degree in ethnomusicology enables students to focus on Native Hawaiian music. The naming of a wing in the music complex after Dorothy Kahananui for her many contributions to the department over an extended teaching career is further evidence of support for Native Hawaiian music. Dorothy Kahananui was a gifted composer, arranger, and performer, as well as an influential teacher. Her daughter, Dorothy Gillette, followed her mother at UHM and was nationally known for her work with young students in both Western and Native Hawaiian styles.

Although the *'ukulele* is of Portuguese origin, its Hawai'i connection is assured because of the development of the instrument in the Islands. The Roy Sakuma *'Ukulele* Studio, a prominent studio in Honolulu, was established in the early 1970s; the faculty of approximately twenty instructors in four locations annually teaches thousands of students. All major music stores stock fine *'ukulele* made by various manufacturers, but the Kamaka factory, which has been turning out *'ukulele* since 1916, sells around 3,500 per year, mostly in the Islands. Public and private schools frequently include *'ukulele* instruction as part of their music offerings. Several high schools in the Islands have Polynesian groups, in which *'ukulele* and Native Hawaiian music are a major part of the activity. Many elementary schools employ *kupuna* (elders or grandparents who uphold Native Hawaiian cultural values and carry on the oral tradition of history) to teach Native Hawaiian music to their students.

Two other forms of music and instruments are the slack key guitar and the steel guitar. Although there are a few theories about how the guitar made its way to the Islands, one of the more acceptable ideas maintains that it was introduced through the influx of Californians and Mexicans to Hawai'i in the early 1800s. The term *paniolo* (Hawaiianized version of *español*) was applied to these visitors, who used the Islands as a provisioning center when crossing the Pacific. The term *paniolo* was later applied to the *vaqueros,* who went from México and California to tend cattle in Hawai'i. Their songs have been chronicled in *Na Mele Paniolo*, a booklet and set of cassettes available from the State Foundation on Culture and the Arts (Trimillos 1987).

The slack key guitar tradition emanates from the returning of the regular Spanish guitar by slackening the strings to sound a major chord. This allows the player to use the lower strings open while stopping the upper strings in various chord and melodic formations. Many tunings exist to adapt to the songs played in this tradition. Presently, the most famous of the slack key guitar masters are Fred Punahoa, Leonard Kwan, Peter Moon, Raymond Kane, and Sonny Chillingsworth (Kanahele 1979, 350–59). One of Chillingsworth's students, Matthew Swalinkovich, a recent graduate from Pearl City High School, is said to have the ability to take his place alongside the greats, including his teacher. Many students study slack key guitar at private studios, through the UH continuing education program, and informally among amateur players.

The origins of the steel guitar are not fully known, save the story of Joseph Kekuku, who claimed to have invented the technique in 1885 at age eleven and then to have perfected the technique within seven years (Kanahele 1979, 367–68). With the development of the steel guitar style and its subsequent electrification in Texas around 1935, the sound instantly became recognizably Native Hawaiian. The steel guitar also took its place in mainland country music to great effect. Presently, there are fewer players than in the heyday (1900–1930), so its future is in doubt. However, the effect of the steel guitar on Native Hawaiian music through the technique and overall quality of sound is too great to allow us to dismiss the instrument; a comeback is inevitable.

Any Native Hawaiian style of music can be found at various hotel and lounge venues, not only in Waikiki but also on the Neighbor Islands. Shows by Don Ho, Danny Kaleikini, Hilo Hattie, and others have been a very important outlet for Native Hawaiian music. The Cazimero brothers, who performed at the Royal Hawaiian Hotel for years, have now moved their act to the Bishop Museum for shorter runs on specific themes. Throughout the Islands, the small lounge group has been an important aspect of Native Hawaiian music; these groups have been essential for *lu'aus* and nightly ship tours of the harbor. While the music they play, sing, and dance is considered to be more for tourists than for aficionados, their roots and spirit are distinctly Native Hawaiian.

Contemporary Native Hawaiian music draws on numerous influences. *Jawaiian* is a combination of Hawaiian and *reggae*. Jazz has influenced some groups as well. The conditions remain dynamic, and the Native Hawaiian spirit prevails through the many different styles adapted for various uses. That spirit is exemplified by *aloha*—described as love, affection, openness, generosity (Kanahele 1979, 10)—which will continue as the force that drives Native Hawaiian music. As Elizabeth Tatar states,

> It is apparent that Hawaiian music is not a simple tune sung to the strum of an *'ukulele*. A typical melody, harmony, or text is not going to define Hawaiian music. Nor is a Hawaiian voice quality without the typical musical trappings to accommodate it going to define the music. It is the right combination of typical musical features,

representative instruments, and unique Hawaiian voice qualities sparked by the creative individual genius of the Hawaiian artist that makes the music unquestionably Hawaiian (Kanahele 1979, xxx).

Native Hawaiians were in the Islands hundreds of years before any others. Their culture absorbed the music of later arrivals. As the base culture, the bulk of this chapter is devoted to Native Hawaiian music, which permeates and transforms all else, directly or in spirit, and remains as dynamic as when Captain Cook first eyed the Islands. The rest of the story will be devoted to the later arrivals and their musical presence in Hawai'i.

SUBSEQUENT INFLUENCES IN HAWAI'I

Other influences came from the West, other parts of the Pacific, as well as Asia. These are described next.

Western Contributions

Although sailors from Captain Cook's ships and their brethren over the next few decades brought a modicum of Western music to the Islands, the music from the West that most influenced the present musical scene arrived only 175 years ago. With Hiram Bingham as the leader, the *Thaddeus*, carrying a large party of New England Congregationalists, landed on the island of Hawai'i on March 30, 1820. Kamehameha the Great had just died the previous year, and Liholiho reigned as Kamehameha II. Within a year's time, the missionaries gained a permanent stay in the Islands and began their slow rise to power. Eventually, the missionaries saw that the only way to convert the large masses of people was to convert their leaders. Liholiho was not a willing student, and his death in 1824 during a visit to England cleared the way for the mission to succeed. In a short time, in addition to the Kawaiaha'o settlement and its thatched-hut church of more than 12,000 square feet, more schools and churches were built, and orders to obey the Sabbath, attend school and church, and to become Christian were put into effect (Daws 1968, 61–74, 85). The solemn and straight-metered hymns were principal staples of conversion material. Native Hawaiians, already musically advanced, learned quickly and *himeni* (hymns) became the fundamental musical style of the new converts.

Other Christian groups followed within a couple of decades, and now the Islands are permeated by a wide array of church groups that include music as an indispensable part of worship. St. Andrews, the Episcopal Cathedral in Honolulu, is a center of musical activity, with frequent organ and choral public concerts held by John McCreary, dean and music director. Another mainstay, the First Lutheran Church of Honolulu, under Carl Crozier's direction, offers a variety of fine Western concert fare from Renaissance through contemporary music. Robert Mondoy of the Honolulu Catholic Archdiocese, though less active publicly, has an effect on thousands of Catholics in the state, with an emphasis on contemporary Catholic music. The Church of Jesus Christ of Latter-Day Saints is prominent, especially through the La'ie campus of Brigham Young University (BYU). BYU's music department, principally the choral groups under Dr. James Smith, is quite active on the north shore of O'ahu and elsewhere, offering patrons a variety of excellent music, Western and Asian-Pacific.

The Honolulu Symphony Orchestra has had a credible and interesting history of music making in the Islands since its establishment in 1902. Begun as an amateur group, concerts were at first given on an irregular basis. One difficulty was in finding wind players. The orchestra had a hiatus from 1914 through 1924, when it was reinstituted with a more solid foundation of support. The 1924 group presaged the present group in ethnic makeup by having a Japanese American violinist. The wind player problem was solved by borrowing from the military bands, always a large presence in Hawai'i. Still functioning with a large number of amateurs, the orchestra became a union closed shop in the 1960s. Although severe problems arose over financial support in the early 1990s, a new permanent music director, Samuel Wong, was appointed in 1996 to revitalize the orchestra. A remarkable feature of the symphony is its ethnic makeup. Although dedicated to a Western repertoire, instrument players are fully representative of a world population. Concertmistress Claire Hazard, for example, is Hawai'i-born of Japanese descent. The symphony started programs for schoolchildren as early as 1906, with a regular program beginning in the 1950s. Tours to the Neighbor Islands began in the 1970s. A recording of composer Dan Welcher's work on the legend of Maui and the sun, part of the Native Hawaiian cosmogony, has been released on compact disk. The symphony has received consistent recognition from the American Society of Composers,

Authors, and Publishers (ASCAP), culminating in an award in 1991 for adventuresome programming of contemporary music, particularly American works.

Allied with the symphony in its initial foray into the operatic area, Hawaii Opera Theater (HOT) began in 1961 with a single production of *Madama Butterfly*. HOT, an independent organization from 1980, had four productions in 1995 and 1996. The repertoire is taken from the usual staples—Mozart, Verdi, Puccini—with Wagner, Stravinsky, Strauss (Johann and Richard), Bernstein, and a miscellany of other operatic composers.

Musical theater has been a staple of musical offerings for some time. Presently, the Diamond Head Theater offers musical productions each year, the most notable of which has been such fare as Gilbert and Sullivan's *Pirates of Penzance* and Stephen Sondheim's *Sunday in the Park with George*. Manoa Valley Theater offers traditional drama and musicals; their recently produced *Sweeney Todd* won local drama awards. On an amateur level, although using professional actors in lead roles occasionally, are musical productions at Fort Shafter, which mount the usual popular Broadway vehicles and have a large following. The schools have their share of attendance and productions. Castle High School, among others, has furnished a workshop for budding actors now active in professional venues. The Hawai'i Theater for Youth is among the producers of children's theater and an outlet for developing playwrights as well as professional talent.

Instructional departments at the University of Hawai'i at Manoa also represent a major source in the Islands for Western art forms as well as many Asian-Pacific events. The symphony orchestra, conducted by Japanese American Henry Miyamura, does excellent standard orchestral repertoire as well as new works by resident composers. The wind ensemble, likewise conducted by a Japanese American, Grant Okamura, also presents well-attended concerts with a balanced offering of standard and contemporary repertoire. The choral groups under Timothy Carney also perform major repertoire, frequently with orchestra. Other performing groups are the Opera Workshop under the direction of John Mount and Larry Paxton, both of which are also active in professional venues outside the university. Combinations of the UHM Drama and Theatre and Dance departments produced a creditable and well-received *West Side Story*. In all these events, the performers are well dispersed across numerous ethnicities.

The Theatre and Dance Department is well known in the Islands for high-level productions, ranging from Shakespeare—in recent years, *Macbeth, Comedy of Errors, The Merry Wives of Windsor*—to such contemporary classics as Nikolai Gogol's *The Marriage.* Such contemporary works as Aleksandr Popovic's *Dark Is the Night* went from UHM's theater to La Mama in New York. New theater is supported as well, as shown by the recent mounting of *Cultivated Lives* by the young Los Angeles-based playwright, Velina Hasu Houston. The annual *Let's Dance* series features choreography by the dance faculty and their graduate students. All these productions play to a large number of Island residents. The recent *Dragonquest*, an original work using masks, puppets, and original music, played host to a large number of young people.

Held on the Manoa campus, although a separate organization, is the Hawai'i Chamber Music Society, whose annual five-concert series regularly presents world-renowned string quartets and other chamber music ensembles. Across town, the Honolulu Academy of Arts sponsors concerts of solo performers through small ensembles.

The Royal Hawaiian Band needs to be included here as a Western ensemble for its instrumentation and for its primary programming. The band can trace its roots to 1836, but in 1872 the band blossomed when the Prussian Ministry of War responded to a request from Kamehameha V by sending Henry Berger. With a huge task before him, Berger managed to perform a concert with just five days of rehearsal (Kanahele 1979, 336). From the meager beginning of just ten young men assigned to Berger upon his arrival, the band grew into a fully professional group that today numbers thirty-five regular members, with others added as needed for special events. Although many pieces written during the Berger and later days had Western instrumentation, the compositions were influenced significantly by stories, subject matter, and texts about Hawai'i. Subsequently, the band moved to more regular Western fare, but still keeps the standard pieces from a century ago within its repertoire.

Jazz is also an important part of the musical fabric. Gabe Baltazar is not only a mainstay at many commercial jazz ventures but also a contributor to an annual summer jazz festival held at various places on O'ahu, most recently at the Turtle Bay resort. In addition, young players receive excellent instruction under Pat Hennessey, the jazz band instructor in the UHM Music Department. Many of these students become public and private school instrumental teachers and continue to foster the jazz idiom among intermediate and high school students. In the line of accessible music, hotel lounges regularly feature outstanding performers, who provide the more popular vocal and instrumental music for listening and dancing while covering most styles of Top 40, jazz-fusions, and other crossover types—ballad, *salsa*, and other Latino musics.

Education in music is an important forerunner of professional musicianship. In addition to the school music program, two groups are worthy of mention: the Hawai'i Symphony for Youth, a statewide organization under the wing of previously mentioned Henry Miyamura, and the Hawai'i Youth Opera Chorus under the direction of Nola Nahulu. Both organizations offer public concerts frequently, have a large following, concentrate on Western repertoire, and develop young musicians, many of whom succeed to professional careers as music teachers and performers. Students represent the full ethnic spectrum in the state.

Regular instruction for youngsters, which ultimately contributes to the state through music performance, also occurs in the private piano studios. The studio of Ernie Chang has produced numerous fine pianists, as has that of Helen Masaki. Their students have won many competitions here and abroad. Peter Coraggio, UHM professor of piano, also operates a studio with various teachers set at different locations that is not limited to piano; the studio assists young people to develop talents in a wide variety of Western instruments and voice. Hiroko Primrose, a former student of Shinichiro Suzuki, has a fine studio of string players, principally violinists, whose many students find professional attainments, as well as contribute to a climate of high-level music making. There is an irony in this return of Western music from Japan with the Suzuki string methodology, considering that Japan had virtually no Western music prior to the Meiji Restoration in 1868.

Finally, to conclude the Western portion of the Islands' musical story, two major outlets that are listened to and watched regularly as a normal part of Hawai'i's receptivity to music and dance are the radio stations and television. Several FM stations program a significant number of hours per day on a wide variety of Western music, from symphony to country music to jazz to rap. The television stations, in addition to local interest programming, carry the same programs as one finds on the mainland but, nevertheless, are important to the Islands' interest in music.

Pacific Island Contributions

Pacific island contributions to Hawai'i are of long duration. Although periods of activity have alternated with quiescence, immigration has increased since World War II. Various groups make their connections with previous immigrants, not infrequently through church attendance.

Natives from Tonga, a nation of approximately 150 islands about 3,000 miles southwest of Hawai'i, arrived in the fiftieth state during the 1960s for better economic opportunities. Their musical styles, prior to any European contact, include multipart polyphonic singing. Adaptation to Christianity in the nineteenth century merely transferred their musical proficiency to a different repertoire. A dozen or more churches now feature Tongan choirs, and their services may be heard easily by tourists at St. Augustine Catholic Church in Waikiki, the First United Methodist Church of Honolulu, and several other churches throughout the Islands. In addition to church music, Tongans gather for a special community event called *hiva kava*, named after the drink made from the root of the *piper methysticum* plant. Songs for these events, laced with metaphors of birds, flowers, and place-names to refer to people, may be accompanied with string instruments or sung without accompaniment (Martin 1994, 40).

Samoans, from American Samoa and the independent nation of Western Samoa, have been in Hawai'i since many young men served in the U.S. Navy during World War II. Subsequently, many came to join relatives, and others arrived to find better economic opportunities. As with the Tongans, Samoans carried on a rich musical tradition prior to Western contact. After Christianization in the 1820s, native traditions joined European hymnody. Samoan music is strongly choral singing, is frequently accompanied with dance, both seated and standing, and is both unaccompanied and accompanied by string instruments (guitars, *'ukulele*, etc.) and various sizes of a slit-drum made of wood called *pate*. Performances with electrified guitar and bass are now common. Music and dance contests are held frequently, and many church services feature Samoan choirs. The Cathedral of Our Lady of Peace, the oldest Catholic community in the Islands, for example, has a

Samoan choir that has been singing regularly at the Sunday evening mass for more than thirty years.

The Polynesian Cultural Center, founded by the Church of Jesus Christ of Latter-Day Saints in 1963, is dedicated to preserving the cultural heritage of Polynesia while providing educational opportunities for students at the adjoining BYU-Hawai'i. Seven villages feature culture—with its integrated music and dance—from Samoa, Aotearoa (Maori of New Zealand), Fiji, Old Hawai'i, Tahiti (including the Marquesas), Tonga, and an 1850s-era missionary complex. Their continually running show, *This Is Polynesia*, although packaged as commercial entertainment in its overall presentation, does feature individually the music and dance cultures of the Fijians, Maori, Native Hawaiians, Samoans, Tahitians, and Tongans. In addition to the standard fare, performers from various Pacific Islands are imported for special events.

Asian and Other European Contributions

A pattern of immigration to Hawai'i was set by the plantation era that lasted approximately eighty years, beginning in the mid-nineteenth century. Young males were brought to work on the sugar plantations with the hope of returning home with a large nest egg of savings. Low wages inhibited these plans; subsequently, young single women from the original nation came to establish permanent family residence, followed later by whole families. Occasionally, the migrants married into the present Island population. The newcomers, feeling isolated, used native arts to establish cultural identity or sent to the home country for performers and teachers to rebuild a miniature culture within the new home. A final phase of sharing with the larger community naturally followed.

Music from Japan is a prominent feature of the Islands in the fashion just described. Representing the largest single ethnic group in the Islands, at close to 25 percent of the population, Japanese first arrived in the late 1800s, largely from rural Japan. The movie *Picture Bride*, released in 1995, tells the story of one young woman who came to Hawai'i in the early 1900s to marry one of the plantation workers. In addition to the mail-order picture brides, the plantation workers also sent for their families, eventually left the plantations, and began many small businesses in the growing Island economy, particularly after

World War II. Japanese music is present in Hawai'i now in many ways: *O-bon* Festivals each summer, festivals held by the Okinawan cultural organizations, music at the many temples associated with Japanese Buddhism and Shinto sects, and the recent emphasis on *taiko* (Japanese drum) groups.

With permanent residence came the desire for the settlers to inculcate their offspring with the home culture. Musicians, dancers, and various artists were brought to Hawai'i to teach the young. Many stayed and established schools for *koto*, for Okinawan music and dance, and for the oldest of traditional Japanese music, *gagaku*, the court and shrine music of some 1,200 year's duration in Japan, the roots of which can be traced back centuries earlier in China and Korea. Of the latter, Tenrikyo Church—connected to the nativist Japanese religion, Shinto—became home to Masatoshi Shamoto, a *gagaku* master. He established a *gagaku* group at the Tenrikyo Church and began to teach *gagaku* in the UHM Music Department. Also a principal musician of the music department for many years was Harry Seisho Nakasone, a representative of the classical music of Okinawa, *koten*. In both cases, attracted to the vibrant programs, many students, representing various ethnicities were tutored by both and became practitioners of Japanese music in the Islands and elsewhere. It must be noted that the instrumental groups stemming from Okinawan classical and folk song repertories have begun playing popular Okinawan music, which blends other Asian and Western idioms into its textures, a further example of the musical mixing that occurs in the Islands.

The *O-bon* festival calls for special mention as well. This celebration, which is for the departed relatives, finds its origins in Indian Buddhism and ancient Sanskrit religious texts that call for honoring the departed spirits on the fifteenth day of the seventh month. Cleaning of grave sites, offerings of food and flowers at *butsudan* (family Buddhist altars), and most especially the *bon odori* (group dances with special music according to the specific styles related to Japanese provinces), are all part of the *O-bon* celebrations. With the permanent establishment by 1915 of the Jodo, Nichiren, Shingon, and Soto Buddhist sects in the Islands, the *O-bon* celebration became a regular part of Island festivals and is now held from late June through early August. The 1996 calendar listed fully seventy-five observances covering six of the eight main islands from June 8 to September 1. At least half are two-day celebrations. Originally held on temple grounds, one can now find *bon odori* in various venues sponsored by hotels as well as cultural groups. Among the celebrants one finds various ethnicities represented, not only because of the now more generalized nature of the celebration but also because families may be mixtures of Japanese and any number of other Pacific and Asian origins.

A more recent facet of Japanese traditional music has come to the Islands via Kenny Endo. An anthropology major on the U.S. mainland, Endo studied with the great *taiko* drummers in Japan, a tradition revitalized by the group Kodo a few decades ago. After several years in Japan, Endo went to UHM for a master's degree in ethnomusicology. While in Hawai'i, he developed a resident *taiko* group, which has performed throughout the Islands for a wide variety of civic and private functions. He now teaches numerous students ranging in age and ethnicity.

James R. Brandon, a respected expert in Japanese and other Asian theater, has brought several Japanese theater troupes as actors and teachers to UHM over the past three decades. Brandon also has written and mounted plays in *kabuki* style which have become successful vehicles for graduate students drawn from the mainland United States and Pacific countries.

Young Korean males also came to Hawai'i to work on the sugar plantations. They first arrived in the early 1900s and then stayed when Japan took over Korea in 1910. From the early 1960s, the number of Korean immigrants has swelled. Community groups emerged in the 1920s and 1930s to offer cultural reinforcement and also to expose the larger community to the Korean arts. In such exposure one finds adherents from outside the ethnic community as well.

Perhaps the most outstanding examples of ethnic crossover are Mary Jo Freshley and the Korean Dance Studio of Halla Pai Huhm. Halla Pai Huhm had many ties to both Japan and Korea. After arriving in 1949, she taught Korean dance at UHM and established her own studio. Freshley, whose residence dates from the early 1960s, obtained such expertise in Korean dance that she continued the studio when Huhm died in 1994. Over the years, many Korean dance experts went to Hawai'i to enhance the instruction already present. More recently, Chun Heung Kim, a national treasure, was in residence for five months in early 1995. In February 1996, Myo Seon Kim, a disciple of Mae Bong Yi, another national treasure, visited and gave workshops and performances. Although the audiences are largely Korean for the dance concerts given regularly, many others have interests and connections to dance and are in attendance at these events. The studio has been a way station for Korean immigrants as they enter the Islands and adapt to new ways.

Other Korean contributions are the traditional musical forms of *P'ansori* (stylized speech, gesture, and song by a soloist accompanied by a drum), *Sanjo* (solo instrumental playing on the plucked zither called *kayagum*), and church music. The traditional musical forms have been enriched by immigrants who went to Hawai'i to establish careers as performers and teachers. The Korean community also supports a large number of Christian congregations, most of which have significant Western performing groups, albeit with Korean language settings of hymnody and contemporary styles. Korean choirs also appear on local television stations.

Chinese presence in the Islands is of long duration, the first groups having arrived in 1789. However, larger groups came in the mid-1800s. By 1896, some 21,000 laborers were in Hawai'i, mostly on the sugar plantations (Martin 1994, 59). Desiring to perpetuate the original culture,

> [t]hey formed fraternal societies, established Chinese language schools, supported Chinese opera, and perpetuated special cultural celebrations. In addition, Chinese families maintained some of their ancestral traditions, such as customs surrounding childbirth, birthdays, marriages, and funerals (Martin 1994, 59).

Chinese music, particularly the Cantonese variety, is heard by the general population through the Lion Dance, which beckons blessing and good fortune, and is most prominent for New Year's celebrations, grand openings, and other joyous occasions. In the dance, several young men manipulate an elaborately decorated large and colorful lion's head with a long body, accompanied by a lively ensemble of cymbals, drums, and gongs: "The drum beats are considered the heartbeat of the lion, while the sounds of the gong and cymbal are intended to frighten away evil spirits" (Martin 1994, 62).

The narrative would be incomplete without noting the musical presence of traditional Chinese music and Chinese opera. Most opera clubs, which are in Honolulu, play host to large audiences. Significantly, the dramatic presentations are accompanied by live music, and are kept current by professional troupes from China traveling to the Islands. Although the performances are in Cantonese or Mandarin, the Chinese community is supportive because both dialects are still spoken among the Chinese population in Hawai'i.

In 1970, an important aspect of Indonesian music was brought to the Islands with the arrival of Hardja Susilo. Susilo was a practicing musician and dancer in the Javanese *gamelan* tradition before enrolling as a graduate student in the Institute of Ethnomusicology at the University of California at Los Angeles (UCLA) under Mantle Hood, noted ethnomusicologist. After developing the UCLA *gamelan*, he moved to Hawai'i to set up the *gamelan*, and he began to train students. For more than two decades, students of various national and ethnic backgrounds have carried their *gamelan* experiences to such venues as Australia, Japan, and mainland U.S. schools and institutes.

Of the Asian musics, none is more important than the contributions of Filipino musicians. The Philippines is most varied in geography and indigenous ethnic groups. Of the more than 7,000 islands that make up the nation, there are three major groups: Ilocanos from northern Luzon, Tagalogs from central Luzon, and Visayans from the central islands. Fewer came from the Muslim-populated southern island of Mindanao. By 1930, some 100,000 Filipinos were in the workforce, mostly on the plantations. Following the usual pattern, the first to arrive were males, followed later by single women and families.

The Filipino culture, although Asian, was permeated by Spanish music and traditions, Spain having ruled the islands for over three centuries. The major musical tradition, *rondalla*, is largely accompanied by plucked stringed instruments, with an occasional accordion added. In recent years, other instruments have been added such as banjo, flute, mandolin, saxophone, *'ukulele*, and violin. Filipinos quickly gained a reputation for fine musicianship, and they frequently appear at birthdays, dances, weddings, and other important events. *Rondalla* music lends itself to a variety of styles of songs and dances and is especially valuable in the multicultural mix in the Islands, where a wide variety of popular music is in vogue. Filipino musicians perform regularly throughout Hawai'i.

Influences in Island music also stem from the importation of workers from Portugal and Puerto Rico. Musically similar, these cultures brought music and dance related to Iberian roots. The Portuguese, mentioned previously because of the ubiquitous *'ukulele*, are an integral part of Island life. From 1878 to 1913, some 12,000 workers, primarily from the islands of Madeira and the Azores, entered Hawai'i. Largely Roman Catholic, they enhanced the growth of Catholicism in the Islands (Martin 1994, 75). Their presence is felt in every avenue of Island life from music to business. The group retains many of the older musical and cultural customs through Holy Ghost organizations, which stem from a special religious celebration.

In the case of Puerto Ricans, the music in the Islands is more related to the Spanish heritage than the subsequent African influence in Puerto Rico, featuring the plucked string variety of instruments. Music for Puerto Ricans is an integral part of everyday life. Some groups have performed commercially, but most are amateur albeit skilled musicians who continue to fill the major celebrations of the extended families with dances and songs of unique flavor.

The East-West Center has become an important resource for Asian and Pacific cultures. Established by the United States Congress in 1960 for the purpose of fostering mutual understanding and cooperation among the governments and peoples of the Asia-Pacific region, including the United States, the Center is valuable not only for its involvement in the economic and political arenas but also for its sponsorship of a strong program in the arts, regularly offering a wide variety of music and dance programs from Asia and the Pacific. Programs range from such locally-generated programs as Raplee K. Nobori's *The Death of Keoua* featuring the music, dance, and chant of John Keola Lake, to musicians and dancers from India, Japan, Korea, and the many nations of the Pacific. A typical program, "Masters of Asian Dance," was presented in July 1992, featuring

> dances from five groups that are part of the multicultural collage that is Hawai'i, [which] honors five individuals who have made important contributions to the artistic and cultural life of the islands for decades. Each of these individual dance artists is recognized as an accomplished master of a dance tradition. All have performed, choreographed, taught, and shared their cultural insights with the Hawai'i community, enriching the lives of all of us (Van Zile and Feltz 1992).

Other Musical Traditions in Hawai'i

Several other cultures need to be mentioned. The African American community, although small in number, makes its presence felt through the church congregations that serve African Americans, both permanent residents and locally based military. Trinity Missionary Baptist Church of Honolulu is well known for its choir. Native Americans in Hawai'i are supported in their culture by the Inter-Tribal Council of Hawai'i on the island of O'ahu. A counterpart organization holds frequent powwows on the island of Hawai'i.

The International Folk Dancers sponsor Eastern European music and dance events. Celtic culture is supported by the Caledonian Society, which sponsors the Highland Games annually. A Swedish dance group performs regularly.

Music and dance from Laos, Thailand, and Vietnam can be found among the offerings. Middle Eastern music is found in various avenues, frequently religious, such as the half-dozen Jewish temples and synagogues. On the secular side, belly dancing and instruction from the practitioners may be found at various Middle Eastern restaurants.

THE LONGER VIEW

Important to all of the above, particularly the nonprofit artistic companies and educational organizations, is the State Foundation on Culture and the Arts, now headed by Executive Director Wendell P. K. Silva. Without the funds allocated by the state legislature and administered through the Foundation—although at reduced levels in the last couple of years because of statewide budget restrictions—the arts in Hawai'i would be less effective in their influence on the Island's population. Grants to a wide variety of dance, music, and theater groups make performances possible and arts education available to a large number of residents and help the arts to be more accessible than through the purely commercial arenas.

Hawai'i is indeed multicultural to a major and important degree, especially as it might be a model for other states to emulate in its awareness, openness, and respect for traditions other than one's own. Public recognition and inclusion is indicative of respect. The annual birthday celebrations of King Kamehameha and Prince Kuhio Kalaniana'ole, which are state holidays, typify the prevailing attitude.

Music, after all, is a reflection of deeper psychic processes than the mere sounds that one hears. Each sound is selected in combination with others; held in specific durations that make up the rhythms of a people in their interpretation of natural and social phenomena that they experience daily; expressed through timbres to which the group claims ownership, adding precise inflections in phrasing that are recognizably theirs; and formed to mirror their innermost psychic needs as a people. While the musics presently exist in Hawai'i in cultural forms that are easily recognized, the future truly belongs to the cross-fertilizations of the people and their newly developing collective psychic makeup. What exactly that holds for the future is impossible to predict, for the millions of variables that enter into the continuing fructifying of this multicultural society are neither controllable nor desirable to shape, except to keep music vibrant and viable and to allow the voice of the people to speak loudly through their chosen pathways that feed the individual and collective soul. That soul, because of the unique experiences of the individual parts put into collective ensemble, will always be Native Hawaiian.

NOTES

1. In addition to the references cited in the text, additional information was derived from conversations with the following: Manu Boyd (Office of Hawaiian Affairs), Mary Jo Freshley (Halla Huhm Studio), Lynn J. Martin (State Foundation on Culture and the Arts), Delsa S. Moe (Sterling Scholar Awards), Jane Freeman Moulin (UHM Music Department), Sharon Pressburg (UHM Theatre and Dance Department), Roy Sakuma Studios, Victoria Takamine (UHM Music Department), Cathy Temanaha (professional dancer), and Noenoelani Zuttermeister (UHM Music Department).

CHAPTER 6

Literature

Rodney Morales

AND WE CALL IT A COMMUNITY

topography: *topos* (place) + *graphein* (to write)

To the visitor, the itinerant viewer of Hawai'i's community of people, we proudly display our homogeneity and our ability to transcend race/class markers and get along with one another. After all, isn't Hawai'i the *"Aloha* State," and isn't its *aloha*-spirit-driven, multicultural lifestyle evident in the workplace, at shopping malls, at sports and cultural events in parks, stadiums, and arenas, at movie theaters, and at the beaches?

Hawai'i is a place claimed as home by many people, both native and non-native, both local and nonlocal. Everyone from the mainstream media to the Hawai'i Visitors Bureau (HVB) likes to promote the image of a warm body of people, peacefully coexisting. On the surface—to the visitor who hasn't felt overly charged for the hotel tab, or harassed by so-called "locals" when cruising the beach, or inundated by people selling T-shirts or passing out flyers that promise something (they always promise something), or turned off by the concrete and the traffic and other evidence of development gone awry—Hawai'i is paradise. A deeper look (to supply a metaphor) reveals the rips and snarls in this seemingly seamless social fabric, this multicultural state we call Hawai'i. (Or is it a state of mind?)[1]

How one chooses to see Hawai'i says much about the beholder. While the itinerant may see the Islands as smooth silk, an illusion that HVB would like to perpetuate, or as an American quilt, made up of pieces of material that represent the wide array of peoples that populate

Hawai'i, U.S.A., those who know the Islands more intimately would perhaps prefer to describe them as *kapa*, a coarser cloth, tough in its uneven heritage, breaking apart yet still one fabric.

Hawai'i's literary community may also present a homogeneous cast to itinerant readers, those who pick up a "local" story every now and then. But, again, to those intimately involved, obvious tears and gaping holes have come to light in the 1980s and 1990s.

A deeper look at Hawai'i's literary community—writers, critics, scholars, voracious readers, and supporters of the literary arts—reveals a contentious community, a community divided by degree of familiarity with place; a community as divided as it is united by ethnicity, gender, and race, a community that has historically privileged the colonizer spirit. And, while the colonized have made great strides (from books published to awards to a growing audience), some, in succumbing to the benefits of compromise and dilution as they play out a distinctly American Dream, show that they have bought into the colonial construct.

Hawai'i is a tough environment for a writer. There's a lack of institutional support, a dearth of grants and the kind of funding one finds in states across the mainland. Still, some writers are moderately successful despite these obstacles. Others are successful partly because they are misinterpreted, just as some are unsuccessful because their work is undervalued, thanks in part to the absence of critical attention to their works. Being a writer in Hawai'i is a challenge; persisting in being one against all obstacles is a triumph.

One of the major entities involved and/or vying for space in the literary topography is the Hawai'i Literary Arts Council (HLAC). HLAC is a volunteer, nonprofit organization that was founded in 1978 to support the literary arts in the Islands. Made up primarily of teachers and writers from the community, HLAC uses grant monies from state and federal agencies to fly writers to the Islands for readings. HLAC also pays writers, both local and nonlocal, to read their works. The organization also helps to publicize such readings, poetry slams, and other literary happenings, and chooses the winner of the prestigious— or dubious, to those who see this as a means to perpetuate that colonizer spirit—annual Hawai'i Writer's Award.

In 1980, local writers associated with the fledgling Bamboo Ridge Press staged a revolution at the polls, voting in a slate of members to HLAC offices. Bamboo Ridge Press, which publishes *Bamboo Ridge:*

The Hawaii Writers' Quarterly, is easily the fiftieth state's most successful literary journal and has received a steady flow of funding from the State Foundation on Culture and the Arts as well as occasional assistance from federal agencies. (Of course, now that the New World Order has shown its face as the New Fiscal Reality, and social welfare programs and education are among its casualties, even Bamboo Ridge faces a loss in funding.)

An adjunct to the press is the Bamboo Ridge Study Group, a workshop group that includes writers who have published book-length works, including Marie Hara, Juliet Kono Lee, Wing Tek Lum, Gary Pak, Cathy Song, Lois-Ann Yamanaka, and press editors Eric Chock and Darrell Lum.

Except for this tightly-knit group of "Asian Americans" (most of whom instead prefer being identified as "local") who are closely linked to Bamboo Ridge Press, most writers in Hawai'i have affiliations that are looser—aligned along evershifting planes: native, gay, woman, while some avoid being categorized altogether. Joseph P. Balaz, Kathy Banggo, Dana Naone Hall, Richard Hamasaki, Mahealani Kamau'u, Dennis Kawaharada, R. Zamora Linmark, Michael McPherson, Wini Terada, Haunani-Kay Trask, and Cedric Yamanaka are names that come up often in discussions about local writing, or locals writing. This list is by no means exhaustive,[2] so it would be erroneous to think that the aforementioned writers produce all the worthwhile literature in Hawai'i. It just seems, especially to the itinerant viewer, that they do.

SOME SAY IT BEGAN WITH "TALK STORY"

> For entertainment there were Hawaiian songs and a ceremonial hula. When later, the Mainlanders began to stroll through the gardens, they found mangoes, ripe and gorgeously multicolored, lying on the ground, theirs for the taking. It was the quintessential Hawaiian Dream! (Newman 1979, 47–48).

A conference that was pivotal (a major step/evolution) in the development of a "local literature" consciousness was held at Mid-Pacific Institute in June 1978. Known more formally as "Talk Story, Our Voices in Literature and Song: Hawai'i's Ethnic American Writers' Conference," this groundbreaking conference brought together many writers of local heritage, who for the first time had an opportunity to network, find some common ground, organize, and become agents of their own fortunes and misfortunes. Following the emergence of ethnic and black studies programs across the continental United States, the local community had begun to assert itself culturally, and now local writers wanted to play their role in, as the media guide stated, "confront[ing] the plantation owner aesthetic of *haole* arbiters in the University of Hawai'i's Department of English." Back in 1978, these *"haole* arbiters" still privileged the likes of A. Grove Day (a former English Department faculty member), who, along with Carl Stroven, edited *A Hawaiian Reader*, a 1959 anthology that presented an exotic collection of ship's logs, diaries, poems, short stories, folktales, and essays, written mostly by tourists who really were both occidental and accidental. (Some, notably Jack London, Robert Louis Stevenson, and Mark Twain, were highly recognizable names on literary maps of the Western world.) These works painted a misleading, often lurid portrait of Hawai'i and its unique multicultural mix. Some of the stories, such as London's *Ko'olau the Leper*, could be viewed as laughably inaccurate if they weren't so painfully influential in their depiction of the Islands and its people. It was no accident that James Michener's *Hawaii* also appeared in the same year as *A Hawaiian Reader*, since 1959 was the year when Hawai'i became the fiftieth state. Michener, a writer of some (some say questionable) literary merit and an excellent marketing strategist, timed the release of his opus to coincide with Hawai'i's admission to the United States, a time when worldwide attention focused on our small group of Islands.

The prime movers of the Talk Story Conference were the cofounders of Talk Story, Inc.: Marie Hara, Arnold Hiura, and Stephen Sumida, the latter going on to become a professor of English who is now ensconced in the American Studies Department at the University of Michigan at Ann Arbor. These three reined in a number of writers with solid literary and dubious local credentials, such as Maxine Hong Kingston, who grew up in Stockton, California, but had lived in Hawai'i for a few years, while teaching at Mid-Pacific Institute and writing her soon-to-be-acclaimed *The Woman Warrior* (1976). Also present were retired University of Hawai'i at Manoa (UHM) microbiologist O.A. "Ozzie" Bushnell, writer of five historical novels centering on Hawai'i; playwright Aldyth Morris, author of *Captain James Cook* (1955) and *Damien* (1980); and novelist Milton Murayama, whose self-published *All I Asking For Is My Body* (1975) became an Island classic, and, validated by sales volume and critical attention, has been printed and distributed for the last decade by the University of Hawai'i Press. Also attending the conference were many aspiring young writers, including several who have come to be associated with Bamboo Ridge Press.[3]

"Agency" was the operative word that emerged from the conference. Local writers learned that they had to take matters into their own hands. One obvious way to do just that, when the outside world is ignoring you and your kind, is to start your own press and publish your own work and that of those whom you support. This is what some founders of Talk Story, Inc. began doing while the conference was still in the planning stages. Thus, almost immediately after the conference, they published *Talk Story: Big Island Anthology* (1979), a collection of drama, fiction, and poetry by writers who had been involved with the conference, as well as by other locals deemed worthy of attention. Soon after, several small, independent journals emerged, publishing some form of local literature. They complemented the already established University of Hawai'i Board of Publications, which supports *Hawai'i Review*.[4]

Undoubtedly the most successful press to come out of this "barrage" *was Bamboo Ridge: The Hawaii Writers' Quarterly.* While just about all the aforementioned independent presses never got beyond a few issues, Bamboo Ridge, on the other hand, has flourished. It has published more than fifty volumes including fiction, poetry, single-writer collections, and special issues that allow for a wider range of groupings and genres—movie screenplays, works by children, compilations of speeches, photographs, and drawings. Many local writers have found their first pieces of poetry, drama, and fiction published by Bamboo Ridge Press.

The press' most recognizable volume is *The Best of Bamboo Ridge* (1986), a collection of what its editors, Eric Chock and Darrell Lum (with the help of an advisory committee), saw as being the best of its first twenty-nine issues. Because of its seemingly representative range, this 325-page volume provides the many currents and crosscurrents found in local literature, the mainstreams and extremes. In its successes and excesses this book has both empowered and marginalized those who claim membership in the local literary community. Furthermore, the book has given Hawai'i's literary community a lot to talk and theorize about. Because of its flagship billing as "The Best of," this anthology, published by what many in Hawai'i have come to see as the "establishment of local literature" (Bacchilega 1994, 9), has been the target of uncritical praise as well as, in recent years (to Bamboo Ridgers and those who have championed the press, and to anyone superficially engaged with the day-to-day doings of the local literary community), discomfiting scrutiny.

Because of its historical timeliness (around the time when colleges everywhere began paying a lot of attention to noncanonical literature, and "multicultural" had become a buzzword), the anthology filled both a community and a scholarly void. *The Best of Bamboo Ridge* has received much attention and use. It is frequently used as a text in sophomore literature classes at UHM, as well as in most classes that deal in any way with Hawai'i's literature. God only knows how many times an essay, a poem, or a story has been photocopied for classroom use at all levels. While not a best-seller by any means, this Bamboo Ridge anthology is studied, not just casually read, and one would be hard pressed to find a more closely read literary text in the Hawaiian Islands.

A GLUT OF METAPHOR: FOOD, FISH, AND FISSURES

Just about every scholarly analysis (and there aren't that many) that deals with Hawai'i's literature presents to us a metaphor, some trope on which to hang the discussion. Darrell Lum's "Local Literature and Lunch," which opens the anthology, is no exception. In "Local Literature and Lunch," Lum defines "local literature" in terms of where and when we shop and what we buy and how we interact with our environment: the things we share and do. We seem to have common tastes in food. Though he doesn't initially mention the ever-present Spam, Lum does offer the recipe for *loco moco*: "a bed of rice topped by an over-easy fried egg and smothered in brown gravy" (Lum 1986b, 3). "Real locals," he continues, "then add salt, pepper, *shoyu*, and ketchup before digging in!" He also links us by our affinity for that "nutritional nightmare," the meal which crosses class and ethnic lines, the plate lunch: "curry stew [or some other main dish] poured over two scoops of rice alongside a scoop of macaroni salad and a bit of *kim chee*." "This is," Lum says, "all a part of living in these islands." At the essay's end, Lum says that the literatures, like the lunches, "are diverse, tasty," and he, like any good host, invites the reader to dig in.

One doesn't have to dig far into the book to find a poem that offers a similar metaphor. Wing Tek Lum's "Chinese Hot Pot" begins,

My dream of America
is like *da bin louh*
with people of all persuasions and tastes
sitting down around a common pot
chopsticks and basket scoops here and there
some cooking squid and others beef
some tofu or watercress
all in one broth
like a stew that really isn't . . . (Lum 1986b)

From a "nutritional nightmare" to an American dream. We again see a tribute to diversity and an appeal to sharing, which one soon finds to be a common theme in this anthology of "local literature." No doubt many readers would find this poem by this other Lum (no relation) to be an appropriate metaphor for multiculturalism.

The sentiments expressed by the poem seem to reflect a magnanimous, some might even say local, spirit—and a democratic one at that. To think that these sentiments truly govern the anthology is to be misled, however. As in the Chinese pot, the preponderance of essays, poems, and stories, multifaceted as they, are by Asian writers. The overall feel of the book is undeniably Asian—from Gary Nomura's carp, or *koi*, cover design (apparently using a familiar symbol for Boy's Day, as celebrated among Japanese) to the last image (a large fish) in the final article.[5] This Asian American Dream privileges certain groups—middle-class Chinese, Japanese, and Korean descendants of plantation immigrants who arrived a few generations ago.

In the aforesaid piece that closes the anthology, "Waiting for the Big Fish: Recent Research in the Asian American Literature of Hawaii," Sumida, the local community's (to the itinerant viewer) "resident" spokesperson (who writes from Ann Arbor), catalogs the sorry history of exclusion that has stifled the local Asian literary community. Much of his diatribe is aimed at the preeminent Pacific anthologizer mentioned earlier, A. Grove Day, who along with cohort Carl Stroven privileged the *exotic* at the expense of the *endemic* (though not indigenous) local Asian community. Whether they were consciously or unconsciously ignored, Hawai'i's Asian writers were indeed silenced. Apparently, they were not even deemed worthy of attention. As Day demonstrated in a 1988 interview in reply to the question, "Why have you not mentioned in your book the contributions of 'Chinese and Japanese Americans' and other writers born in these islands?" Day stated, "I have always been aware that there are excellent but untranslated writings about the Pacific Islands in a dozen languages" (Sibley 1988, 24). They were, in fact, all in English, suggesting that he never even researched the writings.

Sumida's "big fish" metaphor is curious. In his essay he cites a well-known local writer to punctuate a point of concern:

> Hawai'i novelist O.A. Bushnell has charged on many public occasions that "outside" writers have shamelessly raided Hawai'i for materials—and have mostly botched the job of writing them up. Indeed, some keepers of the community's culture in Hawai'i are so sick of being pillaged that they refuse their knowledge to virtually every prospective or already proclaimed expert from the outside (Sumida 1986, 318).

Then Sumida goes on to talk about the elderly man who calls visiting scholars and writers "steal baits . . . . thievish little fish who nibble the bait off the hook," leaving "nothing for the real catch." This Hilo man, whom Sumida calls "the local Japanese American community's self-appointed archivist," is said to have "grown reclusive . . . [and] will not even open his door for any steal bait. . . . [H]e waits still, today, for the Big Fish."

Apparently there's some big local fish out there, waiting to be snagged by this archivist, who will then provide . . . what exactly? The raw material with which to write the great local Asian novel? A critical study that's viewed from the shores of the Great Lakes? Isn't this rather presumptuous? Can the itinerant see this? Can the outsider who, according to Bushnell (1981, 42), "has got to guess, got to feel his way, got to borrow," see this?

Surely a good many readers of this "Best of" collection feel that they have had a feast, as promised; others may feel that they have been had. A feast, yes, maybe even indigestion, but no *lu'au*. Not with certain items consistently left off the plate. We appear to have a troubling multiculturalism that engages the rhetoric of sharing and fair play, but in reality (as *real* locals might say) it may be a new brand of colonialism in which successful Asians have established a hegemonic relationship over those who are less fortunate.

Darrell Lum (1986b, 3), in his "Literature and Lunch" essay, defines "local literature" as being not only "opposed to 'Asian American' literature, largely a mainland term," but also " 'Hawaiian' literature, which the locals know means [N]ative Hawaiian literature." Sumida, in the opening to his book on Hawai'i's "literary traditions," *And the View from the Shore* (1991, xiv), defines the word "local" as a person "usually thought of as nonwhite, for instance an Asian American, Native Hawaiian, Samoan, or Puerto Rican; or a local may be someone historically, ethnically originating in the working classes of Hawai'i, such as Portuguese American or a Spanish American, with a family history on the sugar plantations or the ranches of paniolo country." Later Sumida adds, "A Hawaiian is quintessentially a local, but a local is not necessarily a Hawaiian" (xv).

So what is the verdict? Are Native Hawaiians, the quintessential locals, considered writers of local literature? Are they insiders or outsiders? This ambivalence, also discussed in Candace Fujikane's essay, "Between Nationalisms: Hawai'i's Local Nation and Its Troubled Racial Paradise" (1994), shows that local literature, as defined by the Bamboo Ridge community, stands on shaky ground, and that there are "cracks and fissures" threatening this imagined nation. Furthermore, this noncommittal ambivalence has allowed Bamboo Ridge to remain multifaceted.

Some will wonder, what is the problem? What is wrong with what Bamboo Ridge publishes? So what if it's mostly Asians? What is wrong is that the same *us versus them* construct, which has for two or more generations cast *haoles* (sometimes even if they're born and raised in the Islands) and recent immigrants as outsiders and has helped to create a community, is now being used to position Native Hawaiians as a *they*. Telling a story or writing a poem is one thing. Defining a community that you're less and less a part of, that's something else again. Writers associated with Bamboo Ridge purport to speak on behalf of an entire "local community," thereby imposing their values on that same community.

This assumed role has given middle-class Asians a prominent and dominating place on the topography of Hawai'i; and, in their role as spokespersons, by some geographic and ethnographic sleight of hand, they have *otherized* Native Hawaiians, written them off the map. As

Dennis Kawaharada, a community college professor and staunch
defender of Native Hawaiian rights and values, says,

> In Hawaiʻi, public and private schools were established and a
> university was set up to train natives and immigrants. The children
> and grandchildren of immigrants did relatively well in these schools.
> They were already part of the money economy through the
> immigration experience of their parents, who had left their ancestral
> homelands to make money. It was not easy for Native Hawaiians
> who, still living in their ancestral homeland, had to choose between
> cultural traditions and economic survival (1994, 57).

This is not to ignore that Asians have for a long time been victims
of oppression in America, especially on the continental United States.
Cincinnati Reds owner Marge Schott, who stated in a *Sports Illustrated*
interview, "Well, I don't like it when they come here, honey, and stay
so long and outdo our kids. That's not right (Reilly 1996, 78)," is only
the most recent example of the contemptuous way even successful
Asian Americans are viewed by many white Americans.

But how does that play in Hawaiʻi, where, in the minds of many in
the local community, Asians are more central than marginal, where the
indigenous population is an at-risk group, just as the more recently
arrived immigrants are? With these groups being *otherized* for their
poverty and crime rate, and *demonized* by what is perceived as the
dominant community, what kind of multiculturalism are we getting?

According to Kawaharada, who was managing editor of Bamboo
Ridge Press until the mid-1980s and in recent years founder of his own
press, *Noio*, in part to recover and publish Native Hawaiian folktales
(*moʻolelo*), "If multiculturalism means that all cultures are equal and
can pick and choose which ones we want to study, like a consumer at
the supermarket, that will be potentially harmful because of the
ethnocentric tendency of each group" (1994, 59). He goes on to say,
"How equal is the sharing if one of the groups control publishing and
education? (ibid.)" Sociologist Jonathan Okamura (1996b) echoes these
concerns when he suggests that naïve multiculturalism in Hawaiʻi
works to preserve the *status quo* and all its inequities, especially in
regard to Native Hawaiians.

With the outsider-controlled mass media busy managing the
processes of stereotyping and demonizing disenfranchised minorities

(especially any ethnic group with which the dominant Anglo culture has been engaged at war in the last century); when lives are trivialized by tabloid news, soap operas, and deejays to points beyond excess; and when taking responsibility for your world/town/street/beach is put on hold because you can let go of that dream, because you can't let go of that remote, what kind of society do you end up with?

Neil Postman, author *of Amusing Ourselves to Death: Public Discourse in the Age of Show Business* (1985, vii), says that the problem is not the Orwellian vision of Big Brother and censorship but rather the Huxleyan nightmare that we will be "reduced to passivity and egoism," and that "truth would be drowned in a sea of irrelevance." Consequently, the voice of the marginalized, while present, is lost in the din of masses of information pouring out from the mainstream as well as from such high-tech venues as the Internet, the movie theater, and the Walkman. Increasingly, we in Hawai'i find that our children are being raised on MTV and rap music, and wearing Nike shoes that seem to cost as much as cars used to. Is this "local"?

In our multicultural world the disenfranchised is given voice, but it is a faint and distant cable channel (*'Olelo*) whose reception, due to lack of support, is poor. This channel is decidedly unglamorous when compared to the high-powered channels, the ones that are backed by wealthy advertisers, for whom profit is the only margin of concern. Multiculturalism is not working when the end result is that the individual is still marginalized. One gets a voice but it's muffled in the multicultural mix.

WHEN THE PAINT DRIES

Darrell Lum's contributions to *The Best of Bamboo Ridge*, aside from the already daunting task of co-editorship, are significant. Besides having written the introductory essay, "Local Literature and Lunch" (1986b), Lum is represented by three of his most popular short stories: "Beer Can Hat" (1986a), "Primo Doesn't Take Back Bottles Anymore" (1986c) and "Paint" (1986d). While others have offered excellent critiques of these pieces, I find that the "Primo" story carries the most symbolic weight. This symbolism is echoed in co-editor Eric Chock's poem, "Tutu on the Curb" (1986), where an elderly Native Hawaiian woman is disrespectfully engulfed by exhaust fumes left by a bus—

which is representative of modern technology—as it pulls out from a stop.

"Primo Doesn't Take Back Bottles Anymore" portrays how a down-and-out, young Native Hawaiian, Rosario "Rosa" Kamahele, a nineteen-year-old intermediate-school bully-turned-dropout-turned-unemployed-laborer survives on society's spurned edges. Homeless, though he pays the Filipino bookie named Almazon, ten dollars a month to claim him as a resident, Rosa's main means of survival is bartering. He collects and trades in empty Primo beer bottles for cash. He also regularly gathers and catches fish and seaweed to bring to Harry, the Primo brewery worker who takes care of Rosa by keeping an extra bottle or two on the side to compensate for Rosa's notoriously incomplete cases. One day, Rosa arrives at the brewery and there's no Harry, and he is told by one of the painters involved in the renovation that Primo isn't taking bottles anymore, and, furthermore, is under new management. Rosa, desperate and angry that his one tangible means of support has been taken away, picks up a can of spray paint left by the painter, and writes "F-O-C-K" (which may be read as a typical misspelling, or, as some insist, an accurate pidgin spelling, a cultural coding). His statement reads as a desperate assertion against encroaching dissipation—*I rage, therefore I am*—and, after "defacing" property, Rosa storms away. The problem is that he has used the same paint that was used to paint the wall earlier, so when the paint dries there is no statement; Rosa, as far as we can tell, is never seen or heard from again. He is another casualty of progress, Western hegemony, global capitalism, or, as the story plainly states, new management. He, like the words he sprayed, is buried in the mix (Lum 1986b).

In *The Best of Bamboo Ridge*, the "Primo" story functions as the perfect lead-in for Darrell Lum's "Paint." In this latter story, two characters—Coco and the woman he calls "the hippie lady"—vie for supremacy in what could be termed the "battle for the wall." Coco, whose preoccupation is to spray surf pictures on a freeway underpass wall, is intimidated and overrun by the hippie lady, who covers up his "surf *pikchas*" with revolutionary slogans, which ironically have to do with freedom from oppression. The battle escalates like an arms build-up, and they both lose when the government workers (henchmen who are sent out to erase dissent and free expression) paint over everything in an easy flexing of power. This small story speaks legions in symbolic terms. On one hand, you have the local—say the local writer—fighting for page space, fighting to tell his or her story. (As Sumida and others remind us, before the mid-1970s the notion of a local writer was pretty much nonexistent.) On the one hand, there's the outsider, whether well meaning or mean spirited, who wants to fight the local's battles, or at least articulate them. Coco, representing the local writer, was not all that articulate. And he too got buried in the mix (Lum 1986b).

B. RIDGE OVER TROUBLED WATERS

> Bamboo Ridge is a non-profit, tax-exempt organization formed to foster the appreciation, understanding, and creation of literary, visual, audio-visual, and performing arts by and about HAWAI'I's PEOPLE [my emphasis]—Bamboo Ridge Press's mission statement, imprinted on all its books and cassette tapes.

In recent years, those associated with Bamboo Ridge Press have probably felt that they are victims of a siege mentality. And considering the remarkable accomplishments of the press, the itinerant may ponder, why all the criticism? Why can't we just get along?

ANOTHER LITERARY SHOWCASE

> B.Y.O.B. party. . . . Bring your own book, your bottle, your balls (Hershinow 1994, ii).

Sixteen years after the seminal Talk Story Conference the stage was set for a reassessment, a regrouping, or was it to mark, as Lorna Hershinow (1994, i) wrote, "what is now so obviously a quantum leap forward in Hawai'i's literary history" Bamboo Ridge Press, a fledgling in 1978, had become the dominant, the local establishment press. Some writers affiliated with Bamboo Ridge had even begun to take a watchdog role regarding who was hired to teach anything touching local or Asian American Literature at the university level. In March 1994, spurred on by grumblings and rumblings in the local literary community, HLAC (now a hybrid of English-department types and Bamboo Ridgers) organized, for the first time in many years, a conference on Hawai'i's local literature.

The resulting 1994 Hawai'i Literature Conference reader, *Reader's Guide* (1994), a 128-page spiral-bound collection of essays and poems meant to highlight conference themes and concerns, turned out to be a valuable supplement and resource. One piece in the reader that, in retrospect, could be read as a preemptive strike is Talk Story, Inc., cofounder Marie Hara's essay, "Some Thoughts on the Nature of Exclusionary Activity." As if anticipating the accolades not to come, Hara wrote of the time when she was part of a literary panel of "so-called *hapa* women writers." A woman who, like her, is of mixed ancestry, raised her hand and stated in anger, "I'm tired of hearing all this promotion of Asian Americans." This unidentified woman, according to Hara, "may have also been the person who had voiced her opinion that Bamboo Ridge Press and Kumu Kahua [sponsor of local drama productions] were working far too diligently to promote Asian American artists to the neglect of all other groups here in Hawaii." Hara (1994, 48) then went on to speculate that this woman may have had her work rejected.

At the conference itself, held at the University of Hawai'i's Kapi'olani Community College, Dennis Kawaharada took the stage and summarized, condensed, and expanded candidly on his contribution to the *Reader's Guide*, which was subtitled *Towards an Authentic Local Literature of Hawai'i*. In this essay, he talked about how the "local literature" that had been developed by the "grandchildren of Asian immigrants" was constructed upon a "nostalgia for family and homeland," and then stated, "and if you write it in pidgin English and refer to local landmarks like King Street and Diamond Head or Tantalus, you've got a regional flavor that has some appeal for a local, if not a national, audience. . . . But this literature is not local in the same sense that Hawaiian stories are local" (Kawaharada 1994, 58). Kawaharada went on to claim that this literature was "neo-colonial" partly because it "embodie[d] values of the American way of life" (*ibid.*).

Kawaharada's sentiments were echoed by Richard Hamasaki, Kamehameha Schools teacher and former co-editor of a defunct literary journal, *Seaweeds & Constructions*. He felt that there was a need for non–Native Hawaiians to learn more about and respect the cultures and values of Hawai'i's indigenous people.

There was surprisingly little of substance offered by the other speakers at the various panels. As the above "quantum leap" quote suggests, many attendees probably thought that it would be a gathering in praise of local literature, and then a few "heavy-handed critics" came to spoil the party. In essence, the *Reader's Guide*, within which there are charges and countercharges for the record, has taken on more life than the event that it was meant to commemorate, for media coverage of this event was scant, skewed with mainstream interpretations, but gave credence to Kawaharada's warning about who controls publishing.

At subsequent conferences, other charges and accusations have been leveled. One concern is the appropriation of the term *hapa* by Asian Americans on the West Coast and to some extent in Hawai'i. *Hapa*, the Hawaiian word for half, has been used historically to identify those who are half-white (thus, *hapa haole*). The other half was usually Native Hawaiian. Then the term came to mean "mixed," though usually Caucasian was still part of that mix. Recently, posters spotted at the Berkeley campus of the University of California advertise a *Hapa* club, and to become a member you need to be part-Asian. The problem here is not only one of appropriateness, but also how this notion reinforces the Hollywood stereotype of the Eurasian, exotic beauty, which sets up the models for failure that are explored in the work of several local writers, notably Lois-Ann Yamanaka.

In April 1994, at the Eleventh National Conference of the Association for Asian American Studies in Ann Arbor, Michigan, some of the critical fire was aimed at Lois-Ann Yamanaka, then the brightest new comet in the local literary community. Yamanaka, a gifted poet and fiction writer who had come out with a hot-selling poetry collection, *Saturday Night at the Pahala Theater* (1993), and who has recently published an even hotter novel, *Wild Meat and the Bully Burgers* (1996), was criticized for her negative portrayals of some of Hawai'i's ethnic groups. At Ann Arbor, a roundtable discussion focused on Yamanaka's supposed demonizing of Hawai'i's Filipinos, particularly in the poem "Kala Gave Me Anykine Advice Especially About Filipinos When I Moved to Pahala" (Yamanaka 1996).

A major concern is whether the author's strengths—the way Yamanaka captures the voices and ludicrosities of childhood, with believable children who are both vicious and vulnerable, seeking reprieve from victimization, in contrast to the superficial, naïve "We are *Aloha*," shaka sign waving, smiling people image perpetuated by Hawai'i's banks and the HVB—are enough to counter her penchant to cast certain at-risk ethnic groups one-dimensionally. While the jury may still be out on this one, one has to be wary of *patterns of representation* of an oppressed group by one that is more dominant. If the only place for a Filipino or Native Hawaiian is in the backdrop, and the only available roles are those of bookies, bullies, bums, and criminals, then the writer who perpetuates these notions (rather than shattering them) is no different from Day's favorite nesomaniacs, Jack London and W. Somerset Maugham.

DEFENDERS AND DETRACTORS

Under the rising sun/the enemy came/wearing my face—*Blackout Baby* (KHET-TV 1991)

"We are being attacked from within," Darrell Lum said to the same AAAS conference audience at Ann Arbor in 1994. He defended Lois-Ann Yamanaka's work, saying readers who think her work is racist aren't getting it. "Using a stereotype," he said, "that the narrator rejects may do more toward diminishing the impact of a negative stereotype than pretending that it doesn't exist" (Lum 1994, 2). (Here I think Lum means the author, not narrator, for it is obvious that Lovey and other narrators/speakers employed by Yamanaka buy into the practice of negative stereotyping as much as, if not more than, the other characters.) Because this is a critical and contentious point, this distinction, I believe, is important. Lum also noted that these critics, the same ones who identified *Bamboo Ridge* as being neocolonial at the 1994 Hawai'i Literature Conference, are Asians themselves and labeled them "ground termites" who "tunnel up through the cracks in the concrete and eat at the very foundation of a house" (Lum 1994, 1).

Such discourses as those mentioned above take place in the academic world—at conferences, in colloquiums, in classrooms. As a result, they often fail to note who is left out of the loop in these exchanges. More privileged local Asians (though not only Asians) might inform the itinerant *haole*, for example, that racism does not bother them: *"It's how we are here in Hawai'i. We tease each other."* This neo-*hapa* coalition, the Asian and Caucasian middle class (does "HLAC" stand for "*haole*, local Asian combined"?), throws these issues around, flicks them off their shoulders like so much dandruff, and then goes back to their condos and suburban homes. Regarding issues of racism and demonizing, sociologist Jonathan Okamura

(1996b) asks us to consider, "Would the disprivileged and marginalized share this view?"

Many still would laud Bamboo Ridge's sizable contributions to the ever changing local literary landscape and find that the good things they've done outweigh any seeming slights. Also, Bamboo Ridgers are quick to point to several special issues that do deal with Native Hawaiian issues and themes.[6] The question that a reader might pose is, "Isn't this enough?" What is not apparent to the itinerant viewer is that these works came out in the mid-1980s, published partly under the guiding spirit of then managing editor Kawaharada. After *The Best of Bamboo Ridge* was published, and after the editors received some criticism for the book being too Asian, the press reply seemed to be to publish an even more disproportionate amount of work by Asians. At a recent colloquium, in a paper entitled, "The Neocolonialization of Bamboo Ridge: Repositioning Bamboo Ridge and Local Literature in the 1990's," Eric Chock (1996) was quick to admit that the last five special one-writer volumes published by the press were the work of Asian American authors. What he did not say was that they are all member of the Bamboo Ridge Study Group. When one considers the complaints lodged against Day and other exotic editors/writers ("He never even bothered to look") by Sumida, Lum, et al., one wonders why the reluctance to get beyond the enclave and take a closer look at what Hawai'i's non-Asian writers have to offer.

RE(DIS)COVERING THE LOCAL

The first mainstream press use of the word "local"—the uttering that defined a community—had to do with the Massie Case, a landmark event in 1931, when five young men—Horace Ida, Joe Kahahawai, Henry Chang, Benny Ahakuelo, and David Takai, who were of Native Hawaiian, Chinese, and Japanese ancestry—were identified by Thalia Massie as the men who raped her on the night of September 12, 1931. This alleged rape of Thalia Massie, the Caucasian wife of Caucasian naval officer Thomas Massie, made headlines throughout the continental United States.

The killing of one Native Hawaiian, Joe Kahahawai, by navy men in a revenge plot hatched by Thomas Massie and Thalia's mother, Mrs. Fortescue, "came to represent for many of the white residents of Hawai'i, all 'local boys'" (Fujikane 1994, 50).

But there was one more Native Hawaiian. And his is an interesting story as well. Interrogators could not convince Benny Ahakuelo to turn against the "Orientals" and tell on them. One obvious reason why is because they were innocent, as Pinkerton detectives assigned to the case would later corroborate in evidence that Governor Lawrence Judd kept under seal for years. An equally important reason is that Ahakuelo would not buy in to the divide-and-rule scheme that plantation owners tried to impose on the different immigrant groups on the plantation.

The case was a wake-up call, a consolidation for the local community, as it now calls itself, which realized how the *haole* outsider could literally get away with murder. (Although Fortescue, Thomas Massie, and accomplices were found guilty of murdering Joseph Kahahawai, their up-to-ten-years-in-prison manslaughter sentences were commuted to one hour of detention in the governor's office.) One reaction to this racist spirit, conflated with a need to assert their Americanness, was manifest when *Nisei* Japanese sought to prove themselves in the trenches of World War II.

The 1950s was a time of sweeping change. In 1954, a group of Democrats, mostly of Asian ancestry, many of them Japanese who had fought for America in World War II, came to power. As a result, the *haole*-dominated, mostly Republican Big Five lost the total dominance that they had held over Hawai'i's economy and people for more than half a century. The Japanese and Chinese citizens who came to political power, however, sought economic wealth, the more sordid episodes of which are covered painfully well in *Land and Power in Hawai'i* by George Cooper and Gavan Daws (1985). By the 1980s, Japanese and Chinese, along with descendants of earlier boatloads of Koreans, were among the wealthiest groups in the Islands.

So it was inevitable, as Asian groups emerged as a political power, that their children, who began attending universities in large numbers, would emerge as a class of artists. And, not comfortable with such mainland- or continent-based labels as "Asian American," they called what they produced "local literature."

In many ways this was a wonderful circumstance. With the advent of literary journals, most notably the aforementioned Bamboo Ridge Press, Hawai'i's people finally got to hear authentic voices—the voices of people on the street, and varieties of pidgin that had never been depicted with accuracy by Michener or anything coming out of Hollywood. We had begun to tell our own stories.

We?

Obviously, not all of the story is being told. With a few notable exceptions, we haven't heard nearly as much from, for example, those other Asians, the Filipinos, who are overrepresented in service jobs, especially in the hotel and food industries, or Native Hawaiians, who are overrepresented in Hawai'i's prisons.

"Local male." One of the most telling and ironic circumstances that reveals how this already problematic term can mean something else altogether is when the connotation is negative. Thus, when most Hawai'i residents hear the phrase "Suspect: Local Male," for some reason they visualize neither a Japanese nor a Chinese, let alone a *haole* or a representative of the middle class. Instead, they see a Polynesian pulling out a pistol, a Polynesian (or maybe a Filipino, part Hawaiian, or Puerto Rican) being handcuffed, a decidedly brown-skinned man wearing jeans and no shirt, boasting tattoos of the non-Polynesian variety—in essence, a decidedly different profile than the one many are led to imagine when reading the so-called "local literature" of the so-called "local community."

Similarly, in the surfing community, when *haole* surfer types refer to "locals" they are not thinking about Asians. "Local," to many Caucasians, is a very general term by which to regard and in some cases disparage those perceived as being of Hawai'i, those who hold claim, because of language (Hawaiian or pidgin), skin color (brown, tanned), or what is perceived as a laid-back style. Actually, they see a Rosa Kamahele.

Yet when the itinerant talk about "local literature"—at the universities and community colleges—they are usually talking about a literature written by middle-class Asians, defined by middle-class Asians, a literature in which the major characters (not always middle class, what with the plantation heritage) are Asian. Not to say that the Native Hawaiian or the Filipino are absent. In fact, both groups are represented, albeit in stereotypical fashion, as filler in the backdrop, a situation the now-privileged Asians resented (and still resent) when being cast in the exotic Hollywood films and mainland literature about Hawai'i. Filipinos and Native Hawaiians (and African Americans and Indochinese and Latinos and Portuguese and Samoans, etc.) just have had little chance to tell their own stories.

Sensitivities are high, especially in this age where the word sovereignty takes on more substance and resonance with each passing

day. Native Hawaiians have been left out in these debates—there has
been no *poi* on the mixed plate—and Filipinos have felt the brunt of
ethnic stereotyping.

GROWING PAINS (UNDER NEW MANAGEMENT)

> In the late 1970s . . . an effort [to "regain control of political and
> economic forces in the islands from external sources"] was described
> as *Palaka* Power, named for the durable cloth used to make the work
> clothes of plantation laborers . . . and other working-class people in
> Hawai'i. *Palaka* Power . . . sought especially to promote and protect
> the interests and values of local people. . . . It never developed into an
> organized social movement. State Representative David Hagino, the
> principal theorist of the *Palaka* Power initiative, attributed its failure
> to the yuppie generation of political leaders . . . who are more
> concerned with "grandiose projects, ostentatious spending and
> conspicuous consumption" than with social justice and equality
> (Okamura 1994, 174–75).

Hawai'i's local literature is undoubtedly having growing pains. Is that
why the penchant for paeans to "Small Kid Time"?

My comments may seem severe to some. An overreaction, perhaps.
Fair enough. But because criticism has been discouraged, muted,
relegated to backroom and hallway small talk, because the message
"Take care of each other" has come to mean "help your friends in that
cozy little enclave of yours by promoting their work in mock reviews,
and by having a lock on who gets awards," such an overreaction as
mine, I feel, becomes necessary. One should feel free to applaud
Sumida for his tireless efforts to this place in the map of multicultural
America, just as one needs to feel free to suggest the fishing lure
(perhaps *mana'iakalani*, the fishhook that *'Ai'ai* used to catch the giant
puhi), which his Japanese archivist can use to snare the Big One.

The question is, are we ready for a new stage? How can we get
better if we cannot criticize one another, not in backrooms and hallways
but right at the table where the *kapa* is laid out, torn, frayed on the
edges, like a map of who we are and where we are going?

And, if we don't, outsiders are going to do it for us. Right now, as
we live *under new management*, pencils are being sharpened, fingers
are being stretched for a day at the computer, notes, clippings, books all

around—thanks to institutional support, the kind of support Hawai'i's local writers have rarely received.

And where else can we go? "We," meaning those who are concerned with the future of local literature and want to see it remain/become a vital part of our lives. We hope that we can move in several directions.

* One possibility is that we could get more into indigenous culture, the host culture of Hawai'i. For those who have seen local literature as something that began with the mixing of ethnic groups in the plantations, it may be time to see how far Native Hawaiian literature really goes back, which may mean getting into the histories and folk tales (*mo'olelo*) set down by Samuel Kamakau, David Malo, Moke Manu, Moses Nakuina, and others. Right now, increasing numbers of Hawai'i residents of all ethnicities are learning the Hawaiian language at every level, from immersion schools to the universities, and huge numbers are joining *hula halaus*. There is an increased interest in the recuperation of the ancient Hawaiian culture, and with part Hawaiians being the fastest growing ethnic group in the Hawaiian islands, pre-1990s critical constructs of local literature and local culture, whether by Ann Arbor's resident Asian American scholar, Steven Sumida, or by Bamboo Ridge editor Darrell Lum, or whomever, should be reconstructed in this light.

* We could get into ourselves. *Chailukyu eensei*, Joseph Hadley once wrote in phonetic pidgin. No doubt there are times when we need to point the finger outwards, blaming hegemonic politics. But we need to be most critical of ourselves and our community. What comes out of this complex mediation are the works that truly reflect a time, a place, a people.

* We could shake off that stigma of provinciality as we move out internationally. While Asian American constructs may be useful, they are also a reminder of Hawai'i's anomalous status as one of the fifty states, a condition that binds the Hawaiian Islands to its primary colonizer. By studying the cultures and literatures of Third World nations, such as in the Caribbean, we may find that we share similar colonization experiences and mutliethnic/multi-cultural sensibilities. The region that is really worth our attention

and consideration, however, is the South Pacific. The *Hokulea*
and *Hawai'i Loa* voyages of ancient seafaring craft to the Pacific
Islands from which natives to Hawai'i came, point to new
developments, along with promises of new alignments. These
voyages offer a change for Hawaiian Islanders to recover and
learn from Pacific Island connections. The South Pacific, which
has also had to struggle with its being defined (by the literati
who "did the good work" for the reigning imperial powers) as an
exotic idyll, a tourist mecca, shares with Hawai'i, its northern
counterpart, a strikingly similar mythology. In many cases, the
same deities and demigods, a closely related Polynesian
language, and, equally important, a parallel history of
devastation, exploitation, and recovery (seen most notably in the
struggles for nationhood or independence and against nuclear
testing). Similar to that annual summer swell that we anticipate
all along our southern shores, literatures from such places as
Aotearoa, Fiji, Samoa, Tonga, and other islands and island
continents has come in brilliant, awe-inspiring sets. We can align
ourselves with the postcolonial and resistance-oriented
sensibilities of many gifted South Pacific writers—Alan Duff,
Patricia Grace, Epeli Hau'ofa, Keri Hulme, Sudesh Mishra,
Albert Wendt, to name a few—writers who write back to the
"Empire."

Or we can whine and remain static. We could decide to speak in
voices that are multifaceted and singular, mellifluous and discordant.
We could utilize mythology and revitalize cultural tricksters to combat
Eurocentric and postmodern glut, to demythologize the dominant
cultures and its ever-present noise. We could use all conceits and
gestures and schemes that we deem appropriate. Or we could not. The
choice is ours.

NOTES

1. I want to thank Cindy Franklin for her editorial comments and
suggestions.
2. There is a growing tendency among scholars at such places as the
University of Hawai'i at Manoa to encourage a new generation of local writers
toward what can be termed *post-local*, or *postmodern local*. This recent trend is
a healthy one, hopefully, though one wonders, too, if this is yet another way in

which the mainland scholar can maintain privileged status—sometimes to the detriment of local scholars who seek positions that these "outsiders" hold almost exclusively—"outsiders" whose idea of the local community often seem to come from the mainstream press (rather than direct interaction) and the classroom (where they hold court to mostly middle-class representatives of the community).

3. Much of the write-up on this conference has focused on the influence of Asian Americans from the mainland on the budding local literary movement. Such writers as Jeffrey Paul Chan, Lawson Fusao Inada, and Shawn Wong seemed to function as mentors to the young local writers, many of them Asian. Also intriguing is the attention given to nonattendee Frank Chin for his long-distance (and long-running) attack on Maxine Hong Kingston (for what Chin claimed were inauthentic portrayals of Chinese culture). A related and much-covered "event" is Chin's stint as a Visiting Writer the following year, when he took a number of local writers under his wing. Chin, who constantly emphasized to local writers the need to cast minority characters in heroic light, chastised Darrell Lum for writing stories that put Hawai'i's Creole English into the mouths of losers. Chin stated, "Is pidgin really a language exclusive to the stupid of Hawaii? . . . Is it a matter of prejudice, skill or inadequacy of vision that the Hawaiian writers championing the virtues of Hawaiian pidgin cannot make the language work complexities, communicate intelligence, perform magic?" (Fujikane 1994, 64).

4. For a more comprehensive discussion of Hawai'i's literary journals, see Hamasaka (1993).

5. I'm thinking of the searing look at racism within the local community by Violet Harada, Wini Terada's linguistic range, shown in both prose and poetry, riveting poems by Laurie Kuribayashi and JoAnn Uchida, the rich sampling from Virgilio Felipe's oral history of Bonipasyo, and the authentic yet unique pidgin voices of several writers, including Dean Honma, Darrell Lum, and Michael McPherson.

6. For example, *Ho'i Ho'i Hou: A Tribute to George Helm and Kimo Mitchell*, which I guest edited; *Malama: Hawai'i Land and Water*, guest edited by Dana Naone; and two volumes of Native Hawaiian folktales, *Kaua'i Tales* and *Polihale*, guest edited by Frederick Wichman.

CHAPTER 7

Public Opinion and Cultural Values

Yasumasa Kuroda

A MULTI-ETHNIC COMMUNITY WITHOUT A MAJORITY

Aloha is an attitude, a propensity to act in a friendly manner toward people whom you encounter every day. The spirit of *aloha* has been an important traditional Hawaiian value, a preferred course of action. This chapter attempts to examine whether the assimilation model or the mosaic model of American society applies to Hawai'i. At the beginning of the twentieth century, President Theodore Roosevelt (n.d.) declared that "there is no room in this country for hyphenated Americanism." His definition of *American* is that an "American is an American and nothing else." In short, everyone should assimilate to the mainstream American standard, and minorities should merge with the dominant group of Americans in all areas, from marriage to language, to the point where America becomes a huge melting pot. For example, Japanese language schools were banned in Hawai'i during the 1920s. This ideal of *assimilation* dominated the United States until the 1960s, when even the dominant group started to accept the reality that America must live with pluralism, and when we started to hear such slogans as "small is beautiful" and "black is beautiful." The norm has increasingly shifted toward the *mosaic model*, a salad model of American society wherein each ethnic group is proud of the way it is. An extreme form of the mosaic model, *separatism*, is supported by a very small number of persons.

Is ethnicity a salient factor in separating values and opinions of the population in Hawai'i? This chapter will demonstrate that local-born voters have different attitudes and values from mainland-born Americans who settle in the Islands. I will also show how both groups fare, compared with others in the world. The aim is to move toward the development of a theory of ethnic values by isolating age, gender, and education from ethnicity.[1]

The data source for this study is a longitudinal survey of Honolulu voters initiated in 1971 and repeated in 1978, 1983, and 1988. The population sampled at random consists of registered voters in urban Honolulu.[2] The sample size ranges from 400 to 800. I primarily report results of the 1988 survey below, using only items that produced at least a 20 percent difference between two ethnic groups. Excluded also are apparent differences that are washed out when education was held constant.

CULTURAL CORE AND ETHNICITY: INDIVIDUAL, FAMILY, AND SOCIETY

Culture is a historically created design, explicit and implicit, for living shared by members of a group. Culture and language offer a way of organizing one's life experience. Viewed in this perspective, one of the key aspects of culture is the role that the self plays in experiencing the world. What is the most salient primary unit?

TABLE 7.1
Ethnic Culture by Group

Ethnic Group/Primary Unit	Self	Family
Mainlander	+	−
Local	−	+

American culture has been known for its emphasis on individualism from the days of the Western frontier, whereas Asians and Pacific Islanders stress family life (Table 7.1). Because mainlanders in Honolulu represent an upper sector of American society at large,[3] I hypothesize that the individualism of mainlanders is stronger than that of other ethnic groups in the Islands; their sense of self is defined with clear boundaries. Second, mainlanders consider the family or home life to be less important than do locals, who trust family members but not others in general. Mainlanders are more secondary-group oriented than locals.[4]

Caucasians and Japanese Americans are the two largest ethnic groups in Hawai'i. Census figures for 1990 show the former to be a plurality of 33 percent and the latter to comprise 22 percent, whereas the former constitutes less than a third among the registered voter population and the latter (38 percent) a plurality.[5] Chinese Hawaiians, Native Americans, and others constitute the remaining third of the voter population.

Care was taken to ensure that differences between ethnic groups are not spurious, i.e., a result of education, occupation, and other demographic attributes. The sample was divided into five cultural groups: (1) M*ainlanders*, that is, those who hail from the continental United States, (2) *Islanders*, consisting of Hawai'i-reared voters other than Japanese Americans, (3) *first- or second-generation Japanese Americans*, (4) third- or *later-generation Japanese Americans*, and (5) *immigrants*, mostly recent arrivals. When I use the term "local," I refer to categories (2), (3), and (4).

Earlier studies indicate that Americans in general are individually oriented and optimistic compared with Arabs, Europeans, and Japanese (Kuroda and Suzuki 1991). Two sets of values, as presented in Table 7.1, set mainlanders apart from others, independent of such demographic attributes as the length of formal education and occupation. For example, mainlanders report that they are relatively free from daily worries, but locals are concerned with such matters as car accidents, nuclear power accidents, street crime, unemployment, and war. My findings demonstrate that mainlanders have a much lower degree of anxiety than locals.[6] Older Japanese Americans worry more than others about these mundane matters. To some extent, the level of anxiety is inversely related to the level of formal schooling, but educational attainments do not account for significant differences in types of concerns and worries. Along with their higher educational background, mainlanders are also more likely to hold professional and managerial positions in Honolulu than any other ethnic group and to consider themselves primarily upper middle class (Table 7.2).

Mainlanders are concerned with protecting the environment, men and women sharing housework, and saving energy, and they believe that the arrival of the computer age is desirable and that their health is excellent. Although locals worry, they tend to believe that the American standard of living has improved and will continue to improve; differences disappear when controlling for levels of education. In short, mainlanders' values set them clearly apart from locals, but that is

largely a function of education, not ethnicity (Research Committee on
the Study of Honolulu Residents 1986, 106).

TABLE 7.2
Social Attributes of Ethnic Groups in Hawai'i, 1988 (figures in percent)

Attributes	Islanders	Main-landers	Immi-grants	Older Japanese	Younger Japanese
(a) *Schooling*					
elementary	5	0	12	1	0
junior high	6	2	7	13	3
senior high	27	10	23	35	12
technical/business	12	3	7	22	12
college graduate	38	47	30	23	50
graduate work	12	37	21	5	23
(b) *Occupation*					
professional	16	27	16	7	28
managerial	7	14	7	5	14
skilled	6	5	9	13	7
farmer	1	1	0	0	0
semi-/unskilled	7	0	4	2	1
clerical	25	19	16	23	25
service	5	4	19	8	5
not employed	26	25	25	36	16
small businessperson	8	6	54	6	4
(c) *Social Class Identity*					
upper middle	23	45	26	20	23

Note: "Japanese" are Japanese Americans.
Source: Research Committee on the Study of Honolulu Residents.

DATA ANALYSIS

In this section, I focus on specific attitude dimensions, using data for
1988, when the Cold War was still in progress. After comparing mainlanders and locals on psychological characteristics, I examine sociological differences in order to demonstrate whether differences and
similarities among ethnic groups fit into the local-mainlander model.

Psychological Dimensions

Anxiety. Mainlanders are definitely less concerned with the daily problems that bedevil locals. The problems that "very much" concern mainlanders range from only 4 percent for unemployment, 8 percent for war, 13 percent for car accidents, 16 percent for serious illness, 18 percent for nuclear power plant accidents, and 22 percent for street crime (Table 7.3[a]). Street crime most worries all groups. The foreign-born and Islanders likewise worry much more than mainlanders; their percentages range from 21 percent about war to 44 percent about street crime. The possibility of muggings is the most worrisome problem for Honoluluans of all ethnic backgrounds. The least concern is unemployment, reflecting a favorable state of Hawai'i's economy at that time.

Preferred Way of Life. Mainlanders look for "a feeling of accomplishment" in their job, while locals are less inclined to do so (Table 7.3[b]). Older Japanese are most interested in obtaining safe and secure jobs, whereas mainlanders are scarcely interested in job security, a difference largely explained by the relatively low educational background of older Japanese Americans. However, younger Japanese, who are almost as well as educated as mainlanders, are also less inclined to desire a feeling of accomplishment in their jobs.

I asked respondents to identify their preferred way of life among six alternatives (Table 7.3[c]). Regarding working hard to "get rich," immigrants are much more interested than mainlanders and older Japanese Americans. Mainlanders are more inclined to seek a life that suits their "own taste" over other ways of life than immigrants and first- and second-generation Japanese Americans. I attribute this statistically insignificant but qualitatively meaningful difference to the core of American culture, individualism. Mainlanders, in particular, seek self-satisfaction as a preferred way of life. Older Japanese Americans, on the hand, chose the worry-free way of life ("Live each day as it comes, cheerfully and without worry") by almost two to one over a self-satisfaction lifestyle ("Don't think about money or fame; just live a life that suits your own taste"). It is only logical that older Japanese Americans, who worry so much more about mundane problems than any other group, prefer a way of life free of worries.

TABLE 7.3
Psychological Dimensions of Ethnic Groups in Hawai'i, 1988 (figures in percent)

Dimensions		Questions	Islanders	Mainlanders	Immigrants	Older Japanese	Younger Japanese
Anxiety	(a)	Worry "very much" about					
		car accident	44	13	37	52	28
		nuclear power	41	18	35	42	35
		serious illness	35	16	26	43	33
		street crime	47	22	44	51	39
		unemployment	21	4	23	17	13
		war	36	8	21	33	33
Values	(b)	Job selection criteria					
		a safe, secure job	16	1	19	21	13
		sense of accomplishment	49	79	54	40	51
	(c)	Way of life					
		"Work hard and get rich."	9	7	21	6	13
		"Suit your own taste."	36	39	26	22	36
		"Live each day as it comes. No worry."	35	27	35	56	31
	(d)	Importance of					
		career/work most important	38	23	49	28	36
		religion & church most important	38	28	40	31	18
	(e)	Teach children importance of money.					
		agree	16	5	32	26	16
		disagree	81	89	63	69	78

TABLE 7.3 (*continued*)

(f)	Most important values						
	filial piety	78	54	75	86	71
	individual freedom	24	49	32	16	24
(g)	"Live for today."					
	agree strongly	17	6	14	26	7
(h)	Attitudes toward computer					
	desirable	43	65	39	28	44
	inevitable	51	31	49	63	50
Feelings						
(i)	Will people be happy or unhappy?					
	happier	22	22	51	27	32
(j)	Will people's peace of mind increase?					
	increase	24	25	42	44	32
(k)	Does science decrease human feelings?					
	yes	63	53	56	79	82
Self-Society						
(l)	Go alone to do right or follow custom?					
	go alone	57	71	47	44	57
(m)	To improve nation,					
	country first, then individual	33	13	32	42	26
	country and individual at same time	29	53	39	29	34

Note: "Japanese" are Japanese Americans.

Source: Research Committee on the Study of Honolulu Residents.

How do various ethnic groups value different aspects of life (Table 7.3[d])? Much more than mainlanders, immigrants consider their career to be important. Religion and church are "very important" to Islanders and immigrants alike but less so to mainlanders and Japanese Americans, particularly younger Japanese Americans. Results are only partly a function of education. Other items produced little difference among different ethnic groups.

Should one teach children that money is important? The answer is a resounding "No" for a great majority, especially to mainlanders, but least so among immigrants (Table 7.3[e]). Many immigrants, most of whom today are from the Philippines, leave home to seek a better economic life. Money is important to them, as they remit a large amount to their families back home. Older Japanese Americans, many of whom lived through the depression era, come closest to the immigrant group.

I asked respondents to choose two most important values out of four, consisting of two Eastern and two Western values. Regarding filial piety, a Confucian value, 54 percent of the mainlanders considered rendering respect and love to one's parents to be one of the two most cherished values, while a very high 86 percent of the older Japanese Americans did so (Table 7.3[f]). The second Eastern value, *on* (social obligation), did not yield any group differences.[7] The most preferred Western value was individual rights; however, there was no significant difference among the groups, so percentages are not displayed in Table 7.3. The second Western value, individual freedom, attracted 49 percent of the mainlanders, followed by 32 percent of the immigrants; the first and second generations of Japanese Americans were least impressed with this Western value. Educational attainment explained the results to a large degree, but not entirely.

Does one have "to live pretty much for today and let tomorrow take care of itself"? Only 6 percent of the mainlanders agreed strongly, whereas 26 percent of the older Japanese Americans did so (Table 7.3[g]). Only 12 percent of the Japanese and 30 percent of the mainlanders disagreed strongly.

Is the advent of the computer age welcomed by everyone or simply accepted as something inevitable by different groups? Most felt computers to be either "desirable" or "inevitable" (Table 7.3[h]). The higher the level of schooling, the more one thought the computer age is "desirable." Some 65 percent of mainlanders were most likely to consider the arrival of the computer age as desirable, while only 44 percent of younger Japanese Americans and 28 percent of older Japanese considered computers desirable. Thus, there is more than just the level of education involved in the percentage differences among the different groups.

Age and education correlate with value preferences to some extent, but they are closely related. The older a Japanese American respondent, the shorter the length of formal schooling. These data are not displayed in Table 7.3.

Will life be happier or unhappier in years ahead? Some 51 percent of the immigrant group said that the people will be happier, while only 20 to 30 percent of the native-born groups felt so (Table 7.3[i]). Having hailed from economically deprived parts of Asia, immigrants look for better days in America.

Concerning whether "people's peace of mind" will increase in the future, 42 and 44 percent of the immigrant and older Japanese American groups respectively agreed (Table 7.3[j]). Only 25 percent of the mainlanders said so. This result is relatively free from age and education influences.

The development of science and technology has made life more convenient, but some feel that "a lot of human feeling is lost." Japanese Americans (79 percent and 82 percent) believe that "a lot of human feeling" has been lost, but only 53 percent of the mainlanders agreed (Table 7.3[k]). The remaining Islanders side with mainlanders: only 56 percent of the immigrants agreed. I believe that traditional Japanese culture continues to affect the Japanese American population. Japanese culture values human relations more than the individual (Kuroda and Hayashi 1995).

Self Orientation. Older Japanese Americans, in particular, are most likely to "follow custom." A large majority (71 percent of mainlanders) would go their own way, while only 44 percent of older Japanese Americans, 47 percent of immigrants, and 57 percent of younger Japanese Americans and Islanders choose their way over tradition (Table 7.3[l]). Further analysis reveals that education but not age is a factor in shaping these views to some extent, but so is ethnic culture.

Only 13 percent of the mainlanders thought that the country must improve before individuals can achieve happiness, compared with 42 percent of the older Japanese Americans and 26 percent of the younger Japanese Americans (Table 7.3[m]). The difference between groups was largely a function of aging or cohort and only to some extent education among the Japanese Americans. Some 53 percent of the mainlanders believe that both individual happiness and the improvement of a whole society comes at the same time. Only 29 percent of the older Japanese Americans and Islanders agreed. Education appears to play a minor but not a decisive role; age is unrelated. The responses by different ethnic groups to these two items support the proposed model of mainland versus local culture.

Sociological Dimensions

Thus far I have been concerned with psychological variables. The next set of questions goes beyond the level of individual to a higher level of human relations.

Human Relations. Are people helpful or do they just look out for themselves? A large majority of mainlanders (74 percent) believe that most of the time people are trying to be helpful to others, compared with 68 percent of the immigrant group and 50 percent for older Japanese Americans (Table 7.4[a]). Age more than education is a factor for Japanese Americans, perhaps a reflection of what they experienced before the end of World War II.[8]

A majority of both mainlanders and Japanese Americans is willing to trust most people, whereas immigrants and Islanders are less willing (Table 7.4[b]). Responses to this question are highly correlated with education for non-Japanese.

Religion. A varying majority, ranging from 84 percent of the immigrant group to 67 percent of the mainlander group, claims to have a religious faith (Table 7.4[c]). Younger Japanese Americans and mainlanders are least religious. A majority of all ethnic groups, except older Buddhist Japanese Americans, is Christian (Table 7.4[d]). Among immigrants and their descendants in the United States, Japanese Americans may be the only ethnic group to adopt the host nation's religion to a significant extent.[9] Surveys of Japanese Americans conducted in Honolulu indicate that about one-third are Buddhists, another third are Christians, and the remaining third are without any established religious beliefs.[10]

Politics. How interested are different groups in politics? Naturalized citizens showed the most interest in politics, with 32

TABLE 7.4
Sociological Dimensions of Ethnic Groups in Hawai'i, 1988 (figures in percent)

Dimensions		Questions	Islanders	Mainlanders	Immigrants	Older Japanese	Younger Japanese
Human Relations	(a)	Are people helpful or not?					
		helpful	58	74	68	50	66
	(b)	Can people be trusted?					
		can be trusted	40	62	30	62	59
		cannot be too careful	56	33	65	38	39
Religion	(c)	Do you have a religious faith?					
		yes	80	67	84	74	68
		no	17	32	12	26	30
	(d)	If so, what faith?					
		Protestant	28	29	21	21	29
		Buddhist	1	1	5	41	17
		Catholic	34	18	47	6	10
Politics	(e)	How interested are you in politics?					
		very much	17	30	32	9	15
	(f)	How often do you attend fundraisers?					
		very often or sometimes	26	33	37	22	29
		rarely or never	72	67	61	78	71
	(g)	Attitudes toward capitalism					
		favorable	45	68	46	40	54
	(h)	Party preference					
		Democratic Party	42	30	32	74	67

Note: "Japanese" are Japanese Americans.
Source: Research Committee on the Study of Honolulu Residents.

percent of them claiming much interest in politics, followed closely by mainlanders (30 percent) (Table 7.4[e]). Locals showed the least interest, ranging from only 9 percent for senior Japanese Americans, 15 percent for the younger Japanese Americans, and 17 percent for islanders. Differences between locals and immigrants decreased from 21 percent to 15 percent when I asked whether respondents ever attended political fund-raising events (Table 7.4[f]).

Views of capitalism yielded significant differences. Mainlanders were much more favorable (Table 7.4[g]). This is understandable because many mainlanders went to Hawai'i to accept executive or professional positions.

Yet another dimension of political orientation is party preference. Japanese Americans stand out from other ethnic groups in choosing the Democratic party over the Republican Party: 70 percent chose the Democratic Party compared to only 30 percent of the mainlanders, whereas only 42 percent of Islanders and immigrants chose the Democratic Party (Table 7.4[h]).

Education is not a factor in party choice but instead a consequence of historical events from the days when Japanese Americans in Hawai'i were not welcomed by the Republican Party. Younger Japanese Americans are as inclined as their parents to choose the Democratic Party over the Republican Party.

DISCUSSION: AMERICAN MAINSTREAM AND ISLAND CULTURES

The following are the principal findings of this survey of public opinion in Hawai'i.

More Similarities than Differences. Only one-fourth of the questions asked in the questionnaire yielded a significant difference among different ethnic groups. Thus, there are more similarities in values than differences. In other words, the assimilation model is more applicable to Hawai'i's ethnic groups than the mosaic model, through not totally.

Differences Among All Groups. The differences found are not only between locals and mainlanders but also among different ethnic groups, birthplaces, and generations. For example, religious preference and the extent of such worries as "serious crime" and "street crime" vary by ethnicity, whereas responses to such items as the importance of money and future happiness differ significantly among those born in the United States and those born abroad. Differences between younger and older Japanese Americans are correlated with such demographic factors as education and occupation; for example, a majority of the older generation chose "Live each day as it comes, cheerfully and without worry," while only 31 percent of the younger generation did so.

Island versus Mainland Cultures. Significant differences emerged on anxiety items, job selection criteria, attitudes toward computers, following custom, country before self, and favorable attitude toward capitalism. These findings are consistent with the mainland individualism-Islander communitarianism dichotomy presented above.

Salient Self and Diffuse Self. What must separate the two cultures is the priority placed on oneself as opposed to one's environment. Mainlanders are self-confident and clearly place themselves in the center of their world. On the other hand, the Island culture focuses on human relations. Individual freedom is more important to mainlanders than custom. Locals' perception of self is diffuse and less distinctive, powerful, and salient than that of mainlanders.

Japanese Values. Japanese Americans in Hawai'i, who constitute a plurality of the registered voter population, continue to support the Democratic Party over the Republican Party more than other groups. Another item that sets them apart from the rest is preference for Buddhism, although younger Japanese tend to have no religious faith, similar to mainlanders. Japanese Americans are also significantly more concerned about the possible loss of rich human feelings as the development of science continues, indicating the importance they place on human relations and feelings. Japanese culture does have less confidence in logic and reason than Western culture. Many books on traditional Japanese culture point to emotional elements and the prime value placed on human relations over the individual. Hence, differences found between Japanese Americans and the rest of the groups are largely derived from historical factors.

CONCLUSION

Therefore, Hawai'i is a melting pot as well as a mosaic of ethnic and generational groups, but the mosaic model is less applicable in regard to a wide range of attitudes. Certainly, the sharp rise in outmarriage by

Japanese Americans will contribute to the complexity of ethnic identity in years to come.

My findings confirm the validity of the local-mainlander model introduced at the outset only when the focus is on the mosaic dimension of values in Hawai'i. Mainlanders tend to possess a clear, distinct, positive, and powerful concept of self, whereas the Islanders' self is more diffuse and extensive and less salient. Major sources of the local concept of self are likely to be rooted in the cultures of the Native Hawaiians and East Asians. Such concepts as *aloha* and *'ohana* (family) resemble key elements of Japanese culture, which emphasizes the importance of family and group memberships over the individual. Chinese often speak of keeping dirty linen within the family and prefer the middle way, avoiding extremes. Japanese place a premium on harmony, the most cherished value that Prince Regent Shôtoku enunciated in 704, when he promulgated a seventeen-article constitution that provided a basis for governance. Japanese today avoid open conflict and confrontation and prefer to work out solutions through consultation and mediation.

Thus, Hawai'i has developed a variant of communitarianism (cf. Etzioni 1993). Compared with interviewees in France, Germany, Japan, the United Kingdom, and the U.S. mainland, Honolulu residents are happier, healthier, and more optimistic and relaxed (Kuroda 1993, 17–19). In Hawai'i, personal happiness is shared, and sadness is easier to bear when there are sympathetic ears.

Although no ethnic group is free from discrimination in Hawai'i, the extent of relentless racism is less than in the mainland United States. Islanders pay more attention to the feelings of other ethnic groups. For example, an African American on the mainland may openly and proudly vote for a fellow African American candidate. In Hawai'i, no one will openly declare political support on the basis of race or ethnic origin. Because of historical reasons, Hawai'i has several chambers of commerce based along ethnic lines. However, such groups as the Japanese Chamber of Commerce (JCC) not only admit non-Japanese, but the JCC has even elected a Caucasian as its president. Groups and families play a greater part in the life of individuals in Hawai'i compared to the U.S. mainland.

Mass society has produced a heightened sense of alienation in modern America, as manifested in the rise of such social disorganization indicators as divorce and family violence. While it is true that "mom and pop" stores are disappearing in Hawai'i as well, human bonding remains stronger than on the U.S. mainland. A recent case of two-year-old Alana Dung in Honolulu, a leukemia patient in need of a bone marrow transplant, attracted over 30,000 volunteers, far beyond expectations (Barnett 1996). Entertainers joined in assisting the small child by donating their talents at the place where blood tests were conducted. Perhaps this local value of *aloha*, which cuts across ethnic lines, is what most makes Hawai'i an attractive place to live, as nostalgic Hawai'i-born expatriates on the U.S. mainland readily attest.

NOTES

1. Can we think of an ethnic group without taking into account its members' educational background? Is education a part of being a member of an ethnic group? I decided, when it was possible, to see whether the level of formal schooling yielded any independent effect on items in the study. I decided to separate educational effects from other effects within an ethnic group on opinions and values. However, I could not use both age and education as independent variables, to see their separate impacts on items, since the number of respondents in each cell would be so small as to make data analysis statistically meaningless.

2. Electoral districts have changed over the years from 1971 to 1988. I used the geographic area (Kokohead to the Diamond Head side of Middle Street) as the criterion in defining the population. I used a magnetic tape of the registered voter list made available from the office of the city clerk to draw random samples.

3. Caucasians from the U.S. mainland who reside and decide to register to vote in Hawai'i are largely business people and professionals with much higher educational attainment than the average Caucasian in North America.

4. This trend may be caused by their East Asian cultural heritage and their living on an island.

5. I arrived at the breakdown of Hawai'i registered voters by surveys conducted in the summer and fall of 1990. The self-identification method derived the following percentages: Caucasian (28 percent), Chinese/Korean (8 percent), Filipino (10 percent), Native Hawaiian (10 percent), Japanese (35 percent) and mixed/others (9 percent).

6. This finding is a result of a correspondence analysis called "Quantification III" (Hayashi 1956; Lebart, Morineau, Worwick 1984), which is similar to principal-component analysis but is designed for qualitative data.

For more on this finding, see Research Committee on the Study of Honolulu Residents (1986, 100–29).

7. The Japanese word *on* refers to what a person acquires from birth onward as one becomes indebted to various people: from one's parents, neighbors, and teachers, to others who assist in the pursuit of education and a better life in general. *On* is more than the return of a favor for an act considered favorable. *On* is an indebtedness that one must return in one form or another. Because there are no significant differences, percentages for this question are not displayed in Table 7.3

8. Then, doors to middle-class jobs were closed to Japanese Americans, even in such occupations as bus drivers and certified public accountants. It is difficult to say that people are helpful when, for example, a McKinley High School graduate, after having studied accounting for two years in the 1930s through correspondence was told by authorities that he could not take an exam to become a certified public accountant because he was Japanese. Such is no longer the case, and a large percentage (68 percent) of the recent immigrants perceive people in general to be helpful.

9. The number of Christians has remained at about 1 percent of the total population of Japan since 1868 (Kajimura 1988, 5). Christianity came to Japan in 1548 and became an attractive religion, having about 150,000 converts at its heyday before it was banned in the 1630s.

10. My hypothesis is that many Japanese Americans became Christians in order to prove their loyalty to America and to obtain employment. We must keep in mind that Japanese Americans in Hawai'i during World War II even pretended that they did not know how to use chopsticks in restaurants. They did not want to be recognized as Japanese. However, the situation changed in the 1960s, when ethnic pride rose among many in America. During World War II, Buddhist Japanese Americans in Hawai'i had a unique experience because all Buddhist and Shinto priests were sent to relocation camps. Their mainland counterparts were not separated from their Buddhist priests, since all of them relocated from their homes on the West Coast. How, then, could Japanese Buddhists bury family members who died during the war? The U.S. government made no provision for Buddhist funerals in Hawai'i. In some cases, "instant priests," usually men who knew some Buddhist funeral rituals, resolved the crisis created by the absence of Buddhist priests. In other cases, Christian ministers performed Buddhist rituals, perhaps the first and last time in the history of Christianity when Christian ministers performed funeral services for Buddhists.

CHAPTER 8

Politics

Michael Haas

ETHNIC SUCCESSION

Until recently, politics was the principal means by which a system of ethnic dominance and subordination was enforced in Hawai'i. After the arrival of *haole* settlers in the Hawaiian Islands, the Native Hawaiian monarchs were in control, and they listened to and acted on advice from the *haoles* without prejudice. When Chinese laborers were allowed to enter the kingdom, they had few rights initially, but they were eventually permitted to become citizens. Mutual trust between the ethnic groups ended in 1887, when the king signed the "bayonet constitution," which imposed property qualifications on prospective Native Hawaiian voters, and the fall of the monarchy in 1893 can only be viewed as an example of racism.

In 1900, the Native Hawaiian-backed Home Rule Party swept territorial elections. In 1902, *haole* Republicans captured control with Prince Kuhio Kalaniana'ole at the head of the ticket. *Haole* Republican rule, which particularly involved anti-Japanese campaign slurs and governmental policies before World War II, continued until 1954, when Japanese candidates in the Democratic Party came to power in the territorial legislature. Although the rhetoric of the victorious Democrats was to create a "new Hawai'i" that would end the institutional discrimination against nonwhites dating from the plantation era, no such social revolution occurred. What appeared to be class politics was instead ethnic politics. The dominant Japanese instead used political power to rise to middle-class status (Cooper and Daws 1985), leaving behind Filipinos and Native Hawaiians who joined in ousting the *haole* Republicans but have enjoyed few benefits from their loyalties to the Democratic Party.

TABLE 8.1

Registered Voters in Hawai'i by Ethnic Group, 1887–1990 (in percent)

Year	Caucasian	Chinese	Filipino	Hawaiian	Japanese
1887	31.4 (48)			65.3 (100)	
1890	27.4 (36)			75.4 (100)	
1892	28.0 (40)			69.9 (100)	
1894	77.1 (100)			18.0 (23)	
1897	55.1 (100)			41.8 (76)	
1902	30.0 (44)	1.1 (2)		68.8 (100)	
1904	28.2 (40)	1.3 (2)		69.8 (100)	
1906	22.4 (32)	1.6 (2)		71.0 (100)	
1908	30.4 (45)	2.0 (3)		67.6 (100)	
1910	30.6 (46)	2.7 (4)		66.6 (100)	.1 (-)
1912	34.3 (55)	3.2 (5)		62.1 (100)	.3 (-)
1914	37.4 (64)	3.7 (6)		58.2 (100)	.6 (1)
1916	34.5 (61)	4.1 (7)		56.7 (100)	.9 (2)
1918	39.7 (73)	4.7 (9)		54.2 (100)	1.4 (3)
1920	37.5 (67)	4.3 (8)		55.6 (100)	2.5 (4)
1922	40.1 (77)	4.6 (9)		51.8 (100)	3.5 (7)
1924	41.2 (86)	5.8 (12)		48.0 (100)	4.9 (10)
1926	38.0 (87)	7.2 (17)		43.8 (100)	7.6 (17)
1928	39.8 (97)	8.6 (21)		41.1 (100)	11.7 (28)
1930	39.1 (100)	8.4 (21)		38.1 (97)	13.5 (34)
1932	39.8 (100)	8.4 (21)	.1 (–)	33.8 (85)	17.7 (44)
1936	34.6 (100)	8.6 (25)	- (–)	28.9 (84)	24.9 (72)
1938	32.3 (100)	8.6 (27)	.6 (2)	26.7 (83)	28.5 (88)
1940	30.2 (97)	8.5 (27)	- (–)	24.7 (80)	31.0 (100)
1961	28.9 (73)	13.3 (34)	6.2 (16)	7.5 (19)	39.5 (100)
1970	20.0 (44)	5.3 (12)	9.7 (21)	16.9 (37)	45.8 (100)
1974	32.5 (89)	7.4 (20)	7.9 (22)	9.9 (27)	36.7 (100)
1976	29.0 (75)	7.2 (19)	9.7 (25)	12.2 (32)	38.6 (100)
1990	28.0 (80)	8.0 (23)[a]	10.0 (29)	10.0 (29)	35.0 (100)

Key: - = less than 1%; (-) = less than 1% of top group.

[a]Includes Koreans.

Note: Figures report percentages of voting-age persons within each ethnic group who registered to vote, and add to 100 percent horizontally when other groups are included. For 1961, figures exclude Kaua'i, Lana'i, and Moloka'i. For 1974, figures exclude Lana'i and Moloka'i. For 1990, the combined count of Chinese and Koreans was 10 percent, so I assume that Koreans account for 2 percent of voters. Parenthesized figures are normed, with 100 assigned to the group with the highest percentage of registered voters; other groups are expressed as a percentage of the top figure. "Hawaiian" figures includes persons with any Native Hawaiian ancestry. "Caucasian" figures include Portuguese, Puerto Ricans, Spanish, and other Caucasians.

Source: Coffman (1973, 11); Hawai'i (1932a, 21; 1934, 10; 1940a, 15; 1977b, 87); Kuroda (Chap. 7); Lind (1967, 98); Meller (1955, 265); Oshiro (1976, A3, 10); Schmitt (1961, 5–6; 1977, 55–56).

Today, Japanese are still the largest ethnic group in the electorate (Table 8.1) as well as in the majority Democratic Party (Table 8.2), but their percentage of control has been slipping in recent years. The election of a Native Hawaiian governor and a Filipino lieutenant governor in 1986, their reelection in 1990, and a Filipino governor and Japanese lieutenant governor in 1994 appear to herald the beginning of a new multiethnic era for politics in Hawai'i.

TABLE 8.2
Ethnicity and Party Preference, 1976 and 1986 (in percent)

Ethnic Group	Party Preference	1976	1986
Caucasian	Democratic	49	33
	Republican	30	43
	Independent	26	24
Chinese	Democratic	40	37
	Republican	29	20
	Independent	31	43
Filipino	Democratic	77	41
	Republican	9	24
	Independent	14	35
Hawaiian	Democratic	49	46
	Republican	17	21
	Independent	34	33
Japanese	Democratic	58	68
	Republican	11	9
	Independent	31	23
Total	Democratic	52	45
	Republican	18	27
	Independent	30	28

Source: Boylan (1992, 71).

Ethnic interpretations of Hawai'i elections square with the popular understanding in the Islands of the meaning of electoral eras (Fuchs 1961, chap. 13–14; Honolulu Advertiser 1972; Endicott 1979; Burris 1981; Morita 1986a,b,c; Griffin 1987; Adamski 1988; Borreca 1990; Kresnak 1988, 1990; Boylan 1992; Rosegg 1994a; Yuen 1994a; cf. Rosegg 1994b). Still, documentary evidence is superior to impressionistic conclusions, so the analysis below first focuses on data regarding voters and then on results of elections in ethnic terms in order to demonstrate the arrival of post-ethnic politics in the Aloha State.

ETHNIC BLOC VOTING

Defining *ethnic bloc voting* as existing when a member of one ethnic group votes only for candidates of that group, sociologist Andrew Lind (1957) found considerable bloc voting from 1928 to 1938. When he examined ballots of voters in 1947, however, he found that only 3.2 percent of Japanese voted *only* for Japanese, thus discrediting the belief, held by some opponents of statehood, that an extreme form of nonwhite ethnic bloc voting existed in Hawai'i.[1] The myth that there is no ethnic voting in Hawai'i, which dates from the era of the statehood campaign, still persists (Boylan 1992, 73–77).

What if *ethnic bloc voting* is merely the tendency to support members of one's own ethnic group, other things being equal? Three voting studies, using a technique known as factor analysis, have sought to correlate aggregate percentages of ethnic groups present in voting precincts with the percentage of votes cast for candidates of particular ethnicities. In 1954, when the Democratic Party displaced the Republican Party, there was a clear polarization between pro- and anti-Japanese precincts, but party preference was a better predictor of voting than ethnicity (Digman and Tuttle 1961). In one precinct, voting officials identified each voter's ethnicity; correlating the ethnicity of voters directly with the ethnicity of candidates supported, the researchers were able to validate their aggregate analysis across all precincts. In 1956, they found a similar pattern (Digman and Tuttle 1959).

In 1970, when two *haole* Democrats vied for the governorship, the incumbent John Burns openly courted Japanese and other non-*haole* voters, implying that his Hawai'i-born opponent, Lieutenant Governor Thomas Gill, was the darling of upper-status *haoles* and recent arrivals unassimilated to the local culture of the Islands (Coffman 1973, chap. 17). Burns's victory signaled to many observers that Filipino and Japanese support remained solid. In a factor analysis of aggregate precinct voting in 1970, I discovered a polarization between Caucasian-dominated precincts supporting Caucasian Republican candidates and Japanese-dominated precincts favoring Japanese Democrats, and several other factors linked ethnicity of candidates with the ethnic composition of precincts (Haas 1977). Dan Boylan (1992, 72) offers a similar analysis for 1989.

The main problem with analyses of aggregated statistics of precincts is that they do not measure the opinions of voters directly. Sample surveys are therefore preferable. In 1950, four years before the Democratic landslide, a survey found that Japanese preferred the Democratic Party, and Caucasians showed even more preference for the Republican Party (Territorial Surveys 1950), a finding that has been repeated in many subsequent studies. The next major sample survey of voters in Hawai'i occurred in 1970, when Caucasians preferred Gill to Burns in the primary, and then Native Hawaiian Republican gubernatorial hopeful Samuel King lost to Burns in the general election. Non-Caucasians, especially Filipinos and Japanese, supported Burns in both the primary and the general elections (Table 8.3). With union leaders accustomed to trucking voters to the polls in rural areas, the victory appeared to represent yet another success of the "Burns machine."

In 1973, Burns resigned because of poor health, whereupon Lieutenant Governor George Ariyoshi became the nation's first Japanese governor. In 1974, Gill tried his luck again, but Honolulu Mayor Frank Fasi, a Sicilian American from Hartford who came to Hawai'i as a marine in World War II, threw his hat into the ring as well. Ariyoshi made a bid for the Democratic non-Caucasian voting bloc that had won every gubernatorial election since 1954. Middle-class voters preferred Gill. Fasi made a populist appeal to non-Caucasian working-class voters and to alienated mainland-born *haoles*. At the urging of Ariyoshi's campaign manager, State Senator David McClung, a *haole* from Michigan, entered the race to split the Caucasian vote even more; when he later reported the deal on television, he threw his support to Gill (Burris 1974; Haas 1976, 52). At one point in the campaign, Gill evidently came close to comparing Fasi with Benito Mussolini, the former fascist leader of Italy, whereupon the mayor bristled that a "slur

TABLE 8.3
Gubernatorial Support from Voters in Hawai'i by Ethnic Group, 1970–1978 (in percent)

Election	Candidate	Party	Race	Caucasian	Chinese	Filipino	Hawaiian	Japanese	Other	Total
1970 primary	Burns	D	W	19	NR	NR	NR	33	NR	25
	Gill	D	W	29	NR	NR	NR	36	NR	33
	Burns	D	W	35	NR	55	50	58	NR	NR
	Gill	D	W	59	NR	40	41	35	NR	NR
1970 general	Burns-Ariyoshi	D	W-J	45	48	61	48	59	55	58
	King-Kiyosaki	R	H-J	50	42	33	47	35	39	42
1974 primary	Ariyoshi	D	J	14	NR	21	NR	36	NR	26
	Fasi	D	W	33	NR	31	NR	26	NR	29
	Gill	D	W	35	NR	23	NR	22	NR	26
	Ariyoshi	D	J	13	*	23	*	41	23	35
	Fasi	D	W	35	*	32	*	25	30	31
	Gill	D	W	36	*	25	*	23	27	30
1974 general	Ariyoshi-Doi	D	J-J	25	*	*	*	72	47	49
	Crossley-Dillingham	R	W-W	57	*	*	*	14	31	33
1978 primary	Ariyoshi	D	J	17	*	*	*	59	32	29
	Fasi	D	W	65	*	*	*	17	44	39
	Ariyoshi	D	J	14	*	*	*	55	23	34
	Fasi	D	W	74	*	*	*	19	54	44

Note: Figures report percentages of each ethnic group preferring one of the candidates or candidate slates and add to 100 percent vertically when other candidates and nonascertained preferences are included. When two or more sets of figures are reported for the same primary, the topmost is from the earliest sample.

Key: D = Democrat; H = Native Hawaiian; J = Japanese; NR = not reported; R = Republican; W = White; x-x = ethnicities of gubernatorial and lieutenant gubernatorial candidates; * = included in "Other" column.;

Source: Coffman (1970; 1973, 181, 203); Keir (1974a, A4; 1974b, A4; 1974c, A1, 3; 1978a, A17; 1978b, A4).

on one minority is a slur on every minority" (Kakesako 1974, A1).
When Ariyoshi supporters spread the word that the meaning of the
election was to determine whether Japanese were good enough to be
elected governor (Honolulu Advertiser 1974b), Fasi retorted that
"nobody should get elected to any office in Hawaii because of his racial
or ethnic or national origin" (Kakesako 1974, A1). Then, in a close
vote, Ariyoshi squeaked to victory over his two opponents, who
together garnered more support from all ethnic groups. Japanese even
supported *haole* gubernatorial candidates by a 48 to 41 percent margin
over Ariyoshi, according to the poll, Filipinos went 57 to 23 percent for
the *haole* candidates over Ariyoshi, and Caucasians voted 68 to 14
percent against Ariyoshi (Table 8.3). In the general election, Japanese
overwhelmingly supported Ariyoshi over his Republican opponent,
Randolph Crossley, a *haole* business executive who attracted a larger
share of Caucasian voters than King in 1970.

Had there been one *haole* candidate instead of two in the 1974
primary, armchair observers speculated, Ariyoshi might have lost. In
1978, there was an opportunity to test this hypothesis, since Fasi was
Ariyoshi's major opponent. Opinion polls released before the election
even predicted Fasi's victory (Keir 1978a,b), but there were two
problems with the polling that year (Honolulu Star-Bulletin 1978).
First, some 26 percent of the Japanese voters refused to state a
preference; they were reluctant to confide in pollsters. Second, the
sample was drawn from all potential voters, even from those not
registered to vote in Hawai'i; the influence of respondents in the
military, who voted by absentee ballots in other states, distorted
the sample. Fasi won on O'ahu by a few votes but lost decisively on
the Neighbor Islands, so Ariyoshi was renominated in the primary. In
the general election, State Senator John Leopold, a Republican born in
Pennsylvania, again proved that no Republican could be elected
governor in the Aloha State.

In 1982, Ariyoshi faced opposition from his lieutenant governor,
Jean King. No relation to Samuel King, she became Ariyoshi's
lieutenant governor in a close election in 1978 as "Jean Sadako King,"
so voters correctly suspected that she was of mixed *haole*-Japanese
ancestry. In 1982, however, she inexplicably dropped "Sadako," her
pale face looked more *haole* than Eurasian, and solid backing from
Japanese voters carried Ariyoshi to victory. Fasi, tired of losing in the
Democratic primaries against Ariyoshi, formed the Independent

Democratic Party. In the general election, the Republican challenger, Native Hawaiian State Senator Andy Anderson picked a Japanese running mate, Pat Saiki, another state senator. Together, the Independent Democrat and Republican tickets won majority support from all groups but Japanese (Table 8.4), who had sufficient voting strength to reelect Ariyoshi for a third term.

According to the Hawai'i constitution, Ariyoshi was ineligible for reelection to a fourth term. Back in 1980, in an effort to cultivate a successor, he supported the candidacy of his *haole* director of finance, Eileen Anderson, who defeated Fasi to become mayor of Honolulu; rather than returning the favor by working closely with the Ariyoshi administration, she operated independently. In 1984, when she sought reelection, Ariyoshi support was absent, and Fasi returned to City Hall. In 1986, John Waihe'e, Ariyoshi's lieutenant governor from 1982, then sought to run as the heir to the Burns-Ariyoshi tradition. One of Waihe'e's primary election opponents was Cecil Heftel, a *haole* business executive who bought a network television station, often editorialized on political issues during prime time, then captured the first congressional district (Honolulu) in 1976, and was reelected to Congress four times. A third gubernatorial candidate in 1986 was Japanese: Patsy Takemoto Mink, formerly elected to the second congressional district (rural Hawai'i), who had lost a bid for a U.S. Senate seat in 1976 and now wanted to make a political comeback. Despite an early poll that showed Heftel as the clear winner among all ethnic groups (Table 8.4), Waihe'e mobilized a majority in a primary in which charges of racial prejudice played a role, albeit mostly in private conversations (Hartwell 1987). On the Republican side, Andy Anderson ran again for governor in 1986, but Mayor Fasi encouraged Maria Victoria ("Vicky") Bunye, the Filipina head of his Office of Human Resources, to run for lieutenant governor (Borreca 1985). Fasi said he did not want an "all-Caucasian" Republican ticket (Honolulu Advertiser 1986), but no such slate was in the offing, since Andy Anderson and his preferred running mate, John Felix, were both Native Hawaiians. During the campaign, Bunye cited statistics on Filipino underrepresentation in jobs with Hawai'i state government and urged Filipinos to switch to the Republican Party (Takeuchi 1986a). Ben Cayetano, a Filipino candidate for lieutenant governor in the Democratic primary, then attacked Bunye for injecting the issue of race into the campaign and for dishonoring Japanese Americans, who

TABLE 8.4
Gubernatorial Support from Voters in Hawai'i by Ethnic Group, 1982–1990 (in percent)

Election	Candidate	Party	Race	Caucasian	Chinese	Filipino	Hawaiian	Japanese	Other	Total
1982 primary	Ariyoshi	D	J	30	*	*	45	84	48	52
	King	D	WJ	54	*	*	40	11	37	35
1982 general	Anderson-Saiki	R	W-J	44	*	*	25	17	27	28
	Ariyoshi-Waihe'e	D	J-H	19	*	*	31	65	31	38
	Fasi-Piltz	I	W-H	34	*	*	37	10	33	27
1986 primary	Heftel	D	W	60	*	*	59	44	57	54
	Mink	D	J	13	*	*	3	13	8	10
	Waihe'e	D	H	11	*	*	29	21	15	18
1986 general	Anderson-Felix	R	H-H	59	*	21	49	21	*	39
	Waihe'e-Cayetano	D	H-F	23	*	35	32	60	*	41
1990 general	Waihe'e-Cayetano	D	H-F	46	NR	63	66	78	NR	NR
	Hemmings-Beamer	R	W-H	46	*	*	*	20	29	30
	Waihe'e-Cayetano	D	H-F	42	*	*	*	71	66	60

Note: Figures report percentages of each ethnic group preferring one of the candidates or candidate slates and add to 100 percent vertically when other candidates and nonascertained preferences are included. When two or more sets of figures are reported for the same primary, the topmost is from the earliest sample.

Key: D = Democrat; F = Filipino; H = Native Hawaiian; I = Independent Democrat; J = Japanese; NR = not reported; R = Republican; W = White; WJ = White-Japanese mixed; x-x = ethnicities of gubernatorial and lieutenant gubernatorial candidates; * = included in "Other" column.

Source: Keir (1978b, A4; 1982a, A4; 1982b, A4; 1986a, A1, A3; 1986b, A4); Kresnak (1990, A3); Burris (1990, A4).

TABLE 8.5
Gubernatorial Support from Voters in Hawai'i by Ethnic Group, 1994

Election	Candidate	Party	Race	Caucasian	Chinese	Filipino	Hawaiian	Japanese	Other	Total
1994 primary	Cayetano	D	F	21	*	39	31	23	21	24
	Fasi	B	W	20	*	6	32	8	25	20
	Saiki	R	J	46	*	22	31	48	29	40
	Cayetano	D	F	17	*	51	19	21	20	22
	Fasi	B	W	23	*	14	27	6	16	19
	Saiki	R	J	52	*	31	40	64	56	51
	Cayetano	D	F	13	*	*	17	16	16	18
	Fasi	B	W	24	*	*	26	13	26	22
	Saiki	R	J	39	*	*	30	43	36	36
	Cayetano	D	F	20	16	57	33	29	NR	28
	Fasi	B	W	22	24	8	16	17	NR	20
	Saiki	R	J	38	38	14	25	28	NR	31
1994 general	Cayetano-Hirono	D	F-J	19	NR	42	25	32	NR	30
	Fasi-Kaleikini	B	W-H	25	NR	19	27	16	NR	23
	Saiki-Hemmings	R	J-W	33	NR	11	18	25	NR	34
	Cayetano-Hirono	D	F-J	19	NR	61	45	45	NR	35
	Fasi-Kaleikini	B	W-H	27	NR	NR	21	NR	NR	20
	Saiki-Hemmings	R	J-W	40	NR	NR	21	32	NR	31
	Cayetano-Hirono	D	F-J	16	25	47	33	46	NR	31
	Fasi-Kaleikini	B	W-H	36	24	21	22	10	NR	24
	Saiki-Hemmings	R	J-W	31	28	3	18	26	NR	24
	Cayetano-Hirono	D	F-J	17	16	48	17	41	NR	27
	Fasi-Kaleikini	B	W-H	33	32	17	38	10	NR	26
	Saiki-Hemmings	R	J-W	35	31	6	22	27	NR	26

Note: Figures report percentages of each ethnic group preferring one of the candidates or candidate slates and add to 100 percent vertically when other candidates and nonascertained preferences are included. When two or more sets of figures are reported for the same primary, the topmost is from the earliest sample.

Key: B = Best Party; D = Democrat; F = Filipino; H = Native Hawaiian; J = Japanese; NR = not reported; R = Republican; W = White; x-x = ethnicities of gubernatorial and lieutenant gubernatorial candidates; * = included in "Other" column.

Source: Yuen (1993); Burris (1994a, b); Kresnak (1994); Honolulu Advertiser (1994a, b); Yuen (1994a, c).

applied for government work because of discrimination in the private sector and had become a "great American success story" (Takeuchi 1986b). Whereas Cayetano became Waiheʻeʻs running mate, Bunye lost in the primary. The Waiheʻe-Cayetano ticket then defeated Anderson and Felix in an election in which Japanese votes were again decisive (Table 8.4). The "Ariyoshi/Burns machine" had become a multiethnic "Democratic machine." Republicans remained political dinosaurs at the statewide level despite successes in electing mayors on Maui and Oʻahu.

In 1990, the Waiheʻe-Cayetano team faced token opposition in the Democratic primary. In the general election, they attracted about as many Caucasian votes as the Republican opponents (Caucasian State Senator Fred Hemmings, Jr., and Native Hawaiian Billie Beamer) to win the first overwhelming landslide election since statehood (Table 8.4).

The election of 1994 was accompanied by more published polls than ever before (Table 8.5). For the Democrats to win, Cayetano would have to defeat not only Republican Pat Saiki but also an independent challenge by Frank Fasi's Best Party. The first survey to appear, in November 1993, showed that Saiki was popular within all ethnic groups but Filipinos, who preferred Cayetano; Saiki's overall lead was 2:1 over both Cayetano and Fasi (Yuen 1993). One year later, the polls revealed why Cayetano emerged on top. Although many Caucasians defected from Saiki to Fasi, the biggest switch was Japanese from Saiki to Cayetano. Japanese were evenly split between Cayetano and Saiki in early September, but they were almost 2:1 for Cayetano-Hirono over Saiki-Hemmings two months later. Were Japanese returning to traditional Democratic Party loyalties or instead attracted by the addition of Mazie Hirono as Cayetano's running mate after the primary election? The data strongly suggest that Cayetano needed Hirono to divert Japanese voters from Saiki.[2]

The record of two decades, thus, is of considerable voting solidarity within ethnic groups. Each year, many ethnic groups show a marked preference for candidates of their same background. Japanese voters average nearly 60 percent support for Japanese candidates, although they split their votes in the three-candidate contests of 1974 and 1986; the latter case was the only election when they failed to back one of their own, Patsy Mink. Caucasian and Filipino voters rank next in ethnic loyalty. Whites supported only two tickets with a gubernatorial candidate of a different race, whereas there were no major Filipino candidates until Ben Cayetano became John Waihe'e's running mate in 1986. Filipinos, who cast anti-Ariyoshi votes in 1974, returned to the mainstream Democratic fold in 1986. Native Hawaiians have the lowest ethnic solidarity; until 1990, they failed to give clear support to Native Hawaiian gubernatorial candidates of either party.

Since some polls find respondents reluctant to state preferences, voting solidarity can be recalculated by dividing the percentage of votes for the ethnic group receiving the most votes by the percentage of votes for all candidates each year. When these calculations are performed, the same patterns hold (Haas 1992, Table 4.2).

However, answers to questions in sample surveys that correlate ethnic background of voters with ethnicity of candidates may be misleading. In two of the factor analyses reported earlier, there was a similar correlation indicating ethnic voting patterns, but party loyalties were even greater. Accordingly, I examined nine surveys from 1988 to 1992 administered by the same polling organization that reported most of the survey data reported above (Haas 1995b).[3] What I found was that party orientation is predominant in presidential elections, which are between two Caucasians. In local elections, however, personal attributes about candidates have been more important influences on voting than either ethnicity or party preferences, and both campaign funding and incumbency play a role as well. As Boylan (1992, 78) notes, 39 percent of the incumbents in the state legislature ran unopposed in 1988; most had formidable campaign war chests in case a challenger deigned to emerge.

ETHNIC VOTING SLATES AND ELECTORAL SUCCESS

Because there is no ethnic majority in Hawai'i, open ethnic appeals risk political suicide. Numerous politicians will readily admit that subtle ethnic appeals, nevertheless, are central to their campaigns (Boylan 1992, 73). Candidates seeking office carefully select campaign treasurers of a different ethnic background and then advertise their names in order to assure voters that they have a broad multiethnic base of support.

TABLE 8.6
General Election Voting Slates in Hawai'i, 1959–1996

Year	Party	Governor	Lt. Gov.	Senator		Rep. 1	Rep. 2
1959	D	W	J	W	W	J	
	R	W	H	C	J	W	
1960	D					J	
	R					W	
1962	D	W	H	J		W	J
	R	W	H	W		W	W
1964	D			W		J	J
	R			C		W	W
1966	D	W	W			J	J
	R	W	H			W	H
1968	D			J		J	J
	R			W		H	W
1970	D	W	J	W		J	J
	R	H	J	C		H	
1972	D					J	J
	R					W	W
1974	D	J	J	J		J	J
	R	W	W	W		W	W
1976	D			J		J	J
	R			W		W	J
1978	D	J	WJ			W	H
	R	W	W			W	W
1980	D			J		W	H
	R			W		W	
1982	D	J	H	J		W	H
	R	W	J	W			
1984	D					W	H
	R					W	H
1986	D	H	F	J		S	H
	R	H	H	W		J	W
1988	D			J		W	H
	R			W		J	W
1990	D	H	F	H		W	J
	R	W	H	J		C	H
1992	D			J		W	J
	R			W		W	H
1994	D	F	J			W	J
	R	J	W			W	W
1996	D					W	J
	R					W	W

TABLE 8.6 (*continued*)

Key: C = Chinese; D = Democratic Party; F = Filipino; H = Native
        Hawaiian; J = Japanese; R = Republican Party; S = Samoan; W =
        White or Caucasian; WJ = White-Japanese.
Note: Hawai'i was apportioned one seat in the House of Representatives
        before 1962; it now has two seats. In 1959, two Senators were elected
        with staggered terms.

Primary election voters pick a set of candidates in each party to run as voting slates, which, in turn, can represent one or more ethnic groups (Table 8.6). Often, the slates are deliberately contrived. In 1959, Democratic statewide candidates consisted of three *haoles* and two Japanese, while Republicans balanced the ticket with a Chinese, a Japanese, a Native Hawaiian, and two *haoles*; when the polls closed and the Republicans won the positions of governor, lieutenant governor, and senator, the Democrats won one seat each in the House of Representatives and the U.S. Senate. Learning their lesson (Boylan 1992, 76), the Democrats fielded a more balanced ticket in 1962 and swept all Republicans from office but incumbent Senator Hiram Fong. In 1970, Governor John Burns was eager to have a Japanese lieutenant governor, so he endorsed George Ariyoshi, and the Republicans also ran a Japanese candidate for lieutenant governor. In 1974, Ariyoshi refused to endorse lieutenant governor candidates, but he woke up to the embarrassment that voters had elected a Japanese governor, lieutenant governor, senator, and two members of the House of Representatives, though of course the Republicans ran only *haoles* for the same races. From 1978, the Democrats were more careful to field candidates with a more balanced ticket. As noted above, Fasi tried to outflank the Democrats in 1986 by running Bunye for lieutenant governor in order to attract Filipino voters, but this ploy succeeded only in raising the visibility of the Filipino Democratic candidate for lieutenant governor, Ben Cayetano, who became Waihe'e's successful running mate. In 1990, Republican gubernatorial candidate Fred Hemmings, Jr. urged primary voters to choose Billie Beamer, a Native Hawaiian, as lieutenant governor. Leonard Mednick, who was also a candidate for lieutenant governor, then charged Hemmings with discrimination for turning him down as a running mate because he was Caucasian (Borreca 1990). In 1994, Democratic primary voters selected Mazie Hirono, which served to deter Japanese defection to the

Republican Party, which ran Pat Saiki for governor and stalwart Hemmings for lieutenant governor. Also in 1994, in order to pull the rug from underneath both parties, which failed to have Native Hawaiians on the ticket, Fasi chose entertainer Danny Kaleikini as his running mate on the short-lived Best Party.

TABLE 8.7
Ethnic Representation in General Election Voting Slates in Hawai'i, 1959–1996 (in percent)

Ethnic Group	Democrats	Republicans
Caucasian	26.4	64.2
Chinese	0.0	6.0
Filipino	4.2	0.0
Hawaiian	15.3	17.9
Japanese	51.4	11.9
Samoan	1.4	0.0
Mixed	1.4	0.0
Total	99.9	100.0

Source: Table 8.6.

In short, ticket balancing is a normal part of the political landscape in Hawai'i. The array of candidates for statewide offices and the two congressional districts of Hawai'i reveals a fascinating pattern in which more Japanese candidates are nominated by the Democratic Party and more Caucasian office seekers emerge from the Republican Party. The torch has been passed from Native Hawaiians in the days of the monarchy to *haole*s from 1893 to sometime between 1963 and 1973, to Japanese from 1973 to 1986, and now to various multiethnic combinations (Native Hawaiian-Filipino, 1986–1994, and Filipino-Japanese, 1994–). Politics has become post-ethnic, as the two major ethnic groups no longer visibly hold onto power (Haas 1995a).

Comparing registered voters (Table 8.1) with legislators elected from specific districts (Table 8.8), the overall match appears reasonably close. Caucasians and Filipinos are underrepresented, whereas Japanese and Native Hawaiians are overrepresented. Since the Democratic Party wins most elections, and Japanese dominate the Democratic Party,

TABLE 8.8

Legislators in Hawai'i by Ethnic Group, 1901–1997 (in percent)

Year	Caucasian	Chinese	Filipino	Hawaiian	Japanese
1901	16.7 (0)			73.3 (100)	
1905	37.8			62.2	
1909	37.8			62.2	
1913	42.2			57.8	
1917	37.8			62.2	
1921	37.8			62.2	
1925	42.2			57.8	
1929	46.7	4.4		46.7	
1933	33.3	4.4		51.1	8.9
1937	48.9	6.7		35.6	6.7
1941	42.2	8.9		33.3	15.6
1945	46.7 (63)	6.7 (7)		46.7 (26)	.0 (0)
1949	46.7 (48)	6.7 (3)		20.0 (17)	26.7 (28)
1953	37.8 (56)	6.7 (4)		13.3 (11)	37.8 (30)
1955	33.3 (30)	2.2 (7)	2.2 (0)	13.3 (10)	46.7 (53)
1959	31.0 (25)	7.9 (6)	2.6 (4)	14.5 (6)	46.1 (58)
1963	28.9 (21)	7.9 (10)	2.6 (4)	6.6 (4)	50.0 (62)
1967	26.3 (15)	11.8 (13)	5.3 (6)	5.3 (4)	50.0 (62)
1971	21.3 (14)	10.7 (10)	2.7 (8)	12.0 (4)	50.7 (65)
1975	23.7 (15)	10.5 (11)	1.3 (2)	13.2 (11)	46.0 (57)
1979	15.8 (12)	6.6 (7)	2.6 (3)	14.5 (13)	47.4 (55)
1983	17.1 (14)	7.9 (8)	7.9 (10)	19.7 (22)	38.2 (41)
1987	23.7 (18)	7.9 (10)	6.6 (8)	18.4 (18)	36.8 (45)
1991	21.3 (14)	9.3 (11)	8.0 (9)	17.3 (20)	42.7 (45)
1995	25.3 (20)	9.3 (9)	9.3 (11)	12.0 (12)	44.0 (48)
1997	21.3 (11)	6.7 (8)	8.0 (10)	16.0 (15)	46.7 (55)

Note: Figures report percentages of legislators within each ethnic group and add to 100 percent horizontally when other groups are included. Parenthesized figures are percentages of legislators for each ethnic group in the majority party and add to 100 percent horizontally when other ethnic groups are included. "Hawaiian" figures include persons with any Native Hawaiian ancestry, and "Caucasian" figures include Portuguese, Spanish, and other Caucasians.

Source: Fujiyama (1967, 111, 123, 135, 147, 159, 171, 183, 195, 207, 219, 231, 243); Hawai'i (1932a, 21; 1934, 10; 1976, 181; 1977b, 189; 1979, 246; 1981, 336; 1983, 396–97; 1985, 255; 1987, 280; 1990, 253); Meller (1955, 267; 1958a, 104; 1961/62, 47); personal communications from Abraham Pi'ianai'a, Morris Takushi, and Dwayne Yoshina.

while *haoles* play a similar role within the Republican Party, the only anomalies are the paucity of Filipino and abundance of Native Hawaiians in the state legislature.

CONCLUSION

Ethnic bloc voting in Hawai'i is best explained as a situation in which the two largest groups, Caucasians and Japanese, have respectively sewn up control of the Democratic and Republican parties. Whites in the Republican Party depended upon the Native Hawaiian vote to come to power in 1902 and to retain control until 1954. Republicans did not need Japanese voters, who responded by joining the Democratic Party. When Japanese voting strength mounted after World War II, a few Filipino votes helped. When the *haole* vote increased after statehood, the Democrats had to look beyond Filipinos to secure a new majority. Accordingly, Democrats attracted Native Hawaiian voters from the Republican Party. The election of Waihe'e as Ariyoshi's lieutenant governor in 1982, which served to solidify this coalition of Japanese and Native Hawaiians, did not provide recognition to traditional Filipino support for the Democratic Party. Aware of the lesser role of Filipinos in the Democratic Party, the Republicans then launched a crude effort to attract Filipinos to the Republican Party in 1986, but they failed. Ben Cayetano, first as lieutenant governor and now as governor, kept Filipinos home in the Democratic Party. In 1992, Republican representation among the seventy-five state legislators plummeted to seven seats; the count went up to nine in 1994 and reached fourteen in 1996.

Some researchers of mainland politics argue that ethnic politics fades as ethnic groups become increasingly assimilated to life in the United States (Dahl 1961, chap. 4) or integrated into the social mainstream (Wolfinger 1965). The experience of Hawai'i suggests instead that politicians rely on ethnic coalitions because they are looking for just enough voters to total at least 50.1 percent of the electorate (cf. Haas 1992, chap. 4). Yet there has been no backlash in recent years to the construction of winning ethnic coalitions. From the experience of building ethnic coalitions, politicians have learned not to tread on the toes of any ethnic group too openly, and *haole* candidates have increasingly been successful in the Democratic Party (Table 8.8). Hawai'i politics, thus, has become consociational and communitarian.

The *consociationalism* is the tendency of the ruling Democratic majority to avoid any open harm to the interests of any ethnic group, even if not represented in the legislature (cf. Lijphart 1984). The *communitarianism* is the belief that all groups must coexist through a discourse wider than merely within ethnic enclaves (cf. Taylor 1992).

Ethnic politics has been a major reason why politicians have been able to steer clear of class politics in the United States (Key 1949). Japanese in Hawai'i have benefited economically since the 1954 Democratic landslide, advancing into middle-class status. Rather than moving into the Republican Party, as might be expected of successful ethnic groups on the U.S. mainland, Japanese have remained loyal to the Democrats and gracefully passed the mantle in the 1980s to a Native Hawaiian and a Filipino rather than infiltrating a *haole*-dominated Republican Party that shows little sign of becoming truly multiethnic.

Yet behind the façade of an increasingly multiethnic Democratic Party and a Caucasian Republican Party, which is increasingly embarrassed by race-baiting rhetoric from its own party in national politics, much evidence shows that voters in Hawai'i are more impressed by personal characteristics of candidates than by ethnic or political party loyalties. The political situation is less structured along ethnic lines than it might otherwise appear.

NOTES

1. The failure of Japanese to engage in bloc voting may, of course, have been precisely to demonstrate that they were good citizens (see Boylan 1992, 74). Another reason, however, was that their votes were carefully monitored on the plantation: pencils were tied with string onto an overhead cable, positioned so that the Republican side of the ballot could be marked with ease; any movement of the pencil meant a vote for the Democratic Party and possible disciplinary action (Fuchs 1961, 179).

2. Although Survey Marketing Associates generously has provided me with raw polling data for 1988–1992, they have not released polling data for 1994 that might answer this question.

3. A later analysis, with data collected by Yasumasa Kuroda for 1990, yielded the same result. I am indebted to Atsuko Sato for this later analysis.

CHAPTER 9

Organized Labor

Edward D. Beechert

Sugar plantations have traditionally used coercive labor systems, ranging from the mildest form of indentured labor in Hawai'i to slavery in the United States and Latin America. The range of repression varied greatly according to location and historical circumstance (Tinker 1974; Lal, Munro, Beechert 1993). The gap between Cuba's extreme chattel slavery and the Solomon Islands' savage indentured labor and Hawai'i's indentured labor system was very wide. Sugar plantations customarily used a labor force racially or ethnically distinct from both the indigenous population and the plantation power structure for two reasons. The indigenous population was generally inadequate in numbers and might have had access to political power. Another compelling reason was that "race was a convenient means of controlling labor" (Beckford 1972, 67).

Most plantation economies generated racial notions of superiority and inferiority to create justifications for the acceptance of the labor systems. The groups so defined were assigned traits and customs that would serve to set them apart from the indigenous population and which were used to justify the constraints used to enforce the labor system. Hawai'i was different only in degree from other, more brutal, plantation systems. Edgar Thompson (1975, 115) has put the issue concisely: "one characteristic of the plantation is a labor problem which tends eventually to be defined as a race problem. The plantation is a race-making situation" (cf. Benn 1974; Saxton 1971).

Given these assumptions about sugar plantation economies, the question for Hawai'i becomes, why did multiethnic cooperation among workers emerge from a capitalist economy?

BACKGROUND

In Hawai'i, the term "race" was coupled with expressions of depravity, ineducability, and unassimilability. When arguing for the importation of foreign labor supplies, the planters presented a picture that usually emphasized the docility and efficiency of the proposed labor force. The opponents of immigrant labor stressed the depravity and unassimilability of the immigrant (Beechert 1985, 77–78).

Hawai'i's history was somewhat different from other plantation areas. Native Hawaiian people were caught up in a violent process of political and dynastic struggle when Captain James Cook arrived in 1778. His arrival signaled the injection of Western military tactics and weapons into what had been a traditional conflict. The new type of warfare resulted in drastic changes in land tenure and in the relationship of the Native Hawaiian commoner to the ruling class. Unlike the traditional military commodities, which had been produced by the commoner class, the new weapons had to be purchased from the Westerners. Payment was accomplished with drafts of labor and goods produced by the commoner. Production in Hawai'i lost its traditional social-community character. The new need to purchase weapons severely disrupted the rhythms of the low-technology agriculture. Under normal conditions, the people could have produced easily for their own subsistence and for that required by the political structure (Kamakau 1976, 34; Beechert 1985, 10–11).

The era following Cook's arrival was marked by an increasing flood of ships calling at Hawai'i. The new demand for supplies for these visitors further converted the commoner into a laborer status; rather than sticking to traditional agriculture, Native Hawaiians sold their labor. Production was no longer for the mutual support of the community and ruling class, but was now for the power and prestige of the chieftain class (Sahlins 1958, 1, 412). The chiefs saw only the possibility of gaining new weapons or acquiring what quickly came to be symbols of prestige and power: weapons and Western clothing, furniture, and jewelry. As the Islands became a winter rendezvous for ships trading and fishing the Pacific, a continuous and massive shift in the political economy of Hawai'i took place. The famines induced by the diversion of commoner labor from agriculture and the arrival of European diseases decimated the population.

These changes were swept up in the arrival of New England missionaries, who came to convert the "heathen population" to their particular brand of Christianity. The missionaries summarily rejected the Native Hawaiian culture in almost all aspects. Quickly moving into the position of advisors to the Hawaiian chiefs, they soon came to dominate the emerging, Western-style government. Viewing Native Hawaiians as a childlike race, given to evil behavior, their plans and actions set the tone for generations of notions of racial inferiority and superiority. As one leader put it, "[Native Hawaiians] need more powerful promptings and encouragements to effort and enterprise than they now have" (Bingham 1849, 490–92).

Two steps were needed to convert Native Hawaiian commoners to the status of wage laborers. First, taxes payable in cash were levied in 1839. Then, in the Great *Mahele* of 1848, land was converted to fee-simple holding. The new land distribution system effectively destroyed the *ahupua'a* land utilization system, which allowed the community wide access to land, as needed. The privatization of land resources did not consider water and access rights and thus left the commoner with small plots of useless land in most cases (Kelly 1956, 131). As a result, Native Hawaiians had to resort to wage labor to meet the head taxes imposed.

The decimation of the population and the Native Hawaiian's refusal to work for low wages or under intolerable conditions soon made clear the fact that imported labor would be required to put vast tracts of unoccupied land to profitable use. Various proposals were made by the growing foreign community to deal with the problem of the "reluctant" worker. One representative proposal, made in 1847 by Godfrey Rhodes, suggested compulsory labor, in which all males between ages fourteen and twenty would be defined as wards of the government. Each "person receiving them should pay a moderate tax for each laborer, as well as moderate wages to the apprentice, in proportion to his usefulness" (Goodale 1914, 180).

Ample evidence indicates that Native Hawaiian commoners asserted themselves in the only manner open to them—by simply not responding to the demands of wage hire at exploitive rates. A survey conducted by the missionaries in 1846 revealed the degree of failure of the efforts to convert the commoner to a compliant, wage-working status. Reports from all areas of the Islands demonstrated the Native Hawaiians' refusal to work for low wages. They could be attracted into wage labor for varying periods of time, but only when the offer was attractive enough to persuade them to leave their subsistence activities (Wyllie 1848).

THE LABOR QUESTION

While the general tendency of *haoles* commenting on the labor scene was to decry the dishonesty, greed, laziness, and surliness of workers, some in the urban community expressed more charitable sentiments and recognized the problems inherent in plantation agriculture. The Hawai'i constitution of 1850 prohibited slavery, and a revision in 1864 prohibited involuntary debt peonage and servitude. The Masters and Servants Act of 1850 extended to imported workers the full rights accorded to citizens, but without conferring citizenship itself (Beechert 1985, 41–45).

Much rhetoric on the need for a labor supply before 1861 was largely theoretical. The early sugar industry was marked by low production, primitive technology, and frequent failure. Importation of Chinese, which began in 1852, trailed off as the sugar boom of the 1850s faded. The U.S. Civil War closed off southern sugar production, opening the way for Hawaiian sugar to penetrate the mainland market. The new demand for sugar at high prices renewed the debate over labor supplies. Immediately, new arguments for sharply increased numbers of Chinese workers were heard.

Objections to the Chinese came from the urban nonplantation community, and theories of labor control began to be articulated in the Honolulu press and in political circles. Planters were urged to keep the Chinese apart from Native Hawaiian workers in order to stimulate the latter: "their example will have a stimulating effect on the Hawaiian, who is naturally jealous of the coolie and ambitious to outdo him" (quoted in Glick 1980, 8). One planter-government official observed that the "indolence of the native is not irremovable. I believe it is not greater than what prevailed amongst the Anglo-Saxon race in the early periods of their history, when only a just comparison could be made between that race and the Polynesians" (Wyllie 1858, 4).

Attempts in the 1870s to placate the increasingly virulent anti-Chinese political movement on the West Coast of the United States meant the replication of the ideological arguments of the total inferiority of the Chinese. Typical of the underlying rhetoric of inferiority is the following statement of Hinton Helper in 1852:

> No inferior race of men can exist in the United States without becoming subordinate to the will of Anglo-Americans. . . . It is so with Negroes in the South . . . it will be so with the Chinese in California" (quoted in Saxton 1971, 19).

The debate over labor was intensified by the signing of the Reciprocal Trade Treaty between Hawai'i and the United States in 1876. The principal point of the treaty was to admit Hawaiian sugar to the U.S. market duty-free. Given the protective tariff on imported sugar from other parts of the world, this amounted to a bonus profit to Hawaiian growers (19 *U.S. Statutes at Large* 200; Kuykendall 1967, vol. 3, chap. 2).

Plantation acreage increased rapidly, as did the numbers of imported Chinese workers, bringing into play new forces of opposition. Anti-Chinese sentiments in Hawai'i and the U.S. mainland prompted the search for non-Asian labor. Portuguese from the Azores and Madeira and small numbers of other European workers were recruited. The legislature, nominally controlled by Native Hawaiians, was a center for anti-Asian agitation. This façade of Native Hawaiian sovereignty limited the power of the controlling planter class. Frightened by increasing attempts of the legislature to restrict Chinese recruiting, the planters forced a new constitution in 1887 on the king and the legislature, backed by the threat of armed insurrection. This so-called "Bayonet Constitution" effectively disenfranchised Native Hawaiian commoners and limited the power of the king.

ANNEXATION

When the McKinley tariff of 1891 ended the subsidy of the 1876 treaty, Hawai'i suffered a severe depression, and the importance of becoming a territory of the United States was abundantly clear. The uncertainty of labor supplies meant only the threat of higher wages and some restriction of production; the loss of the subsidy, roughly two cents per pound of raw sugar, was an economic reality (Taylor 1935, 68).

In 1893, the monarchy was overthrown by what amounted to a joint conspiracy between the sugar planters and the U.S. military. The purpose was the annexation of Hawai'i to the United States. The move was precipitated both by the McKinley tariff of 1891, which eliminated the preference for Hawaiian sugar and by the growing militancy of Queen Lili'uokalani. Thwarted by President Grover Cleveland's veto of annexation, the plotters formed a provisional government. Ruling by executive committee decree, the Republic quickly reduced labor indenture to a condition of servitude, restricting imported workers to plantation work on threat of deportation. The importation of Chinese and Japanese workers was accelerated in the hope of establishing a sufficiently large workforce before annexation that would cut off the Chinese source due to the U.S. Chinese Exclusion Act (Kuykendall 1967, vol. 3, 582–605; Beechert 1985, 83–84). Given the rate of expansion of sugar acreage from 1876 to 1900 and the high rate at which imported indentured workers left the industry, sugar planters faced a continual shortage of labor, resulting in a competition for labor and higher wages than were thought desirable.

Annexation dramatically altered the pattern. Despite elaborate theories of race, planters were never able to achieve a multiethnic work force of sufficient magnitude that would enable them to substitute workers as a means of controlling wage demands. They took what was available. The struggle is reflected in the number of workers imported before annexation (Table 9.1).

TABLE 9.1
Plantation Workers Imported in Hawai'i, 1852–1899

Ethnic Group	Number	Peak Period	Percent
Chinese	56,700	1852–1897	38.5
Japanese	68,279	1885–1899	46.3
Portuguese	17,500	1878–1886	11.9
Pacific Islanders	2,500	1878–1885	1.7
Germans	1,300	1882–1885	.9
All Others	1,099	1853–1896	.7
Total	147,378		100.0

Source: Schmitt (1977, 25); Reinecke (1979, 540); Glick (1980, 12).

Annexation to the United States had long been a goal of the Honolulu business community. The inescapable fact was that the West

Coast was the only feasible market for Hawaiian sugar. The certain loss of Chinese labor sources and the likely loss of Japanese workers, either from changes in Japanese government attitudes or the rising resentment of the Pacific coast states to Japanese immigration, had to be weighed against access to the market.

Despite draconian efforts of the Republic of Hawai'i to impose strict controls on indentured labor and to impose indenture on all imported workers, slightly more than half the plantation workforce were free day workers. The presence of the indentured workforce limited the degree of worker resistance. After annexation, the U.S. Constitution and U.S. law opened the possibility of labor organization with some protection of civil rights. Accordingly, the struggle to control the job site was fought vigorously from 1900 forward.

Dire predictions of chaos and anarchy did not materialize:

> So the contract labor system of fifty years was at an end. Labor was free to move about and bargain as it pleased—subject to the limitations of poverty, ignorance, language barriers. . . . Haoles remained completely in the economic saddle. . . . The task of building an American commonwealth out of such a heterogeneous lot was difficult; to many it appeared hopeless. It is little wonder that the old oligarchical outlook persisted in the dominant class for another two decades (Reinecke 1979, 17–18).

The period from 1900 to 1920 was marked by such extremes and ambivalence that generalizations are difficult. Governor George Carter in 1905 expressed no fear of Japanese and Chinese becoming American citizens: "I believe that they [Japanese and Chinese children born in Hawai'i] will show a greater appreciation of the right of suffrage and use more intelligence in its exercise than is exhibited here today" (quoted in Reinecke 1979, 37). In contrast, an attorney who defended the Japanese strikers in 1909, upon learning in 1911 that his daughter was being taught by a Japanese teacher, proclaimed, "I don't care how qualified the girl may be, she is a Jap and no Jap can be properly qualified to teach white children. The Japanese fifty years ago were barbarians, and our civilization is the growth of a thousand years" though the editor of the newspaper strongly disagreed (Pacific Commercial Advertiser 1911a, b).

What began as an anti-Chinese attitude became transformed into an anti-Japanese view when, due to massive importation of laborers, the Japanese population increased from 24,407 to 61,111 from 1896 to 1900. Their numbers continued to increase until 1907, when the Root-Takahara agreement slowed the flow to a trickle.[1]

The Hawaiian notion of *aloha*, which combines the ideas of compassion, greeting, and mercy, when applied to race relations, connoted tolerance. The idea was explicitly stated in commentaries on the California controversies of 1907 over Japanese children in San Francisco schools (Damon 1907; Inglis 1907). Despite its widespread appeal and persistent usage, the *aloha* spirit "coexisted with a considerable distrust of [the Japanese immigrant] and with the plantation system's ideal of a static, docile labor force" (Reinecke 1979, 38). This gap was reinforced by the maintenance of both an economic and social gap between Japanese and the *haole* community.

The careful control that the planters managed to exert for some fifty years was severely challenged by the arrival of free labor and federal courts. For example, the O'ahu strike of Japanese workers in 1909 was nominally unsuccessful when measured in the traditional way. The union was not recognized, no bargaining took place, and the demands were not met; the leaders were prosecuted under a variety of charges and jailed. When looked at in a different perspective, the strike brought a high degree of unity to the Japanese worker community and managed to inflict considerable damage on sugar production. Japanese forced changes in the discriminatory wage structure and prompted the planters to improve social and living conditions. Japanese strikers won the sympathetic support of the fledgling Honolulu Central Labor Council, which was an important step toward ethnic unity (Beechert 1985, 174–76). The social demands of the workers outnumbered the economic demands. The growing number of married workers created a pressing demand for better housing, roads, and schools. Above all, the workers demonstrated that they could organize, formulate demands, and take action, demonstrating skills and power that surprised plantation owners.

One outcome of the strike was a renewed search for new labor supplies to "dilute" the Japanese strength. Puerto Rico was the scene of the first effort. Grossly mismanaged, these efforts were costly and stimulated a strong political backlash, both in Puerto Rico and in Washington, D.C. The pacification of the Philippines by 1909 opened the door to a second possibility, a last resort for the beleaguered sugar industry managers.

Despite theories of control of the workforce by using different races or ethnic groups and of using segregation and ethnic rivalries to divide workers, little or no action was ever taken to implement such notions in the face of the chronic labor shortage that characterized the Hawai'i sugar industry. The strikes of 1909 and 1920 clearly demonstrated that scab labor was unable to produce sugar efficiently. The skill of the experienced plantation worker was not easily replaced. Throughout the Pacific, the increasingly severe restrictions imposed on labor recruiting and the elimination of indentured labor created an upward pressure on wages.

Thus, spurred by the strike of 1909, planters began to import Filipino workers. By 1920, Filipinos formed a significant portion of the workforce. When the Federation of Japanese Labor presented demands for higher wages and improved living conditions, the Filipinos joined, forming a somewhat impromptu Filipino Labor Union. The worst fears of the planters were confirmed by this dual action. Although marked by serious confusion on the part of the Filipinos, nonetheless the rank-and-file Filipino struck and remained out as long as the Federation of Japanese Labor was able to provide rations and housing (Beechert 1985, 196–215).

The strike created a wave of hysteria in the Honolulu press and the Hawaiian Sugar Planters' Association (HSPA), who portrayed Japanese as conspiratorial, degraded, evil, and stupid. Their leaders were denounced as gangsters preying on the otherwise docile workers. The Filipinos were largely portrayed as primitives with little understanding. The thoroughly frightened establishment resorted to repressive labor legislation, including a criminal syndicalism act modeled on mainland laws. Nevertheless, borrowing from the notion of welfare capitalism so popular on the mainland, Hawai'i's plantations instituted a wide-ranging program of community building designed to focus the loyalty of the plantation worker on the company (Beechert 1985, 206). This program, along with a speeded-up effort at mechanization of field processes, was thought to be sufficient to contain any labor discontent (Beechert 1988).

The Filipino sugar strike of 1924, the most massive and lengthy strike in Hawai'i up to that point, put an end to such ideas. Over a period of eight months Filipino workers struck twenty-three of the forty-five plantations. Ill planned, conducted with little or no leadership, the strike was technically lost (Reinecke 1997). The impact on the industry, however, was sharp.

The industry was shocked to find that elaborate plans of loss-sharing, stepped-up labor imports from the Philippines, and vigorous prosecution of strikers and strike leaders did nothing but prolong the strike. Nonstruck plantations were discovered to have greater losses in production due to the steady diversion over nine months of new labor supplies and the steady out-migration of Filipinos from the sugar industry. HSPA (1926) then contracted a massive study of the industry to the industrial relations staff of Curtis, Fosdick & Belknap.

A further problem quickly arose. The steady movement of Hawai'i's Filipino workers to the mainland resulted in efforts to restrict the movement of these noncitizens who were, nonetheless, American nationals, needing no visa to enter. Rising opposition to this immigration resulted in congressional efforts in 1928 to end this source of labor. Eventually, this goal was reached in the Philippine Independence Act of 1934, which cut off Filipino emigration and promised independence by 1944. As a result, the plantations could only import citizen labor—a condition always before held to be impossible for any plantation economy (Benn 1974; Thompson 1975, 115).[2]

Particularly disturbing to the plantation owners in the 1924 strike was the evidence of considerable economic support from the non-striking Japanese community in the form of money and food supplies. HSPA's draconian measures to control the situation are evident in this message:

> The police at this time are prepared to jail a large number of men and are arresting the Filipinos on the slightest indication of wrong doing. The police have forbidden any of the strikers to hold meetings in town or elsewhere (Ola'a Sugar Company manager 1925).

In general, the Curtis, Fosdick & Belknap report cited serious inefficiencies in both mill and field operations. The report noted the contradiction between the welfare-community programs and the day-to-day operation of the plantations. The recommendations for improvement in managerial personnel was particularly strong. Field foremen were held to be responsible for many of the difficulties in production efficiency (HSPA 1926, vol. 1, iv–v). The basic recommendations, too radical for the industry, were rejected. Improvements in medical care and housing were instituted, and efforts to mechanize the more difficult tasks increased.

The underlying element in labor relations was the racist attitude of the plantation management. The Filipino, and to a lesser extent, the Japanese, were regarded as inferior, incapable of managing their own affairs or of requiring dignity and respect.

Prominent psychologists, commissioned to write a report on the Filipino in Hawai'i for the survey, concluded that Filipino workers had the mentality of fifteen-year-old boys, prone to wild fluctuations in emotions and inclined to criminal behavior (Porteus and Babcock 1926, 61–67). Their analysis was only more extreme than one made by an "expert" in 1916: "The Filipino is something of an overgrown boy. He requires a certain amount of looking after. . . . They are a totally different people from the Chinese or Japanese. They require some amusements" (HSPA 1916).

With the cutoff of immigration from the Philippines in 1934, the labor situation for the planters changed dramatically. The only possible source of new labor would be the nonfarmworkers of Hawai'i. Although minimal by comparison with the plantation workforce, the nonfarm labor force was molded by and drawn largely from the plantation. For many plantation workers, Honolulu or Hilo offered a transition to better employment and to migration to the mainland.

Craft unions were established at the Pearl Harbor naval base since the beginning of construction in 1911. Traditional American Federation of Labor (AFL) excluded Asians from membership and, due to federal requirements, also excluded noncitizens. Shortly after annexation, Honolulu had a Central Labor Council, made up entirely of AFL craft unions, with a majority of the membership based at Pearl Harbor. The exceptions were the construction industry in Honolulu and on the waterfront. Although the national construction unions, principally carpenters, barred Asians from membership, Hawai'i Carpenters' Local 745 began admitting Chinese as early as 1906. Such names as "Young" appeared to the parent organization as Caucasian, but they were very likely to have been Hawaiian-Chinese. The first explicitly Chinese name appears on the membership roles in 1919, followed by a Japanese name in March 1920, along with eight Hawaiians, six Portuguese, and one Chinese (Beechert 1993, 16–17). These admissions were in defiance of an order from the International

Brotherhood of Carpenters and Joiners and Samuel Gompers, AFL president, to exclude such members.

The dockworkers of Hilo and Honolulu joined the International Longshoremen's Union (ILU) as early as 1911, when charters were issued. Although the ILU locals subscribed to the parent union's anti-Asian resolutions in 1912, they asked for permission to admit Japanese workers to the union in order to prevent the plantations from using them as strikebreakers. The delegate, Moses Keohokalole, succeeded in gaining permission to admit Japanese members, with the proviso that they would be denied transfer-membership into mainland locals. Japanese members were then admitted to the union, despite the prohibitions of the parent union (ILA 1912, 73). Following a strike by dockworkers in Honolulu during 1916, the ILU local demanded the rehiring of several Japanese dock foremen who had been fired for sympathy toward the strikers.

A significant step toward racial unity, though a temporary one, was the emergence of George Wright, chairman of the Central Labor Council, who worked actively to support the Filipino and Japanese sugar strikers in 1920. Following that strike, he formed the Hawai'i Workers Union in 1921, dedicated to the inclusion of all workers, in a "Rank and File" union (Beechert 1985, 212–14; cf. Reinecke 1979, 318–19).[3]

Hawai'i soon followed the pattern of mainland unions in the face of a concerted attack on labor during the decade of the 1920s and the savage antilabor legislation of the period. What remained of the early organizing efforts was a spirit of racial unity; what was lacking was any formal organization to implement the unity. In 1929, there were "no union contracts in force in Hawai'i," according to the U.S. commissioner of labor.

THE TRANSFORMATION OF LABOR RELATIONS

The Great Depression of the 1930s soon brought a new element to the local political economy of Hawai'i. The Roosevelt administration's effort to cope with the depression brought a new power to Hawai'i—federal regulation of local economic affairs. The subsidy arrangements for sugar, the Agricultural Adjustment Act, the National Labor Relations Act, and the Social Security Act, all of which came in 1935, transformed industrial relations and the economy of Hawai'i. Although the conventional wisdom of sugar industry lawyers suggested that these were passing fantasies that would be declared unconstitutional, they nonetheless required compliance if the sugar industry were to receive a subsidy. The Fair Labor Standards Act required compliance with minimum wage standards. Hearings to determine compliance soon brought about major changes.

The labor turmoil that marked the mainland economic scene soon arrived in Hawai'i. Dockworkers in Hilo and Honolulu were again in the vanguard of organizing. They applied for charters in the ILA. The drive was sparked by the experience of some of their members in the San Francisco waterfront strike of 1934. Harry Kamoku returned to Hilo, determined to organize his fellow workers along the lines of the San Francisco dockworkers. Caught up in the intra-union dispute between Harry Bridges and ILA president, Joe Ryan, the Hawai'i locals were not recognized until the newly formed International Longshoremen's and Warehousemen's Union (ILWU) was organized in 1936. The racial situation in Hawai'i in the 1930s is described by ILWU leader Jack Hall (1968):

> In the past, Hawaii's power structure has dealt as badly with minorities as the white power structure in Alabama, Mississippi or Chicago. It was not until the minorities themselves did something about their situation that this was changed and we have finally ended up today where there is no serious discrimination based on race per se either economically, politically or socially—where Hawaii's minorities are now hailed as the "golden people." . . . It was not always so.
>
> From 1932 until I permanently settled in, I was a merchant seaman and had the opportunity to visit the colonial countries of Asia and see the contempt of the white Anglo-Saxons for the oriental people. Hawaii was not much different. . . . In 1930 the then president of the Hawaiian Sugar Planters' Association, R.A. Cooke, told a Congressional committee, "I can see no difference between the importation of foreign laborers and jute bags from India."
>
> . . . Island workers of an earlier day had to protest, organize and fight for power to liberate themselves from shameful deprivation.

Plantation organizing began in 1937, when the United Cannery, Agricultural, Processing, and Allied Workers of America issued a charter for organizing on Kaua'i. Jack Hall, who made sophisticated use of the new federal legislation, added a new element to Hawaiian politics. He successfully organized political action and ousted two of the leading planter politicians from the Territorial Senate in 1938 and 1940. In 1940, a contract was successfully negotiated with Kaua'i Pineapple Company.

The full impact on Honolulu labor was felt in 1938, when the Roosevelt administration undertook a major overhaul and expansion of Pearl Harbor naval base. The Pacific Contractors' Consortium brought mainland construction workers and their union contracts and wages to Hawai'i to convert Pearl Harbor into a major naval base.

Evidence of the transformation is seen in the first National Labor Relations Board (NLRB) hearing in Hawai'i, held in 1937. The ILWU local in Honolulu filed unfair labor-practice charges against Castle and Cooke, the stevedoring firm, supposedly distinct from Castle and Cooke, Inc., the sugar factor and operator of plantations. The field examiner, however, found a carefully constructed façade of companies and legal entities which masked a very few people. He concluded:

> The relationship is so close, the acts of one melt into the acts of another, with no line of demarcation, that it is impractical when discussing the occurrences to separate in each case the different companies (NLRB 1937, Region 12, Case XX-C–55, 3).

World War II would add the finishing touches to the transformation of Hawai'i's political economy. The oligarchical power, so long exercised, was rudely pushed aside by mainland intruders, eager to exploit a market booming with construction. Soon, chain-store and other commercial interests, which brought mainland construction practices and wage scales to the Islands, effectively broke the longstanding monopoly of the Big Five on the retail sector of the economy.

Most important of all was the arrival of effective organizing of the agricultural economy under the leadership of the ILWU. Immediately after the lifting of military rule over Hawai'i in 1944, the ILWU International Executive Board, pushed by insistent demands of Hawai'i dockworkers, set up a Hawai'i division under the leadership of Jack Hall as division director and Frank Thompson as field organizer.

The ILWU recognized the importance of bringing all ethnic groups into the organization. All past efforts at plantation organizing had focused on one ethnic group, excluding others. All failed in the sense that union objectives and union recognition were not achieved, although the workers did bring about major changes in industrial relations. Despite vigorous opposition, the ILWU won overwhelming victories in 1945–1946, winning union recognition elections at all plantations but one small company on Kaua'i (Beechert 1985, 289–310).

The strike of 1946 provided a uniform contract for the sugar industry, uniform job classifications, and the end of the perquisite system. More important, the union was recognized as the bargaining agent for all workers in the sugar industry. The unity of the workforce was an impressive demonstration of the union's effort to eliminate ethnic rivalries that had plagued some earlier strikes. When the planters hastily imported 6,000 Filipino workers to counter the impending strike (U.S. Dept. of Labor 1948, 51–55), they all joined the union and went out on strike (Beechert 1985, 299).

The urban unions, primarily in construction and the tourist industries, nevertheless made progress toward ethnic unity. In August 1943, the Honolulu Central Labor Council adopted a motion, made by Art Rutledge of the Hotel Employees and Restaurant Employees and the Teamsters unions, calling for the naturalization of Chinese and Filipino aliens. Rutledge also represented the largely Japanese American dairy workers. In 1944, he defied the president of the Hotel Workers' International, who objected to his placing Japanese Americans in culinary jobs (Stern 1986, 15). When challenged in 1947 by the AFL, Rutledge replied to charges that he favored Asians over Caucasian bartenders as follows:

> The largest percentage of our membership is composed of Orientals, Hawaiians and other nationalities, known as "local people." . . . We have a small, vociferous group of white bartenders who seek to use the organization for their own benefit without being willing to go out and fight for working conditions shoulder to shoulder with local people (Stern 1988, 17).

The climax came in 1958 in the settlement of the so-called "*Aloha* Strike." After the union won improvements to the pension plan and generous severance pay for workers displaced by advancing mechanization, the union's presence was not seriously contested by management. The strike was in many ways the culmination of union strength and maturity. The ILWU doctrine of equality quickly spread to other sectors of the community. The union's insistence on including a statement of nondiscrimination in all contracts was fiercely resisted by employers. To the general public, it made sense as a way out of the discrimination that the multiethnic community had long suffered.

Coupled with the steady decline of sugar and pineapple employment through mechanization of the work processes, thousands of workers were pushed into urban and public sector employment. Gone were the small plantation communities, with an ease of communication and feeling of solidarity that had been at the heart of ILWU's organizing strategy.[4] The anonymity of urban life made for a much different labor-organizing situation. No longer were there conveniently large units of workers engaged in a compact situation, with easy access to the workers' homes.

As early as 1952, the ILWU foresaw the effects of mechanization on plantation employment. They began a serious effort to organize the service sector, primarily the tourist industry. The union now found itself losing as many recognition elections as it won. Other unions, notably Rutledge's Hotel Employees and Restaurant Employees (HERE), vigorously contested these elections and frequently won. Citing the preferences of mainland visitors, hotels had long confined Filipino and Japanese workers to "back of the house" positions. Both HERE and the ILWU emphasized the importance of ending the crude, racist practices of the tourist industry.

The organization of the tourist industry was not easy. Both HERE and the ILWU were able to organize only the larger hotels by 1970 (Reinecke 1970, 25–26; Stern 1988). According to the ILWU (1965, 28),

> In our organizing, we made the discovery that there is no magic in the letters ILWU as far as the younger generation is concerned. In many cases some of those we are organizing weren't even born at the time of the 1946 sugar strike. . . . These younger people have to be convinced. They demand full explanations and they are not prone to take orders from their parents that they have to automatically vote ILWU or else.

The fragility of the tourism economy, one subject to severe seasonal fluctuations, has meant a deterioration in wages and the quality of jobs offered. Nevertheless, despite "the low wage and poor working conditions tradition of Hawai'i and the tourism industry, the unions have managed to preserve the wages and working conditions to a greater extent than in most resort destinations" (Stern 1988, 10–11, 126).

If the tourism–service sector economy was the "new plantation" for workers, public employment became a second major source of employment in Hawai'i. A state law permitting the organization of public employees, passed in 1970, created overnight a major labor union sector. Two unions now dominate this field, the Hawai'i Government Employees Association (HGEA) and the United Public Workers of Hawai'i (UPW).

HGEA was originally a traditional government employees association, specializing in insurance, political lobbying, and travel. Originally, it heavily represented supervisors, but, as reorganized in 1970, HGEA now dominates the clerical sector of public employment (Johnson and Miller 1986, 91ff.).

When road workers in Hilo, spurred by the activities on the plantations, wanted to organize, the AFL in Honolulu sent Don Owens. The road workers were tired of the old system of being at the disposal of county politicians, being hired in election seasons and laid off after the election. They refused the AFL, wanting to join their plantation friends. The ILWU refused their request, pointing out that there was a Congress of Industrial Organizations (CIO) government employees union, which they promptly contacted. Henry Epstein of the State, County, and Municipal Workers of America, CIO, then arrived in Hawai'i on May 2, 1947, with a charter for Local 646, which later became the United Public Workers of Hawai'i.[5] From that beginning, Epstein went on to organize hospital workers, refuse collectors, custodial people, prison guards, and private hospital workers, becoming basically a blue-collar union. As it evolved, the union was a good mixture of the Hawai'i population:

> There are probably more Japanese than any other group, but we have a lot of Hawaiians, part-Hawaiians, and we have a considerable group

of Filipinos in the hospitals. Our leadership is pretty well mixed and our staff is mixed (Epstein 1975, 8).

Important changes in the construction unions came during the 1980s. Under the leadership of Walter Kupau, the Carpenters Union Local 745 initiated far-reaching programs of change, including a Community Service Program to bring families closer to the union. An effective apprenticeship program took advantage of the construction boom of the 1970s. The Joint Training Program, with the employers, enrolled over 1,000 students through the community college system of the University of Hawai'i. A special effort in the program was made to reach out to women and minorities in 1987 (Beechert 1993, 74–75).

Both HGEA and UPW engaged heavily in political lobbying, since bargaining was largely a matter of convincing legislators and the governor to make the desired concessions. From the decade of the 1970s to the late 1980s, bargaining seemed always to result in higher wages, improved benefits, and liberalized work rules. In the 1990s, however, the pattern is sharply reversed. A massive state budget deficit and falling tax revenues of local governments resulted in major layoffs in 1995 (Honolulu Advertiser 1996).

THE FUTURE

One is tempted to use the popular phrase "back to the future" in describing the present. The tourist industry, particularly large hotels, has come to rely heavily on part-time labor, frequently made up of mainland *haoles* who are financing short-term visits with work in hotels and restaurants and who tend to regard the unions as unimportant. Local residents regard the transients' attitudes as hindering their achievement of reasonable working conditions.

Rising resentment among some of the ethnic groups threatens the outwardly calm labor and social situation. Filipinos resent the domination in the state civil service by Japanese Americans, and other minorities are demanding a better share of opportunities. The Native Hawaiian nationalist movement has gained impressive strength in recent years. Underlying demands for sovereignty is the fact that many have been systematically shut out of adequate housing, denied access to land, and shunted into low-paying occupations. Coalescing into a new movement, Native Hawaiians have been able to raise public consciousness on these issues, which remain unresolved, frustrated by fiscal crises.

Construction, public and private, and the continuous expansion of the tourist trade are no longer viable means for sustaining employment. Faced with economic and political obstacles to organizing, labor now confronts the rising demands of ethnic groups left behind the post–World War II advances.

The observations of Jack Hall of the ILWU in 1968 remain a valid observation of the situation today:

> It is important to realize that the Aloha Spirit grew out of struggles to eliminate injustice. New forms of injustice, which are present in Hawai'i today, can destroy it if they are not remedied. Even today certain deprived groups among us tend to fall into racial categories . . . . The Aloha Spirit will flourish to the extent that all elements of our community are able to participate in the good things of life . . . (Hall 1968, 5–6).

Clearly, ethnic tensions in Hawai'i are growing as the global economy worsens. The tourist industry is particularly vulnerable to economic downturns. A mistaken belief is that tourists would flock to Hawai'i if only there were more advertising, a "solution" which implies that "those who lack the means for an Hawaiian vacation might be persuaded to come to Hawai'i to spend money they don't have for a vacation they can't afford" (Stern 1988, 124).

A wide-ranging survey of the challenges facing Hawai'i today presents a very mixed bag of conclusions. One of the more perceptive analyses concludes:

> The crucial point is to recognize the existence of some positive ethnic and racial patterns; the persistence of some long-standing negative ones; the threats imposed by new developments; and, most important, the need for policy considerations to protect and enhance our ability to tolerate and respect different heritages and aspirations (Odo and Yim 1993, 229).

Hawai'i, similar to the rest of the United States, is moving toward a structure of employment ever more dominated by jobs that are poorly paid, with little or no future. Workers are not generally successful in coping with the rapid development of the service sector and low-wage, low-security employment. Although labor organizing and collective bargaining face massive hostility from all fronts—corporations busily "downsizing," government, and the media—one cannot assume that history has stopped or that the basic struggle of class interests has ceased. Organized labor, for all its faults and weakness, is the only point around which ethnic minorities can continue the struggle so long in the making.

NOTES

1. Rising resentment of Asian immigration to the United States as well as the rapidly changing position of Japan sparked the "Gentlemen's Agreement," which ended the flow of workers, except for "picture brides." All Japanese immigration ended when Congress adopted the Immigration Act of 1924 (Wakukawa 1938, 143–44).

2. Hawai'i plantation workers, from 1853 forward, suffered no restrictions on their movements in and out of plantation work. Such agricultural areas as cattle farming, coffee farming, dairying, independent cane planting, and pineapple cultivation offered considerable opportunity to non-sugar plantation workers.

3. Both employers and the anti-union press wrongly assumed that this meant the IWW goal of "One Big Union."

4. See, for example, the interviews with Kenji Omuro and Yasuki Arakaki, Puna Sugar Co., Kea'au, Hawai'i, April 20, 1966, and May 4, 1966, Pacific Regional Oral History Program, Center for Labor Education and Research, University of Hawai'i.

5. The State, County, Municipal Workers of America became the United Public Workers of America in 1946. Anti-Communist harassment forced the dissolution of UPWA in 1952. The Hawai'i local was the sole surviving unit.

CHAPTER 10

Social Stratification

Jonathan Okamura

DEFINING "STRATIFICATION"

In this chapter I will describe and analyze ethnic and racial stratification in Hawai'i according to occupational, income, and educational status. The analysis includes eight of the larger ethnic/racial groups—African Americans, Caucasians, Chinese, Filipinos, Japanese, Koreans, Native Hawaiians, and Samoans—and is based on socioeconomic data from the 1990 U.S. census of Hawai'i. My analysis, the most recent in a longitudinal study that includes previous analyses of 1970 (Okamura 1982) and 1980 (Okamura 1990) census data, has been primarily concerned with identifying the organizing principles of the stratification order that regulate the distribution of socioeconomic opportunities and rewards among ethnic/racial groups.

Despite the centrality of studies of race and ethnic relations in Hawai'i, surprisingly few analyses of ethnic/racial stratification have been conducted in recent years. These studies have provided generally consistent views of the status ranking of groups in the stratification order. James Geschwender and Rita Carroll-Seguin (1988, 194, 204) have contended that "*haoles* continue to be the most privileged" group and that "Asian Americans" in Hawai'i lack "equal opportunity to achieve economically," since they are subject to "some discrimination" in the form of not receiving the same degree of economic benefits from their education compared with Caucasians. In an analysis of family-income data from the 1975 Census Update Survey, Joyce Chinen (1984, 100) also placed Caucasians at the apex of the stratification system, followed by Japanese and Chinese, and then Native Hawaiians and Filipinos. According to various "quality of life" and socioeconomic and political status indicators, Michael Haas (1992, 47) considers Filipinos, Guamanians, Native Hawaiians, Puerto Ricans, Samoans, and Vietnamese as "disadvantaged minorities," while Caucasians, Chinese, Japanese, and Koreans are more privileged "nonminority" groups, and African Americans occupy a position between those two sets of groups. Based on 1980 census data on occupational, income, and educational status, my analysis of the stratification order has groups in the following positions: Caucasians and Chinese with the highest status; Japanese, Koreans, and African Americans (in descending order) in the intermediate range; and Native Hawaiians, Filipinos, and Samoans (in descending order) at the lower end of the status hierarchy (Okamura 1990, 9). According to Herbert Barringer and Nolan Liu (1994, 96), who analyze the 1990 census, Native Hawaiians "invariably suffer" in comparison with Caucasians and Japanese. In sum, while there might be differences in terms of the relative social status of the dominant groups, there is considerable agreement that Filipinos, Native Hawaiians, and Samoans are among the subordinate groups in the stratification order.

Despite such common recognition of a highly stratified socioeconomic status system, other observers (i.e., Fujii and Mak 1985; Lind 1980) have maintained that equality of opportunity is more characteristic of the fiftieth state. Andrew Lind (1980, 90), for many years the foremost scholar of race relations studies in Hawai'i, has contended that there has been a

> steady trend toward an equalization of opportunity and status across
> ethnic lines with reference to the occupational life of the Islands.
> Obvious inequalities, based in part on the order of arrival, the length
> of residence in Hawai'i, and the cultural traditions of each group, still
> exist and will continue for some time in the future, but the difference
> becomes less apparent with each passing decade.

Unfortunately, the decades have been passing, and the inequities are still evident without regard to when groups arrived in Hawai'i, to how long they have been resident in the Islands, and to what their cultural values and beliefs might be.

In previous studies of ethnic/racial stratification in Hawai'i, I have emphasized that institutionalized inequality of opportunity and reward is a fundamental condition of the socioeconomic status system

(Okamura 1982, 1990). I have argued that ethnicity is the primary organizing principle of the stratification order, insofar as it structures or regulates the distribution of social status among ethnic/racial groups. In other words, access to socioeconomic benefits and privileges is very much racialized in the Islands, certainly to a greater extent than being open to competitive achievement and individual merit. If the latter were the case, there would be a much more equitable distribution of educational, income, and occupational status among ethnic/racial groups. My conclusion concerning the "racialization" (cf. Omi and Winant 1986, 64) of the stratification order also was based on the lack of any significant change in the relative position of groups from 1970 to 1980. Particularly noticeable was the absence of upward social mobility on the part of any disadvantaged group, thus indicating the extent to which collective socioeconomic status is virtually ascribed by ethnicity (Okamura 1990). I also have maintained that Hawai'i's economy plays a major constraining role in the stratification system, since the state's overdependence on the service-oriented tourist industry cannot provide the occupational and income opportunities necessary for socioeconomic mobility by disprivileged groups.

Studies of ethnic/racial stratification or of the social status of specific groups in the Islands have focused on family and personal income as the principal indicator of socioeconomic status, and income is viewed as primarily determined by educational and occupational status. Given Hawai'i's historical and contemporary high intermarriage rate, the methodological limitations of using family/household income data by race, when spouses oftentimes do not share the same racial/ethnic identity, have been noted by Chinen (1984, 90). Furthermore, Chinen (1984) and Geschwender and Carroll-Seguin (1988) have emphasized the differential female labor force participation rate among ethnic/racial groups in the Islands and the significance of women's labor, particularly that of wives/mothers, for understanding the varying socioeconomic status of groups. Thus in my own analyses and the current study, I describe and analyze the ethnic/racial stratification system as a structural composite of the educational, income, and occupational status orders. By including these three dimensions of socioeconomic status without privileging any one in particular, a more complete understanding of the stratification system is obtained than with a primary focus on income alone.

My analysis of the ethnic/racial stratification order is primarily concerned with specifying the organizing principles of that order rather than with the mere hierarchical ranking of groups. Using such objective indices as family income, previous studies of stratification in Hawai'i have provided analyses of the ranking of groups or of the relative status of particular groups, but they have been less concerned with offering an overall analysis of the stratification order in terms of the allocation and maintenance of socioeconomic status. In viewing the stratification order primarily according to organizing principles, I seek to explain how socioeconomic status is distributed. As stated by Michael Smith (1975, 272),

> Inequalities in the distribution of social assets, opportunities and values are thus central to stratification; but the concrete empirical distribution of these inequalities presupposes some principle or principles to regulate, integrate and order the differentiation. Analytically, then, the stratification can be reduced to a set of specific principles that generate and organize the prevailing distribution of resources and opportunities.

I argue that ethnicity is the primary regulating principle of the stratification order in Hawai'i because of the substantial inequality in social status among ethnic/racial groups and the institutionalized nature of that inequality.

OCCUPATIONAL STATUS

Racial stratification in Hawai'i began to emerge in the second half of the nineteenth century, when Asians, Europeans, and Latino peasants were brought to the Islands in order to labor on the sugar and pineapple plantations. On the plantations, workers from different nationality groups were paid differing wages for doing the same work and had differential access to skilled and supervisory positions, which were initially reserved for Caucasians. Over time and particularly over the generations, as groups moved off the plantation, they entered urban and other nonplantation employment, taking advantage of economic boom periods after the turn of the twentieth century, during and after World War II, and following statehood in 1959. Chinese and Japanese, as will become evident, have made tremendous socioeconomic progress since their arrival as contract laborers, but Filipinos, Native Hawaiians, and other minorities have not.

The data for this section are from the U.S. census report entitled *Social and Economic Characteristics, Hawaii* (1993), which is based on a 5 percent sample from the 100 percent tabulation data set for the state. It will become evident that very little change has occurred in the ethnic/racial stratification system since 1980. Groups continue to hold the same relative position in the socioeconomic status hierarchy, with very little evidence of upward social mobility among Filipinos, Native Hawaiians, and Samoans.

Occupational Distribution: Vertical Percentages

Since 1980, there has been an increase of about 52,000 male and 61,000 female workers in the Aloha State, and the latter have been steadily closing the employment gap with men over the years. Hawai'i is distinguished by a very high female labor participation rate of 63.3 percent (of females 16 years and over) (U.S. census 1993, 59), which can be attributed to a cost of living that is almost 40 percent higher than in the continental United States (Hawai'i 1993–94, 339). Among women, the greatest increases were in technical, sales, and administrative support (referred to as TSAS) (24,000), administrative, executive, and managerial (14,000), and professional specialty (13,000) employment. Among males, the largest numerical gains were in TSAS (16,000), service (12,000), and professional (9,000) work. Thus, women had much greater access to white-collar occupations than men during the past decade; however, it still needs to be determined whether women benefited equally from these occupational opportunities.

An indication of the relative occupational status of a group can be obtained by comparing its representation in a particular occupational category with that of Hawai'i workers as a whole (Table 10.1). A group is considered at *parity* if its representation in an occupational category is within a 20 percent margin of difference (either above or below) of the average percentage for the total labor force. One can compare white-collar with blue-collar employment profiles—ethnic/racial groups that are better represented in the three higher-status and generally better-paying employment categories (administrative, executive, and management; professional; and TSAS), versus those better represented in the lower levels of the occupational scale (craft

TABLE 10.1
Occupational Distribution Within Ethnic and Gender Groups in Hawai'i, 1990 (in percent)

Occupational Category	Total M	Total F	Black M	Black F	Caucasian M	Caucasian F	Chinese M	Chinese F	Filipino M	Filipino F	Hawaiian M	Hawaiian F	Japanese M	Japanese F	Korean M	Korean F	Samoan M	Samoan F
Administrative, executive, managerial	13.4	12.3	10.9	10.8	16.4	15.0	15.5	14.2	5.6	6.8	8.3	10.9	16.9	13.6	13.2	9.4	5.3	5.9
Professional	11.8	15.4	9.5	12.9	16.8	21.5	14.6	15.3	3.3	6.2	6.3	10.9	12.8	17.6	10.4	8.2	7.4	8.3
Technical, sales, administrative support	21.4	45.1	31.2	52.9	21.1	41.4	25.3	46.8	15.4	42.5	15.1	47.3	26.7	50.0	26.3	43.4	12.1	43.0
Craft, precision production, repair	18.5	1.7	13.8	1.1	18.0	1.2	13.1	1.7	18.4	2.2	21.4	1.5	19.6	1.7	15.1	2.7	15.8	.6
Fabricators, laborers, operators	14.9	4.7	14.8	2.3	11.1	3.0	10.0	4.6	23.4	9.2	24.5	6.1	10.7	3.4	15.2	3.0	28.2	10.8
Service	15.9	19.4	19.0	19.1	12.8	16.7	19.6	16.7	25.3	29.7	19.3	22.4	10.5	12.7	17.2	32.1	28.0	29.9
Farming, forestry, fishing	4.2	1.4	.8	.9	3.7	1.1	1.8	.8	8.6	3.3	5.1	.9	2.8	1.0	2.6	1.1	3.3	1.5
Total	100.1	100.0	100.0	100.0	99.9	99.9	99.9	100.1	100.0	99.9	100.0	100.0	100.0	100.0	100.0	99.9	100.1	100.0

Note: Figures do not always add to 100 percent due to rounding errors.
Source: U.S. census (1993, 60, 130–31).

and repair; fabricators, laborers, operators, and precision production; service; farming, forestry, and fishing).

In the administrative/executive and professional categories, Caucasians (males only), Chinese, Japanese, and Koreans are well represented, with percentages greater than or at parity with those for their respective Hawai'i counterparts. In contrast, Filipinos, Native Hawaiians, and Samoans have far lesser proportions of their workers in such employment. African Americans are better represented as executives/administrators and professionals than the latter groups but are below parity.

In TSAS work, the most outstanding feature is the very high proportion of women employed. In fact, the great majority of women in this occupational category work either in sales or administrative support rather than in technical positions. In particular, about 15 percent of Hawai'i females work in sales and over one-fourth in administrative support, which consists primarily of such clerical jobs as financial records clerks, secretaries, stenographers, and typists. Clearly, administrative support, an area of work that has become socially defined as predominantly for women, can be expected to offer relatively lower wages.

Among male TSAS workers, a greater proportion work as proprietors and supervisors in sales, as sales representatives, and as technicians and technologists (particularly in nonhealth fields), than as administrative support workers. African American, Chinese, Japanese, and Koreans are well represented in percentages generally greater than those for their respective Hawai'i counterparts. While Filipino, Native Hawaiian, and Samoan males are not proportionately represented in TSAS occupations, females of these groups are employed in percentages comparable to that of Hawai'i women.

Blue-collar levels of the occupational scale, craft, precision production, and repair work, which can be considered skilled work, employ males predominantly. Caucasian, Filipino, Japanese, and Native Hawaiian men are found in percentages comparable to that for all Hawai'i males, while African American, Chinese, and Korean men are represented below the state average.

Among semiskilled operators (fabricators and laborers), Filipino, Native Hawaiian, and Samoan males and females are employed to a much greater extent than their respective Island counterparts. In contrast, men and women from the other groups are employed in percentages generally lower than those for Hawai'i workers.

A similar situation prevails in service work. Filipinos, Koreans (females only), Native Hawaiians, and Samoans are found in proportions greater than the state average. Among women of these groups, service work is the second largest occupational category after TSAS employment. Service work is especially prominent among Filipinos and Samoans; for both groups, one out of every four males and nearly one of every three females are service workers. The other groups are represented in service work in percentages lower or only slightly higher than those for their male and female Hawai'i counterparts.

Farming, forestry, and fishing are not especially significant industries in Hawai'i in terms of the number of persons employed (15,300). Only Filipino men and women and Native Hawaiian men are substantially involved.

Occupational Distribution: Horizontal Percentages

The occupational distribution across various ethnic/racial groups in Hawai'i in 1990 sums to 100 percent when all groups are included (Table 10.2). A group is considered *overrepresented* in an occupational category if it exceeds its proportion of the labor force by 20 percent or more. Conversely, a group is deemed *underrepresented* should its percentage in an occupational category not meet its proportion of the labor force by 20 percent or more. A group is considered at *parity* if its representation in an occupational category is within a 20 percent margin of difference (either above or below) of its percentage of the labor force.

In the administrative/executive and professional categories, Caucasian, Chinese, and Japanese men and women are either overrepresented or at parity. Chinese males are well represented as professionals, Japanese males as administrators/executives, and Caucasian males and females are overrepresented in both upper-level categories. White men hold nearly one-half of the professional positions, as they also did in 1980. In contrast, Filipino, Native Hawaiian, and Samoan males and females are underrepresented as executives/administrators and professionals. Korean women also are employed below parity as executives/administrators and professionals,

TABLE 10.2
Occupational Distribution Across Ethnic and Gender Groups in Hawai'i, 1990

Occupational Category	Black M	Black F	Caucasian M	Caucasian F	Chinese M	Chinese F	Filipino M	Filipino F	Hawaiian M	Hawaiian F	Japanese M	Japanese F	Korean M	Korean F	Samoan M	Samoan F
Administrative, executive, managerial	1.0	1.2	*40.1*	*36.4*	8.0	7.9	6.5	9.5	6.7	9.6	32.3	29.1	1.9	*1.9*	.4	.4
Professional	1.0	1.1	*46.0*	*42.2*	8.5	6.8	4.4	6.8	5.8	7.6	27.7	29.9	1.7	*1.4*	.6	.4
Technical, sales, administrative support	*1.8*	1.5	31.6	27.0	8.2	7.0	*11.2*	16.0	7.7	11.3	32.0	29.1	2.4	2.4	.6	.7
Craft, precision production, repair	.9	.9	30.5	20.8	4.9	6.7	15.5	23.0	12.5	9.7	27.1	26.7	1.6	4.1	.9	.3
Fabricators, laborers, operators	1.2	.6	22.7	*18.7*	4.7	6.6	24.3	33.2	17.8	13.9	18.4	18.7	2.0	*1.6*	1.9	*1.7*
Service	1.4	1.3	24.6	24.6	8.5	5.8	24.7	26.1	13.2	12.5	17.0	17.2	2.1	*4.2*	1.8	*1.2*
Farming, forestry, fishing	.2	.8	26.8	24.4	3.0	3.8	31.3	40.2	13.1	6.9	17.0	18.4	1.2	*2.0*	.8	.8
Total	1.2	1.3	31.6	29.5	6.9	6.8	15.5	17.0	25.6	26.2	10.8	10.8	1.9	2.5	1.0	.8

Key: Underscored numbers are for overrepresented groups (20 percent more than the group's percentage of the workforce).
        Italicized numbers are for underrepresented groups (20 percent below the group's percentage of the workforce).

Note: Figures add to 100 percent across for each sex when all other ethnic groups are included.

Source: U.S. census (1993, 60, 130-31).

while African American males and females and Korean men are at parity.

In TSAS work, only African American, Japanese, and Korean men are overrepresented, while Filipino, Native Hawaiian, and Samoan males are underrepresented. Despite the obvious gender bias in this occupational category, surprisingly no group of women was excessively found in TSAS employment, not even Japanese, who are commonly stereotyped as clerical workers in Hawaiʻi.

Craft, precision production, and repair work, held primarily by men, is relatively evenly distributed among ethnic/racial groups. Only African American and Chinese males are employed below parity in this field, while female Filipinos and Koreans are overrepresented.

Filipinos, Native Hawaiians, and Samoans are overrepresented as fabricators, laborers, operators, and service workers, whereas Caucasians and Japanese are underrepresented. Filipino men and women, particularly immigrants, comprise the largest groups in these two occupational categories. Chinese males, who are overrepresented as administrators/ executives and professionals, are also above parity in service work, very likely due to the employment placement of recent immigrants from China and Hong Kong. Korean women, who tend to be underrepresented in white-collar work, are overrepresented as service workers; stereotypically, they are considered to be bar hostesses and restaurant workers. The picture that emerges of these semiskilled and unskilled occupational categories is of a sector where immigrants, especially Chinese, Filipinos, Koreans, and Samoans, and also Native Hawaiians, can find employment. However, a substantial proportion of service jobs are held by Caucasians and Japanese. The overrepresentation of Filipinos, Native Hawaiians, and Samoans as blue-collar operators/laborers and service workers is directly related to their underrepresentation in white-collar administrative/executive, professional, and TSAS positions.

In farming, forestry, and fishing, most groups are below parity. The notable exceptions are male and female Filipinos and male Native Hawaiians. Filipinos, notably women, comprise the largest group in this occupational category, and are especially employed as farm and plantation workers, though there are few sugar plantations left today. Native Hawaiian men, many living on Hawaiian homestead land, work in both farming and fishing.

Discussion

The data in Tables 10.1 and 10.2 can be used to provide a hierarchical ranking of ethnic/racial groups in the occupational status order in Hawaiʻi. Clearly, Caucasians, Chinese, and Japanese hold dominant positions in the three upper-level occupational categories. White males and females are especially overrepresented as executives/administrators and professionals. Conversely, Caucasians, Chinese, and Japanese are employed below or at parity in the lower levels of the occupational scale in farming/fishing, operative/laboring, precision production/craft, and service work.

African Americans and Koreans have intermediate positions in the occupational status hierarchy, as they did in 1980, insofar as they are generally proportionately represented in most occupational categories. With the exception of the overrepresentation of Korean women in service work, these two groups predominate in midrange occupational categories (craft/precision production and TSAS) rather than in the upper or lower levels of the occupational scale.

As in recent decades, Filipinos, Native Hawaiians, and Samoans continue to hold subordinate positions in the occupational order. They are underrepresented as executives/administrators, professionals, and TSAS (males only) workers and greatly overrepresented as blue-collar operators/laborers and service workers.

Comparing this occupational ranking of ethnic/racial groups with that in 1980, not much change has occurred over the past decade. This result should not be surprising, given Hawaiʻi's increasing dependence on tourism during the 1980s, which ended during a temporary period of massive foreign investment by Japanese corporations in the local economy, particularly in hotel and resort development. A tourism-dependent economy creates primarily low-wage and low-security service and sales jobs, employment that can hardly provide for significant occupational and income mobility for socioeconomically disadvantaged groups.

Women greatly increased their numbers in administrative/executive, professional, and TSAS work during the 1980s. However, in the two former occupational categories, Caucasian, Chinese, and Japanese females accounted for more than two-thirds of the increase. On the other hand, among service and TSAS workers, Filipinos, Native Hawaiians, and Samoans held a majority of the gain in positions. Thus, even though there were considerable opportunities in the two higher-status occupational categories, the subordinate groups remained in lower occupational positions.

INCOME LEVELS

On the whole, the income status hierarchy of ethnic/racial groups in the Islands, which is based on earnings in 1989, is somewhat comparable with occupational rankings (Table 10.3). In terms of median family income, only Japanese and Chinese are above the median for Hawai'i families, while the other groups are below. Except for the reversed positions of Caucasians and Filipinos, the exact same ranking of groups by median family income existed in 1979.

TABLE 10.3
Median Income of Ethnic Groups in Hawai'i, 1989

Ethnic Group	Family Income	Female Income	Male Income
Black	$27,338	$14,478	$17,019
Caucasian	41,878	21,488	26,881
Chinese	48,518	21,954	31,889
Filipino	41,955	16,455	21,871
Hawaiian	37,960	18,282	26,029
Japanese	52,982	22,429	33,501
Korean	37,420	17,023	30,214
Samoan	23,914	13,950	19,901
Total	43,176	20,073	27,147

Note: For females and males, data are for full-time workers aged fifteen and over. "Caucasians" are non-Hispanic Whites.

Source: U.S. census (1993, 63, 132–33).

A factor in the higher income rank of Chinese, Japanese, and Filipino families is their high female labor force participation rates (Geschwender and Carroll-Seguin 1988, 195). Caucasians and Filipinos both have family incomes slightly less than the Hawai'i median despite their very different occupational statuses. Filipino families rank third in family income, in part because both females and males work. Whites have a lower family income ranking despite their high occupational status because of the substantial number of lower-paid military personnel in their population (Geschwender and Carroll-Seguin 1988, 195). Thus, Chinese, Filipino, and Japanese families seem to need a much higher rate of female labor force participation in order to attain the same standard of living as Caucasian families (Geschwender and Carroll-Seguin 1988, 204).

The large military segment also contributes to the relatively low family income of African Americans despite their intermediate occupational status. The lesser income of Native Hawaiian and Samoan families is consistent with their lower occupational position, while that of Korean families is reduced by the lesser earnings of Korean women.

With regard to median female income, Caucasians, Chinese, and Japanese have higher earnings than the Hawai'i median, while African Americans, Filipinos, Koreans, Native Hawaiians, and Samoans have lower incomes. With the exception of the lower position of African Americans and Caucasians, this income ranking is relatively consistent with the occupational ranking of women. Although the income differences among Caucasian, Chinese, and Japanese females are not great, the latter may have lower personal income than the two former groups, in spite of their high occupational status, because of their younger median age and lower percentage of full-time workers. The above data also demonstrate that women continue to be paid less than men despite their comparable occupational status and higher educational attainments, particularly in the white-collar occupational categories. Except for the reversed positions of Filipinos and Native Hawaiians, the current female income ranking is similar to that in 1980.

For median male income, Caucasians, Chinese, Japanese, and Koreans are above or at the Hawai'i median, whereas African Americans, Filipinos, Native Hawaiians, and Samoans are below. With the exception of the Caucasians and Samoans, both of whom have large percentages of military service personnel, this income ranking approximates that for occupational status among males. The high income position of Chinese is somewhat surprising, given their overrepresentation as service workers, probably indicating substantial earnings of Chinese white-collar workers. In 1980, the same income ranking of ethnic/racial groups was found.

EDUCATIONAL ATTAINMENTS

Education is commonly viewed as a means for social mobility. Structural changes in the ethnic/racial stratification order in the future might first be indicated by increasing access of certain groups to post-secondary education.

A clear ranking of ethnic/racial groups is evident from the percentage of persons (25 years and over) with a bachelor's degree or higher (Table 10.4). Caucasians, Chinese, and Japanese are above the Hawai'i average. In contrast, African Americans, Filipinos, Koreans, Native Hawaiians, and Samoans are below the state median.

TABLE 10.4
Persons with Bachelor's Degrees or Higher in Hawai'i by Ethnic Group, 1990 (in percent)

Ethnic Group	Total, Ages 25 or More	Females, Ages 25–34	Males, Ages 25–34
Caucasian	31.0	25.3	25.9
Chinese	30.3	39.9	37.9
Japanese	25.2	39.8	33.3
Korean	18.6	19.4	26.0
African American	15.2	14.5	9.3
Filipino	11.6	17.3	10.1
Native Hawaiian	9.1	8.9	9.5
Samoan	5.0	3.3	4.4
Total	22.9	24.0	22.2

Source: U.S. census (1993, 57, 122–23).

To determine future patterns, the same statistics were divided into age groups (Table 10.4). Among a younger cohort of females (ages 25 to 34), the ranking of groups is similar to that presented above. Caucasians, Chinese, and Japanese are again above the Hawai'i average, while African Americans, Filipinos, Koreans, Native Hawaiians, and Samoans are below average. A similar rank order obtains among males. Caucasians, Chinese, Japanese, and Koreans are above the Hawai'i average, and African Americans, Filipinos, Native Hawaiians, and Samoans are below average.

In terms of gender, at least for those aged 25 to 34, women have higher percentages of college degrees than men, with the exception of Koreans. However, females have lower personal income than males despite their comparable occupational status. Among these age groups, Chinese and Japanese males and females, female Filipinos, and male Koreans have a higher than average percentage of college completion. In contrast, the younger cohorts of Native Hawaiians and Samoans fall below, suggesting possible discrimination against those groups in gaining access to a college education.

TABLE 10.5
College Enrollment by Ethnic Group in Hawai'i (18–24 Years), 1990 (in percent)

Ethnic Group	Persons Enrolled in College
African American	13.4
Caucasian	20.8
Chinese	53.7
Hawaiian	22.2
Japanese	52.3
Korean	47.0
Filipino	30.7
Samoan	22.4
Total	30.0

Note: Figures may include out-of-state students.
Source: U.S. census (1993, 57, 122–23).

Data for an even younger cohort of persons (those aged 18 to 24) indicate somewhat greater access of the most subordinate groups, i.e., Filipinos, Native Hawaiians, and Samoans, to higher education (Table 10.5). However, an overall differential ranking in educational status is markedly evident. Chinese, Filipinos, Japanese, and Koreans have proportions higher than the Hawai'i average, whereas African Americans, Caucasians, Native Hawaiians, and Samoans are below average. The comparatively low percentage for Caucasians is due to the considerable number of young females and males associated with the military, both as enlisted personnel and as dependents. The college enrollment of Samoans, which exceeds that of Caucasians and Native Hawaiians, is very encouraging, although the figure refers more to enrollment in community colleges than in four-year institutions. The position of Filipinos, slightly above the Hawai'i average, can be attributed especially to their community college representation, since they are the largest group at community colleges but very underrepresented at University of Hawai'i campuses that offer baccalaureate degrees (see Chapter 12).

Data on age-specific educational attainments indicate that not much change in the ethnic/racial stratification order can be expected in the coming years. The dominant groups, i.e., Caucasians, Chinese, and Japanese, continue to have greater access to and achievement in higher education. In contrast, African Americans, Filipinos, Native Hawaiians, and Samoans have significantly lower levels of college access and completion.

The presence of far too many college-educated cab drivers, restaurant servers, secretaries, and other underemployed and underpaid workers in clerical, sales, and service jobs clearly demonstrates the severe limitations of Hawai'i's economy to provide appropriate employment for its residents, particularly its young college graduates. A recent study by Hawai'i's Department of Labor and Industrial Relations predicted that service, clerical, and sales work would have the greatest numerical growth, and tourist-industry jobs were expected to be the fastest growing from 1992 to 1997 (Honolulu Star-Bulletin 1993). These occupations include cashiers, cleaners and janitors, office clerks, retail salespersons, and sales supervisors, hardly meaningful and rewarding opportunities for Hawai'i's young people, especially college graduates. But the drastic downturn in the Hawai'i economy during the first half of the 1990s, which was clearly evident in the tourist industry, very likely nullified the above predictions concerning job growth. Perhaps more ominously, Hawai'i was the only state that had a decline in the number of available jobs in 1995. Indeed, the local economy was rated the weakest in the nation by a national insurance information agency (Lynch 1996).

RACIALIZATION OF THE STRATIFICATION ORDER

Considering the rankings of ethnic/racial groups in Hawai'i on the three indices of socioeconomic status, i.e., educational, income, and occupational attainments, a significant degree of correspondence is apparent. An overall ranking of groups in the ethnic/racial stratification order would have Caucasians, Chinese, and Japanese holding dominant positions. Chinese, who have the highest educational attainment in terms of college completion and enrollment rates among both males and females, rank second to Japanese in family and personal income, and they have a relatively high position in the occupational status order with substantial representation as executives/administrators and professionals. The continued high socioeconomic status of Chinese is all the more remarkable, given ongoing immigration of almost 1,000 persons each year from China, Hong Kong, and Taiwan, resulting in considerable numbers of lower-paid and -educated service workers in their population.

Japanese, who have the highest family and individual income, rank a close second to Chinese in educational achievement. They rank second to Caucasians in occupational status, since males are overemployed in administrative/executive and TSAS work.

Whites hold the dominant position in the occupational hierarchy, with both men and women considerably overrepresented as executives/administrators and professionals. They rank above the Hawai'i median on both male and female personal income despite the large military segment of their population and the lower labor force participation rate of Caucasian women. They also surpass the Hawai'i median on most indices of educational attainment, again despite their young military population.

The midrange of the ethnic/racial stratification order is occupied by Koreans and, to some extent, by African Americans. The former have an intermediate occupational status, with proportional male representation in white-collar employment, particularly in TSAS work, and women represented below parity as executives/administrators and professionals and overrepresented in service work. In both educational achievement and income, Korean men surpass the average on college completion and personal income, while women are below average.

African Americans have an intermediate position in the occupational status order. Both males and females are proportionally represented in white-collar categories, except for male overrepresentation as TSAS workers. African Americans are employed below parity in blue-collar occupational categories. However, very likely because of their young military population, they are well below the Hawai'i average in educational attainment and, especially, in family and individual income, where they rank last or second to the last.

The lower levels of the ethnic/racial stratification order continue to be occupied by Filipinos, Native Hawaiians, and Samoans, a situation that appears unlikely to change in the next generation. Filipinos remain underrepresented in white-collar jobs, with the sole exception of women in TSAS work, and both males and females are greatly overemployed as farmers, operators/laborers, and service workers. On most educational achievement and income indices, they rank below the Hawai'i median, although their family income approaches the state norm.

Similarly, Native Hawaiian men and women are represented below parity in the three upper occupational categories, with the exception of female parity as executives/administrators and TSAS workers. In contrast, men are overrepresented as operators/laborers and service workers. They rank above Filipinos in personal income but are below on family income. Native Hawaiian educational achievement is considerably below the state median on all our indicators.

Samoans continue to be the most socioeconomically disadvantaged of the subordinate groups, ranking last or near to the last on all indicators. Both male and female Samoans are overrepresented in blue-collar work while underrepresented in white-collar employment. A small percentage, far below the state average, has obtained a college education, even among those aged 25 to 34. Samoan family and individual income levels are generally the lowest of the ethnic/racial groups in this study.

The similarity between the above ethnic/racial stratification order with that in 1970 and 1980 is clear and is a further indication of the continued salience of ethnicity as the primary organizing and integrating principle of the social status system in Hawai'i. As a structural principle, ethnicity appears to regulate the distribution of socioeconomic opportunities, rewards, and benefits by privileging some groups and disprivileging others. Members of the former groups can use their privileged position to acquire the educational and occupational qualifications and skills necessary to compete and succeed, and thus they are able to reproduce themselves socially in their dominant status. In contrast, the disprivileged groups are collectively denied the advantages, opportunities, and resources that are generally available to the dominant groups. Through laws, plans, policies, practices, and procedures that have the effect or result of treating groups of people unfairly and unequally, although that might not be their specific intent, such minority groups as Filipinos, Native Hawaiians, and Samoans are not provided with the same privileges and benefits enjoyed by others in such larger institutions of society as the economy, educational institutions, government, and the law. Discrimination is evidenced by the continued underfunding of the state Department of Education (DOE), the negative consequences of which many Caucasian, Chinese, and Japanese parents are able to avoid by enrolling their children in private schools, while minority parents are less able to afford that option. According to a recent DOE report, while Hawai'i ranks second in the nation in per-capita state revenue and sixth in per-capita income, it ranks last among the states in the percentage of state funding for kindergarten through twelfth-grade education (Donnelly 1996). In employment, institutional discrimination is evident in government hiring practices (Forman 1991, 6–7; Haas 1992, chap. 5). Institutional discrimination also occurs through the nonenforcement of federal and state equal employment opportunity laws and affirmative action policies. The cumulative and ongoing result is a racialized stratification order and thus the institutionalization of inequality among ethnic/racial groups in Hawai'i.

At the same time, socioeconomic mobility is still very possible in Hawai'i. Because of the pervasiveness of ethnicity as a regulating principle in society, mobility is limited to individuals (rather than groups) through their own personal merit and achievement and acquired qualifications. It is still very possible for someone from a minority group, whose parents work in low-paying, blue-collar jobs and never attended college, to earn a college degree and to obtain a managerial, professional, or technical position in Hawai'i. However, individuals from subordinate groups who do so are not sufficiently numerous to alter current patterns in the ethnic/racial stratification order.

CONCLUSION: MULTICULTURAL HAWAI'I 2000?

As Hawai'i enters the next millennium in the next few years, the overall structure of its ethnic/racial stratification order is clearly discernible. Barring major changes in the political economy of Hawai'i, the stratification system in the year 2000 will not be appreciably different from what it was in 1990. Hawai'i society will remain highly unequally stratified. Since at least 1970, ethnicity has emerged as the dominant organizing principle that regulates the allocation of socioeconomic status, resulting in the maintenance of the socioeconomic *status quo*, with ethnic/racial groups continuing to hold their relative positions. Most significantly, this institutionalized inequality has meant and will continue to mean the subordination of Filipinos, Native Hawaiians, Samoans, and such recent immigrant groups as Laotians, Tongans, and Vietnamese. Having a Native Hawaiian state governor for eight years (1986–1994) did not result in significant gains in political and economic power for Native Hawaiians, even though there was an economic boom during the 1980s. Having a Filipino American governor in the mid-1990s also is leading to greater power and privileges for Filipinos because of the strong resistance of the stratification system to change. Opportunities for collective social mobility, which were available to minority groups during the post-statehood economic expansion of the 1960s, appear less likely with each passing decade as the economy becomes further mired in the tourist industry, with jobs that have low mobility, low pay, and low security (Okamura 1994, 168). There is a striking correlation between the decline in socioeconomic opportunities for all Hawai'i's people and the development of the Native Hawaiian sovereignty movement from the 1970s.

The institutional inequality and discrimination prevalent in the Islands present a glaring contradiction with the widely held perception of Hawai'i as a "multicultural model" for other societies. Promoters of this sanguine view of the Islands as a veritable racial paradise commonly boast about the Aloha State in such terms as "the nation's experiment in multiculturalism" and as an "ethnic rainbow of shining colors." The fiftieth state is said to be blessed with a tradition of tolerance and peaceful coexistence based on the proverbial "*aloha* spirit," harmonious race relations, as evident in cordial social relationships, high rates of intermarriage, and a broadly shared local culture and identity (Okamura, in press). A seemingly harmonious, peaceful, and tolerant society in which a majority of its people share a common culture and identity and intermarry with one another, nonetheless, may still be highly unequal and unjust. While loudly and proudly embracing its ethnic/racial diversity, multicultural Hawai'i has yet to confront its perverse social inequities.

NOTES

I would like to express my appreciation to Mary Yu Danico and Michael Haas for their very useful comments and suggestions for revision of a previous draft of my paper.

CHAPTER 11

Elementary and Secondary Education

Michael Haas

THE EDUCATIONAL GAP

Through education, a person may rise in social status from a job that requires few skills to a position with managerial or professional responsibilities. The continuing gap between rich and poor, which appears to distinguish lighter- from darker-skinned ethnic groups in Hawai'i appears to be correlated with an educational gap. However, the 1990 census reports that more than 80 percent of all persons in the Islands aged twenty-five and over completed high school, so at least three explanations for the gulf in social stratification are possible. First of all, the occupational structure of Hawai'i may result in underemployment, as Jonathan Okamura (Chapter 10) and Ibrahim Aoudé argue (Chapter 14), so that high-school graduates are performing low-skill jobs. A second explanation is that the home environment for certain ethnic groups fails to prepare children adequately for school, and indeed a Carnegie Foundation (1991) study found that Hawai'i public schoolteachers estimated that 47 percent of all kindergarten children were not ready for first grade, a level much higher than in any other state in the United States. A third possibility, explored in this chapter, is that some groups receive inferior schooling and thus pass along lower educational expectations to their children. With 15.8 percent of all primary and secondary students enrolled in private schools in Hawai'i (U.S. census 1993, 57), it is clear that many parents are willing to spend a lot of money on prebaccalaureate education because they concur that something is wrong with the public schools. This chapter will provide details of monocultural problems and multicultural innovations.

SCHOOLING BEFORE STATEHOOD

Before the arrival of Captain Cook, a system of traditional education operated to prepare the nobility to rule, while the mass of the population engaged in food gathering and related activities. When Protestant missionaries from New England arrived in the 1820s, the nobility was eager to gain the knowledge of the *haoles*, who set up mission schools.[1]

After a decade of educating adults of the Native Hawaiian nobility and royalty, the missionaries turned their attention to the younger generation, for whom they established two types of schools. *Common* schools enrolled Native Hawaiian children of the nonelite classes; as indicated in the Board of Missions guidelines, instruction was in the vernacular. *Select* schools, privately funded at first, consisted of boarding schools (to get children away from the "corrupting" influence of parents), the English language government-run Oʻahu Charity School (from 1833) for offspring of mixed Native Caucasian-Hawaiian parentage (some were abandoned by seafaring fathers), and various private schools for the *haoles*. The first government boarding school, started in 1839, was the Chiefs' Children's School; designed for children of the *aliʻi* who wanted to learn English, the school was renamed Royal School in 1846.

In 1841, Punahou School, the oldest private school west of the Mississippi, opened as an English language missionary school. Today, Punahou remains a top college preparatory school in the Islands. Native Hawaiians, allowed to attend Punahou as early as 1848, began to enroll increasingly within a decade, but they had to be "wealthy and civilized" (Pennybacker 1991, 121). The first Chinese student entered Punahou in 1867, and the first Japanese in 1885 (Forbes 1991, 461), but there was a ceiling of 10 percent for Asians from 1896 until 1945, when the quota increased to 12 percent. The entire quota system ended in 1955, one year after the U.S. Supreme Court ruling in *Brown v Board of Education of Topeka* (347US483), which suggested that Punahou might otherwise lose its tax-exempt status (Newport 1991, 157; Pennybacker 1991, 120–21). Other private schools, such as ʻIolani and St. Andrew's Priory, which began in the last half of the nineteenth century, were primarily for Native Hawaiians; since they had no racial quotas, they became multiethnic as soon as Asian parents could afford to send their children to private schools.

In the 1830s, teacher training started at Royal and two private boarding schools, Hilo Boarding School for vocational education (Clement 1980) and Lahaina Mission Seminary. The latter, renamed Lahainaluna in 1840, became a common school a decade later, then focused on vocational education after 1877, and was fully integrated into the public school system in 1961.

In 1837, when the Board of Missions began to cut aid to the Protestant mission schools in Hawai'i, Horace Mann coincidentally became the head of the state educational system in Massachusetts. Responding to the new financial reality, under which all mission aid was to cease within a decade, the monarchy decided in 1841 to follow Mann's example by establishing a system of tuition-supported public education throughout the Islands. Since Protestants in effect ran the public schools, Catholic and Mormon missionaries undertook to compete by operating small tuition-free private schools on funds provided from their own missionary boards on the U.S. mainland. The influence of the Protestant missionaries over the king was so considerable that no sectarian schools with fewer than twenty-five pupils were allowed after 1854. Parents were taxed $2 per child enrolled in common schools and $3 per child in select schools. Public funds raised in this manner defrayed all tuition costs of common schools and half the tuition costs at private schools. Tuition for elementary common schools ended in 1888, and public funds were denied to private schools after 1896.

Attendance in the English language select schools soon began to outstrip the vernacular common schools. In 1854, all select schools had authority to teach English to Native Hawaiians, a practice extended gradually to the common schools. By 1857, more funds went to the select schools than to the common schools (Reinecke 1935). Linguistic monoculturalization accelerated from 1878, with the arrival of Portuguese laborers: as the first immigrant group recruited to work in the sugar cane fields that was allowed to bring wives and children in any quantity, Portuguese parents wanted their children to learn English, not Hawaiian, and school administrators saw the wisdom of having English as the vehicle to homogenize a population that already consisted of large numbers of Chinese and Japanese as well as *haoles* and Native Hawaiians.

In 1887, the will of Princess Bernice Pauahi Bishop led to the establishment of Kamehameha Schools. One school was for boys; seven years later, a school for girls was added. Initially offering tuition-free elementary and secondary instruction, Kamehameha Schools soon eclipsed Royal School, which then became a multiethnic select school. Although nothing in the will specifically restricted attendance at Kamehameha to children of Native Hawaiian ancestry, the first students were children of Native Hawaiian parentage, and the practice has continued ever since.[2] Standard English was emphasized so that the education would be on a par with students in the common and select schools. Today, Kamehameha Schools enroll one-fourth of all Native Hawaiian children; most of the rest attend public schools (Hannahs 1983, 170).

There were only three vernacular Hawaiian schools by 1896. The decline of Hawaiian language schools, according to the Republic of Hawai'i's school authorities, amounted to a "linguistic revolution" (Hawai'i 1896, 22). English became the official language of government in 1896 and thereafter prevailed in the public schools. Monolingualism and monoculturalism became official policy.

Although a few Chinese, German, and Portuguese language schools opened in the 1880s, a flood of Japanese language schools, financed largely by Buddhist missions in Hawai'i, opened in the last decade of the nineteenth century (Brieske 1961, 305–8). Since the children were unsure which language to learn in any depth, yet attended public schools where teachers stressed rote learning and exams more than oral class participation (Stueber 1964, 239), improvised forms of communication developed as the basis for communication between classmates of the various ethnic groups. In due course, immigrant children developed a pidgin tongue, which originally consisted of an amalgam of non-English words, into a language of its own, known by Derek Bickerton (Chapter 3) as Hawaii Creole English (HCE). Children then taught their parents the new language. For more than a half century, many non-*haoles* grew up relatively isolated from *haoles* and thus had more exposure to HCE than to standard English. Other non-*haoles* lived in urbanized areas, where they came into contact with English-speaking *haoles*, and the gradual urbanization of the Islands enabled English to predominate in due course. In 1980, nonetheless, the

Hawai'i Department of Education (1980, 4) acknowledged that HCE "is the first language of many children," and in 1987 more than half the students in certain rural parts of the Islands were considered monolingual in HCE (Reyes 1987). Over the past century, many non-*haoles* have regarded the use of standard English as a form of snobbery, a tradition that continues to the present among members of working-class families, whose children sometimes call better English speakers "fags" or "damn *haoles*" for using standard English (Meredith 1965).

Because of HCE's prevalence among increasing numbers of Native Hawaiians as well as second-generation Americans of Asian and Portuguese ancestry, *haole* parents wanted to keep their children away from the so-called contaminating influence of HCE. Thus, nearly one-fourth of the schoolchildren attended private schools by the 1890s – (Table 11.1).

After World War I, Washington-appointed Hawai'i governors subscribed to the assimilationist stress on Americanization. Adopting a recommendation of Frank Bunker (1922), the author of a federal survey of education in the territory, a novel system of segregated education began in 1924. Children certified competent in oral standard English were to enroll in "English standard schools," where *haole* teachers prevailed. The remaining public schools were then attended and taught increasingly by non-*haoles*; even when non-*haole* students and teachers had exemplary English, an HCE accent was a sufficient ground to assign them to "nonstandard" schools (Stueber 1964, 254). School conversations in Hawaiian and HCE were actively discouraged.

Meanwhile, the Hawaiian Homestead Act provided plots of agricultural land to be settled by persons with at least 50 percent Native Hawaiian ancestry. Because of this *de jure* system of residential segregation, schools located inside the homestead areas almost entirely enrolled Native Hawaiian children. Other schools were deliberately located within monoethnic residential areas, both rural and urban (Bunker 1922, 2).

The new segregated system of public instruction, which disproportionately assigned non-*haole* children to inferior schools but did not exclude them on basis of race *per se*, provided an opportunity for *haole* parents to send their children to public schools of high quality. *Haole* support for the new system of segregation provided an expanded tax base on which the entire system of public schools operated. *Haoles* contributed some 80 percent of the tax revenues, but

TABLE 11.1
Private School Enrollment in Hawai'i by Ethnic Group, 1874–1990
(in percent)

Year	Caucasian	Chinese	Filipino	Hawaiian	Japanese	Korean	Puerto Rican
1874	29.8			70.2			
1878	29.8			70.2			
1896	75.1	7.7		16.0	1.2		
1899	41.9	11.9		42.6	3.6		
1900	42.8	13.6		39.5	3.6		
1902	32.5	12.1		34.1	12.9		8.4
1904	41.8	9.5		35.9	9.0		2.3
1906	39.7	11.5		35.1	13.7		NA
1908	40.4	12.7		35.4	10.0	1.2	.3
1910	35.6	12.6		36.2	12.7	1.8	1.1
1912	34.6	13.0		34.3	15.1	1.9	1.1
1914	33.6	15.5	.6	27.6	18.7	2.0	.8
1916	29.0	13.4	.7	25.9	27.9	2.4	.7
1918	34.4	15.5	1.0	28.4	18.0	1.8	.9
1920	34.4	14.6	1.2	29.2	17.1	2.6	.9
1922	34.0	12.4	1.3	28.0	19.8	2.3	.8
1924	35.4	11.1	2.2	26.7	22.1	1.4	1.1
1926	32.0	11.8	2.3	25.8	23.3	1.8	.7
1928	39.1	10.0	2.1	24.9	21.6	1.5	.8
1930	36.0	10.4	2.7	25.2	23.1	2.1	.5
1932	36.0	11.1	2.4	26.5	21.5	1.8	.7
1945	25.9	13.3	1.3	25.0	25.3	1.3	.7
1946	30.6	11.6	6.5	28.9	16.7	1.2	1.0
1970	43.8	6.0	8.2	11.7	27.1	1.3	NA
1975	44.0	13.0	8.0	11.0	21.0	NA	NA
1980	40.0	10.0	9.6	14.7	19.4	1.6	2.2
1990	33.7	10.3	12.8	13.8	21.1	3.3	1.9

Note: Figures add to 100 percent horizontally when other ethnic groups are included. For 1970, data for Koreans applies only to Honolulu.

Key: NA = not available.

Source: Gulick (1937, 156); Honolulu Advertiser (1957); Hawai'i (1874, 2; 1878, 2; 1896, 19; 1899, 116; 1900, 103; 1906, 73; 1908a, 55; 1910, 55; 1912a, 80; 1914a, 9; 1916a, 68; 1918a, 55; 1921, 70; 1922a, 67; 1922b, 4; 1924b, 113; 1926, 130; 1928b, 161; 1930, 159); Kaser (1975b); U.S. census (1972, 211–12, 214–15; 1973, 11, 70, 129, 178, 180; 1983, 40, 64, 70; 1993, 57, 122, 140).

private schools spent twice as much per student as public schools (Stueber 1964, 249, 302). The desired academic result, preparing *haoles* for college while retarding the educational attainments of non-*haoles*, was achieved thereby (Stueber 1964, 255–56). The social result was to foster a community of interest among yet another generation of non-*haoles*, who learned to despise those who were denying them an opportunity to receive the best education possible.

Bunker's recommendation for English standard schools came two years after his survey, which was published by the Bureau of Education of the United States (1920). A second recommendation was to regulate foreign language schools, consistent with so-called principles of Americanization. Arguing that Japanese language schools, which enrolled nearly all Japanese children, were fostering patriotism to Japan, he urged that they be closed, and in 1925 the territorial government sought to do so by imposing various regulations (Stueber 1964, 276). Two years later, the Supreme Court of the United States, however, ruled such efforts unconstitutional in *Farrington v Tokushige* (47StCt406). Nevertheless, shortly after December 7, 1941, Japanese language schoolteachers were interned, their schools were closed, and from 1943 students below the fifth grade were statutorily prohibited from taking a foreign language. After the war, the ban on foreign language schools remained, so a Chinese language school took the territorial government to court, but the ban was upheld by the U.S. Supreme Court in *Stainback v Mo Hock Ke Lok Po* (336US368) in 1949. Although the territorial legislature later amended some of the more objectionable provisions of the 1943 law, which was finally repealed in 1959, foreign language schools never regained their earlier rates of attendance.

Since there was a shortage of teachers for public schools, the Department of Public Instruction operated from 1895 a two-year postsecondary teacher training program at Honolulu High School, which was renamed the Normal and Training School in 1897. When the University of Hawai'i opened a Teacher College in 1931 (the College of Education from 1957), the Normal School was abolished, and prospective teachers enrolled at the university to be certified. Because Normal School degrees were no longer honored unless teachers were recertified at UH, the percentage of Native Hawaiian teachers dropped sharply; Japanese, who were eager to go to four-year institutions of higher learning, took up the slack (Table 11.2).

TABLE 11.2
Public Schoolteachers in Hawai'i by Ethnic Group, 1888–1994
(in percent)

Year	Black	Caucasian	Chinese	Filipino	Hawaiian	Japanese	Korean
1888		42.4			57.6		
1890		50.0			50.0		
1892		45.7			54.3		
1894		47.6			52.4		
1896		63.6	.4		36.1		
1898		68.4	.0		31.6		
1900		70.6	NA		28.4		
1902		69.3	.3		30.4		
1904		62.0	1.0		37.0		
1906		57.3	2.0		40.6		
1908		54.6	1.6		43.8		
1909		55.6	1.6		42.8		
1910		51.5	3.2		44.9	.4	
1912		56.6	5.0		37.3	1.1	
1914		57.6	5.6		35.3	1.4	
1916		56.6	6.1		35.0	2.2	
1918		53.6	7.6		34.1	2.9	
1924		54.5	11.1		14.2	5.1	
1948	.0	47.0	**	.8	5.7	46.4	**
1967	NA	35.0	10.0	4.0	11.0	38.0	NA
1974	.3	18.7	8.9	2.2	7.0	57.9	1.4
1976	.4	17.4	8.5	2.4	7.0	59.6	1.2
1978	.3	17.2	8.4	2.5	7.0	59.4	1.2
1980	.3	17.1	8.2	2.7	7.0	59.5	1.2
1981	.4	16.9	8.1	2.8	7.0	59.4	1.2
1983	.4	16.3	7.8	3.4	7.0	59.3	1.1
1984	.4	16.3	7.5	3.3	7.2	59.4	1.1
1986	.4	17.1	7.8	3.6	7.4	58.3	1.1
1988	.5	18.4	7.9	4.0	7.3	57.2	1.1
1990	.6	20.9	7.5	4.0	7.5	54.6	1.0
1993	NA	26.2	6.9	4.5	8.2	48.7	*
1994	NA	25.7	6.9	4.7	8.4	47.7	*

Note: Figures add to 100 percent horizontally when other ethnic groups are included.
          For 1967, data are for O'ahu only.
Key: NA = not available; * = counted with Chinese; ** = counted with Japanese.
Source: Hawai'i Department of Education; Hawai'i (1888, 16; 1890, 18, 19; 1892, 21,
          22; 1894, 16; 1896, 16; 1897,54; 1898, 112; 1899, 112; 1900, 99; 1902b, 24;
          1904, 87; 1906b, 58; 1908b, 59; 1910b, 78; 1912b, 192; 1914b, 61; 1916b, 64;
          1918b, 53); Honolulu Star-Bulletin (1971).

Franklin Roosevelt's New Deal brought many educational reforms. In 1933, the territorial legislature adopted a policy of "equal educational opportunity," the cornerstone of which was the requirement to equalize per-student expenditures for all schools. Previously, only the top 75 to 80 percent of all elementary school graduates were allowed to enroll in secondary schools; in 1936, this requirement was dropped in favor of a policy of open admission. Fees for books, courses in home economics and typing, kindergarten, and even library cards were finally abolished in 1942.

Inconsistent with the policy of equal educational opportunity, a disproportionate percentage of *haole* students were still bused from their homes past "nonstandard schools" to the English standard schools. After the attack on Pearl Harbor in 1941, private and public schools closed for eight weeks, and many buildings were converted to war purposes. During the war, patriotism was stressed, and special classes in English began in the schools. Since many *haoles* left for the mainland, the number of *haole* children in English standard schools fell from 4,024 in 1941 to 1,261 in 1942. So many Chinese, Japanese, and Koreans were admitted to the English standard schools during the war that they outnumbered the *haoles* by 1946 (Stueber 1964, 342, 344). Standard English tracks for non-*haole* students were even established in nonstandard schools during the war. Although some public school desegregation had already begun to occur because of increasing residential integration in Honolulu, the social stigma associated with the division between standard and nonstandard schools was the primary motivation behind a campaign to abolish the English standard schools (Hormann 1947). In 1947, the territorial legislature decided to phase out assignment to schools on the basis of language ability, starting in grade 1; the process of desegregation was to last twelve years. The last class enrolled on the basis of *de jure* language segregation graduated in 1960. Patterns of racial segregation, established by dint of the pattern of rural residential settlement into Filipino plantation camps, Hawaiian homestead lands, and *haole*-dominated military bases were not remedied by a reversion to neighborhood patterns of enrollment, however. Since school attendance zones continued to coincide with ethnic enclaves, especially in elementary rural schools, the result was as before—to isolate minorities from the mainstream. Military buses continued to take military dependents past schools with predominantly non-*haole* enrollment to public schools operated on military bases in central Oʻahu, a practice that stopped in 1968, when Congress prohibited the use of federal funds for busing students to schools.

Integrated schools enrolled a few bright students along with those of lesser abilities. Whereas formerly the stress in "nonstandard" schools was to prepare students vocationally, integrated schools offered new courses for students seeking to go to college. To satisfy competing demands for instruction, the school system established ability grouping, which, in turn, resegregated students so that darker-skinned ethnic groups (mostly Filipinos and Native Hawaiians) tended to be located in the lower tracks (Haas 1992, Table 6.3). By the 1970s, many schools had as many as five tracks, and at least one school operated seventeen. Indeed, in 1991 Hawaiʻi public schools reported more tracking than any other school district in the United States.

PUBLIC SCHOOLS IMMEDIATELY AFTER STATEHOOD

When Hawaiʻi became a state, the Department of Public Instruction was renamed the Department of Education (DOE). The fiftieth state, thus, became the only state to have a single, statewide school district. Soon, dramatic changes occurred to narrow educational opportunities for less-affluent groups within the public schools.

Demographic Polarization

In 1963, the state legislature abolished a provision, in force since 1893, allowing students of Native Hawaiian ancestry in the public schools to take courses in the Hawaiian language. Thereafter, courses in Hawaiiana replaced the former Hawaiian language courses, but they were taught by larger percentages of teachers of Japanese ancestry (Table 11.2). Instruction in the Japanese language, which reached a low point because of the decline of the Japanese language schools from World War II to statehood, began in public schools in 1959 and grew rapidly among students of Japanese ancestry (Kaser 1975a), while courses in European and minority languages declined (Maier 1975), reflecting the changing language abilities of the new composition of public schoolteachers. A Japanese teaching staff was, in effect, closing down language teaching for other ethnic groups in a quieter manner than the crackdown on Japanese language schools in the 1920s.

After statehood, the economic level of the Japanese community rose to the plateau previously achieved by Chinese and *haoles* in

Hawai'i. An increasing percentage of Japanese schoolchildren, accordingly, entered private schools, although they enrolled in some private schools more than others (Haas 1992, Tables 6.4–6.5). As a result, Japanese teachers in the public schools faced classes where the percentage of students of their own ethnicity has been on the downswing in relation to students of other ethnic groups, especially Filipinos (Table 11.3). Moreover, to sociologist Lawrence Fuchs, schooling is increasingly based on social class, with Chinese, *haoles*, and Japanese predominant in private schools other than Kamehameha, whereas Filipinos, Native Hawaiians, Portuguese, and Samoans largely enroll in public schools (Wilcox 1974a).

During the early 1970s, federal authorities defined the term "segregation" more precisely to determine when schools in a district reach integration. According to *Adams v Richardson* (351FSupp636), a *segregated* school was defined to exist whenever the enrollment of any ethnic group at a school deviates more than 20 percent from the percentage of students of that group in the school district as a whole. Using the *Adams* algorithm, about half of Hawai'i public schools in 1974 were segregated (Haas 1992, Table 6.6). Most segregated schools were at Filipino plantation camps, within homestead lands, and on military bases. Although Hawaiian homestead school segregation is clearly *de jure*, no formal segregation complaint has yet emerged in the fiftieth state. Although no one wants to "make waves," segregation has a measurable effect on educational performance, the next topic to be discussed.

Unequal Educational Performance

In 1964, Congress authorized a study of barriers to equal education opportunity. The study, soon contracted to a team of sociologists (Coleman et al. 1966), did not analyze Hawai'i separately to ascertain whether national findings were applicable locally, but lower academic performance of Filipinos and Native Hawaiians was soon identified in several studies (Werner, Bierman, French 1971; Gallimore, Boggs, Jordan 1974; Hawaii Association for Asian and Pacific Peoples 1974, 23–57; Werner and Smith 1977). These early studies attributed lower academic attainment to such factors as a lack of cultural sensitivity toward the needs of educational minorities on the part of teachers and

TABLE 11.3

Public School Enrollment in Hawai'i by Ethnic Group, 1874–1995 (in percent)

Year	Cauca-sian	Chinese	Filipino	Hawaiian	Japanese	Korean	Puerto Rican
1874	70.1			12.9			
1878	70.1			12.9			
1892	28.3	3.3		67.4	.6		
1894	29.3	4.7		64.4	1.0		
1896	32.7	5.9		58.7	2.1		
1899	30.4	7.3		52.8	8.7		
1900	29.2	6.4		52.3	10.5		
1904	27.5	8.2		44.1	17.2		2.6
1908	25.3	10.6		34.4	27.1	.9	1.7
1912	24.6	10.4		26.2	35.2	1.2	2.4
1916	22.1	9.6	1.5	21.2	41.6	1.1	3.1
1920	17.6	9.7	2.5	19.3	45.8	1.3	2.6
1924	15.7	9.8	3.4	16.9	51.0	1.8	1.9
1928	14.5	9.3	4.2	16.8	52.1	2.2	1.5
1932	12.4	8.6	5.3	14.3	54.5	2.5	1.7
1936	11.2	7.8	6.3	14.8	54.0	2.4	1.9
1945	8.1	5.3	9.6	19.9	49.1	1.5	1.5
1946	28.6	4.8	10.1	21.3	47.0	1.1	2.0
1970	NA	6.0	14.8	11.3	27.1	1.2	NA
1974	28.6	4.7	16.9	18.1	22.4	1.4	1.8
1977	26.6	4. 1	16.9	19.6	NA	1.7	NA
1980	28.4	4. 1	18.5	17.9	19.7	1.8	3.4
1984	19.8	3.5	19.6	21.2	16.5	1.9	2.0
1988	22.9	3.5	18.9	22.2	14.4	1.8	2.1
1992	19.0	3.2	17.8	23.4	13.2	1.7	NA
1995	17.5	3.2	18.5	24.4	12.4	1.6	NA

Note: Figures add to 100 percent horizontally when other ethnic groups are added. Korean 1970 data are for Honolulu only.

Key: NA = not available.

Source: Hawai'i Department of Education; Hawai'i (1874, 2; 1878, 2; 1892, 21; 1894, 21; 1896, 20; 1898, 94; 1899, 115; 1900, 102; 1905, 27; 1907, 40; 1908a, 55; 1909, 63; 1911, 70; 1912a, 80; 1913, 77; 1915, 58; 1916a, 68; 1917, 74; 1919, 57; 1920b, 62; 1921, 70; 1923, 68; 1924a, 70; 1925, 71; 1927, 87; 1928a, 86; 1929, 77; 1931, 80; 1932b, 92; 1933, 36); U.S. Congress (1946, 717); U.S. census (1972, 212–15; 1973, 11, 70, 129, 178, 180; 1983, 40, 64, 70).

school administrators, HCE's prevalence at home, and the mono-culturalist destruction of the self-concept of the less-affluent groups, whose educational and occupational futures were dead-ended because of tracking. In later studies, Christopher Melahn (1986, 489) found that Native Hawaiians had lower aspirations about going to college principally because they were marked down by their teachers, and Rosalind Mau (1986) found that minority student alienation could be attributed primarily to a perception that teachers were unfair in giving them low grades.

Yet another study found that test scores of Filipinos and Native Hawaiians were far below those of Caucasians, Chinese, and Japanese (Morton, Stout, Fischer 1976). The test scores of Filipinos and Native Hawaiians even declined from grades 2 to 6, so the inference was that school experiences were responsible for lowering academic attainments of minority children.

In a later study, I found that schools with abnormally large percentages of Filipino and Native Hawaiian students had the lowest test scores (Haas 1988), thereby confirming the finding that segregation is associated with lower academic performance (Coleman et al. 1966). Although DOE officials tried to argue that Filipinos and Native Hawaiians scored poorly because of their lower socioeconomic standing (Port 1979; Savard and Araki 1965; Verploegen 1986), using more advanced statistical techniques, my study refuted this contention.

Discrimination Against Language-Minority Groups

Title VI of the Civil Rights Act of 1964 attached a string to all federal grants to school systems and other public agencies—the requirement that all ethnic groups must derive equal benefit from the institutions thus supported financially. Federal agencies were empowered to terminate funding to state and local governments that engage in flagrant ethnic discrimination. Accordingly, all school districts had to provide annual counts of enrollment by ethnicity to Washington, D.C., in order to facilitate civil rights monitoring. Since the state's single school district did not fit the black/white pattern of the mainland, members of Hawai'i's congressional delegation secured an exemption for the DOE from filling out federal forms on the ethnicity of students in each school (Gereben 1970a). As a result, the Aloha State was exempted from civil rights monitoring for a decade.

In 1965, Congress advanced the civil rights revolution again by abolishing discrimination in immigration policies based on national origin. Families separated for decades between a distant homeland and the United States received preference in immigration, with equal quotas for all countries. A flow of Chinese, Filipino, and Korean immigrants then came to Hawai'i, bringing some children with limited or no English background into the public schools. By 1991, these children accounted for at least 6.25 percent of DOE enrollment. Following familiar monoculturalist procedures, the DOE assigned new immigrant students to lower tracks, and many intelligent immigrant students found themselves in classes with native English speakers of lesser academic aptitude. In some cases, immigrants of average intelligence were even assigned to classes for the mentally retarded.

In 1972, Congress passed the Emergency School Aid Act (ESAA), which aimed to facilitate desegregation and to provide language assistance to students whose home or primary language was other than English. Although public schools in the Islands had the largest percentage of immigrant children among the fifty states, DOE personnel thought that ESAA funds were not relevant to Hawai'i, so they did not submit a grant application (Wilcox 1974b). Congresswoman Patsy Mink then urged the DOE to apply, so that programs for language-minority students could be developed. ESAA guidelines required that the DOE submit an initial count of its students at the various schools by ethnicity, since later funding was contingent on a reduction of segregated patterns of pupil assignment. Accordingly, annual ethnic counts of students, discontinued in 1946, resumed in 1974, and an unheralded "mini-busing program" began (Honolulu Advertiser 1974a).

School Violence

My statistical study also found that violence was most intense in secondary schools that enrolled disparate streams of students from ethnically identifiable ("segregated") elementary schools and in schools where immigrants were disproportionately classified as "mentally retarded" (Haas 1988). Sociologist Eldon Wegner (1976, 14–15), analyzing attitudes of seniors in four O'ahu high schools in 1976, found that the schools with higher percentages of college-bound students and fewer cross-ethnic friendships had the most ethnic tension. He also reported that ethnicity, not social status, was related to the lower educational attainments of Filipinos and Native Hawaiians (Wegner, Sakihara, Takeuchi 1976; Wegner 1977).

School violence was not new to Hawai'i, however. The only school violence of any consequence, in the recollection of former School Superintendent Techiro Hirata, consisted of organized gangs that roamed from school to school to cause mischief (Verploegen 1974). After the bombing of Pearl Harbor in 1941, Japanese American children became victims of "rap a Jap" attacks on frequent occasions, mostly involving Filipino, Korean, and Portuguese bullies (Lind 1946, 59). After the war, violence stabilized on the campuses of public schools, and less than 1 percent of DOE students were referred to counselors for misconduct in the 1952–53 school year (Hawai'i 1953, 6, 21). After statehood, as mainland-born *haoles* increasingly enrolled in public schools, they learned of a mythical "kill a *haole* day" if they failed to assimilate to more deferential Island ways. Upset parents then responded by routing their children to private schools, where they met students of other affluent groups. By 1974–75, some 13.3 percent of all DOE students were cited for disciplinary infractions on three or more occasions, according to data supplied to a national study of school violence (cf. Haas 1988).

The situations that triggered school violence in Hawai'i varied considerably, but a pattern was evident. Children seeking to define their identities at schools that were not providing relevant instruction formed cliques based on ethnicity and language, and then laid territorial claims to trees and other portions of schoolyards. Little violence took place inside the classroom. Instead, students who, in the words of former Deputy Police Chief Eugene Fletcher, found school "totally unrewarding and totally boring" (Armstrong 1975; cf. Verploegen 1989a; Wegner, Sakihara, Takeuchi 1976, 20) either were absent from class but present on the schoolgrounds or asked a teacher to be excused to go to the bathroom and then never returned to class. Students who hung around the bathroom, in turn, extorted money from students seeking to use the toilet by threatening them with a beating. Most students at four schools under study in the mid-1970s reported a fear of violent incidents (Wegner, Sakihara, Takeuchi 1976, 54). Teachers observed acts of violence but cited their union contract as a reason for not trying to stop the more brutal incidents, leaving crisis intervention to a passive school administration. At the end of the school day, students might emerge from classes divided into ability-grouping sections; those in the lower tracks might then interact with verbal abuse, such as "dumb *haole*," "Buddhaheads," and "here come the *bago'ongs*."[3] Although those with the most cross-ethnic friends reported the most ethnic tension, children in more ethnically homogeneous upper-status tracks most feared violence (Wegner 1976, 31, 36). Lower-track students, whose honor or pride was challenged by the snobbish bearing of an upper-track or mainland-born student, whom they doubtless did not know, might resort to fisticuffs (Wegner 1976, 47). At this point, the police would be called, an arrest made, and all students would be told to leave the campus immediately. Although juvenile arrests skyrocketed in the 1970s (Haas 1988, 731), Filipino immigrants were less likely to be arrested than Hawai'i-born students (Agbayani-Cahill et al. 1975), so the violence was predominantly blamed on local students who resented the attainments of upward-mobile groups.

School violence reached a climax in the 1970s, when two Filipino students were killed in the public schools (Haas and Resurrection 1976, chap. 5). In 1974, a group of Japanese boys assaulted a few Filipino immigrants at a high school in Honolulu, and one of the Filipinos died of an aneurysm. In 1975, a prearranged fight between a Hawai'i-born Filipino and an immigrant Filipino at a rural O'ahu intermediate school developed into a melee, and an immigrant fatally stabbed the local student.

These incidents called attention to a rise in acts of vandalism, arrests, fires, and other measures of violence that had been soaring during the 1970s. Comparing Hawai'i public schools with those on the mainland in 1974–75, there were 21.2 offenses of violence per thousand students, the highest rate of school violence among the fifty states (National Institute of Education 1978, I-B6). In 1985–86, an average of eighteen cases of disorderly conduct occurred per day in Island public schools (Glauberman 1988). In 1988, Hawai'i ranked highest among the fifty states in teacher concerns over absenteeism, disruptive behavior, parental and student apathy, racial discord, theft, vandalism, and violence (Verploegen 1988). An educational task force reported in 1989 that the most unruly students were those who perceived that they were rejected by school personnel (Verploegen 1989a). Unlike problems of assault on teachers reported on the mainland, the main target of violence in the public schools of the Islands has been fellow students (Infante 1991c).

CIVIL RIGHTS RESPONSE

The Filipino community, which sent its offspring to schools where they were treated as outsiders, responded quickly when the first Filipino died. As several studies noted, immigrant parents place a higher value on education than local parents (Melahn 1986; Research Information Services 1977; Wegner, Sakihara, Takeuchi 1976, 20; Wegner 1977, 7). In 1974, the O'ahu Filipino Community Council formed a task force of Filipino educators, who prepared a report with twenty-five recommendations (OFCC 1975). When OFCC issued a report in February 1975 and sent copies to public school officials and the governor, they waited in vain for a response. After OFCC took its report to a meeting of the Board of Education (BOE) in June 1975, there was still no follow-up. In the fall, after the second Filipino died, members of the OFCC task force reconvened, decided that local remedies had failed, identified twenty-two DOE policies and practices that adversely affected Filipinos, circulated a petition calling for a federal civil rights compliance review of the DOE, garnered some 750 signatures on the petition, and sent the petition to the BOE (Honolulu Star-Bulletin 1975, A1). Again, the OFCC was ignored, and a high-ranking DOE official of Japanese ancestry even told a television reporter that he "didn't understand the need for special programs. After all, we made it without them" (Haas 1976, 43). The statement vindicated the OFCC complaint.

The petition was also sent to the Office for Civil Rights of the U.S. Department of Health, Education, and Welfare (HEW). Upon receipt of the class-action complaint, HEW contacted DOE Superintendent Charles Clark, who initially threatened not to cooperate with any investigation. When civil rights officials pointed out that noncooperation would result in prompt termination of all federal funds to the DOE, Clark relented and received two investigators in May 1976. One month later, the federal agency issued a report citing the DOE for violating Title VI of the Civil Rights Act of 1964 by failing to provide appropriate language assistance to Filipinos, Koreans, Samoans, and other immigrants.[4] The DOE was thus ineligible to renew its $2.5 million ESAA grant, pending negotiation of an agreement to establish better procedures for identifying students in need of English language assistance, and to provide these students with special language programs (Verploegen 1976).

In response to the noncompliance finding in 1976, OFCC renewed its call for a full review of all aspects of DOE operations covered in the original petition. Again, there was no BOE or DOE response to the Filipino community. Later in 1976, I accepted an invitation from the Hawai'i Federation of Teachers to present results of my statistical studies to audiences of teachers; afterward, the press reported my remarks. People's Party senatorial candidate Tony Hodges, after reading press reports about my research, asked me for my list of "segregated schools." Soon he released the list to the press, charging the DOE with racism; he also called for an HEW compliance review, agreeing with the original OFCC petition.

Reacting to mounting pressure, Superintendent Clark charged that OFCC was inciting violence by complaining, and he refused to meet with the Filipino educators to discuss their call for an HEW compliance review. At this point, Governor George Ariyoshi intervened (Woo 1976). Clark reversed his stand and asked HEW to do a compliance review (Honolulu Advertiser 1976). HEW civil rights officials, busy with a full schedule of complaints in California, then replied that if the DOE wanted to exercise voluntary compliance with the law, it should review itself. Rather than coming into compliance, HEW officials cited the DOE for continued language discrimination in 1977, 1979, 1980, 1981, 1982, and 1990 (cf. Ong 1980), and thus HEW continued to monitor the DOE's programs for language-minority students, which were serving only half the eligible students by 1981. What was occurring was paper compliance without a sincere commitment of resources to equip immigrant students to enter the educational mainstream.

Many immigrant students, meanwhile, were dropping out of school without an educational experience that they regarded as useful for earning an income. When immigrants arrived home from school each day, adults were at work, so they lacked parental guidance. In the intervening years since the first complaint from the Filipino community about public education in Hawai'i, the sporadic yet persistent campus violence of the 1970s gradually turned into organized gang violence during the 1980s. Some immigrant students, aware that opportunities for upward mobility were blocked in the public schools, went into the business of importing and selling small amounts of narcotic drugs (cf. Chesney-Lind et al. 1992). As rival gangs battled for control of the market, they attracted more young members, engaged in turf battles, and executions of gang members began to occur on and off the grounds of public schools. By 1991, there were an estimated forty-five gangs on O'ahu, mostly composed of Filipinos and Samoans, and at least six murders from 1988 were attributable to gangs, some on the grounds of public schools (Infante 1991a).

In 1982, at the insistence of members of the Hawai'i State Advisory Committee to the U.S. Commission on Civil Rights, public hearings were held to determine why the DOE was making no progress to hire schoolteachers from ethnic groups other than the dominant Japanese. The resulting report charged the DOE with deliberate discrimination, especially against Filipino applicants, who had risen from 2 to only 3 percent of the teachers during a decade of obvious lackluster affirmative action (U.S. Commission on Civil Rights 1983).

AFFIRMATIVE ACTION RESPONSE

During the 1980s, efforts to improve equal educational opportunity competed for attention with innovations aimed at advancing the overall quality of education. Promotion from one grade to another was limited to students with passing grades; automatic "social promotions" ended. A passing score on competency tests became a requirement for a diploma, and course requirements increased.

Nevertheless, with the appointment of Francis Hatanaka as the new DOE superintendent in 1984, civil rights compliance increased. The DOE agreed to a decision rule that "preference" in hiring would thenceforth go to groups underrepresented in the jobs to be filled. The percentage of Japanese teachers then began a steady decline, and other groups, including Caucasians, increased.

While Filipinos were struggling to succeed in a society whose norms they accepted, yet found themselves treated as if they were not good enough to enjoy the constitutionally mandated equality of educational opportunity, many Native Hawaiians were ambivalent about wanting to be a part of American society (Wegner 1976, 44). Instead of equal treatment to take their place in the United States as yet another successful minority, Native Hawaiians were trying to cling to a culture that was in danger of extinction. In 1974, Congress recognized this quest, granting Native Hawaiians the same status as American Indians in the Native American Programs Act. A further breakthrough came in 1978, when the legislature mandated that all DOE students take courses in Hawaiian Studies. Since there were insufficient qualified teachers for the new program, the DOE hired *kupuna* (Native Hawaiian elders) on a part-time basis from 1980.

Meanwhile, Native Hawaiian leaders formed needs assessments task forces in several areas, one of which was education. Whereas the Filipino task force of the mid-1970s operated on a shoestring to identify a set of problems and solutions, the Native Hawaiian task force on education had sufficient federal funding to prepare a 234-page report with considerable documentation (Hannahs 1983). As in the case of the earlier Filipino report, DOE implementation of recommendations from Native Hawaiians was almost nonexistent during the early 1980s.

In the 1986 campaign for lieutenant governor, candidate Vicky Bunye raised the issue of DOE discrimination against Filipinos. Her main focus was on employment of Filipino teachers, with the aim of improving the quality of instruction through the hiring of more culturally sensitive schoolteachers. Although she lost the election, the issues at last received the attention that they deserved.

After the election, Charles Toguchi became DOE superintendent; he was eager to reverse any unequal educational opportunities in the public schools. The BOE, in turn, decided to set up the Citizens' Task Force on Affirmative Action for Filipinos, the first BOE response to matters raised by the OFCC in 1974 and 1975. When the task force presented its report in 1987, the BOE agreed to several new programs. Some focused on employment; most were efforts to promote equal educational opportunity directly with programs for students.

Several new programs were launched in the late 1980s. Teaching as a Career clubs were started in high schools in order to attract more Filipinos and other underrepresented groups to become schoolteachers. A Career Shadowing Program provided mentoring to help new minority hires to become successful teachers. Since Filipinos who formerly taught school in the Philippines disproportionately flunked the National Teacher Examination (NTE) test upon arrival in the Islands, the DOE set up NTE Preparation Workshops.

To assist HCE speakers, the DOE used federal funds to support the Hawai'i Creole Project (*Holopono*) and Project *Akamai* in the 1980s. Although neither program was renewed, they have been models of interest to educators who are concerned about African American children who speak Ebonics, a tongue that is based on West African languages that were perpetuated by slavery, segregation, and substandard schools on the U.S. mainland (Honolulu Advertiser 1997). For immigrant children, the Bilingual Intensive Basic Skills project was set up in 1988 to provide language assistance, and Project *Anuenue* (rainbow) from 1991 was designed to provide cross-cultural counseling.

The DOE also undertook more sophisticated methods to identify and to prepare students with college potential through the project Assistance in Cross-Cultural and Career Education for School Success (ASSESS). In conjunction with the University of Hawai'i at Manoa (UHM), the Hawai'i Opportunity Program in Education (HOPE) was launched to provide academic enrichment from grade 3, with an incentive of eventual scholarships to encourage younger minority children to aim their sights for college. Both projects began in 1990. Several DOE-UHM projects, also begun in the 1980s, were designed to provide some college experience to minority high school students (Haas 1992, Table 6.8b).

In 1984, Native Hawaiian instructors at the University of Hawai'i's main campus organized a pilot program of total instruction in the Hawaiian language at a private school. In 1987, the BOE approved a trial of this "immersion program" at three elementary schools; the program expanded to five schools in 1991. Despite criticism of the program from Lawrence Fuchs (Smyser 1992), the BOE agreed in 1992 to expand the program to include all grades, with one hour of English language instruction from grades 5 to 12.

In 1989, the Wai'anae Coast School Concerns Coalition protested unequal school facilities for Native Hawaiians (Viotti 1989). Although the group's leader, Michael Kahikina, threatened a lawsuit, the DOE responded in a few months with promises of increased funding to Wai'anae schools (Verploegen 1989b).

Also in 1989, the Board of Education established a program of special learning centers in twenty-eight of the thirty-eight high schools. The aim of these "magnet schools" is to provide specialized career-oriented curricula articulated to particular professions. Performing arts learning centers, for example, were located at Kaimuki High School in Honolulu, Castle High School in Windward O'ahu, Hilo High School on the island of Hawai'i, and Baldwin High School on Maui.

Recently, "academies" with even more intensive training have been developed. In 1991, Farrington High School, located in one of the poorest areas near downtown Honolulu, opened a High School Health Academy with fifty-four sophomores enrolled as aspiring health care workers, a field of employment with a labor shortage (Infante 1991b, A1). The program seeks to graduate nurse's aides and prepare students for entry to a professional degree in nursing. An Academy of Travel and Tourism opened at Waipahu High School in 1992, with funding from the National Academy Foundation. Both schools enroll large percentages of Filipinos.

In 1991, the BOE decided to respond to complaints that the DOE's powerful central bureaucracy stifles initiative in individual schools. The Board began to consider a form of decentralization known as School/Community-Based Management, under which principals would be freer to act in a wide variety of matters without approval from the central office. Whether this innovation, now adopted at about half the public schools, will make schools less accountable for civil rights violations or more able to respond to problems of immigrant and other students remains to be seen.

CONCLUSION

The political succession from ruling *haole* governors, mostly Republican, to the ruling majority of Democrats, mostly Japanese, was paralleled within the public school system in Hawai'i. *Haole* children increasingly exited from public schools to attend private schools, joined in due course by affluent lighter-skinned classmates, leaving the public schools as the last resort for those who could not afford to receive better education. Upward-mobile public school students, whose ethnicity most closely matched the staff, were able to attend college-bound classes, while darker-skinned pupils encountered low teacher expectations. Test scores declined, and more students exited from the public schools.

What broke the downward spiral toward educational disaster was political protest. Filipino complaints of educational isolation led to federal civil rights intervention, which eventually shored up problems regarding language discrimination. When the issue of the nearly monoethnic composition of the school administration and teaching staff was raised in the 1986 election, the Board of Education responded with a large set of new programs for Filipinos. Meanwhile, Native Hawaiians developed a new program to revive the Hawaiian language within public schools, and others protested shortchanging of funding for schools attended by Native Hawaiians. Again, the BOE listened and agreed. In due course, exciting magnet school innovations were developed to provide quality education.

Problems of public education are by no means resolved today. The pattern of community protest and BOE response, followed by professional program development and BOE acceptance of such innovations, has turned the corner. Public education in Hawai'i has become more responsive to the needs of its multiethnic and multicultural population. Rather than a backlash to affirmative action, the new educational multiculturalism has gained wide acceptance and has no vocal critics in the Islands.

Japanese sought teaching positions in mid-century Hawai'i as middle-class jobs to which they were admirably suited. By the end of the century, the low pay of teaching attracted fewer Japanese. For reasons to be identified in the next chapter, however, Filipinos and Native Hawaiians did not emerge to fill the gap. Currently, the public schools have a serious teaching shortage that must be overcome by trips to the U.S. mainland to recruit applicants. Increasingly, *haole* teachers from monoethnic and monocultural parts of the mainland are entering Hawai'i public schools, often unprepared for a multiethnic student body and a multicultural curriculum. Thus, those leaving the mainland to teach in the fiftieth state are now destined to learn about important multicultural innovations.

NOTES

1. For more details on the history of education in Hawai'i, see Brieske (1961), Midkiff (1935), Stueber (1964), and Wist (1940).

2. Presumably, any child can apply for admission to Kamehameha. Non-Hawaiian children of Kamehameha teachers, for example, attend the school. An orphan or abandoned child, for which there is no information on ancestry, could not be denied admission to Kamehameha, according the school's admission office. The only problem, the staff tell me, is that a non-Hawaiian child may have to endure hazing from students unhappy that an obvious non-Hawaiian is enrolled. Although attacked in the press from time to time for maintaining segregated enrollment (Jones 1967), Kamehameha Schools have received

federal funds and tax-exempt status despite an overwhelming enrollment of students of Hawaiian ancestry because it is serving a minority community.

3. *Bago'ong* is a condiment used in the Philippines distinguishable by smell. The term refers pejoratively to immigrant Filipinos.

4. Filipinos accounted for 44 percent of the with limited English language proficiency students in 1986, according to the DOE.

CHAPTER 12

Higher Education

Michael Haas

THE EMERGENCE OF HIGHER EDUCATION

The first efforts to provide higher education in Hawai'i came in 1857, when what is now Punahou School, a prep school originally set up to educate *haoles*, instituted a private two-year institution known as O'ahu College, which lasted until 1934. There was no university in the Islands during the nineteenth century.

The impetus for public higher education came from Honolulu Postmaster William Kwai Fong Yap, who wanted his daughter and son to go to a four-year state-subsidized college. Since he could not afford to send them to the U.S. mainland, he launched a petition drive to gain support for the establishment of a four-year college with public funding from the Territory of Hawai'i. In 1907, despite some opposition from *haole* ruling circles, the territorial government agreed, and the College of Agriculture and Mechanic Arts opened its doors in 1908. After a retitling in 1911 as the College of Hawai'i, the institution was renamed the University of Hawai'i (UH) in 1920. By the end of the century, UH branched out from the high-enrollment campus at Manoa Valley in Honolulu to encompass two four-year campuses (at Hilo and West O'ahu), four two-year community colleges on O'ahu (Honolulu Community College, Kapi'olani Community College, Leeward Community College, Windward Community College), and three two-year community colleges on islands other than O'ahu (Hawai'i Community College, Kaua'i Community College, Maui Community College).

A few other institutions of higher learning began later. A Catholic institution near UH, St. Louis Junior College, started in 1955, and became four-year Chaminade College in 1957 and Chaminade

University in 1977. Church College of Hawai'i, operated by the Mormon Church on the North Shore of O'ahu from 1955 as a junior college, was upgraded to a four-year institution in 1958, and became a branch of Brigham Young University in 1974. Nondenominational Hawai'i Pacific College opened at downtown Honolulu in 1965, became Hawai'i Pacific University in 1990, and in 1992 absorbed nondenominational Hawai'i Loa College, which had been operating independently at Kailua, O'ahu, from 1965. Although these universities fill important needs in the community, the rest of the chapter will discuss developments within UH, the largest institution of higher learning in the Islands.

In multiethnic Hawai'i, one might expect a multicultural university; that is, admission and enrollment patterns should be diverse, curriculum and research should support multiculturalism, graduation rates should be nondiscriminatory, and employees, especially faculty, should represent diversity. What may be surprising, as documented below, is that UH is one of the least multicultural institutions in the Islands. Alternative explanations abound. Some observers believe that ethnic groups differ in their desire or aptitude for higher education. Others cite institutional racism, that is, barriers to higher education placed in the way of ethnic minorities by UH administrators and faculty.

The analysis below focuses on enrollment disparities, difficulties in encouraging multicultural curriculum and research, lower graduation rates for certain ethnic groups, disinterest in multiculturalism by university administrators, and faculty resistance to diversity. As we shall see, a tradition of legislative intervention and student mobilization, both on behalf of just causes, has moved UH toward greater multiculturalism.

ADMISSION AND ENROLLMENT

Initially, UH enrollment was restricted ethnically (Wist 1940, 168, 210). More than two-thirds of the students were Caucasian, and Chinese constituted the largest minority (Table 12.1a). Considerably more students of Japanese ancestry began to attend UH from the mid-1920s, but Filipino and Native Hawaiian students remained largely outside.

When Hawai'i became a state, the University of Hawai'i enrolled only 7,312 students (including 225 at its branch in Hilo) and granted only 812 undergraduate, 80 master's degrees, and 5 doctorates. Summer enrollment (8,334) exceeded figures for the regular school year. In 1959, Congress approved an appropriation for the establishment of the East-West Center as an autonomous unit within the university,[1] thereby bringing UH into the rank of the top ten universities in amounts of federal funds received. Soon, hundreds of students from Asian and Pacific countries, many with important academic and political connections, were attending the main campus, the University of Hawai'i at Manoa (UHM).

TABLE 12.1
Enrollment at the University of Hawai'i by Ethnic Group, 1915–1994 (in percent)

(a) Manoa Campus

Year	Black	Caucasian	Chinese	Filipino	Hawaiian	Japanese	Korean
1915	NA	84.7	8.3	.7	1.4	3.5	1.4
1918	NA	67.8	16.1	.0	4.2	9.1	1.4
1921	.0	50.0	22.6	.9	7.8	16.1	2.6
1924	NA	47.0	14.6	.7	9.8	25.9	2.1
1927	NA	43.4	14.3	.9	11.5	27.6	1.5
1930	.0	23.0	23.0	1.0	14.0	37.0	2.0
1933	NA	28.0	19.0	.7	11.0	39.0	2.0
1936	NA	23.0	25.0	.5	11.0	35.0	5.0
1939	NA	22.0	23.0	.4	10.0	40.0	4.0
1961	NA	22.1	14.3	2.4	1.4	53.5	1.9
1968	NA	32.0	8.0	1.0	1.0	44.0	NA
1971	.6	31.9	11.2	2.1	3.2	40.7	1.6
1973	NA	32.0	11.0	2.0	4.0	39.0	NA
1978	.4	21.0	9.6	3.0	1.6	31.1	1.4
1981	.6	24.8	11.7	4.1	3.9	35.8	2.1
1984	.7	24.8	13.2	5.2	4.9	35.4	2.6
1987	.6	23.9	12.3	6.3	5.1	33.7	2.7
1990	.8	23.0	11.4	7.9	6.0	29.8	2.8
1992	.9	22.8	12.0	8.7	6.7	27.3	3.0
1994	.8	21.7	12.2	9.4	7.6	25.2	3.5

TABLE 12.1 (*continued*)
(b) Community Colleges

Year	Black	Caucasian	Chinese	Filipino	Hawaiian	Japanese	Korean
1978	1.1	22.4	6.5	12.2	5.0	30.0	1.6
1979	.5	20.3	6.8	12.9	6.1	30.1	1.9
1980	1.2	22.4	6.8	13.1	7.9	29.5	2.0
1981	1.2	22.0	6.9	14.0	10.0	27.8	2.3
1982	1.4	21.8	6.8	14.7	10.6	27.0	2.2
1983	1.3	21.3	6.8	15.4	10.6	27.4	2.3
1984	1.3	21.2	6.9	16.2	10.8	26.9	2.3
1985	1.3	21.9	6.9	16.6	10.5	25.5	2.4
1986	1.3	22.0	6.7	16.7	10.7	25.3	2.5
1987	1.5	22.6	6.4	16.4	10.9	23.4	2.4
1988	1.2	22.5	6.3	16.2	11.2	23.3	2.5
1989	1.4	23.1	6.3	16.0	10.8	22.9	2.6
1990	1.2	22.3	6.0	17.0	12.2	20.5	2.7
1991	1.2	21.9	5.9	17.8	12.9	19.5	2.5
1992	1.1	22.0	5.7	18.1	13.6	18.2	2.5
1993	1.2	20.8	5.6	18.8	14.4	17.1	2.4
1994	1.1	19.6	5.4	19.5	15.5	16.3	2.7

Note: Figures add to 100 percent horizontally when other ethnic groups are added. After spring 1978, figures refer to fall enrollment. "Caucasian" figures include Portuguese and other Caucasians but not Puerto Ricans. Only undergraduates are counted from 1929 to 1939.

Key: NA = not available.

Source: Dannemiller (1973); Gereben (1970b); Gulick (1937, 78); Hawai'i (1915, 60; 1916,a 72; 1918a, 56); Martorana and Hollis (1962, 71); Institutional Research Office, University of Hawai'i; *University of Hawaii Quarterly Bulletin*, 3 (December 1924, 5, 11); *University of Hawaii Quarterly Bulletin*, 6 (January 1927, 13).

With the election of John Burns as governor of Hawai'i in 1962, when the postwar "baby boom" was graduating record numbers of high school students, the state legislature dramatically increased the budget of the university, and the Board of Regents authorized an increase in enrollment at the Manoa campus to 25,000. After reaching a peak attendance in the era of the Vietnam War, enrollment fell somewhat and has leveled off. As of 1996, UHM enrolled 18,232 students; other four-year campuses (Hilo and West Oʻahu) had 3,371 students, and community colleges counted 25,472 students. The out-of-state student quota varies from 10 to 20 percent of total enrollment at the various campuses.

PROGRAMS TO INCREASE STUDENT DIVERSITY

Title VI of the Civil Rights Act of 1964 requires educational institutions receiving federal financial support to provide equal opportunities for all ethnic groups. Accordingly, all universities operating with federal funds are required to make annual counts of enrollment by ethnicity to facilitate civil rights monitoring. When UHM surveyed its attendance profile in the1960s for the first time in decades, the conclusion was that affirmative measures were needed to recruit more Filipino and Native Hawaiian students. Since community colleges were attracting more of a cross section of high school graduates around the state (Table 12.1b), there was clearly no aversion to higher education among any of the ethnic groups.

A principal requirement for admission to the University of Hawaiʻi at Manoa is a minimum score on the Scholastic Aptitude Test (SAT), which is often blamed for skewing ethnic enrollment patterns. The earliest special program aimed at increasing ethnic diversity in UHM enrollment, the College Opportunities Program (COP), began in 1970. COP recruits ethnically disadvantaged students who are denied admission because they have SAT scores just below the minimum and thus have academic potential. COP offers a one-year scholarship, subsidized student housing, a summer orientation program including a basic skills review, college survival techniques after classes begin, and a place to gather together to build a sense of community. Although COP has enjoyed success in recruiting minority students, immigrant students have additional needs. Accordingly, with a small grant from a local church in 1971, Amefil Agbayani developed a program called Operation Manong.[2] Targeting college-bound Filipinos in certain high schools, she paired them with existing UHM Filipino students, in an effort to attract more Filipinos to apply for admission to UHM. In due course, Operation Manong expanded to recruit immigrant Koreans, Samoans, and refugees from Indochina. Other UHM programs operate in collaboration with the Hawaiʻi Department of Education (Haas 1992, Table 6.8b), and several programs in the health and science fields focus on preparation of minorities for entry into the Manoa campus (Haas 1992, Table 6.8c). As a result of these programs and other factors, the percentage of Filipino students at UHM rose from 1.7 to 9.4 percent and Native Hawaiian increased from 3.1 percent to 7.6 percent from 1969 to 1994 (Table 12.1a).

Because the representation of Filipinos and Native Hawaiians has increased only halfway to parity after a quarter century of special programs, several explanations have emerged to account for why Filipinos and Native Hawaiians are well represented at community colleges but not at Manoa. One fact is the tendency of some public high school counselors to steer Caucasian, Chinese, Japanese, and Koreans into UHM, while either discouraging other ethnic groups from taking college-preparatory courses or steering the latter to community colleges (Campos 1991; Agbayani 1994, 9). Secondly, community colleges do not stress preparation of students for Manoa (Astin 1982, 192; Junasa 1982; Okamura 1991, 19–22). A third explanation flows from an analysis of admission criteria, as developers of the SAT admit that the test is biased against minorities (Hanford 1982), and Filipinos and Native Hawaiians indeed disproportionately score lower (Wegner 1978, 37; Cablas 1991). Evidence that Filipinos enrolled at UHM have the lowest SATs but respectable grade point averages (Ikeda, Pun, Torro 1984, 3) suggests that greater weight in admission might be assigned to high school grades. Nevertheless, in 1984 a UHM faculty review committee on admission standards obstinately insisted on maintaining SAT scores as the principal screening criterion. A fourth factor is that parents of Kamehameha Schools graduates insist that their children observe a long tradition of attending certain colleges on the U.S. mainland (Wong 1975). Fifth, Filipinos and Native Hawaiians, who tend to live far from Manoa Valley, find commuting difficult and rental housing expensive near campus (Agbayani 1994, 9). Student housing is available for only 16 percent of students, compared to an average of 47 percent at comparable mainland universities (Sherman 1984).

Some UHM departments and professional schools, comparing the ethnic composition of their students with the state population, have realized that extra efforts are needed to encourage minorities (Hawai'i 1988). Notable among these efforts are programs for education, engineering, law, medical, nursing, psychology, and social work students. The only backlash to these programs has come

TABLE 12.2

Composition of Selected Professions in Hawai'i by Ethnic Group,
1920–1991 (in percent)

(a) Elementary and Secondary Educators, 1980–1990

Year	Black	Caucasian	Chinese	Filipino	Hawaiian	Japanese	Korean
1980	.8	32.5	8.6	5.9	6.7	45.3	1.5
1990	.8	41.4	7.3	5.2	8.7	39.7	1.0

(b) Engineers, 1980–1990

Year	Black	Caucasian	Chinese	Filipino	Hawaiian	Japanese	Korean
1980	.8	31.4	15.2	2.7	4.8	41.2	1.5
1990	.7	32.5	11.8	4.7	4.0	42.0	1.0

(c) Lawyers, 1970–1991

Year	Black	Caucasian	Chinese	Filipino	Hawaiian	Japanese	Korean
1970	.1	58.0	14.4	1.3	1.3	23.0	2.0
1974	1.0	55.0	15.0	1.0	1.0	24.0	2.0
1991	.3	49.5	14.9	2.6	2.9	27.9	1.7

(d) Physicians Licensed, Living in Hawai'i, 1920–1989

Year	Black	Caucasian	Chinese	Filipino	Hawaiian	Japanese	Korean
1920	NA	64.7	2.6	.0	1.3	30.7	NA
1965	.0	49.4	19.9	2.5	1.4	24.5	2.2
1966	.0	49.0	19.8	2.7	1.4	24.1	2.1
1967	.0	49.8	19.7	2.6	1.7	23.7	2.1
1968	.0	49.9	19.6	2.8	1.6	23.6	2.1
1970	.0	51.2	19.0	2.6	1.3	23.0	2.0
1971	.0	53.4	18.0	2.6	1.3	21.4	2.1
1973	.0	54.6	16.0	3.2	1.2	20.7	2.1
1974	.0	49.6	15.6	3.7	1.1	20.1	2.0
1975	.0	46.7	14.8	3.7	1.1	18.8	1.9
1976	.0	42.4	13.6	3.4	1.0	17.2	1.7
1978	.0	33.6	12.4	3.1	.8	14.2	1.6
1989	--	49.7	18.6	4.2	1.3	23.9	1.2

Key: NA = not available; — = more than 0 percent but less than 1 percent.

Note: Figures report percentages of persons employed in each profession by ethnic group and add to 100 percent horizontally when other ethnic groups are included. Many Caucasians have declined to state an ethnic identification in recent years.

Source: Hirata (1971, 54); Hawai'i (1964, 1; 1965, 1; 1966, 1; 1967, 1; 1968, 1 ; 1969, 1; 1970b, 4; 1971, 7; 1972, 6; 1973, 8; 1974, 8; 1975, 8; 1978, 7); Hawai'i State Bar Association (1991); Hawai'i Medical Association (1990); Vernon Kim; U.S. census (1923, 1278; 1980, 44, 67, 71; 1993, 60, 130–31).

from a *haole* male who was denied admission by the Law School; in *Knowles v University of Hawai'i* (1993), he lost due to lack of evidence.

Nevertheless, most special programs for minorities have been financed too modestly to produce an increase in representation, reflecting lesser administrative support than needed to achieve greater parity. The only success stories appear to be considerably more Native Hawaiian lawyers and somewhat more Filipino engineers and Native Hawaiian schoolteachers, but the field of medicine seems unaffected by decades of special programs for minorities (Table 12.2). Most college and professional school deans, in short, have paid little attention to the need for greater student diversity, and the higher administration has rarely demonstrated interest.

CURRICULUM AND RESEARCH

Multicultural instruction existed from the beginning. A year of world history has long been a requirement; currently, the course devotes as much as 40 percent of the content to African, Asian, Hispanic, Native American, and Polynesian civilizations. Most students attend classes in the daytime, work in the afternoons, and study at home in the evening, so campus events are not well attended, and student activism on issues of diversity is infrequent.

Research on ethnic relations in Hawai'i was an important focus in the early years of the Department of Sociology, which launched a journal, *Social Process in Hawaii*, to record social practices unique to the Islands. World-famous sociologist Robert Ezra Park visited and taught at the university in the 1920s. From his experience in the Islands, Park (1928, 196) developed the theoretical model of an integrated society that swept the imagination of leading thinkers in the United States, ultimately resulting in the landmark Supreme Court decision in 1954, *Brown v Board of Education of Topeka* (347SpCt483), which declared an end to segregated schooling.

The bombing of Pearl Harbor on December 7, 1941, was particularly agonizing for Japanese Americans, whose allegiance was suspect, though they had unquestioned loyalty to the United States. To prove their patriotism, *Nisei* (second-generation Japanese American) students at UH formed the Varsity Victory Volunteers (VVV) in February 1942 and proceeded to assist the war effort, establishing thereby a tradition of student solidarity and activism for just causes. The VVV so impressed Washington that a change in national policy occurred: from January 1943, Japanese Americans throughout the country were allowed to serve in combat during the war. Many UH students did so and compiled an unparalleled record of heroism.

By the late 1960s, Ethnic Studies departments had sprouted at universities around the United States. In 1970, with pressure from the state legislature,[3] UH President Harlan Cleveland appointed a committee of all-Caucasian faculty to plan such a program (Gladwin 1972). Since the composition of the committee occasioned a student protest, a temporary faculty hire, African American English Bradshaw, was named director of the new Ethnic Studies Program in 1971. Meanwhile, Fijian James Anthony, an outspoken former UHM student, who had just completed a Ph.D. at Australian National University, returned to Hawai'i as a part-time member of the program. When the program faculty asked to have Anthony reappointed full-time for the following year, Cleveland blocked his appointment.[4] When Bradshaw supported Anthony, he was fired. Arts and Sciences Dean David Contois then named Dennis Ogawa, an instructor in the program, as the new director. When Ogawa backed the discharge of Anthony, he came under attack from faculty and students, and the future of the program itself appeared in doubt. Contois then appointed an all-*haole ad hoc* committee to make recommendations on the future of the program. Contois's action led to a student sit-in, supported by a few faculty, a campus petition for Ogawa's resignation, successful administrative pressure on *haole* faculty to withdraw their names from the petition, and Ogawa's eventual resignation to accept a position to teach in the Department of American Studies. Ethnic Studies faculty were all probationary, because the Board of Regents had not approved the program on a permanent basis, and the program lost about half its positions and barely survived during budgetary cutbacks in the mid-1970s. As a result, the program lacked sufficient numbers to develop a coherent baccalaureate program, though Ethnic Studies courses had high enrollment.

Yet another episode underscores the cultural insensitivity of the era. In 1974, a UHM administration-appointed faculty committee recommended that the newly constructed social science building should be named after Stanley Porteus, a psychology professor hired in the 1920s who accepted stereotypes of plantation supervisors as scientific evidence of the inferiority of most non-*haoles* (Porteus and Babcock 1926). When the Board of Regents accepted the recommendation, faculty and student protests arose. After the Board of Regents agreed to hold a public hearing on the matter (Steinberg, Johnson, Cahill 1975), they announced that the naming of the building was irrevocable, and campus protests petered out. The name Porteus Hall remains to this day, and the episode has been long forgotten.

From the mid-1970s to the mid-1980s, the university was led by two presidents whose fields of specializations were engineering. Wallace Fujiyama, a member of the Board of Regents, occasionally railed against alleged misconduct by the predominantly *haole* faculty, morale dropped, and enthusiasm regarding issues of diversity and multiculturalism evaporated. Meanwhile, administrators and faculty developed about a dozen special-curricular programs with federal and state funds to assist minorities in the fields of biomedical science, education, law, library science, and natural sciences, though with little awareness that despite these programs the ethnic composition of the professional workforce in the state remained virtually unchanged in these fields (Table 12.2).

After the election of Governor John Waihe'e in 1986, attention to multiculturalism skyrocketed. Most dramatically, faculty positions were gradually restored to the Ethnic Studies Program, and the program was granted departmental status in 1995.

Although an emphasis on Asian studies began early, and a short-lived Oriental Institute began in 1935, Native Hawaiian studies were almost nonexistent until the 1970s. Over the years, scholars specializing in various regions in Asia and the Pacific formed study committees. In 1987, the study committees were promoted to the status of centers within the new School of Hawaiian, Asian, and Pacific Studies (SHAPS), which then created the degree-granting Center for Hawaiian Studies.

During the Waihe'e years, the university began to support research on ethnic relations once again. In 1987, the Center for Studies of Multicultural Higher Education opened as a locus for institutional research on problems of ethnic relations at the university. In 1991, the Social Science Research Institute decided to allot some of its overhead resources in order to sponsor a Center for Research on Ethnic Relations, which formed to study why ethnic relations in Hawai'i are relatively harmonious as well as to identify ethnic problems that threaten to tear that harmony asunder because they have not been satisfactorily addressed. Lacking the commitment of staff that was earlier provided to the Romanzo Adams Laboratory, the Center co-directors were required to apply for external funds, but mainland foundations and Washington government agencies were uninterested in state-of-the-art research proposals from Hawai'i, and the Center languished until awarded a grant by the Black Foundation to produce this book.

STUDENT RETENTION AND GRADUATION

Statistics have long showed that some minorities drop out of UHM before graduation (Table 12.3). In the Waihe'e era, several task forces were formed to prepare reports outlining problems to be addressed. One study, entitled "A Study to Improve Access to Public Higher Education Programs and Support Services for Minority Students" (University of Hawai'i 1986b), was a response to a legislative request. A second report, by the UH Task Force on Hawaiian Studies (University of Hawai'i 1986a), recommended a Hawaiian Studies Center. Other task forces have identified problems of Filipinos (University of Hawai'i 1988), Indochinese (Sananikone 1991), African Americans (Takara 1992), and Samoans (Agbayani 1994). No reports have yet been issued for Native Americans or Hispanics.

Among the problems identified in these reports, one of the most serious findings was that Native Hawaiian students disproportionately receive lower grades and drop out at a higher rate than students of most other ethnic backgrounds (Table 12.3; Ikeda, Pun, Torro 1984, 7; Okamura 1991, 8). Counseling and tutorial programs, provided at the medical school through the Kulia Program from 1970, thus seemed warranted. Accordingly, tutorial programs for students in psychology and social work began in 1986, and English and mathematics followed suit in 1987, but other disciplines did not express interest. In 1988, Kua'ana Student Services was set up to provide academic counseling for Native Hawaiians.

Other problem areas were also identified in various related reports. White professors often give extra credit for articulate class participation, unaware that they are penalizing non-Caucasian students who might excel in written work yet believe that it would be rude to express an unusual opinion in class (Chattergy 1992, 5). More

TABLE 12.3

Student Performance at the University of Hawai'i at Manoa by Ethnic Group, 1988–1989 (in percent)

(a) Course Completion Rate

Year	Black	Caucasian	Chinese	Filipino	Hawaiian	Japanese	Korean
1988	93	92	95	91	87	94	89
1989	87	93	95	94	92	95	94

(b) Grade Point Average

Year	Black	Caucasian	Chinese	Filipino	Hawaiian	Japanese	Korean
1988	2.56	2.86	2.92	2.64	2.58	2.81	2.56
1989	2.54	2.89	2.90	2.74	2.70	2.87	2.85

(c) Freshmen Completing Baccalaureate Degrees Within Five Years

Year	Black	Caucasian	Chinese	Filipino	Hawaiian	Japanese	Korean
1988	50.0	33.9	55.0	36.1	28.2	50.6	37.5
1989	10.3	31.1	54.1	40.0	32.0	46.8	38.6

Source: National Center for Higher Education Management Systems (1991).

innovative instructors have discovered that Native Hawaiian students do better when the classroom environment is aligned with values of peer cooperation and teacher-learner apprenticeship rather than competition (Sing 1986).

Filipinos, who also have a low rate of college completion, drop out for lack of finances, not poor grades (UH Task Force on Filipinos 1988). Although scholarships exist for minorities in biomedical fields, education, and library studies, Filipinos receive UHM financial aid at rates substantially below other ethnic groups (Okamura 1992, 6). There is a Native Hawaiian Scholarship Program, but no parallel scholarship opportunities exist for other ethnic groups in need. Finally, two reports indicated that Indochinese and Samoans were alike in disproportionately dropping out not only for financial reasons but also because campus support services in their languages are inadequate (Sananikone 1991; Agbayani 1994, 9).

UNIVERSITY GOVERNANCE

The Board of Regents, appointed by the governor to be the supreme authority of UH, sets general policy, leaving the university administration to operate daily affairs without undue overt interference, though in recent years with a majority of Japanese appointees that have been accused by former Vice President David Yount (1996, 118) of interfering in the autonomy of the university. Unlike the elective Board of Education, which governs public schools, the Regents have never established a committee or task force to deal with minority affairs. Instead, Regents have been accused of privately intervening to insist upon the employment of aging well-connected "old boys" from earlier political eras (Yount 1996, chap. 5). Patterns of governance change with management styles of the UH president, and progress in diversity is generally associated with a more open style. Currently, however, UH President Mortimer is noted for a closed management style; that is, he consults with few subordinates and works on only one issue at a time (Yount 1996, 349–60).

Although degree programs are reviewed by faculty every five years, they seldom focus on problems of unequal educational opportunity. The UHM administration, which is predominantly but decreasingly *haole* (Table 12.4), has never developed a plan to achieve equal educational opportunity for minorities. The higher administration, which often seeks to protect UH autonomy from political pressure (Yount 1996), leaves the task of promoting ethnic equality mostly to deans, most of whom ignore the plight of Filipinos, Native Hawaiians, Samoans, and other less-advantaged groups. Instead, many complacently consider UHM to be a university more diverse than any they have previously encountered.

The burden of addressing problems of minority students, therefore, has fallen on the Special Student Services program, the Center for Hawaiian Studies, the College Opportunities Program, Operation Manong, and on students themselves. Academic advisers within instructional departments have rarely taken advantage of workshops on how to service the needs of minority students that have been provided by some administrative units. From 1988, new faculty received such an orientation from the Center for Studies of Multicultural Higher Education, but that unit was abolished in 1995.

TABLE 12.4
University of Hawai'i Administrators by Ethnic Group, 1908–1995
(in percent)

(a) Manoa Campus

Year	Black	Caucasian	Chinese	Filipino	Hawaiian	Japanese	Korean
1908	.0	100.0	.0	.0	.0	.0	.0
1950	.0	100.0	.0	.0	.0	.0	.0
1952	.0	95.7	.0	.0	.0	4.3	.0
1953	.0	91.3	.0	.0	.0	8.7	.0
1955	.0	87.0	.0	.0	.0	13.0	.0
1956	.0	88.0	.0	.0	.0	12.0	.0
1958	.0	88.5	.0	.0	.0	11.5	.0
1975	NA	70.9	8.7	.4	.0	17.8	*
1977	NA	70.0	6.6	.9	1.3	19.2	*
1981	NA	67.3	9.8	.5	.5	19.5	*
1983	1.3	71.0	8.9	1.1	.6	16.2	*
1987	1.1	70.7	9.0	1.2	.6	15.6	*
1989	NA	60.6	12.2	.7	1.9	21.9	*
1991	.8	53.5	NA	NA	NA	NA	NA
1993	1.9	56.1	NA	NA	NA	NA	NA
1995	.8	48.0	10.4	1.6	4.0	34.4	*

(b) Community Colleges

Year	Black	Caucasian	Chinese	Filipino	Hawaiian	Japanese	Korean
1975	NA	37.9	9.1	.0	6.1	43.9	*
1984	2.0	32.7	4.1	2.0	6.1	57.1	*
1987	1.6	34.4	3.1	6.3	1.6	51.6	*
1989	NA	47.2	.0	9.0	2.2	51.7	*
1991	1.9	47.1	NA	NA	NA	NA	NA
1993	2.3	37.2	NA	NA	NA	NA	NA
1995	NA	39.6	NA	NA	NA	NA	NA

Note: Figures add to 100 percent horizontally when other ethnic groups are included.
Figures for 1995 include the UH system offices.

Key: NA = not available
* = included with Chinese.

Source: University of Hawai'i affirmative action plans and catalogs.

Lacking leadership from top management, there should be no surprise that problems of faculty racism surfaced in the early 1990s. In 1990, a Caucasian student from Louisiana wrote a letter to the editor of the campus newspaper, expressing outrage that he had been slurred too long by being called a *haole*, which he perceived to be a cussword, in a state that he believed to be excessively race conscious (Carter 1990). The director of the Center for Hawaiian Studies, Haunani-Kay Trask (1990; cf. 1992, 48), replied in the letters column that *haoles* encounter hostility in the Islands because Native Hawaiians have never accepted their colonization and marginalization; moreover, she said, if Carter did not like Hawai'i, he could always return to the mainland. Next, faculty from the UHM Philosophy Department called upon Trask to resign as head of the Center for Hawaiian Studies because her letter allegedly constituted "racial harassment" (Laudan et al. 1990). The three missives led to more letters to the editor, a rally attended principally by students opposed to the temerity of the Philosophy Department, sound bites on evening television news programs, newspaper editorials, and invitations for Trask to speak. She then persuasively made the case that Native Hawaiians awaited justice and that UHM was a hotbed of "institutional racism." In due course, Trask was cleared of charges filed by the Philosophy Department, and the furor died down.

The Hawai'i State Legislature, hoping for athletes that would bring national talent to win sporting events, had long been generous in allocating funds to the university's athletic programs. Most sports administrators were able and levelheaded, but as recently as the mid-1980s some openly referred to African American athletes as "boys" and subjected them to disciplinary action for alleged misconduct without following proper procedures. In 1991, the situation came to a head when athlete Terry Whitaker was peremptorily suspended for participating in an off-campus altercation. Whitaker, told by UHM staff not to disclose to the press that he was part African American, retained David Schutter, a top attorney in the state. In *Whitaker v University of Hawai'i* (1991), Judge Simeon Acoba ordered the university to reinstate Whitaker because he had not received a hearing before the suspension, as prescribed by university regulations. While events in this saga made headlines, the Afro-American Association of Hawaii (1991) and three similar organizations complained that there was a "very disturbing" pattern of discrimination over the years against UHM African American athletes (Associated Press 1991). UH President

Albert Simone then agreed to provide more counseling for African American athletes, to develop fairer and more uniform disciplinary procedures (Tsai 1992), and to commission a study on problems of African American students in general (Takara 1992). In 1995, when an African American athlete complained to the football coach about racial problems that affected team performance, the student was summarily dismissed from the team, but the coach was soon fired due to poor team performance, the athlete was reinstated, and racial tensions appeared to subside.

PROBLEMS OF FACULTY DIVERSITY

While the few administrative efforts to cope with problems posed by UH's multiethnic student body are easily documented, faculty initiatives have lagged far behind. One reason for faculty indifference to the needs of local students is that the ethnic composition of UHM instructors consists overwhelmingly of mainland-born Caucasians (Table 12.5). Often, new faculty positions emerge because academic stars leave for more lucrative employment elsewhere, so academic departments want to maintain national reputations by hiring the best qualified from a pool of applicants after nationwide recruitment through professional association contacts. However, when Hawai'i-born applicants lack nationwide reputations through extensive publications in professional journals, their qualifications are evaluated negatively. Politically well-connected friends, unaware of the selection criteria, are displeased when UHM fills openings with either mainland *haoles* or Asians from Asia rather than those born in Hawai'i.

Most *haole* faculty, however, believe that UHM, with nearly 30 percent Asian professors, has the most diverse faculty in the United States (Kaser 1990). Transplanted from the U.S. mainland, faculty tend to form all-*haole* cliques in many academic units, which operate as if they were British clubs in a foreign country, and instances of open racial harassment of students by faculty sometimes occur in class (Hippensteele and Chesney-Lind 1995). However, if the university responded to public pressure to hire substantially fewer Caucasians, federal guidelines about nondiscriminatory hiring might support lawsuits from faculty applicants for discrimination based on race.[5] Instead of confronting the issues more creatively, UH administrators

TABLE 12.5

University of Hawai'i Faculty by Ethnic Group, 1908–1995 (in percent)

(a) Manoa Campus

Year	Black	Caucasian	Chinese	Filipino	Hawaiian	Japanese	Korean
1908	.0	100.0	.0	.0	.0	.0	.0
1920	.0	100.0	.0	.0	.0	.0	.0
1921	.0	94.0	3.0	.0	.0	3.0	.0
1930	.0	91.8	4.8	.0	.0	4.8	.0
1940	.0	89.3	6.1	.0	.0	3.1	1.5
1950	.0	88.0	4.7	.0	1.9	5.1	.3
1960	.1	82.7	4.6	.1	1.2	11.0	.3
1975	NA	72.1	9.3	1.0	1.4	14.7	*
1977	NA	70.4	10.0	.8	1.2	14.8	*
1979	NA	70.0	8.9	1.8	2.0	16.3	*
1981	NA	70.9	9.2	.7	1.3	15.5	*
1983	.2	73.8	8.9	.8	1.4	14.7	*
1985	.3	70.8	9.6	1.0	1.6	14.4	*
1987	.3	71.8	9.2	1.1	1.6	13.8	*
1989	.5	71.3	9.2	1.2	1.8	14.0	*
1991	.2	66.9	NA	NA	NA	NA	NA
1993	.3	69.6	9.6	1.0	1.9	12.9	*
1995	.3	69.3	10.5	1.0	1.8	12.6	*

(b) Community Colleges

Year	Black	Caucasian	Chinese	Filipino	Hawaiian	Japanese	Korean
1975	NA	50.5	8.7	2.0	3.8	32.	*
1983	NA	53.8	10.9	3.2	4.9	28.3	*
1984	.0%	51.9	8.9	3.6	5.0	30.1	*
1987	.0	45.4	10.1	2.6	5.7	29.5	*
1989	NA	47.6	9.5	2.8	5.5	30.0	*
1991	.2	53.5	NA	NA	NA	NA	NA
1993	.2	55.6	NA	NA	NA	NA	NA
1995	4.5	63.6	NA	NA	NA	NA	NA

Note: Figures add to 100 percent horizontally when other ethnic groups are included.

Key: NA = not available;

* * = included with Chinese.

Source: University of Hawai'i affirmative action plans and catalogs.

have failed to develop a coherent policy regarding ethnic employment patterns.

There is some background to the tendency for *haole* faculty to exclude certain minorities from their ranks. In 1967, during the height of American participation in the civil war in Vietnam, UH President Thomas Hamilton decided to turn down the application of political scientist Oliver Lee, a visible antiwar critic, for a tenured appointment. Lee's Chinese appearance doubtless added to the resonance with local students.[6] During the following year student support was mobilized, including an eleven-day sit-in the administration building, resulting in the eventual resignation of Hamilton and the later reinstatement of Lee. As in the case of the Ethnic Studies Program, local students enjoyed a key role in reversing arbitrary action by *haole* authorities.

Although instances of ethnic discrimination against UH faculty based on race might have led to court action over the years, the first important employment discrimination case emerged in 1972. Joan Abramson (1975), a UHM English instructor, filed a sex discrimination complaint with the U.S. Department of Labor. Since UH President Cleveland had merely issued a brief equal opportunity policy statement in 1971, federal authorities responded to Abramson's complaint by asking the university to develop a comprehensive affirmative action plan. Cleveland placed a *haole* male in charge of affirmative action and proceeded slowly. Abramson was then reinstated with an increase in pay, but soon she was fired again by the university in apparent retaliation for complaining. Failing to mobilize student support on her behalf, she undertook costly litigation for the next six years, ultimately receiving a cash settlement (Glauberman 1979).

In December 1972, several UHM female faculty members filed a class-action complaint, alleging inequality in pay, promotions, tenure, and many other issues, with the U.S. Department of Health, Education, and Welfare (HEW). After an investigation in 1973, HEW insisted on a more extensive UHM affirmative action plan. In 1974, when UHM assembled data and drafted a new plan, HEW indicated that neither plan was adequate to answer the charges. Therefore, HEW suspended UHM federal contracts in 1975 until administrators agreed to present a more thorough analysis of recruitment, selection, placement/assignment, promotion, tenure, transfer/reassignment, fringe benefits, training, separation/termination, and rates of pay to identify discrepancies based on ethnicity and sex. By 1976, when a salary analysis resulted in back pay for a dozen or so female faculty members, UHM reported several underutilized ethnic groups. Statistics revealed that most UHM faculty and administrators were Caucasians, but clerical and other civil service personnel were primarily non-Caucasians (Table 12.6): blacks were underrepresented in most positions; Caucasians and Chinese were underutilized in clerical and blue-collar jobs; Filipinos, in clerical, skilled labor, and professional work; and Japanese, in custodial and technical positions. UHM officials then contacted the state civil service to urge a more diverse pool of civil service applicants, and HEW inexplicably closed the case regarding ethnic employment patterns. Student pressure was again absent on the matter.

TABLE 12.6
University of Hawai'i at Manoa Civil Service Personnel by Ethnic Group, 1975–1995 (in percent)

Year	Black	Caucasian	Chinese	Filipino	Hawaiian	Japanese	Korean
1975	.3	11.3	7.1	9.3	8.1	55.0	*
1983	.1	8.4	7.0	4.9	8.4	66.2	*
1985	NA	6.7	7.7	4.9	8.4	66.7	*
1987	NA	7.9	7.7	5.4	8.5	63.6	*
1989	NA	7.6	8.0	4.9	9.9	62.9	*
1991	.3	7.1	NA	NA	NA	NA	NA
1993	.6	7.7	NA	NA	NA	NA	NA
1995	.3	7.9	7.7	8.0	10.6	56.7	*

Note: Figures add to 100 percent horizontally when other ethnic groups are included.
Key: NA = not available;
      * = included with Chinese.
Source: University of Hawai'i affirmative action plans.

In 1979, an official newly assigned to the U.S. Department of Labor (USDOL) in Honolulu ruled that the UHM affirmative action plan was negligent in several respects. The statistical analysis was judged inadequate; the plan was faulted because it was not being updated annually and was not disseminated to deans, who, in turn, were not informing department heads of the requirements. Since UHM was the only campus with an affirmative action plan, USDOL mandated all UH campuses to develop acceptable affirmative action plans and then undertook regular monitoring for the first time.

Nevertheless, matters of UHM ethnic and gender balance were relegated to paper compliance. For example, a form was designed in 1983 for all departments requesting to fill vacant positions, and the Equal Employment Opportunity (EEO) officer alerted all hiring units before screening applicants that they would be monitored for conformity to the affirmative action plan. When this pressure resulted in hiring more Caucasian females but not more minorities, the 1984 affirmative action plan identified the source of the problem in seeking greater ethnic diversification as the failure of African Americans and Filipinos to apply. Thus, the plan appeared to blame minorities for their own underrepresentation, contrary to the spirit of affirmative action, which puts the burden of recruiting underutilized minorities on the employer. The 1984 UHM affirmative action plan also noted that policies had been disseminated (though clearly compliance was not adequately monitored) and that the university offered courses for minorities to take to upgrade their skills if they wished (thus irrelevant to minorities with appropriate qualifications). Under USDOL pressure, the university then amended its affirmative action plan to provide that preference would go to underrepresented groups whenever qualifications for applicants were otherwise equal. Rather than an aggressive effort to hire African Americans and Hispanics, the most underrepresented ethnic groups, this directive was instead interpreted to mandate an effort to find some basis, however vague, for claiming that nonminorities were better than minorities. Students, as before, were deprived of an exposure to the intellectual vitality of African American and Hispanic scholars.

In 1985, comprehensive guidelines for nondiscrimination in recruitment were disseminated throughout UHM, and forms to monitor how well each job applicant satisfied stated criteria were disseminated to hiring units for the first time. At the same time, the campus EEO officer, who previously held a temporary appointment, was then given a permanent assignment with civil service protection, but the task of monitoring employment decisions was transferred from the EEO officer to deans and directors, who in turn lacked resources to carry out affirmative action responsibilities. Although some deans were progressive, others ignored the need to hire minority faculty. When some minority faculty were hired, as Haunani-Kay Trask (1992) reports in her chilling experience as an assistant professor in American Studies, mistreatment often resulted. She was able to mobilize community and student support behind her persistent critique of the colonial status of Native Hawaiians, and she left American Studies to join the new Center for Hawaiian Studies, but more timid female and minority faculty continued to suffer from discrimination.

In 1990, the U.S. Department of Education cited inadequacies in the university's complaint procedures regarding the handicapped and victims of sexual harassment. In the following year, an accreditation team from the Western Association of Schools and Colleges (1991) noted a lack of standardization in personnel selection procedure as well as a failure in affirmative action. Asked to study UHM employment patterns, the state legislative auditor's office noted that the proportion of minorities on the payroll of UHM had declined from 29 to 28 percent from 1979 to 1989, Filipinos and Native Hawaiians were considered the most underutilized, and staff resources committed to affirmative action were deemed inadequate (Sue 1991). Also in 1991, one judge found the university insensitive to issues of sexual harassment (*Austen v Hawai'i*), whereas another pointed out procedural irregularities in the failure to hire Maivan Lam, a Vietnamese-French instructor, to administer a program at the law school (*Lam v University of Hawai'i*). Although some student support for Lam emerged, she left the Islands to pursue a Ph.D. degree elsewhere and later lost her day in court.

With employment issues in the forefront, the university administration decided to study problems of discrimination more systematically. Two studies revealed that minorities and women were disproportionately denied tenure, received lower pay, and got promotions a few years later on the average than Caucasian males (Ikeda and Johnsrud 1991, 1993), while other studies documented reasons why females tended to be denied promotions and tenure and then left the university in disgust (Johnsrud and Atwater 1991; Johnsrud and Sadao 1993; Johnsrud and Des Jarlais 1994). The chief reason cited for discrimination was intellectual and social isolation, that is, the tendency for monoethnic male departmental in-groups to snub ethnic out-groups and females, professionally and socially, and then to discount their academic performance. A procedure was established for a few female and minority faculty to obtain back pay in cases where departments could not justify paying them less than nonminority male counterparts, but amounts of increased salary were small. Student pressure to eliminate unequal treatment of individual female and minority faculty was absent on this issue.

One problem noted in the 1992 report on the status of African Americans at the University of Hawai'i was an almost total absence of African American faculty members (Takara 1992). Moreover, marginalization of minority faculty is well summarized by the fact that no Filipino or Native Hawaiian instructor has ever received an award for community service or research, though a Vietnamese faculty member received a "best community service" award in 1982. The first "best teacher" award went to a Native Hawaiian in 1989, the first Filipino received this Board of Regents award in 1993, and the only African American faculty member on campus was honored for teaching excellence in 1996. Most awards have gone to Caucasians, Chinese, and Japanese faculty over the years.

In 1995, newly elected Governor Ben Cayetano asked all agencies of state government to cut costs. UH was required to reduce expenditures by about 20 percent in two years. All part-time instructors, including Asian and Pacific language faculty, were pink-slipped, though a social science department was allowed to hire an expert on Turkey. Native Hawaiian students and supporters soon mobilized in the spring to have funds restored so that they could learn Hawaiian, and the university administration caved in after a half-day sit-in. In the fall, a one-day sit-in reversed administration budget allocations that had limited access to the campus library to five hours per day, only from Monday to Friday. When faculty and students led a march of about 2,000 to the state capitol in the fall to demand fewer budget cuts, however, Cayetano responded by characterizing leaders of the rally as ill mannered. He doubtless knew that Islanders would understand the remark to mean that *haoles*, as if still on the plantations, were trying to dictate state priorities. Later, his press secretary publicly identified a particular *haole* faculty member who hurled obscenities.

CONCLUSION

The University of Hawai'i exists because of the efforts of a Chinese American and thrives in a state supportive of ethnic diversity. Problems of discrimination at the university have long existed, largely due to an inability to pinpoint complex issues. The legislature, which created UH, has intervened creatively to mandate new academic programs, but the

Board of Regents has largely been asleep on these issues. Administrative efforts to achieve greater diversity have been present, but the effects have had little impact. Most faculty are unaware of the scope of campus problems relating to ethnic discrimination because few are interested.

Student efforts to overcome injustice, albeit rare, have been overwhelmingly successful. The issues that mobilize students have been clear and narrow, and student demonstrators have been extremely well behaved. Violence and name-calling have generally been avoided on both sides. Showing dignity on behalf of just causes, students have won victories from the university administration, which has often agreed to specific demands. In contrast, the student newspaper on campus focuses on sensational issues but fails to press the university on the more insidious yet pervasive problems of institutional racism.

The University of Hawai'i operates in the context of Asian and Native Hawaiian cultures, which stress cooperation, respect for others, and a tendency to focus on specific problems rather than on confrontational expressions of contempt and protests for abstract reforms (Haas 1989a, chap. 1; 1989b, chap. 1). White faculty, generally unassimilated upon arrival in the Islands, pose significant problems to students but are not held accountable on a systematic basis. Administrators fail to exercise clear leadership on matters of ethnic justice, but they make concessions in response to well-organized but respectful student protests. Institutional racism remains, as elsewhere, but does not produce malaise. Multiculturalism advances because some units of the university are progressive, but serious coordination and monitoring are absent. Complacency reigns among most administrators and faculty, but the legislature and the student body have done much to enable the university to increase multiculturalism on campus.

NOTES

1. In 1975, the East-West Center became a nonprofit corporation (The Center for Cultural and Technical Interchange Between East and West, Inc.), independent of the University of Hawai'i. Most East-West Center funds have come from congressional appropriations, though these have declined considerably in recent years. The Center also receives donations from private and public sources, domestic and foreign.

2. The Filipino word *manong* means older brother. Although the word connotes respect in the Philippines, the colloquial use in Hawai'i is derogatory. One aim of Operation Manong is to reverse the pejorative connotation of the word and thus to counteract some of the negative stereotyping of Filipinos in Hawai'i.

3. The state legislature also mandated such university initiatives as the Hawai'i Research Center for Future Studies and the Filipino Studies Program (later retitled the Center for Philippine Studies), both in 1972, and the Center for Labor Education and Research and the Center for Oral History in 1976.

4. Anthony then sued Cleveland and received a cash settlement.

5. In 1979, the former federal Office of Revenue Sharing hinted that there was no merit to any allegation of discrimination by Caucasian UHM faculty based on statistics of underrepresentation in comparison with ethnic percentages at comparable universities on the U.S. mainland. UH has more instruction on Asia and the Pacific than any other university in the United States, and a large percentage of appropriately qualified Asians and Pacific Islanders fill these positions.

6. Oliver Lee's father was Chinese, his mother German.

CHAPTER 13

Crime and Justice

A. Didrick Castberg

INTRODUCTION

Crime and justice in Hawai'i are closely related to the multicultural nature of the state. The various ethnic groups making up the Islands' population are not proportionately represented in the state's criminal justice system, ranging from police officers to convicted felons. Determining why this is the case is difficult at best, for while discrimination in hiring, arrest, conviction, and sentencing might seem a reasonable hypothesis, there is little evidence to suggest that any such explanation is plausible. On the mainland, Caucasians constitute a majority of the population and a majority of those employed in most criminal justice systems, while "minorities" are disproportionately represented among the arrested, convicted, and sentenced. In Hawai'i, there is no majority racial or ethnic group, and the representation of ethnic groups in the criminal justice system is quite complex. Despite this complexity and lack of clear explanations for ethnic disparities, several hypotheses are suggested below.

Are certain ethnic groups arrested and convicted for some offenses but not others? Are the various ethnic groups, even though disproportionately represented among criminal justice professionals (judges, police, and prosecutors), sufficiently represented to ensure nondiscrimination? Finally, are strictly legal criteria the major factors in criminal justice decision-making?

One might expect, according to traditional criminological theory, that those with the highest family income, and therefore the highest socioeconomic status, would be disproportionately represented in the legal profession, while those at the bottom would be disproportionately represented in the prison population. One might also expect those of high status to have a certain amount of prejudice toward those of lower status, which might result in discrimination that would have the effect of disproportionately representing lower-status groups in the prison population. These propositions will be examined below.

DISCRIMINATION AND THE CRIMINAL PROCESS

Let us briefly examine the criminal justice process. Arrest decisions may be made by a police officer who observes a crime being committed or who has probable cause to believe a crime has been committed. Alternatively, a grand jury may issue an indictment after having been presented with evidence by a prosecutor. While some data suggest that arrest decisions by police officers on the mainland may be based to some extent on ethnic or racial factors (Kappeler et al. 1994), no studies to date have documented such discrimination in Hawai'i. Ethnicity may play a role in arrest decisions in the Islands, as the disproportionate crime rate of certain ethnic groups is well known by police officers, and that knowledge is likely to result in increased attention being paid to such groups due to their perceived criminality. Prosecutors and grand juries, on the other hand, are much less likely to take ethnicity into account when seeking an indictment, as they may neither know the ethnicity of the defendant nor have any personal interest in those whom they may indict.

Should plea bargaining[1] occur, however, ethnicity might affect a prosecutor's willingness to be generous, either with respect to the defendant or the defense attorney, but no evidence supports such a proposition to date. Instead, personal factors are most likely to affect plea decisions, notably the attitude of the defendant and prior working relationships between a defense counsel and a prosecutor. In the unlikely event that a case goes to trial, a judge's ethnic bias could affect legal decisions, including rulings on motions, findings of guilt (in bench trials), and sentencing.

ETHNICITY AND CRIME

Although Caucasians, Chinese, Filipinos, Japanese, Koreans, and Native Hawaiians may be considered the "major" groups in Hawai'i, other groups are represented in the criminal justice system, including Hispanics other than Puerto Ricans, Pacific Islanders other than Native Hawaiians, and Vietnamese. As increasing numbers of these groups take up residence in the state, their presence in criminal justice statistics becomes noticeable. Ethnically based youth gangs in Honolulu, for example, have been involved in numerous acts of violence (Table 13.1).

TABLE 13.1
Ethnic Representation in Hawai'i's Youth Gangs, 1988 (in percent)

Ethnic Group	Gang Members
Filipino	44
Samoan	26
Hawaiian/Part Hawaiian	13
Vietnamese	1
Japanese/Chinese/Korean	1
Other	15
Total	100

Source: Chesney-Lind et al. (1992, 17).

Mexicans, some of whom may have immigrated illegally, are increasingly being arrested for drug offenses. The ethnic makeup of criminals is, therefore, changing over time. Comparing the ethnicities of offenders in the 1960s with those in the 1990s, we find some differences, with the appearance of new ethnic groups (Mexicans, Vietnamese), as well as increases in the percentages of arrests of Caucasians, Native Hawaiians, and Samoans (Hawai'i 1977a; Hawai'i 1995). Unfortunately for research purposes, official figures on arrests and dispositions lump these new ethnic groups into the "other" category.

Notable also is the greater ethnic diversity found among the state's judges, police officers, and prosecutors. Increasing diversity is reflected in the changing ethnic composition of the Hawai'i bar (Table 13.2).

TABLE 13.2
Ethnic Composition of the Hawai'i Bar, 1974 and 1992 (in percent)

Year	Black	Caucasian	Chinese	Filipino	Hawaiian	Japanese	Korean
1974	1.0	55.0	15.0	1.0	1.0	26.0	2.0
1992	.3	43.7	10.8	2.7	8.7	27.1	1.7

Source: Haas (1992, 103).

Historically, judges in the Islands came primarily from Caucasian, Chinese, and Japanese ethnic groups, whereas today there are increasing numbers of Filipinos, Koreans, Native Hawaiians, and those of mixed heritage (Table 13.3). Although no official figures are available on the ethnic composition of the Hawai'i judiciary, observations based on family names and photographs, as found in annual reports of the judiciary, indicate an increasingly diverse bench. The Hawai'i Supreme Court in 1971, for example, was composed of five males, including one Caucasian, three Japanese, and one Native Hawaiian. In 1996, the Court was composed of one woman of Japanese ancestry, and one man each of Caucasian, Filipino, Korean, and Native Hawaiian ancestry. In 1971, almost all Circuit Court[2] judges were Caucasian, Chinese, or Japanese men, with only two of the fourteen of Filipino ancestry, and only one Caucasian woman. In 1996, there were two judges with Filipino names and eight female judges, but the total number of Circuit Court judges (excluding those assigned to family court) has risen to twenty-seven, thereby reducing the percentage of Filipino judges somewhat. Caucasians and Japanese continue to dominate the Circuit Courts, but their relative rankings have reversed.

TABLE 13.3
Ethnic Composition of Hawai'i's Highest Courts, 1971 and 1996

(a) Supreme Court

Year	Caucasian	Chinese	Filipino	Hawaiian	Japanese	Korean
1971	1 (20.0)	0 (0.0)	0 (0.0)	1 (20.0)	3 (60.0)	0 (0.0)
1996	1 (20.0)	0 (0.0)	1 (20.0)	1 (20.0)	1 (20.0)	1 (20.0)

(b) Circuit Court

Year	Caucasian	Chinese	Filipino	Hawaiian	Japanese	Korean
1971	2 (14.3)	2 (14.3)	2 (14.3)	2 (14.3)	6 (42.9)	0 (0.0)
1996	10 (45.5)	3 (13.4)	2 (9.1	1 (4.5	5 (22.7)	1 (4.5)

Note: Parenthesized figures are percentages of the total and sum to 100 percent.
Source: Office of the Administrative Director, Hawai'i Department of the Judiciary.

Prosecutors, which have come from the same ethnic groups as judges historically, now reflect the same diversity as judges. Perhaps both groups are more representative of the current legal community, although it has been clear that the Judicial Selection Commission and present and past governors have made a concerted effort to appoint judges from underrepresented groups, and prosecutors have sought greater diversity in their offices (Haas 1992, 116). Fifty years ago, police departments were made up primarily of Native Hawaiian and Portuguese officers, although the higher administrative positions tended to be held by Caucasians, Chinese, or Japanese. Today, however, one finds much greater diversity at all levels of police work. Although police departments are not representative of Hawai'i's society as a whole, ethnic occupational self-selection may be occurring rather than any discrimination in hiring. Discrimination cannot altogether be discounted, as a Kaua'i police officer won a discrimination case in 1993 against his former department (Kobayashi 1993).

ETHNICITY AND VICTIMIZATION

Are some ethnic groups victimized to a greater extent than others? This is certainly the case on the mainland, where African Americans and Hispanics are more likely to be victimized than Caucasians. As might be expected, the situation in Hawai'i is somewhat more complicated.

Results of a random sample of 3,000 Hawai'i residents, conducted in 1994, shows that there is a wide variation in victimization by ethnicity (Table 13.4). Native Americans, who constitute less than 1 percent of the population, had the highest victimization rate, while Japanese had the lowest. African Americans were the least likely to be victims of violent crime, followed by Japanese. Differences between Native American Indian African and American victimization is striking, but reasons for the disparity are not obvious. Native Hawaiian victimization is second only to that of Native Americans. Socioeconomic status may well explain property crime victimization; generally, the higher the income, the greater the likelihood of being a victim of property crime. There is much less of a relationship, however, between income and violent crime.

TABLE 13.4

Victimization by Ethnicity and Income, 1994 (in percent)

(a) Race/Ethnicity

Ethnic Group	All Crimes	Violent Crime	Property Crime
African American	35.3	5.9	29.4
American Indian	71.4	57.1	71.4
Caucasian	39.0	12.7	34.6
Chinese	41.8	16.5	35.2
Japanese	33.2	6.1	30.5
Filipino	43.8	11.5	38.5
Hawaiian	50.8	17.7	43.8
Korean	40.0	15.0	40.0
Mixed Asian	36.8	15.8	36.8
Other	43.2	10.8	40.5

(b) Income

Income Group	All Crimes	Violent Crime	Property Crime
Under $15,000	31.9	14.3	26.9
$15,000 - $24,999	34.7	9.8	29.9
$25,000 - $34,999	37.1	9.3	32.5
$35,000 - $49,999	42.1	13.4	38.9
$50,000 - $74,999	43.6	12.2	39.9
$75,000 - $99,999	42.4	11.2	39.2
$100,000 +	45.5	13.6	40.0

Source: Hawai'i (1994a, 4–5).

ETHNICITY AND ARRESTS

The greatest disparities for Part I offenses[3] are among the Japanese, with 22.3 percent of the population and 6.3 percent of the arrests, and the African Americans, with 2.5 percent of the population and 4.9 percent of the arrests (Table 13.5). Native Hawaiians and Samoans had a disproportionate number of arrests for almost all categories. The relationships found for Part I offenses also hold true for Part II offenses. Although Filipinos do not have disproportionately high arrest rates in general, they constitute 70.6 percent of those arrested for manufacture or sale and 43.5 percent of those arrested for possession of synthetic narcotics (usually crystal methamphetamine, or "ice"). Filipinos constitute 58.2 percent of those arrested for gambling

TABLE 13.5
Arrests by Ethnicity, 1994 (in percent)

(a) Selected Part I Offenses

Crime	Caucasian	Black	Indian	Chinese	Japanese	Filipino	Hawaiian	Korean	Samoan	Other
Murder	25.9	3.7	.0	3.7	5.6	13.0	27.8	1.9	9.3	9.3
Rape	33.3	10.6	.0	.8	5.7	6.5	22.8	.0	4.1	16.3
Robbery	27.0	5.7	.3	2.9	4.1	4.8	30.8	2.2	9.2	13.0
Assault	31.9	9.3	.0	1.6	3.2	14.1	21.0	2.8	7.3	8.9
Burglary	32.6	2.6	.1	2.1	7.4	11.8	27.4	1.2	3.8	10.9
Larceny	43.0	5.1	.1	2.6	6.6	9.0	18.5	1.2	2.8	10.8
Auto Theft	22.5	3.8	.0	2.5	5.6	14.3	32.3	.9	6.3	11.9
Arson	55.2	3.4	.0	.0	10.3	6.9	20.7	.0	.0	3.4
Total	37.1	4.9	.1	2.4	6.3	10.3	22.4	1.3	4.0	11.0

(b) Part II Offenses

	Caucasian	Black	Indian	Chinese	Japanese	Filipino	Hawaiian	Korean	Samoan	Other
Total	35.3	5.6	.2	1.6	5.9	11.8	22.2	1.7	5.0	10.7

(c) Population

	Caucasian	Black	Indian	Chinese	Japanese	Filipino	Hawaiian	Korean	Samoan	Other
Percent	33.4	2.5	.5	6.2	22.3	15.2	12.5	2.2	1.4	3.8

Source: Hawaii (1993-94, 39; 1995, 104, 106).

(primarily cockfighting). Caucasians are disproportionately arrested for negligent manslaughter (66.7 percent of the arrests), arson (55.2 percent), and prostitution (50.9 percent). African Americans and Koreans also have disproportionately high numbers of arrests for prostitution (2.5 percent of the population with 10.4 percent of the arrests and 1.3 percent of the population with 6.8 percent of the arrests, respectively).

Cultural explanations are suspect, as they inevitably touch on stereotypes. However, Filipinos are more likely to be involved in illegal cockfighting, a sport that is popular in the Philippines. As arrest figures show, Filipinos are also more likely to be involved in the sale and use of crystal methamphetamine because the Philippines is a primary manufacturing center for the drug, with smuggling and distribution working along ethnic lines. Korean prostitution arrests are most likely associated with "Korean Bars," that is, cocktail lounges that feature Korean bar-girls, who offer companionship and sometimes sex to single Korean males who are imported without their families by the fishing industry in Hawai'i. African American arrests are usually of Waikiki streetwalkers, most of whom are from the mainland. Negligent manslaughter is almost always associated with deaths caused by automobile accidents, and most of those are the result of driving under the influence of alcohol (DUI). In 1979, 77.2 percent of the alcoholism clinic admissions were of Caucasians, indicating a possible link between drunk driving, fatal accidents, and negligent manslaughter arrests (Haas 1992, 222). Although official figures do not indicate whether Caucasians arrested for DUI were civilian or military, anecdotal evidence from newspaper articles on fatal automobile accidents involving alcohol would lead one to believe that Caucasian military personnel are disproportionately represented.

What accounts for these disparities? Discrimination or cultural explanations? As noted above, discrimination on the part of law enforcement in Hawai'i is difficult to document, yet there is reason to believe that the same process at work on the mainland also operates in the Islands: certain identifiable groups, almost always based on ethnicity, are perceived as less law-abiding than others and are therefore given more attention by police. Are these perceptions accurate, or are they self-fulfilling prophesies? The answer depends to a large extent on whether the arrests are valid arrests, and one way to measure discrimination is to find disparities from arrests to prosecutions and convictions.

ETHNICITY AND PROSECUTION

One study found a relationship between race/ethnicity and arrests for some offenses, but it found none with respect to the charging decision by the prosecutor or the sentence by the judge (Hawai'i 1982, 16–17, 55). Yet the fact that 99 percent of all cases referred to the prosecutor's office by the police result in charges (ibid., 16–17) suggests that any discrimination at the arrest stage could well be continued at the charging stage. Given the virtually unchecked power of the prosecutor to charge (or not charge), there is certainly an opportunity for decisions to be made on the basis of extralegal criteria. The study did not find a relationship between prior convictions and age, employment and marital status, and gender; instead, the data showed that the arrest charge and a person's prior criminal history are much better predictors of being charged than personal characteristics, even though personal characteristics other than race and ethnicity do have an effect on the charging decision (ibid., 55). Why these personal characteristics affect charging is not known, and it is beyond the scope of this chapter to discuss these characteristics, inasmuch as race/ethnicity is not among them. Similar studies of the criminal process on the mainland have found that race is not a factor in prosecutorial decision-making (Eisenstein and Jacob 1977, 284).

Given the diversity of the arrestee population and prosecutors' offices, the likelihood of systematic discrimination against any one ethnic group is quite small. While a Caucasian prosecutor might seek more serious charges against Filipino defendants, for example, a Filipino prosecutor might be less lenient with Caucasian defendants. For such discriminatory charging to have any effect, the defense attorney either would have to be incompetent or equally prejudiced, as overcharging can be easily dealt with by opting for trial. A much more likely explanation of the relationship between personal characteristics and charging decisions involves legal criteria that are associated with personal characteristics but which cannot be isolated in research designs.

ETHNICITY AND ADJUDICATION

Nationwide, only a small percentage of criminal cases go to trial. About
90 percent of defendants plead guilty, usually after plea bargaining. In
the 1982 study, only 179 of the 6,747 Part I arrests resulted in felony
trials (Hawai'i 1982). Most trials are jury trials; few defendants opt for
a bench (judge only) trial. The role of the judge in a criminal case, then,
depends upon a number of factors. With respect to guilty pleas, the
judge's sole role is in sentencing, whereas in a jury trial the judge rules
on matters of law during the trial and, should the defendant be found
guilty, imposes the sentence. The jury determines guilt or innocence. In
a bench trial, the judge rules on law, determines guilt or innocence, and
sentences. There are, then, opportunities for race or ethnicity to play a
role in the adjudication process. Most studies have focused on racial
disparities in sentencing (Spohn et al. 1981–82), as sentencing data are
readily quantifiable, and other judicial decisions are not.

A comprehensive study of sentencing in a large mainland city from
1968 to 1979 found no evidence of racial discrimination in severity of
sentencing; race accounted for 4 percent of the variation in determining
whether to sentence to probation or prison, with Caucasians more likely
to receive probation and African Americans more likely to receive a
prison sentence (ibid., 87). However, the cultural dynamics of Hawai'i
are unlike those of the mainland. A study that attempted to determine
the influence of social distance on sentencing in Hawai'i's criminal
courts during the 1960s, when most judges were Caucasian, Chinese,
and Japanese, and most defendants were Filipino, Native Hawaiian, and
Samoan, found that social distance was a factor in sentencing only
when the defendant's criminal history was ambiguous (Castberg 1971).
A study in the late 1970s failed to find a link between ethnicity and
sentencing, although it did find considerable variation among judges in
sentencing behavior (Keller 1978). A third study, completed in 1982,
found almost no relationship between arrests and ethnicity:

> Holding all other variables constant, Whites and Chinese were more
> likely than the base group (comprised of all other races not
> individually listed) and Hawaiians, Blacks and Samoans were less
> likely to be arrested for larceny. Whites, Chinese and Japanese were
> less likely to be arrested for violent crimes, while Samoans were

more likely than the base group to be arrested for a violent crime (Hawai'i 1982, 15–16).

The latter study also found no ethnic correlates with charging or sentencing and ethnicity.

The issue of ethnic bias in sentencing is complicated in Hawai'i not only by the many different ethnic groups represented among defendants and judges but also by the fact that Hawai'i's law gives judges little latitude in sentencing. For more serious felonies, judges must sentence the convicted person to the maximum term prescribed by law, with the actual time served to be determined by the Parole Board. Thus, the major discretion exercised by judges in most felony cases is whether to sentence to prison or to probation; in some cases, judges also decide whether to extend the term of imprisonment on the basis of aggravating circumstances. There is no evidence that ethnicity plays a role, once other factors are held constant.

TABLE 13.6
Sentenced and Incarcerated Felons by Ethnicity, 1990–1991
(in percent)

Ethnic Group	Sentenced Felons	Inmate Population
Black	6.2	4.7
Caucasian	20.5	25.4
Chinese	0.6	0.6
Filipino	8.0	8.4
Hawaiian	37.6	33.9
Japanese	3.3	3.2
Korean	0.8	0.8
Samoan	4.6	3.6
Other	17.3	16.7
Unknown	1.0	2.7
Total	99.9	100.0

Source: Hawai'i (1994b, 288, 290).

The ethnic composition of sentenced felons shows the same disparities present in arrest figures (Table 13.6). Compared to population percentages, African Americans and Native Hawaiians are overrepresented among those convicted, while Caucasians, Chinese,

Filipinos, Japanese, and Koreans are underrepresented. Thus, very little change with respect to ethnicity appears to take place from arrest to sentencing. The filtering process, which releases arrestees or reduces the charges against them to misdemeanors without regard to race or ethnicity, is based on other factors. Of course, not all convicted felons are sentenced to jail. Judges may sentence felons to probation, except in the case of certain offenses and circumstances, as determined by law. Discrimination in sentencing, then, will most likely occur when a judge decides between probation and incarceration (or some combination thereof). Comparing the sentenced felon population with the inmate population, there are ethnic disparities. Caucasians tend to be incarcerated at a higher rate than conviction figures would predict, whereas African Americans, Native Hawaiians, and Samoans are incarcerated less frequently. Just why this is so is difficult to determine, but many factors are taken into consideration at sentencing.

Hawai'i's judges are required by law to order a pre-sentence diagnosis and report for all convicted felons, a right that is seldom waived by agreement of the defense attorney and prosecutor. This comprehensive report provides information to a judge on the defendant's criminal history, educational background, family and social situation, work history, and other factors that may be aggravating or mitigating. The report generally contains a sentence recommendation, which judges tend to follow. In addition, the law affords an opportunity for victim(s) of the crime (or their family in homicides) to be heard with respect to sentencing. Thus, many issues are considered by a sentencing judge, and cultural as well as socioeconomic factors may well play a role in judicial decision-making. Perhaps those from less advantaged backgrounds (African Americans, Native Hawaiians, and Samoans) may be seen as having more excuses for the commission of felonies than those from more advantaged backgrounds. However, Chinese and Japanese, usually from advantaged backgrounds, disproportionately receive less severe sentences than Caucasians, so local identity may play a role in accounting for leniency in sentencing.

CONCLUSION

Ethnic disparities exist in Hawai'i's criminal justice system, but the reasons are unclear. Do groups that are overrepresented in arrest and incarceration statistics commit more crimes than other groups? Is overrepresentation the result of discrimination on the part of judicial, law enforcement, and prosecutorial personnel? Since there is very little evidence of discrimination, the inference is that members of overrepresented groups do, in fact, commit more crimes. Why that is so is beyond the scope of this chapter, but there are invariably a multitude of factors. Those overrepresented in the system tend to be at the lower end of the socioeconomic ladder, but that in itself does not explain why they commit more crimes.

One is tempted to blame drugs for some of the disparities found, but arrest data do not bear out this explanation. Native Hawaiians are arrested for drug offenses at a rate higher than their percentage in the population, but they are also arrested at a higher rate for all Part I offenses. The same holds true for African Americans and Samoans. Filipinos, also on the low end of the socioeconomic ladder, are overrepresented in some drug offenses but not in overall arrest statistics. Perhaps, then, cultural factors play a role as well, but it is difficult to find empirical evidence to support this proposition. What is clear is that the disparities that exist at the arrest stage of the process continue through the trial stage, but are somewhat ameliorated during sentencing. It is also clear the ethnic diversity of criminal justice professionals has been increasing over the years.

The three hypotheses suggested at the beginning of this chapter seem to be supported by the data. There would seem to be cultural propensities for certain offenses, but the multiethnic actors in the criminal justice process would seem to counterbalance or negate any ethnic biases that might account for disparities in arrest, charging, conviction, and sentencing. Finally, legal criteria seem to be overwhelmingly the basis for decisions made by the key actors in the process.

Disparities in criminal justice are more difficult to explain in Hawai'i than on the mainland, but groups on the lower rungs of the socioeconomic ladder are overrepresented in the courts and prisons of our nation, with aboriginal peoples being among the most overrepresented. Despite efforts to eliminate these disparities, they continue to exist and in some cases increase. Whether it is within the power of the criminal justice system to change this trend is a major public policy issue awaiting resolution.

NOTES

1. *Plea bargaining* is the informal but widespread process whereby prosecution and defense negotiate a plea of guilty. Typically, the prosecutor offers to drop or reduce charges in return for a plea of guilty from the defendant.

2. There are four levels of courts in Hawai'i: the Supreme Court, the Intermediate Court of Appeals, the Circuit Courts, and the District Courts. The Circuit Courts are the trial courts where felony criminal cases are heard.

3. The Federal Bureau of Investigation (FBI) collects arrest data from police departments across the United States and uses it for the FBI's annual *Uniform Crime Reports*. *Part I offenses* tend to be the more serious felonies; *Part II offenses* include misdemeanors and less serious felonies. Part I offenses include Aggravated Assault, Arson, Burglary, Forcible Rape, Larceny-Theft, Motor Vehicle Theft, Murder, and Robbery. Part II offenses include Disorderly Conduct, Driving under the Influence, Embezzlement, Forgery and Counterfeiting, Fraud, Gambling: Bookmaking, Gambling: Lottery, Gambling: Other, Liquor Laws, Manufacture or Sale of Marijuana, Manufacture or Sale of Opium or Cocaine, Manufacture or Sale of Non-narcotics, Manufacture or Sale of Synthetic Narcotics, Negligent Manslaughter, Offenses Against Family/Children, Other Assault, Possession of Marijuana, Possession of Stolen Property, Possession of Opium or Cocaine, Prostitution, Possession of Synthetic Narcotics, Possession of Non-narcotics, Sex Offenses, Suspicion, Vandalism, Weapons, and All Other Offenses.

CHAPTER 14

Political Economy

Ibrahim G. Aoudé

This chapter discusses the political economy of Hawai'i since statehood. It will give an historic backdrop on the economic structure of the Islands, how these new structures developed, and their effects over time on Hawai'i's multiethnic population. The chapter also deals with the development of the political and economic crisis of the 1990s. The response to this crisis by Governor Ben Cayetano and Hawai'i's ruling circles will also be examined. Who benefits? Who loses? What can be done, given the parameters of the Islands' political economy in a global context? Finally, I will advance some thoughts concerning grassroots political action to confront the crisis.

HISTORICAL BACKGROUND

The destruction of the communal, self-sufficient Native Hawaiian system, including its social stratification, is an example of the violence by which capitalism was historically established through the colonization of native peoples. Complete *haole* domination of Hawai'i occurred in 1893, when the Hawaiian monarchy was overthrown.

The development of a plantation system was an integral part of the transformation of the Native Hawaiian pre-contact system to full-fledged capitalism. By the time Hawai'i was annexed to the United States in 1898, the plantation society had developed into a caste-like system with the *haole* oligarchy in power and ethnic minorities on the plantations, mainly Chinese and Japanese, at the bottom. The *haole* oligarchy was also able to drive a wedge between the Native Hawaiians and the other nationalities.

The establishment of the Home Rule Party in Honolulu on June 6, 1900, sounded alarm bells for the *haole*, as Native Hawaiians at that time comprised about two-thirds of the voters in the Territory, as noted in the chapter on politics by Michael Haas (Table 8.1). To check this potential threat, planter Henry Baldwin met Prince Kuhio Kalaniana'ole in 1901 to convince him to run as a delegate to Congress against Robert Wilcox, the candidate of the anti-*haole* Home Rule Party. Baldwin argued that Native Hawaiians and *haoles* needed to join forces against "the rising Oriental tide" (Fuchs 1961, 159). Kuhio agreed. The deal was made in order to have the Native Hawaiians serve the interests of the *haole* oligarchy (ibid., 158). Until 1922, Native Hawaiians were the voting majority, and they comprised more than half the candidates for office. Bribery and jobs in government and on plantations and ranches persuaded most Native Hawaiians to be Republican Party loyalists. As late as 1935, Native Hawaiians, who comprised less than 15 percent of the population, held about one-third of the government jobs in the Territory (Haas 1992, 46). The Japanese, on the other hand, were denied government jobs and were "discouraged from opening homesteads." The percentage of Japanese registered voters jumped from a low of 2.5 percent in 1920 to 31.0 percent in 1940 (Table 8.1), when Japanese voters equaled their *haole* counterparts. However, Japanese only held 1.6 percent of appointive positions in the Territory in 1930 and 2.9 percent in 1940 (Fuchs 1961, 181).

After World War II, workers of all nationalities, but primarily Japanese, wanted to rid themselves of the oppressive plantation system. Allied with urban Japanese professionals and liberal *haoles*, the workers brought about the so-called "Democratic revolution" by first gaining control of the Democratic Party and then capturing power from the Republican *haole* oligarchy in 1954, when Democrats captured majorities in both houses of the territorial legislature. Democrats challenged the big estates and the Big Five corporations (Alexander & Baldwin, American Factors, Castle & Cooke, C. Brewer & Co., and Theo H. Davies), ostensibly promising to effect land reform and to restructure the political economy.

Since statehood, Hawai'i's political economic development has been praised by both mainstream writers (e.g., Fuchs 1961; Hitch 1992) and decision makers in the private and public sectors. Opposing views rarely returned to the radical discourse of the 1950s. Instead, the ruling circles were able to squelch such early reform efforts as Democrat Tom Gill's bid to displace mainstream Governor John Burns in 1970 (Coffman 1973).

Structural changes that occurred in Hawai'i's political economy after World War II transformed the Islands from a sugar economy to a tourism economy (Fuchs 1961; Kent 1983). This transformation was facilitated when *haole* oligarchic rule gave way, as a result of the 1954 Democratic "revolution," to a more open, democratic political system. A depiction of this transformation may be seen in the changing structure of employment from 1960 to 1980 (Table 14.1). Hawai'i's economic transformation can also be observed in the changing share of the gross state product (GSP) from agricultural to military to tourism dependency, as indicated in Chapter 2 (Table 2.5).

TABLE 14.1
Employment Structure in Hawai'i, 1960–1990 (in percent)

Job Category	1960	1970	1980	1990
Professional, Managerial and Technical	21	25	23	30
Farming, Skilled Craft, Operator, Laborer	42	35	27	23
Sales, Clerical, Service	32	40	50	47
Other	5	1	0	0
Total	100	101	100	100

Source: U.S. census (1962, 185–88; 1972, 295–301; 1983, 152–61; 1993, 35).

Hawai'i's boom years (1959–1990), therefore, were the result of global capitalist transformation and its attendant local Democratic "revolution" (Kent 1983). Corporate investment, jet airplane travel, and the political apparatus were essential ingredients for transforming the Islands into a major tourist attraction, with such supportive economic activities as construction, finance, and real estate development. In the boom years, GSP real growth averaged 5 percent annually (Smith 1995). From 1986 to 1990, a wave of Japanese investment contributed to the maintenance of annual growth rates. However, this enviable economic performance occurred at the expense of the lower rungs of the multiethnic working class, especially Native Hawaiians and Filipinos (Aoudé 1994; 1995), a fact of little concern to the ruling circles who oversaw a fast-growing economy.

Over the years, Hawai'i has become characterized by uneven development, not only through its heavy dependence upon tourism, but also due to an increasing dependency upon offshore capital. This inherent weakness in capitalist development has not presented a serious threat to economic performance overall. However, planners in both the public and private sectors have been cognizant and concerned about this situation. Since 1962, planners responded by favoring "diversification," a concept that soon became "a problematic for all seasons" (Aoudé 1995). How could the Islands create a new economic sector so as to become significantly less dependent upon tourism?

By the 1980s, when diversification was cast in a positive light, establishment figures increasingly warned of the dangers of relying on one industry. At that point in time, diversification rhetoric was reinvigorated, and a phantom high-technology sector dominated the propaganda waves of the discussion on development. But Hawai'i's economy was tied by a thousand threads to the global economy from the beginning. And its economic structures were "locked in" to this uneven development favoring tourism (Aoudé 1995).

THE CONTEMPORARY GLOBAL CONTEXT

The confluence of internal and external economic and political forces that brought about the 1954 Democratic "revolution" is quickly dissipating. Organized labor, a pillar of the "revolution," has lost its edge and much of its steam, as demonstrated by the recent attacks of the *Haku* Alliance, a small business lobbying group supported by big business, on significant gains (minimum wage, unemployment insurance, and worker's compensation) that labor had won in the early period, especially since statehood.

Meanwhile, global changes in production have propelled the capitalist economy into crisis (Peery 1993). Robert Reich (1991) and Jeremy Rifkin (1995), who recognize the revolutionary shift in production from electromechanics to electronics, have called for a restructuring of work within the capitalist relations of production. Nelson Peery (1993) argues, to the contrary, that qualitative shifts (from electromechanics to electronics) in the means of production require qualitative shifts (private to communal) in the relations of production.

National policy responses to the socioeconomic changes afflicting American society, notably those under presidents Ronald Reagan and George Bush, have exacerbated the dismal economic situation. The end result of the Reagan-Bush years was a huge national debt and the disqualification of tens of thousands of needy people from social services programs, which, in turn, resulted in such negative social consequences as homelessness and crime of all sorts. More recently, Republicans in Washington have sought to cut social services even more. In addition, President Bill Clinton, and the Democratic Party generally, have increasingly accepted Republican policies.

Global and national changes have affected the state's politics and its economy. Were it not for the wave of Japanese foreign investment in the 1980s, Hawai'i's economy would have been in the doldrums much earlier than 1991. The Cayetano administration's projected state budget deficits for 1996 took into account national public policy, which is driven in large measure by the Republican majority in Congress.

Budget cuts, a higher cost of living, and unemployment in Hawai'i's tourist markets have negative impacts on state revenues. Japan's sluggish economy also has a negative impact on foreign investment and tourism.

THE HAWAIIAN ECONOMY AND ITS SOCIAL EFFECTS

The state's economy was doing very well at the macrolevel during the 1980s. In nominal dollars, the GSP increased from about $19.7 billion in 1987 to $26 billion in 1990 (Aoudé 1995, 227). Visitor expenditures increased from $5.5 billion to $10.4 billion in the same period. In 1982 dollars, the GSP for 1992 and 1993 was $19 billion and $18.6 billion, respectively ($29.3 and $30 billion in nominal dollars, respectively). For 1995, the GSP is estimated to be the same as for 1993 (Bank of Hawaii 1995, 7). In fact, real growth was –0.03% in 1994 compared with 1993 (Bank of Hawaii 1996, 7).

In the 1990s, however, the Gulf War and the recessions in both Japan and California adversely affected the state's economy. Japanese investment slowed to about $200 million per year. In addition, the recessions in the state's two major tourist markets, Japan and California, lowered tourism's contribution to the GSP (Kent 1994, 183–84).

In 1988, the cost of living in Hawai'i averaged 17 percent higher than that of the continental United States, while per-capita disposable income was only 2 percent higher (Hammes, Oliveira, and Sakai 1992, 45). Trade, services, and state and local government sectors have been traditionally known for low wages or low productivity (ibid., 40). From 1985 to 1987, some 11.1 percent of families earned less than $10,000, while 32.3 percent of families earned under $20,000. Although these figures improved over time, over one-third of Hawai'i's families are in poverty or hover around the poverty line (ibid., 39). Most distressing is the fact that 80 percent of pre-tax income expended by individuals in the Islands goes to the purchase of necessities (Crane and Okinaka 1992, 60).

From 1988 to 1992, the cost of living for a family of four on O'ahu jumped to 39.6 percent higher than that of the continental United States (Hawai'i 1993–94, 339). Hawai'i's average wage was 1.1 percent lower than the U.S. average, and 40 percent lower, adjusting for cost of living differences (ibid., 301).

While the state government puts the number of homeless at about 8,000, the number is actually closer to 12,000 (Aoudé 1994, 71–84). In 1980, 8.5 percent of the population (81,000) was below the poverty line. In 1992, 11 percent of the population (129,000) was below the poverty line (Witeck 1995, 17).

Social inequality in Hawai'i is severe (chapter 10) and, given the economic crisis in which the state finds itself, will probably worsen. Ethnicity and class are strongly correlated. Filipinos and Native Hawaiians are overrepresented in service occupations. Native Hawaiians are also overrepresented in transportation occupations and unskilled labor (Barringer 1995, 12). Native Hawaiians and Filipinos have high poverty levels, compared with other ethnic groups (ibid., 15–21).

JAPANESE DIRECT INVESTMENT IN HAWAI'I

Hawai'i has been very much dependent upon outside capital for its economic growth. From the 1950s, foreign capital made some significant inroads. In 1959, the Tokyu Corporation invested one million dollars in the opening of Shirokiya, a department store at the Ala Moana Shopping Center. Next, Kenji Osano purchased the Princess Ka'iulani and Moana Surfrider hotels in 1963. In 1973, Japanese investors purchased eight hotels in the state, in part to alleviate discrimination against Japanese tourists in other hotels (Haas 1992, 247). After purchasing the Royal Hawaiian and Sheraton Waikiki, in 1974, Osano owned all Sheraton hotels in Waikiki, and he bought the Sheraton Maui for $105 million in that year as well.

However, despite the influx of Japanese capital, the dominant source of outside investment in the fiftieth state during the 1970s was American capital. In the mid-1980s, the situation changed: Economic growth in the state was increasingly dependent upon foreign capital. Hawai'i had entered the era of the "New Big Five"—Australia, Canada, Hong Kong, Japan, and the United Kingdom (Jokiel 1988).

From 1970–1989, foreign investment amounted to $8.4 billion. Japan accounted for $6.8 billion (Kim 1994, 42), and Hong Kong was a distant second, with only $231 million invested from 1973–1988. By 1988, Australia, Canada, and the United Kingdom had total investments of $193 million, $167 million, and $162.9 million, respectively (Jokiel 1988). Of the $6.8 billion of Japanese investment in Hawai'i, $5.2 billion (76 percent) was invested from 1986–1989. The impact of Japanese economic activity on the state's economy should also take Japanese tourism into account. In 1988, for example, Japanese investors injected the equivalent of $1.9 billion into Hawai'i's economy, which was about 10 percent of GSP. Adding the 1.4 million Japanese tourists who visited the Islands in that year, the total impact of Japanese economic activity was $9.5 billion or 45 percent of a total GSP of $21.3 billion. From 1980–1985, Japanese investment in Hawai'i averaged $168 million per year; but there was a dramatic jump to $1.3 billion per year in the period from 1986–1988 (Pai 1989, 6–7).

Two related questions arise: (1) Why did the Japanese invest in Hawai'i? (2) Where did they invest? According to economist Gregory Pai (1989, 2–3), "largely as a result of realignments in the balance of global economic power following the oil crisis of the 1970s, the emergence of Japan and the newly industrialized economies . . ., and the shift in the structure of world exchange rates that occurred in 1985, the sources of investment capital in Hawai'i have increasingly become internationalized." Other researchers point out the following variables to explain Japanese investment in the period 1971–1989: (1) the favorable yen/dollar exchange rate, (2) the skyrocketing price of commercial land in large Japanese cities, and (3) the number of Japanese tourists who come to the Islands (Kim 1994, 45). The dollar dropped in value from 349 yen in 1971 to 138 yen in 1989. "The most rapid period of depreciation occurred between 1985 and 1986, when the dollar dropped in value from 239 yen to 169 yen in one year alone" (ibid., 46). This steep decline in the value of the dollar fueled a mad rush to invest in commercial real estate and tourism. Japanese nationals, who constituted over one-fifth of all tourists going to Hawai'i in 1985 and 1986, are only "one tenth of Japan's 10 million citizens that the government has been encouraging to travel abroad as a way of helping to correct its trade imbalances with the U.S. and other countries" (Yoneyama and Hooper 1990, 60).

Some Japanese have invested in residential real estate and other businesses, including manufacturing, as it was only logical to invest in certain growth industries that present low risk and high return on investment. For Hawai'i in that period, Japanese investments brought more employment in construction projects, real estate, and tourism, all interrelated sectors of the economy.

However, the bulk of Japanese investment was speculative (e.g., the $2 billion Ko'Olina project and the Waikiki Convention Center), so the investments have adversely impacted Hawai'i's population by increasing the cost of residential property beyond what most residents can afford. The negative reception of such investment by the state's population and the increased dependency of the economy on foreign speculative investment prompted economists and state planners to discourage "speculative" and instead to encourage "productive" investment. *Speculative investment*, especially in tourism, has traditionally created low-quality jobs (low wages and little or no fringe benefits). *Productive investment* is associated with the creation of high-quality jobs. According to Pai (1989, 11), the "overall position of state policy toward investment, in general, and foreign investment, in particular, is to encourage the growth of investments that help to diversify Hawai'i's economy and contribute to the overall social welfare of the people, while at the same time taking steps to control those investments that are known to generate negative social impacts."

Foreign investment was actively sought not only to decrease the Islands' dependency on tourism through diversification of the economic base but also to maintain the growth of the tourist industry. Presumably, the Hawai'i State General Plan was created to achieve "balanced" development to benefit the people. State intervention is needed, some argue, so that the vagaries of the "free" market would not work counter to the desired goal of economic diversification. "[F]oreign investment needs to respond to the larger social and cultural needs of the community, rather than simply the private profit-maximization motives of individual businesses" (ibid., 12). But such noble intentions and exhortations, desirable as they may be, run counter to the inherent dynamic of the profit motive in capitalism.

DIVERSIFICATION AS AN ILLUSION

Economic diversification has not taken place thus far to any significant degree. As stated earlier, the bulk of foreign investment went into hotel and commercial and residential real estate acquisitions as well as into the development of major resorts, which have increased dependency on tourism and related economic sectors. In addition, the much-touted diversification through high technology was confronted with virtually insurmountable economic and political hurdles. In the economic arena, Hawai'i could not hope to compete with such countries as México and Singapore for obvious reasons: (1) An oversupply of electronic commodities existed on the global market. (2) Wage rates in those countries are so low that the Islands could not even dream of producing (or assembling) electronic commodities at competitive prices. (3) Contrary to what some contend, electronics production is not clean; environmental pollution would endanger the well-being of the number one industry.

Having recognized the above limitations, Hawai'i's policy makers turned their attention to other high-technology areas in order to find a niche that would emphasize research and development in biotechnology, electronics, geothermal, and space industries. But such projects require long periods of development before they actually come on line (Herbig and Kramer 1994). Even if, for some reason, venture capital were to finance such projects on a grand scale, the fact remains that these developments by their very nature are not labor intensive. They would not be able to generate sufficient employment to decrease significantly the dependency on tourism. Since advanced technology industries require the employment of specializations that are not available in the state, these projects would rely on imported skilled labor, which would also put pressure on such scarce Island resources as housing, land, and water. Finally, the economic efficacy of these projects, beyond what has been mentioned, is dubious in the context of global competition in the fields of biotechnology, electronics, and space.

Over the past several years, significant opposition has developed against high-technology projects. While the environmental impact is of much concern, another important factor, in terms of political stability, is the issue of Native Hawaiian land rights. The opposition to high-technology development is simply a logical and natural extension of opposition to economic development in general, which has been in large measure at the expense of Native Hawaiian land rights. What is potentially dangerous for the political elites is the potential mobilization of a majority of voters opposed to development who want to address environmental concerns, problems of homelessness and housing, Native Hawaiian rights, unemployment, and welfare issues.

DEVELOPMENT AND LOSS OF CONTROL

Since the arrival of the *haole*, Hawai'i's history has been a chronicle of disenfranchisement and oppression of an entire people as well as exploitation and oppression of plantation workers. The transformation of plantation society to the modern structures of corporate capitalism underscores the fact that the majority of the Islands' people have never enjoyed political and economic control over Hawai'i's resources. By the 1850s, *haoles* had significant control, which developed into effective and then full control by the time of the "Bayonet Constitution" of 1887 and the overthrow of the monarchy in 1893. Curiously, the *haole* oligarchy developed its political and economic control through its dependency on the outside world. Plantations became viable economically through the development of U.S. markets for sugar; ultimately, plantation society was stabilized through annexation, which gave the *haole* oligarchy full control of Hawai'i.

After World War II, "U.S. corporations formed the leading wedge of the penetration of international capital in the Pacific" (Kent 1983, 99). Hawai'i had a major role to play in this Pacific Rim Strategy. "The Great Corporate Transformation" (ibid., 122) of the Islands was relatively quick. Henry Kaiser, for instance, became the biggest landowner in Waikiki by 1955, just one year after he had established his residence in the Islands. He built the Hilton Hawaiian Village, developed a 6,000-acre residential project known as Hawai'i Kai, and established a cement plant.

The 1954 Democratic "revolution" had its social base in the plantation workers. At that time, workers attempted to wrest control from the *haole* oligarchy. In fact, however, the reins of power were transferred from one set of capitalists to another.

The role of the "revolutionary" Democrats was no different from that of Republican William Quinn, the first governor after statehood. Both Quinn and his successor, Democrat John Burns, were successful in attracting U.S. mainland capital, notably for such infrastructure development as the H–1 Freeway, Honolulu International Airport, the Magic Island extension of Ala Moana Beach Park, and volcano roads. "In October 1963 . . ., a Bank of America consortium purchased $39.6 million worth of state bonds, while a Chase Manhattan syndicate snapped up $15 million of a subsequent issue. Between 1958 and 1968, the state's outstanding public bonds increased sharply from $212 million to $528.9 million, while an average of $48 million in bonds was sold annually between 1960 and 1967" (ibid., 142).

Mass infusion of capital in the 1970s transformed the Big Five, which sold out to and became subsidiaries of multinational corporations. As Laura Brown and Walter Cohen (1975, 3) state, "multinationalization has led either to outright acquisition by outside interests or to a greater dependence on more dominant centers of international trade and investment."

From the 1970s, economic and political elites began to envision a new role for the Islands as the "hub of the Pacific," imagining that, by the year 2000, Hawai'i would have a great role to play both in commerce and finance. However, after over forty years of economic growth, the fiftieth state is nowhere near becoming the "hub of the Pacific." For example, airplanes increasingly fly from the U.S. mainland to Asia without stopping in Hawai'i.

The Islands also lost control in a more profound way due to the "increased vulnerability of the economy to external economic conditions" (Pai 1986, 7). According to Pai, the 1980–1982 severe recession demonstrated that Hawai'i's dependency on mass tourism means that the economy is prone to cyclical economic fluctuations due to external factors.

THE CURRENT SOCIAL STRUGGLE

After the 1954 "revolution," the *haole* oligarchy saw that it was in its interest to merge with the much more formidable external capital. Lately, a section of local capitalists, mostly a large section of the petty bourgeoisie in Hawai'i, have become vociferous against foreign capital. This opposition has translated into anti-Japanese capital investment sentiment. Grassroots social movements, which have emerged in opposition to the consequences of capitalist development on their daily lives, see loss of local control in a broader historic sense. Leading activists in those movements consist primarily of Filipinos, Native Hawaiians, and, to a lesser extent, Japanese. The tactics have consisted of demonstrations, visits to legislative bodies and offices of developers, pickets, and sit-ins; police have been forced to make arrests on occasion, as when a cordon of demonstrators held hands to block bulldozers.

Several movements have opposed the conversion of farmland into real estate developments. The abortive Makua Valley struggle of 1969 informed a second important anti-eviction fight of Native Hawaiians, the Kalama Valley struggle of 1971. In both instances, Native Hawaiians were trampled upon. But there were later successes. In the early 1970s, Chinatown and Ota Camp were sites of anti-eviction struggles, primarily of Filipino workers, and Waiahole Waikane was the site of a struggle against evictions of Japanese and Native Hawaiians by real estate developers who owned agricultural land and wanted windfall profits through residential rezoning (Geshwender 1980–81). This stage of the social struggle was primarily defensive, fighting evictions; it was based primarily in working-class communities, which were inspired by the civil rights and anti-war movements.

The University of Hawai'i's Ethnic Studies Program, itself a product and an integral part of the social struggle, played a key role in the development of grassroots movements. The fight to establish the Program at the University of Hawai'i was, in fact, the proactive dimension of the movement in its first stage. That dimension also continued in the second stage and enabled the Program to gain permanence as a Department by 1995.

The mid-1970s also witnessed the beginnings of a grassroots Native Hawaiian social movement. The issue was land; the target was the island of Kaho'olawe. The movement quickly galvanized around the issue of ceded lands, and the social struggle in Hawai'i entered its second stage, with Native Hawaiians at the center. The two stages overlapped but were distinct. In this second stage, the social struggle took the offensive, producing many grassroots Native Hawaiian leaders.

It was only logical for Native Hawaiian sovereignty to become central to any discussion on development of the Islands. Native Hawaiians have been the most exploited and oppressed nationality by the multiethnic capitalist class and its system. Land is power in Hawai'i (Cooper and Daws 1985). A majority of Native Hawaiians own no land, and many are organizing to reclaim their nation. Most Native Hawaiians are members of the working class (chapter 10). They have much in common with the rest of the multiethnic working class, which has been hit hard by the recent economic crisis in the state. Linkage between the land and social ills, such as discrimination, employment, homelessness, and a shortage of low-cost housing, is logical for three reasons: (1) The Native Hawaiian movement seeks to link the fight to regain ancestral lands with the broader quest for better health care, housing, and jobs. (2) Progressives are increasingly working alongside Native Hawaiians for the broader quest, having come to the realization that resolution of the Native Hawaiian land issue is central to the alleviation of misery and poverty for the multiethnic working class. (3) Ruling circles are trying to find ways to co-opt, derail, or divide the movement in order to prevent the movement from developing into a significant challenge to the *status quo*.

CAMPAIGN 1994

Pat Saiki (1994a; 1994b), the Republican candidate for governor in 1994, concentrated on two main points in her campaign: (1) Yes, John Burns had a vision for Hawai'i, but John Waihe'e and the rest of the Democrats were unimaginative nonleaders who "screwed up big" on the economy and were extremely corrupt. (2) The time had come to restore Burns's vision by kicking the rascals out. Her strategy was similar to Newt Gingrich's assault on the Democrats nationally, as Gingrich invoked Franklin Roosevelt, and, although he did not want to go back to the New Deal's "big government," he wanted to "throw the rascals out."

Due to the lethargic performance of Hawai'i's economy, Saiki concentrated on the theme of Hawai'i becoming a "Pacific Partner." But that theme was flat. First of all, the Islands had been trying to become the center of the Pacific in investment, technology, and trade since before the days of Burns, whom Saiki had invoked as a great visionary, and all such efforts came to naught for reasons having to do with transnational corporate strategies, including the Pacific division of labor and the dearth of capital and natural resources in the state (Kent 1983; Aoudé 1995). Ben Cayetano, a "new Democrat," articulated the same theme, but his message was more concrete. Finally, Saiki blamed the Democrats for everything that went wrong in the state while dismissing economic and political global influences that are so clearly crucial to the state's economic health. In short, Saiki underestimated the intelligence and knowledge of the electorate by providing advertising stimuli without substance.

While Saiki concentrated on Hawai'i's international role, Cayetano (1994) linked that role with issues near and dear to the people, such as attracting investment, cleaning up government, educating the children, helping small business, reforming the land use planning process, and reforming worker's compensation law and health insurance. Cayetano's plan indicated that he understood the politicoeconomic context. He believed that a solution to the economic crisis was within reach if only he could reform the political process. For Cayetano, political will was essential to overcoming most problems by creating niches for Hawai'i in various international markets. Cayetano won, with 134,978 votes, independent candidate Frank Fasi polled 113,158, and Saiki came in last among the three major candidates, with 107,908 votes.

CAYETANO'S POLICIES TO AVERT CRISIS

Cayetano knows that he lacks a mandate from the majority of voters. His victory was by a plurality. For Cayetano, reforming the government also means downsizing, facilitating the way for business, especially small business, to create jobs. Thus, the costs of doing business must be cut. Consequently, health care costs and worker's compensation are being reduced for employees. Proposed incentives for business are tax breaks and enterprise zones.

Conventional wisdom attributes the inability of the state to extricate itself from the economic crisis to state budget deficits and a soft construction industry (Honolulu Advertiser 1996). However, there is a larger underlying economic problem. One of Governor Cayetano's first acts was to declare that the state's financial picture was more grim than he had originally expected. The projected deficit for the state budget 1995–97 biennium was first estimated at $250 million (Kresnak and Botticelli 1995), but was later revised upward. Cayetano responded by severely cutting the state budget and yet having the state embark on subsidies for large development projects. A Democratic chorus echoed that "Hawai'i's easy days are over" (Griffin 1994). The ruling circles realize that the economic crisis could eventually express itself on the political level. Therefore, it is imperative to reinvigorate the economy, which is now growing at less than 1 percent GSP annually. Cayetano estimates that the economic growth he is hoping for would allow him to fulfill his campaign promise of cutting the "paradise tax" (the differential between Hawai'i's cost of living and that of the continental United States). He also has promised to create programs that are in everyone's interest in order to convince the people that current sacrifices are for their future benefit. He believes that he is exercising true leadership in hard economic times (Cayetano 1995, 20).

The campaign promises of 1994, however, soon gave way to the economic realities of 1995. It was not possible to institute programs in everyone's interest. Nor was it possible to eliminate the budget deficit at the expense of the capitalist class. In a capitalist system, one main economic assumption is that capitalists create jobs; since they are the dynamos who energize the economy, they need incentives. Consequently, Cayetano has balanced the budget on the backs of the working class, especially those at the lower rungs.

In *Restoring Hawaii's Economic Momentum* (1996), Cayetano has asserted that the economic crisis in Hawai'i is essentially due to structural problems and is not merely cyclical (xi). True to mainstream economic wisdom, he contends that there are three pillars for economic recovery: (1) correcting fiscal balances, (2) encouraging production in the business sector, and (3) reducing barriers to doing business (xii). All three steps are directly or indirectly related to privatization and "free enterprise." Cayetano admits that in 1995 he was consumed with attending to deficit-spending problems. His program in 1996 was to pay attention to the two other above-mentioned steps within the context of "diversifying" the economy, a goal that for decades has failed to materialize to any significant degree (Aoudé 1995, 238).

Compared with his predecessors, Cayetano has a more realistic vision of diversification. Earlier, the planners (both public and private) were looking at a high-technology sector large enough to compensate for the dwindling agricultural (pineapple and sugar) and military sectors as well as to decrease the state's dependency on tourism. Cayetano (1996, xii) modified the theme somewhat: "This Administration envisions a strong diversified economy, built around our competitive strengths in tourism and Pacific location." Six goals are targeted: (1) promoting a positive business environment, (2) encouraging new investment to reinvigorate our economic base, (3) reaching out through science and technology to new areas of economic growth, (4) focusing on Asia and the Pacific, (5) reinforcing Neighbor Island economic growth, and (6) investing in education and human resources (ibid., xii-xvi). Cayetano, thus, heroically seeks to diversify on all fronts of the plan along two lines of attack: (1) to take steps to shift the economy into the expanding phase of the business cycle and (2) to take measures (already begun) "to respond to structural changes that have emerged in our economy" (ibid., 14).

A more detailed examination of the plan to restore economic momentum reveals dependency on capital improvement projects (CIP) funds to take advantage of the business cycle expansion. As for the long-term approach to respond to structural problems in the economy, the recipe calls for more investment and privatization. Coupled with more cuts in the state budget, the hope is that the economy will begin to grow at a healthy rate.

However, an unintended subtext of the plan reads that Hawai'i has limited options. Cayetano will probably have some success in expanding health services, the finance, insurance, and real estate (FIRE), and tourism sectors—but all at the expense of the multiethnic working class. Incentives to business, a cornerstone of the plan, have been translated into cuts in health care for many indigent families, who can no longer access free non-emergency dental services; cuts in welfare benefits, which have already been passed by the state legislature (Honolulu Advertiser 1996, 1); enterprise zones that could be free from union contracts; tax holidays; and a watered-down worker's compensation law.

However, Cayetano's plan is silent about carrying-capacity arguments that challenge many of the rosy scenarios. Urban planner Luciano Minerbi (1994), who notes limits on physical infrastructre, social services, and water, argues for quality of life and not merely for growth.

However, more serious problems have to do with the nature of the economic crisis. To his credit, Cayetano has recognized structural problems in the economy. But these problems are primarily consequences of a global economic crisis and are not merely internally engendered. In addition, problems exist in all areas of society, including crime, drugs, and education. The crisis is general and systemic, one that cannot be overcome by addressing symptoms, no matter how sophisticated the plan.

Cayetano may be able to curtail corruption and patronage to a large degree, but politics is about horse-trading, and some of that will remain. It would be difficult to rid the state of its entrenched political culture, especially since many Democrats are tied to corporate business interests.

To maintain its grip on power, the Democratic Party, especially the Cayetano administration, is becoming more conservative. It is privileging capital to the detriment of workers.

CONCLUSION

The political expressions that the state has been witnessing of late are but small examples of what the future portends in the way of grassroots political movements. The direction in which Hawai'i politics is moving is liable to bring about a serious counterreaction at the grassroots level. The orientation of that reaction would very much depend upon leaders, as a populist movement could very well make a turn to the right or the left.

Disagreements among various factions of the ruling circles provide a window of opportunity for progressive community leaders to form a core that could begin to respond politically to attacks on the working class. Spontaneous outbursts by workers, whether as individuals or groups, would amount to naught and could be counterproductive unless channeled into a political movement. Consequently, I expect that an increasingly large section of the multiethnic working class will mobilize to defend itself.

CHAPTER 15

Conclusion

Michael Haas

The various chapters present somewhat different visions of Hawai'i, but they all agree that a multicultural transformation has occurred over the years. There have been three major eras, each with important transitions—the periods of the monarchy, the Territory of Hawai'i, and the State of Hawai'i. Using the same convention as in Chapter 1, with dominant groups capitalized, we can agree that during the era of the monarchy, Anglo-Europeans (a) were politically subordinate to Native Hawaiians (B), but rose economically after importing Chinese (c) and Japanese (d) workers to work on the plantations:

$$a + B \rightarrow A + b + c + d.$$

With the fall of the monarchy, the *haoles* dominated all other groups, economically and politically. *Haoles* sought to divide and conquer other groups, importing Filipinos (e) as the latest major group of plantation workers, but non-*haoles* were allowed to intermingle. By the end of the 1950s, Chinese had achieved a favorable economic position:

$$A + b + c + d \rightarrow A + b + C + d + e.$$

In the third era, with the advent of statehood, Japanese (D) displaced *haoles* politically while making significant economic progress, but upward mobility was not achieved by Native Hawaiians (b), Filipinos (e), and many smaller non-*haole* groups. Meanwhile, the rate of marriage across ethnic lines increased considerably, blurring statistics based on ethnicity, but by the end of the twentieth century Filipinos,

Native Hawaiians, and many other non-*haole* groups had not reached a position of equality:

$$A + b + C + D + e \rightarrow A + b + C + D + e.$$

The various transformations require further analysis. An analytical summary of the main contributions of each chapter, therefore, will focus both on multicultural innovations and on alternative explanations advanced to account for the development and flourishing of multiculturalism.

MULTICULTURAL INNOVATIONS IN HAWAI'I

That multiethnic Hawai'i is multicultural has been demonstrated in this volume. Some commentators on multicultural initiatives on the U.S. mainland are fearful that the United States will fall apart unless a monocultural unity binds together diverse ethnic groups and cultures. Although such thinking also existed among *haoles* in Hawai'i in the first half of the twentieth century, the reality is that the Islands became more multicultural and did not collapse. Indeed, multicultural Hawai'i is more harmonious today, despite many social problems, than in the days when *haole* ruling circles tried to impose monoculturalism.

What adjustments were made in Hawai'i to move from monoculturalism to multiculturalism, while attaining greater interethnic peace? Each chapter provides a different answer.

For Derek Bickerton (Chapter 3), the development of Hawaii Creole English is a unique adaptation. When *haole* leaders decided to replace the Hawaiian language with English, plantation workers stopped speaking Hawaiian but were not educated in standard English, so HCE arose by necessity. Ridiculed as "pidgin English" instead of recognized as a separate language, HCE speakers were able to communicate behind the backs of *haole* bosses, and the content of the messages was often one of defiance of oppressive rule. Today, fluency in HCE still separates local-born residents from mainland- and foreign-born residents and thus is an important element that defines the unique culture of the Islands. Nevertheless, as *haole* leadership has been displaced and plantations have been closed, HCE speaking has declined. Standard English prevails in the mainstream, though the population still speaks many languages at home and hears many tongues at cultural events, and Native Hawaiians are reviving their language. The idea that a language might be suppressed is unthinkable in Hawai'i today.

In the media, Helen Geracimos Chapin (Chapter 4) reports, Native Hawaiians were eager to use a printed version of their language, and the existence of many languages in the plantation era also guaranteed media diversity. Plantation workers were often highly literate, though not in English, so efforts of *haole* elites to impose monoculturalism were doomed to failure as newspapers emerged from the various ethnic groups. With different groups deriving news from different sources, multiculturalism was inevitable. Although radio stations have catered to the various ethnic groups, television was largely a mainstream medium, with mainland-originated entertainment predominating until the arrival of public television and cable programming, when Hawai'i-based shows increasingly appeared. The overwhelming success of radio and television over news media, in turn, inspired coverage of more news from ethnic communities in the mainstream press in the 1990s. Thus, the various cultures are celebrated in the major media of Hawai'i. Rather than tearing apart the social fabric, multicultural media have brought everyone together into a mutual cultural admiration society.

The music of Hawai'i, according to Anthony Palmer (Chapter 5), has offered to the world three new musical instruments—the slack key guitar, the steel guitar, and the *'ukulele*. Still, the music of the Islands has long been rooted in Native Hawaiian culture, which is constantly being rediscovered and renewed. While each culture celebrates music appropriate to its festivals and traditions, new musical genres have arisen: *hapa haole* music, in such compositions as *Pearly Shells*, features Westernized lyrics with a relaxed and soothing instrumental accompaniment and *Jawaiian* music combines Native Hawaiian and *reggae*. Residents of Hawai'i can indulge themselves, either as performers or as listeners, through a wide variety of musical offerings without the sharp dichotomy between "Western versus ethnic" that often prevails on the U.S. mainland.

Amid diversity, whether in the media or in music, where is the mainstream? Chapin acknowledges the centrality of mainstream media but finds that the nonmainstream ethnic press is alive and well. Palmer reports that a musical mainstream is difficult to discern. Literature in Hawai'i today, as described by Rodney Morales (Chapter 6), may appear divided into three separatist camps—*haole*, local, and Native

Hawaiian, though the reality is that there is much interaction between the latter two. Students of local literature enroll in courses at the University of Hawai'i taught by *haoles* and ask embarrassing questions. Native Hawaiians accuse the premier local literary outlet, Bamboo Ridge Press, of editorial bias. Bamboo Ridge editors protest that they practice inclusiveness. Such tensions suggest vitality in the Island literary scene. Self-questioning and debates are always helpful in achieving growth and in preventing the rise of a new literary hegemony that would be the antithesis of multiculturalism. At the same time, *haole* literature remains aloof, unwilling to join in the dialog on the basis of equality. Thanks to the 1995 film *Picture Bride*, gatekeepers in Hollywood and elsewhere may begin to read and to appreciate the real Hawai'i, which is distinctively portrayed in the innovative regional literature reviewed by Morales.

Yasumasa Kuroda (Chapter 7) infers from public opinion surveys that a unique local culture exists in the Islands, though there are differences between ethnic groups as well. When he compares mainland-born with Island-born residents, he finds that they hold similar values on most issues, but local people and Asian immigrants stress family over the individualism of the mainland. Traditional values from Asia and among Native Hawaiians have created a culture of *aloha* that can cope successfully with hardships of various sorts, whereas individualistic mainlanders are not so equipped. The unique spirit of *aloha*, which involves respect for other ethnic groups and pride in the multiculturalism of the Islands, is certainly one element that makes the Islands a special place. Fears of attitudinal balkanization amid multiethnic diversity are unfounded in Hawai'i.

Ethnic politics, once virulently polarized, has all but ended in statewide races in Hawai'i, according to Michael Haas (Chapter 8). Ticket balancing, as practiced since statehood, informs voters that Democrats are more multiethnic than Republicans. Republicans have not elected a governor since 1959, rarely represent the state in Congress, and account for less than one-fifth of the state legislature. The displacement of *haole* Republicans by a *haole* Democrat in 1962 was a move toward greater diversity, as the latter chose non-*haole* lieutenant governor running mates. After a Japanese sweep at the polls in 1974, embarrassed Japanese Democrats carefully crafted ticket balancing again, gave up the position of governor to a Native Hawaiian and supported a Filipino gubernatorial successor. Hawai'i politics involves multiethnic cooperation today as never before; self-restraint by ethnic groups applies both to relations with other groups and to policies developed inside each group. For example, while some Native Hawaiian sovereignty advocates stretch the limits of tolerance by demanding independence, moderate sovereignty proponents prefer to work for reforms within the existing political system.

Plantation workers in Hawai'i joined forces through organized labor against *haole* elites, who were forced to make concessions because of a continuing labor shortage, according to Edward Beechert (Chapter 9). Although plantation owners would have preferred to segregate workers from one another, they did not have the space to do so. Because unions along monoethnic lines would create divisions that could be exploited by management, only multiethnic unions could be successful in the Islands, and union organizers gained the trust of workers by providing opportunities for multiethnic social and sporting events. Mainland-based unions, which initially would not accept non-Caucasian workers, did not fear that Islanders would desegregate mainland unions by moving *en masse* to Alabama, New Jersey, or elsewhere. Hawai'i, thus, had some of the earliest multiethnic unions in the United States and was an example of successful integration for the rest of the country to follow. The solidarity among workers was so great that the economic power of the *haole* elites was undermined by strikes soon after World War II, even before the triumph of the Democratic Party in 1954. In recent years, however, union solidarity in hotels, the principal source of employment, is being eroded with the arrival of single *haoles* from the U.S. mainland, who seek to work for a few years to enjoy their youth and then return home, having formed no ties with those born in Hawai'i who seek a decent living in order to feed their families and to purchase overpriced housing.

During the twentieth century, Hawai'i gradually changed from a caste system on the plantations to a class system with managers and professionals on top, clerical and technical workers in the middle, and blue-collar employees at the bottom. The rise of Chinese and Japanese from plantation serfs to the highest levels of affluence within less than a century is a remarkable achievement, due both to a determination to advance toward higher education and to a shrewd accumulation of capital. The Republican *haoles* tried but failed to control every aspect of upward mobility in order to keep these and other groups on the plantations, but educational and employment opportunities converged during World War II and in the 1960s to propel Chinese and Japanese into middle-class status. However, as Jonathan Okamura (Chapter 10) notes, since statehood a gap has become evident between lighter-skinned Caucasians, Chinese, and Japanese, on the one hand, and darker-skinned Filipinos, Native Hawaiians, and Samoans. The gap seems to have developed into a permanent feature of the Islands, and some groups, notably Native Hawaiians, have become increasingly bitter about lack of upward mobility. As later chapters indicate, one consequence of social immobility is increased crime in these latter groups, another is the forging of grassroots political organizations to stop rezoning agricultural land to make way for golf courses, hotels, and suburban bedroom communities. Rather than ethnic rivalry, Hawai'i is increasingly experiencing class envy. The poor are joining forces, regardless of ethnicity.

Despite the lingering effects of institutional racism imposed by *haoles* during the first half of the twentieth century, Michael Haas (Chapter 11) reports that the public schools have done much in recent years to move from monoculturalism to multiculturalism. Although political pressure was needed to break free from the monocultural legacy of the early part of the twentieth century, the form of the pressure has been largely nonconfrontational. One interesting experiment is the revival of education in the Hawaiian language in the public schools, which has attracted students from all ethnic groups. Native Hawaiian professionals first developed a pilot project on an experimental basis, and they later gained support from public schools to regularize the program. Filipinos were willing to cooperate with the public schools, but their needs were ignored until they called upon the federal government to intervene, whereupon the public schools asked Filipino professional educators to implement new programs that would transition immigrant students to greater facility in English. Yet another experimental program, which dealt with monolingual Hawaiian Creole English speakers, has even served as a model for instruction on the U.S. mainland that takes into account problems associated with Ebonics monolingualism.

At the University of Hawai'i, argues Michael Haas (Chapter 12), the role of state legislators has been of considerable importance in moving *haole* administrators and faculty into a multicultural direction. The mobilization of student pressure on behalf of particularistic grievances has been consistently effective in changing insensitive administrative policies, but there is no unrelenting long-term pressure for greater multiculturalism on the commuter campuses. Some *haole* professors have been socialized to Island ways of professionalism, which involve collaborative more than competitive teaching strategies, but these are exceptions. It should be perhaps be no surprise, therefore, that the overwhelmingly *haole*-dominated administration and faculty are complacent about the social responsibility of the university to increase ethnic equality.

Crime statistics, as presented by A. Didrick Castberg (Chapter 13), unmistakably show ethnic correlates. When the criminal justice system was dominated by *haoles*, many non-*haoles* believed that "*haole* justice" meant locking up a disproportionate share of non-Caucasians. Over time, however, there has been greater ethnic diversity within the bar, the judges, the parole boards, and the police; in addition, new laws have insisted on uniformity in sentencing, thus limiting judicial discretion. As a result, there appears to be no evidence whatever that any ethnic groups are victims of racial discrimination in the criminal justice system. Greater diversity has not set one group against another but instead has allayed suspicions.

Regarding the political economy of Hawai'i, Ibrahim Aoudé (Chapter 14) argues that the dispossession of land of the Native Hawaiians by *haole* entrepreneurs is one of the saddest events in the Islands. In the nineteenth century, *haole* commerical interests wanted to make profit from selling sugar cane, but start-up costs required bank loans, and the *haoles* had no collateral. Laws were then changed so that land could be offered as collateral. In time, there was so much profit that the loans were repaid, and *haole* businesses were financially independent within the Kingdom of Hawai'i, a first for a Third World nation. Thereafter, *haole* interests not only sought to protect the Islands from an invasion of mainland capital but also conspired to limit the entrepreneurial aspirations of upwardly mobile Chinese and Japanese. The accumulation of capital within the Chinese and Japanese communities before World War II, thus, is a marvel despite great odds, but after 1954 the increasing prosperity of the two groups can be attributed in part to a takeover of the political system by non-*haoles*. Rather than a division of the economy between *haole* and non-*haole* interests, however, the trend has been toward greater ethnic diversity in private sector employment, such that fewer retail businesses are identifiable ethnically. Nevertheless, the pursuit of prosperity for the

Islands as a whole has been frustrated by the globalization of capital, which has meant ownership of major hotel properties by interests largely outside Hawai'i. The long-term future of the economy of the Islands appears bleak because the private and public sectors in Hawai'i lost control of the local economy long ago.

EXPLANATORY THEORIES

The reality of multicultural Hawai'i is complex. Each author has sought to identify factors that account for relative success in sewing together the fabric of a multicultural society from multiethnic raw materials. It is appropriate to summarize these observations at this point, followed by an attempt to apply broader theories of ethnic relations. In so doing, it is possible to apply the various theories of ethnic relations to a concrete case.

A review of the key elements of alternative theories is therefore in order. In the case of *social distance theory*, an important factor is the extent of interethnic contact, as prejudice is assumed to result from ignorance. For *functionalists*, social discontinuities are supposed to cause system breakdown. *Mass society theorists* look for social isolation as a source of deviant behavior. *Racial equalitarianism* and *social constructionism* both assign responsibility for ethnic inequality to artificial barriers. *Primordialists* account for the persistence of ethnic identifications in the biological needs of humans. *Pragmatists* find practical reasons for various choices by members of ethnic groups.

Derek Bickerton (Chapter 3) carefully documents that after English and other languages entered previously monolingual Hawai'i, a macaronic pidgin, pidgin Hawaiian, and Hawaiian Creole English arose, and efforts to impose a monolingual English mold on the good people of Hawai'i have utterly failed. Instead, polylingualism is alive and well. He cites the following factors: (1) *Commercial Necessity*. Foreigners wanted to trade, so they needed to communicate. Since Hawaiian initially was the dominant language, outsiders picked up some words in Hawaiian, resulting in a pidgin tongue. When speaking of the Hawaiian language was discouraged, Hawaiian Creole English (HCE) emerged, again for pragmatic reasons. (2) *Inaccessibility*. Hawaiian was the dominant language up to 1893, and for many decades thereafter English was the primary language of only a few persons. When *haole* authorities sought to impose English upon those who spoke Hawaiian and other languages, there were no classes for adults to learn standard English. In the 1920s, when the children of immigrants flooded public schools, *haole* authorities constructed the category of "standard English proficiency" as an artificial barrier to prevent most non-Caucasians from attending schools where they would learn standard English. As racial equalitarians and social constructionists would argue, there was a deliberate effort to create a gap between haves and have-nots through an unworkable monolingual language policy. (3) *Social Necessity.* Imported plantation laborers were not expected to learn much English, so they continued speaking the languages of their home countries. Insofar as they needed some minimal basis for communication in the fields and the company store, pidgin Hawaiian developed. The children of plantation workers, who attended school together, broke down barriers of social distance and developed cross-ethnic friendships. Few plantation children acquired English proficiency, which after all was not required for plantation work. Having pragmatic needs to communicate with classmates, nevertheless, the children developed HCE and taught it to their parents. (4) *Backlash to Official Policies.* Efforts to stamp out Japanese language schools in the 1920s were declared unconstitutional by the Supreme Court. *Haole* disdain of HCE was viewed by non-*haoles* as yet another form of oppression to resist. Rather than accepting the monolingual mass society that *haoles* were attempting to forge, HCE flourished as a method for uniting non-*haoles* and thus reduced social distance. When *haoles* lost political power in 1954, they were replaced by groups who had long opposed monolingualism. Moreover, efforts to stamp out Hawaiian ultimately failed in the latter part of the twentieth century, as Native Hawaiians asserted the primordial imperative of maintaining their own culture. Contrary to functionalism, crude efforts to impose official linguistic uniformity resulted in social conflict, and ethnic harmony has resulted from linguistic heterogeneity. At the same time, Bickerton notes that standard English is gaining in prominence as the pragmatic key to upward mobility, while HCE is fading away, possibly because *haoles* are no longer supremely dominant, thereby removing the motivation to resist linguistic oppression.

Helen Geracimos Chapin's (Chapter 4) report on the multiplicity of media in various languages focuses on five influences: (1) *Linguistic diversity.* The languages represented in Hawai'i are distant enough from one another that a segregated press emerged early; a mass society,

with only one permissible language, could not flourish. (2) *Literacy.*
Consistent with the notion of a primordial imperative, Native
Hawaiians were eager to have publications in their own language, and
plantation groups that were more literate from the time of their
recruitment were most likely to develop print media in their own
languages. (3) *Market Forces.* Media flourish wherever there is a
market to tap; a multiethnic society, thus, may have more media per
capita than a monoethnic society, since pragmatic considerations lead
those who own printing presses to seek profits by providing products to
every possible sector of society. For the same pragmatic reason,
mainstream media seek to tap primordial loyalties by covering news of
the various ethnic groups, hoping thereby to increase market share. (4)
Political Motives. As mass society theorists know well, media are
capable of establishing or contesting a dominant discourse. In Hawai'i,
plantation elites sought to maintain political hegemony by printing
special publications in the languages of their workers, but they soon
competed with an opposition press run by non-English-speaking
publishers. (5) *Democratic Rights.* Despite efforts of ruling circles to
maintain control over the media, by a social constructionist
characterization of the "rapid Japanese press," the Bill of Rights
ultimately guarantees the right of media diversity for minority groups
and thus is on the side of racial equalitarianism in regard to the media.
Functionalists, who might point out the dangers of media diversity for
the maintenance of public order, are refuted by the example of Hawai'i,
where the majority of residents speak languages other than English,
have diverse cultural perspectives, and sometimes support the political
establishment. During World War II, when media were subjected to
censorship, the military still allowed publications in languages other
than English, recognizing their pragmatic necessity.

In the field of music (Chapter 5), Anthony Palmer reports that there
is no division between a Western mainstream and a set of ethnic
musical enclaves, as often found on the U.S. mainland. He attributes
musical multiculturalism to several factors: (1) *Cultural Necessity.*
Consistent with primordialist expectations, music is so central to the
cultural rituals and identity of many ethnic groups in Hawai'i that
musical talent is encouraged and loyal attendance is customary. (2)
Musical Innovation. Certain musical forms (*hapa haole and Jawaiian*)
and instruments (slack key guitar, steel guitar, and the *'ukulele*) were
developed in Hawai'i, becoming vital to the identity of an amalgamated

Island culture. (3) *Intermarriage.* Island residents are exposed to several musical genres as they grow up in families wherein the parents have different ethnic backgrounds, consistent with social distance theory. (4) *Cross-Ethnic Performers.* Flowing from the reality of social proximity of ethnic groups in Hawai'i, non-Caucasians perform Western music; non–Native Hawaiians enjoy dancing the *hula*; Caucasians perform non-Western music; and members of each cultural tradition expand their horizons to other musical traditions because of an appreciation for the contributions of various ethnic musical traditions. This crossover phenomenon applies much more to music than to the printed and electronic media. (5) *Accessibility.* Rather than having music available only at high concert prices or performed in relative secret within ethnic enclaves, a scenario that would characterize a mass society, various forms of music are available in parks, at schools, on television, and to preface nonmusical events. There has been no effort to impose artificial barriers to restrict access to musical diversity. (6) *Financial Support.* There is a pragmatic reason for musical heterogeneity. In addition to music for tourists, which keeps many musicians more than a paycheck away from poverty, funding by local foundations and the East-West Center has been crucial in keeping music diverse. Once again, functionalist fears of diversity are unfounded.

Literary diversity (Chapter 6) emerged in Hawai'i, according to Rodney Morales, for the following reasons: (1) *Mainstream Arrogance.* The *haole* literary establishment, hardly exponents of racial equalitarianism, failed to encourage or even perceive local literature, disparaged and ignored nascent trends, and is still rewarded by mainland scriptwriters and others for presenting distorted images of Hawai'i. The very attempt to establish a monocultural mass society in the field of literature, thus, boomeranged. (2) *Native Hawaiian Renaissance.* John Dominis Holt's *On Being Hawaiian* (1964) was a primordialist wake-up call to Native Hawaiians and others to create a new literary genre, and Native Hawaiian writers have arisen to the occasion. (3) *Social Distance.* The third and fourth generation of Chinese and Japanese in Hawai'i, many of whom grew up in the secure middle class while George Ariyoshi was governor, have very different experiences and visions of Hawai'i from those of the monoculturalist *haoles*, struggling immigrants, and troubled Native Hawaiians. The Bamboo Ridge movement filled a deep need to express what might be called a contemporary, local, multicultural, and regional literature. (4) *Commercial Support.* The Bamboo Ridge movement succeeded in attracting foundation funds as well as subscriptions, whereas efforts to establish other local literary outlets failed commercially. The increasing affluence and political power of non-*haoles* crashed through barriers to literary diversity erected by racial inequalitarians. However, the pragmatic reason for literary diversity is of much lesser significance, as there is only meager financial aid to local and Native Hawaiian writers, and both communities have a deep desire to express themselves apart from remunerative motives. Once again, the functionalist fear of diversity is misplaced; alternative literary traditions provide cultural enrichment and opportunities for dialog that can serve to reduce divisive conflict within Hawai'i.

Yasumasa Kuroda's (Chapter 7) study of attitudes demonstrated that there are more similarities than differences among those who live in Hawai'i, though he does not focus on opinions toward ethnic in- or out-groups. In accounting for the differences, he identifies the following factors: (1) *Socioeconomic Status.* Educational levels account for more optimistic outlooks, especially when comparing those from the U.S. mainland with those born in Hawai'i. (2) *Cohort.* Older Asian/Pacific voters tend to be more traditional and have their views shaped by past traumas more than younger persons in regard to some but not all values. (3) *Culture.* Kuroda finds a set of values that distinguish Island-born residents from mainland-born arrivals. The local culture of Hawai'i assigns primacy to family over the individual, whereas mainlanders have an opposite view. Thus, mainland culture tends to assume a mass society, whereas Islanders have a more communitarian, equalitarian orientation.

The politics of Hawai'i, which Michael Haas describes (Chapter 8), could not ignore ethnicity for the following reasons: (1) *Group Solidarity.* In keeping with the primordialist perspective, each group recognizes that it has different cultural styles and economic interests to protect. (2) *Group Antagonism.* In some cases, especially the *haole/* non-*haole* cleavage, group interests have been diametrically opposed; *haoles* dominated the Republican Party, and Japanese joined the Democratic Party in order to further their pragmatic interests. (3) *Desire to Maximize Power.* The two largest ethnic groups have seized leadership roles in the opposing political parties; the Republicans, the party long associated with racial inequalitarianism, have a history of placing artificial barriers in the way of non-*haoles*. (4) *Imperative of Coalition Building*. Since no ethnic group has comprised a majority of the votes during most of the twentieth century, the dominant ethnic group of each political party has sought to corral votes of other ethnic groups. To obtain a winning coalition, quiet appeals to leaders of ethnic groups with lesser numbers, involving pragmatic promises of government contracts and employment, have been successful. (5) *Pseudo-Class Politics*. Although campaign rhetoric appeals to many interests, political leaders since statehood have advanced the fortunes of some ethnic groups over others, and politics has worked to the advantage of the affluent over the less fortunate ethnic groups. From the malaise due to the increasing gap between haves and have-nots, as mass society theory predicts, Frank Fasi formed third parties to mount challenges, hoping to attract disaffected Filipinos, *haoles*, and Native Hawaiians who believe that they have little access to political power, but he has been unsuccessful.

The ethnic divisions within Hawai'i politics may appear to provide grist for the functionalist mill. Having explained why ethnic politics exists, however, Chapter 8 also accounts for the rise of a more integrative post-ethnic multicultural politics: (1) *Ticket Balancing*. The tradition of running representatives of all major ethnic groups for statewide offices has enabled voters to choose the most multiethnic political party, the Democrats, thus continually repudiating pre-statehood racial inequalitarianism. (2) *Intermarriage*. As ethnically mixed voters increase in numbers at the polls, candidates likewise represent more than one ethnic background, decreasing social distance and washing out primordialist considerations. (3) *Candidate Orientation*. Voters increasingly select office seekers more on the basis of personal characteristics other than on ethnicity, and there is a more pragmatic issue-oriented electorate nowadays. (4) *Mathematics*. From a pragmatic point of view, open appeals to ethnic groups will boomerang; since no group has a voting majority, the era of ethnic dominance is over. (5) *Communitarian Ideology*. Perhaps the main reason for a post-ethnic politics is that politicians are so responsive to ethnic interests that they will defer to the sensitivities of groups that object to discriminatory policies. Political leaders guard against the dangers of a mass society.

Ed Beechert's (Chapter 9) history of efforts to organize labor poses the following question: Why did multiethnic cooperation among workers in Hawai'i emerge from a capitalist economy, in which the central organizing principle is competition, and among various ethnic groups that were unaccustomed to trade unions? His answers are the following: (1) *Labor Shortage.* Native Hawaiians were not eager to work for low wages on land from which they were displaced, and they saw their identity threatened as a people, so primordial considerations prompted them to avoid plantation labor. Recruitment of foreign laborers was therefore in earnest, leaving workers in a good bargaining position; pragmatically, non-*haoles* realized the advantages of working together, a factor now absent among workers imported from the U.S. mainland. (2) *Exploitation.* Plantation workers came primarily to accumulate capital yet were paid less than expected, while plantation owners got rich, so multiethnic labor organizing served pragmatic objectives. (3) *Integration.* Management sought to divide the races by a social constructionist classification of the population by ethnicity and differential rates of pay based on ethnic categories, but these efforts boomeranged. Interethnic social patterns, such as ethnic intermarriage, integrated schools, and multiethnic bowling leagues organized by the unions lessened social distance, though the current tendency is for a mass society to pull groups apart. (4) *Human Rights Orientation.* For many years, management was committed to a racial inequalitarian perspective, but eventually New Deal legislation ensured that unions could organize, and racism became unpopular. Indeed, functionalist logic dictated that management make concessions in order to preserve industrial peace.

Jonathan Okamura (Chapter 10) begins his narrative at 1970, when Chinese and Japanese had already risen to the level of Caucasians, thus disproving any notions of inherent Caucasian superiority. He then explains the continuing gap between these three lighter-skinned Hawai'i residents from the darker-skinned Filipinos, Native Hawaiians, and Samoans in several ways: (1) *Employment Structure.* Practically speaking, few middle-class jobs exist in today's tourism-based economy, which employs a mass of workers in dead-end jobs, so there is little opportunity for entire ethnic groups to rise from working-class to middle-class status. (2) *Institutional Racism.* Educational opportunities are not equally available for the less affluent ethnic groups; consistent with racial equalitarian theory, he notes that public schools are denied adequate funding, and he cites evidence that there are insufficient minority teachers to provide role models. (3*) Pseudo-*

Meritocracy. Although he concedes that some Filipinos, Native Hawaiians, and Samoans have moved into middle-class positions on the basis of qualifications, he asserts that many members of these groups are underemployed, that is, they are unable to secure work appropriate to their qualifications and instead settle for jobs that require lesser educational and skill levels. In short, also consistent with racial equalitarianism, the existence of barriers to equal treatment in employment refutes the thesis that meritocracy has prevailed in Hawai'i since statehood. (4) *Group Conflict.* Clearly, affluent groups see the pragmatic advantages of investing resources in their children to go to private schools. Okamura stops short of charging that current discrimination is intentional, suggesting instead that ethnic groups which benefited from the educational route to social mobility before statehood are under the illusion that the less affluent groups can rise as easily as they did in times past.

Michael Haas (Chapter 11) documents how efforts to provide monocultural education in elementary and secondary education ultimately failed in multiethnic Hawai'i. Several reasons are enunciated: (1) *Civil Rights.* According to the equal protection clause of the 14th amendment to the U.S. Constitution, Japanese language schools could not be closed in the 1920s, and bilingual instruction for Filipino and other immigrants was mandated in the 1970s. Constitutional requirements, backed up by federal enforcement agencies, checkmated exponents of racial inequalitarianism and their efforts to construct a homogeneous mass society in the name of maintaining social order. (2) *Political Pressure.* Flagrant denials of equal educational opportunities mobilized the Filipino and Native Hawaiian communities, ultimately embarrassing the Japanese-dominated public school system to provide special programs appropriate to their needs. For both, the goal has been pragmatic—to enable the next generation to achieve greater social status. (3) *Professionalism in Education.* Educational professionals were eager to design innovative minority programs and multicultural curricula. (4) *Monetary Incentives.* Funds were available from the federal government to support multicultural education; athough some public school officials initially turned down the funds, pragmatic considerations won out.

Noting that the University of Hawai'i is much less multicultural than other institutions, Michael Haas (Chapter 12) explores several possible explanations: (1) *Elitism.* University administration and faculty have constructed an image of academia as a Darwinistic arena in which only the best minds of each generation survive, so they resist changes that emerge from democratic norms of equality; monocultural administrators and faculty prefer to treat students as an undifferentiated, socially distant mass and then do not question why some ethnic groups do so much better than others. (2) *Institutional Racism.* Artificial barriers adversely impact the ability of some ethnic groups to complete college, such as rigid ethnically biased entrance tests, grading based on competitive norms that discriminate against persons from cooperative cultures, and insufficient scholarship funds for the poorest ethnic groups. (3) *Resistance to Legislative Innovations.* Innovations mandated by the state legislature, when supported by progressive faculty and students seeking to break free from the monocultural mass society of the past, have often promoted multicultural aims over a recalcitrant university administration. (4) *Student Quiescence.* Generally reactive more than proactive, students have mobilized on occasion to stop nefarious administrative decisions and practices that have impeded multiculturalism on campus, but they have failed to apply continuing pressure because of the pragmatic need to go off campus in order to earn a living.

A. Didrick Castberg's (Chapter 13) search through the labyrinth of the criminal justice system encountered some ethnic correlates in arrest statistics. The following explanations are advanced: (1) *Cultural Propensities.* Filipinos are disproportionately arrested for cockfighting, possibly an assertion of primordial identity on the part of those who have recently left the home country. (2) *Economic Circumstances.* African Americans, Caucasians, and Koreans account for higher rates of prostitution arrests, finding a ready market in the tourist industry and among Korean deep-sea fishing personnel. Caucasians in the armed forces predominate in arrests for negligent manslaughter because they often drive under the influence of alcohol on weekend passes from military bases. Poorer Filipinos are disproportionately arrested for possession of synthetic narcotics, which are sold for profit. (3) *Alienation.* Recently arrived groups, such as Filipinos, Mexicans, and Vietnamese, disproportionately join youth gangs and end up engaging in such offenses as drug dealing.

Castberg also analyzes whether ethnic disparities amount to discrimination against those charged of crimes who are later convicted and incarcerated. He encounters no evidence of institutional discrimination for the following reasons: (1) *Multiethnic Criminal Justice Personnel.* As expected by racial equalitarian theory, previous barriers to employment for previously underrepresented ethnic groups have been removed, so most ethnic groups are found at every stage of the criminal justice system, reducing the social distance between those who operate the criminal justice system and those who commit crimes. (2) *Lack of Judicial Discretion.* The state legislature has erected barriers to judicial whim by passing mandatory sentencing laws.

Ibrahim Aoudé (Chapter 14) asserts that the political economy of Hawai'i has always been based more on class than ethnicity, but some ethnic groups have succeeded while others, notably Filipinos and Native Hawaiians, have failed to progress in recent years. Explanations advanced include the following: (1) *Capitalist Darwinism.* In order to continue to operate businesses, capitalists are very pragmatic: They must make profits, which, in turn, means that workers without lucrative employment alternatives will be exploited. (2) *Waning of the Democratic Party's "Revolution."* Whereas the victorious Democratic Party in 1954 promised a "New Hawai'i" that would bring social democracy to the Islands, successive governors have not given substance to the spirit of 1954, instead preferring to mouth the socially constructed concept of a "diversified economy" in order to mask inattention to the needs of Filipinos and Native Hawaiians. Aoudé finds that the Democratic "revolution" became a counterrevolution after the election of Governor Cayetano, who decided to ape Republican themes of downsizing government and giving tax breaks to business executives (who are expected, as usual, to use the windfall in order to invest elsewhere). (3) *Ineffective Social Movements.* One way to resist excessive exploitation is for affected persons to protest. Aoudé notes that most so-called development projects of the 1970s evicted tenant farmers and others, despite some grassroots agitation regarding the negative social consequences. The mass society created by capitalism meant that victims of development were often too marginalized and socially distant to join forces with other groups, and trade unions favored the jobs that development (and displacement of Native Hawaiians) would create. He expects that social movements will grow as the gap between rich and poor increases. (4) *Global Economy.* A primary reason why grassroots movements have failed is that the economy of Hawai'i is not controlled inside the state but instead increasingly at boardrooms of multinational corporations around the world, which have pragmatic desires for profit, are uninterested in the social problems of Hawai'i, and are beyond the reach of the state legislature.

THEORETICAL IMPLICATIONS

The challenge of the book has been to identify a model of ethnic relations from the experience of Hawai'i. At this point the utility of alternative theories can be assessed in regard to the major transitions identified above: (1) the period of the monarchy to the era of *haole* dominance, (2) the transition from *haole* dominance to the rise of Japanese political dominance, (3) the rise of multiethnic politics, and (4) the nontransition of Filipinos and Native Hawaiians to greater social mobility since statehood.

Clearly, the monarchy embraced multiculturalism. Rather than blocking the *haoles*, Native Hawaiians were eager to learn the English language and to become a part of the world economy. Pragmatic considerations played a role, but the commitment to racial *aloha* was a more primordial imperative for Native Hawaiians.

After private property was instituted in the 1850s, a mass society increasingly developed. The *haole* elites overthrew the monarchy for pragmatic reasons (they wanted to get rich), and they were wired into racist centers of political power in Washington, D.C., that viewed non-Caucasians as inferior and undeserving of self-rule. Monoculturalization was the principal means by which the *haole* upstarts sought to impose colonial rule on non-Caucasians, but each ethnic group insisted on maintaining its cultural, linguistic, and musical traditions. Although the U.S. Supreme Court would not allow a closure of Japanese language schools, and the press flourished in many languages, the *haole* oligarchy not only blocked the growth of trade unions but also constructed artificial barriers to block the advancement of non-*haoles*, such as the English standard schools. Such developments as Hawai'i Creole English attested to the resiliency of non-Caucasians, who were determined never to accept an inferior status in the Islands.

Ultimately, many non-*haoles* advanced to middle-class status, and leaders from these communities were able to mobilize enough support for union recognition and for Democratic Party candidates to topple the *haole* Republicans after World War II. Thoroughly discredited were the English standard schools and other elements of the mass society that Republicans had constructed for so long. Even in the field of literature, *haole* hegemony eventually ended with the rise of the Bamboo Ridge movement.

With the Democrats in command, political power shifted to the Japanese community, which achieved extraordinary upward social mobility. The failure of Filipinos and Native Hawaiians to benefit from Democratic Party rule, however, has posed a threat to continued racial *aloha* in Hawai'i. Democrats, in turn, have responded to the demands for justice from both communities by rolling back some policies and practices of institutional racism in the criminal justice system and the public schools (but ineffectively at the University of Hawai'i) and by fielding multiethnic voting slates in order to defuse tension.

Reviewing the applicability of various theories, the residents of Hawai'i are fortunate that Native Hawaiians established the principle of racial *aloha* before the arrival of Captain Cook. Efforts of the *haole* oligarchs to establish social distance, which were enforced by economic and political power, only set them apart from non-*haoles*, who developed an amalgamated culture and language, formed trade unions together, intermarried, ultimately arose to control political power, and now have captured the imagination of the local literary scene. Social distance theory may even explain why Filipinos and Native Hawaiians have not achieved upward social mobility, as teachers in public schools and at the University of Hawai'i are drawn from the affluent ethnic groups.

Functionalist theory is thoroughly refuted by the example of Hawai'i. Efforts to homogenize the Islands in the name of "better social order" have themselves been the principal source of disruption. "Better social order for whom?" is the question that we must ask when functionalists urge adoption of a single national or state language, want trade unions to stop striking, and the like.

Mass society theory provides keen insights into the history of Hawai'i. The downfall of Native Hawaiians came when private property was instituted in the 1850s, and the common people were tricked into being a mass of tenants on ancestral lands, while the *ali'i* sought economic advancement rather than maintaining solidarity with their own people. *Haole* rule entailed efforts to deprive the masses of institutions that could mediate on their behalf with the citadels of economic and political power, whether by shutting down language schools, refusing to recognize trade unions, establishing English standard schools to ensure that non-Caucasians would be denied an opportunity to learn the *lingua franca* of business and government, by staffing higher governmental positions only with *haoles* and Native Hawaiians, and by ignoring the literary excellence of non-*haoles*. However, the effort to impose a mass society failed, not only through the development of HCE but also the rise of media in several languages, musical innovations, the Bamboo Ridge and Native Hawaiian literary movements, ticket balancing in elections, multiethnic trade unions, and diversity in a multiethnic criminal justice system that is untainted by ethnic discrimination. Currently, tracking in public schools, individualistic *haole* attitudes in the private sector, and University of Hawai'i faculty elitism keep enclaves of a mass society alive, thereby frustrating efforts of Filipinos and Native Hawaiians to achieve the kind of social mobility experienced by other non-*haole* groups in the Aloha State. The individualism of mainlanders transplanted to the Islands assumes a mass society, but local residents subscribe to communitarian views.

Racial equalitarianism is vindicated by the material presented in this book as well. The modern social history of Hawai'i is a story of artificial barriers erected by *haoles* in criminal justice, education, employment, land ownership, and trade union organizing, which, in turn, provoked opposition. When many of these barriers were cast aside by the multiethnic Democrats, the result was upward mobility for Chinese, Japanese, and Koreans. That institutional racism persists in the public schools and the state university is one reason why Filipinos and Native Hawaiians have not advanced.

Social constructionists can find much grist for their theoretical mill in Hawai'i. Ethnic and other artificial classifications were, until the advent of affirmative action, used primarily to privilege the most affluent groups. The term "standard English," for example, was used in an invidious manner. Scores on ethnically biased tests have held back certain groups from teaching in the public schools and attending the University of Hawai'i at Manoa even when their prior performance was exemplary. However, most non-*haoles* were not fooled by invidious classifications; on securing political power, *haole* (an unflattering socially constructed category) social constructionist experiments ended.

Certainly, the distinctiveness and resilience of ethnic groups in the fiftieth state may appear to strengthen the primordialist perspective. Ethnic groups, despite monoculturalist efforts, have maintained themselves by celebrating their ancestral languages and musics. However, the high rate of ethnic intermarriage, lesser levels of ethnic bloc voting, and the tendency for crossover musicians in Hawai'i tends to refute primordialist presuppositions. The people of the Islands respect one another's cultures rather than contributing to an exclusivist primordial imperative.

Pragmatism (or instrumentalism, if you prefer) accounts for much ethnic conflict as well as ethnic cooperation. *Haole* missionaries, cut off from church subsidies, pressured the king to establish private property so that they would have an economic base. Both the macaronic pidgin and Hawaiian Creole English developed out of necessity, since ethnic groups on the plantations were in such close contact. The nonmainstream language press has flourished because it has been profitable. In 1901, the *haole* oligarchs stirred up Native Hawaiians against the Chinese and Japanese for the pragmatic goal of securing political power. Pocketbook considerations explain why *haoles* opposed trade unions and why non-*haoles* achieved solidarity. Chinese and Japanese devoted considerable effort to achieving higher educational attainments, eventually dominating the public school system to the detriment of Filipinos and Native Hawaiians, in order to ensure social mobility for themselves. Japanese opted for multiethnic voting slates in the Democratic Party in order to forestall defections to the Republican Party. Bamboo Ridge Press has been more successful than other nonmainstream literary ventures because it is profitable. Nonetheless, the resurgence of the Hawaiian language lacks any practical payoff and is clearly an assertion of primordial identity.

The Marxian variant of instrumentalism should not be ignored. The pragmatic choices just identified above can be viewed as premised on retaining economic power. Social mobility for Chinese and Japanese was available when middle-class jobs were created during the New Deal, the Cold War, and the transition to statehood. With the globalization of capital and commerce, Hawai'i's high cost of living precludes further economic expansion. Accordingly, most Filipinos and Native Hawaiians seem destined to remain indefinitely in the low-paying jobs of the tourist industry. Still, the seamy side of ethnic inequality has not been translated into ethnic turmoil, as some theories would lead us to believe.

In short, as perhaps might be expected from a volume representing diverse voices, an eclectic approach explains multiculturalism in the Islands. A new theory, based on the experience of Hawai'i, would doubtless stress the primacy of the culture of *aloha*.

CONCLUSION

Some chapters of the Ku Klux Klan reportedly seek to rescind Hawai'i statehood. For vested interests on the mainland, whatever success the Islands enjoy is a threat to the continuation of Caucasian dominance. Meanwhile, scholars who either decry multiculturalism or advance multiculturalism in theoretical terms usually do so without drawing upon the wisdom of an actual model. This volume should put an end to such foolishness.

Hawai'i, once the model of racial integration for the nation and the world, has become multicultural without a formal movement by leaders from education or government. The people have insisted that no dominant group has the right to trample on the cultural values of another group, and they developed multiculturalism without an explicit model. Instead of the ethnic arrogance, confrontation, and violence that is often practiced on the U.S. mainland, the people of Hawai'i have tried dialogue, friendship, and humility as primary methods for addressing problems. Although Hawai'i has many serious problems, and there is a tendency toward complacency in the Islands with regard to issues of ethnic inequality, those on the mainland who favor or oppose multiculturalism must now take the Hawai'i model into account. The Islands have been united, not disunited, by a multiculturalism in which there is a lack of social distance between ethnic groups, a refusal to allow a mass society to take root, a resistance to institutional racism, and a strongly held belief that all persons are entitled to be treated with dignity, fairness, and respect—in other words, with *aloha*.

References

Abbott, William L. (1967). *The American Labor Heritage*. Honolulu: Industrial Relations Center, University of Hawai'i.

Abramson, Joan (1975). *The Invisible Woman*. San Francisco: Jossey-Bass.

Adams, Wonda (1991). "KCCN-FM Takes over Top Spot in Arbitron Ratings Battle," *Honolulu Advertiser*, October 11, C8.

Adamski, Mary (1988). "Panelist Says Bloc Voting by Race in Hawaii Is a Hard Reality," *Honolulu Star-Bulletin*, September 30, A4.

Afro-American Association of Hawaii (1991). "Report on the University of Hawaii and the African-American Athlete." Reprinted in Honolulu: Center for Research on Ethnic Relations, University of Hawai'i at Manoa, *Document Series*, #8.

Agbayani, Amefil (1994). *O Le Sulufa'iga: Report of the University of Hawai'i Task Force on Samoans and Pacific Islanders in Higher Education.* Honolulu: Office of Student Equity, Excellence and Diversity, University of Hawai'i at Manoa.

Agbayani-Cahill, Amefil, et al. (1975). "A Study of Immigrant and Non-Immigrant Youth on Oahu." Honolulu: unpublished manuscript, Behavioral Research Group, Office of Human Resources, City and County of Honolulu.

Altschull, J. Herbert (1984*). Agents of Power: The Role of the News Media in Human Affairs*. New York: Longman.

Anthony, J. Garner (1955). *Hawaii under Army Rule*. Stanford, CA: Stanford University Press.

Aoudé, Ibrahim (1994). "Hawai'i: The Housing Crisis and the State's Development Strategy," *Social Process In Hawaii*, 35, 71–84.

Aoudé, Ibrahim G. (1995). "Tourist Attraction: Hawai'i's Locked in Economy." In *Social Process in Hawai'i: A Reader*, ed. Peter Manicas, 226–42. New York: McGraw-Hill.

Ariyoshi, Koji (1953). "Into the Sixth Year," *Honolulu Record*, August 6, 60.

Armstrong, Diane (1975). "Police Report on Student Crime: 669 Arrests Here in 7 Months," *Honolulu Star-Bulletin*, September 26, A1.

Ashizawa, Becky (1990). "Hawaiians Get Legal Help to Hang onto Their Land: The Land Title Project Has Saved Many Family Tracts," *Honolulu Star-Bulletin*, June 18, A6.

Associated Press (1991). "UH's Treatment of Blacks Questioned: Black Athletes Have Been Involved in a Series of Incidents," *Honolulu Star-Bulletin*, October 4, D1.

Astin, Alexander W. (1982). *Minorities in American Higher Education*. San Francisco: Jossey-Bass.

Bacchilega, Cristina (1994). "Multilocality and Local Literature." In *Hawai'i Literature Conference Reader's Guide*, ed. Lorna Hershinow, 8–12. Honolulu: Hawai'i Literary Arts Council.

Bank of Hawaii (1995). "Selected Economic Indicators," *Business Trends*, 40 (January/February), 7.

Bank of Hawaii (1996). "Selected Economic Indicators," *Business Trends*, 41 (January/February), 7.

Barnett, Greg (1996). " Donor Found at Last for Little Alana," *Honolulu Advertiser,* May 30, A1.

Barringer, Herbert (1995). "The Educational, Occupational and Economic Status of Native Hawaiians." Paper presented at the Ethnic Studies Community Conference, Honolulu, May 20–21.

Barringer, Herbert, and Nolan Liu (1994*). The Demographic, Social and Economic Status of Native Hawaiians, 1990*. Honolulu: Alu Like.

Barth, Frederik (1969). "Introduction." In *Ethnic Groups and Boundaries*, ed. Frederik Barth, 10–17. Boston: Little, Brown.

Bateson, Gregory (1936*). Naven: A Survey of the Problems Suggested by a Composite Picture of the Culture of a New Guinea Tribe Drawn from Three Points of View*. Cambridge, UK: Cambridge University Press.

Beckford, George (1972). *Persistent Poverty: Underdevelopment in Plantation Economies in the Third World*. London: Zed Books.

Beechert, Edward D. (1985). *Working in Hawai'i: A Labor History*. Honolulu: University of Hawai'i Press.

Beechert, Edward D. (1988). "Technology and the Plantation Labour Supply: The Case of Queensland, Hawai'i, Cuba, and Louisiana." In *The World*

Sugar Economy in War and Depression, 1914–1950, eds. Bill Albert and Adrian Graves, 131–42. London: Routledge.

Beechert, Edward D. (1993). *Aupuni I La'au: A History of Hawai'i's Carpenters Union, Local 745.* Honolulu: Center for Labor Education and Research, University of Hawai'i at Manoa.

Benn, Denis M. (1974). "The Theory of Plantation Economy and Society: A Methodological Critique," *Journal of Commonwealth and Comparative Politics*, 12 (November), 249–60.

Bickerton, Derek (1983). "Creole Languages," *Scientific American*, 249 (1), 116–22.

Bickerton, Derek, and Carol Odo (1976). *Final Report on NSF Grant No. 39574.* Honolulu: Department of Linguistics, University of Hawai'i at Manoa.

Bickerton, Derek, and William H. Wilson (1987). "Pidgin Hawaiian." In *Pidgin and Creole Languages: Essays in Honor of John E. Reinecke*, ed. Glenn G. Gilbert, 61–76. Honolulu: University of Hawai'i Press.

Bingham, Hiram (1849). *A Residence of Twenty-One Years in the Sandwich Islands.* Hartford, CT: Huntington.

Bishop, Artemus (1854). *Na hua'olelo a me na 'olelo kikeke ma ka 'olelo Beretania a ma ka 'olelo Hawai'i.* Rutland, VT: Tuttle, 1968 [reprint].

Bishop, Isabella Bird (1874). *Six Months in the Sandwich Islands.* Honolulu: University of Hawai'i Press reprint, 1964.

Blount, James (1893). *Papers Relating to the Mission of James Blount.* Washington, DC: Government Printing Office.

Bonacich, Edna (1980). "Class Approaches to Ethncitiy and Race," *Insurgent Sociologist*, 10 (Fall), 1–15.

Borreca, Richard (1985). "Wooing the Filipino Vote," *Honolulu, 20,* November, *24.*

Borreca, Richard (1990). "Mednick Says 'Balanced Ticket' Are Actually Words of Racism," *Honolulu Star-Bulletin*, July 13, A4.

Borreca, Richard (1991). "Dec. 7: Military Replaces Civilian Rule," *Honolulu Star-Bulletin*, December 2, A8.

Boylan, Daniel (1992). "Blood Runs Thick: Ethnicity as a Factor in Hawai'i's Politics." In *Politics and Public Policy in Hawai'i*, eds. Zachary A. Smith and Richard C. Pratt, chap. 4. Albany: State University of New York Press.

Bradley, Harold W. (1942). *The American Frontier in Hawaii: The Pioneers, 1789–1843.* Stanford, CA: Stanford University Press.

Brieske, Phillip R. (1961). *A Study of the Development of Public Elementary and Secondary Education in the Territory of Hawaii.* Seattle: Ph.D. dissertation, University of Washington.

Brown, Laura, and Walter Cohen (1975). *Hawaii Faces the Pacific.* Palo Alto: Pacific Studies Center.

Bunker, Frank F. (1922). "The Education of the Child of the American-Born Parent in Hawaii," *Hawaii Educational Review*, 11 (September), 1–2.

Burris, Jerry (1974). "If He Weren't Running . . . McClung Would Back Gill over 2," *Honolulu Advertiser*, October 2, A1.

Burris, Jerry (1981). "Ethnic Political Tradition Lives," *Honolulu Advertiser*, June 22, E2.

Burris, Jerry (1990). "Undecided Voters Hold Key to Senate Victory," *Honolulu Advertiser*, October 31, A1, A4.

Burris, Jerry (1994a). "The Battle for Your Vote for Governor—and Some Clues as to Who Will Win It: Ethnicity, Party Do Matter, But Issues May Matter in '94 . . .," *Honolulu Advertiser*, October 23, B1.

Burris, Jerry (1994b). "Who's Seen as Most Caring, Honest, Able? Opinion Poll Gives Saiki Best Marks," *Honolulu Advertiser*, February 20, A3.

Bushnell, O.A. (1981). "O.A. Bushnell: Questions and Answers." In *Writers of Hawai'i: A Focus on Our Literary Heritage*, eds. Eric Chock and Jody Manabe, 33–42. Honolulu: Bamboo Ridge Press.

Cablas, Armando (1991). "Pilipino Americans and the Scholastic Aptitude Test at the University of Hawai'i at Manoa: A Review of the Literature," *Social Process in Hawaii*, 22, 91–106.

Campos, Danilo (1991). "Operation Manong Program for Minority Students." Paper presented at the annual convention of the Association for Asian-American Studies, Honolulu, May 30.

Carey, James W. (1989). *Communication as Culture: Essays on Media and Society.* Boston: Unwin Hyman.

Carmichael, Stokely, and Charles V. Hamilton (1967). *Black Power: The Politics of Liberation in America.* New York: Vintage.

Carnegie Foundation for the Advancement of Teaching (1991). *National Survey of Kindergarten Teachers.* New York: Carnegie.

Carr, Elizabeth B. (1972). *Da Kine Talk: From Pidgin to Standard English in Hawaii.* Honolulu: University of Hawai'i Press.

Carter, Joey (1990). "Being Haole in Hawaii," *Ka Leo O Hawai'i*, September 5, 6–7.

Castberg, A. Didrick (1971). "The Ethnic Factor in Criminal Sentencing," *Western Political Quarterly*, 24 (September), 425–37.

Cayetano, Ben (1994). *This Is What I Believe; This Is What I'll Do.* Honolulu: Cayetano for Governor Campaign.

Cayetano, Ben (1995). "Better for Business?" *Hawaii Business*, 40 (January), 15–21 [interview with Ben Cayetano].

Cayetano, Ben (1996). *Restoring Hawaii's Economic Momentum.* Honolulu: Department of Business, Economic Development, and Tourism, State of Hawai'i.

Chapin, Helen Geracimos (1984). "Newspapers of Hawai'i 1834–1903: From 'He Liona' to the Pacific Cable," *Hawaiian Journal of History*, 18, 47–86.

Chapin, Helen Geracimos (1996). *Shaping History: The Role of Newspapers in Hawai'i.* Honolulu: University of Hawai'i Press.

Chattergy, Virgie (1992). "Complexity and Challenge: Asian Americans in Higher Education," *Teaching & Learning*, 5 (Spring), 4–5.

Chesney-Lind, Meda, et al. (1992). *Gangs and Delinquency in Hawaii.* Honolulu: Center for Youth Research, Social Science Research Institute, University of Hawai'i at Manoa.

Chinen, Joyce (1984). "Working Wives and the Socioeconomic Status of Ethnic Groups in Hawai'i," *Humboldt Journal of Social Relations*, 11 (2), 87–105.

Chock, Eric (1986). "Tutu on the Curb." In *The Best of Bamboo Ridge: The Hawai'i Writers' Quarterly*, eds. Eric Chock and Darrell H. Y. Lum, 6. Honolulu: Bamboo Ridge Press.

Chock, Eric (1996). "The Neocolonialization of Bamboo Ridge: Repositioning Bamboo Ridge and Local Literature in the 1990's." Paper presented at an English Department colloquium, University of Hawai'i at Manoa, May 2.

Chock, Eric, and Darrell H. Y. Lum, eds. (1986). *The Best of Bamboo Ridge: The Hawai'i Writers' Quarterly.* Honolulu: Bamboo Ridge Press.

Clement, Russell (1980). "From Cook to the 1840 Constitution: The Name Change from Sandwich to Hawaiian Islands," *Hawaiian Journal of History*, 14, 50–57.

Coffman, Tom (1970). "Burns' Best Support from Women, AJAs," *Honolulu Star-Bulletin,* January 15, A1.

Coffman, Tom (1973). *Catch a Wave: A Case Study of Hawaii's New Politics.* Honolulu: University Press of Hawaii.

Coleman, James Samuel, et al. (1966). *On Equality of Educational Opportunity.* Washington, DC: Government Printing Office.

Compaine, Benjamin, ed. (1982). *Who Owns the Media?* 2nd ed. White Plains, NY: Knowledge Industry Publications.

Conan, Katherine (1946). *The History of Contract Labor in the Hawaiian Islands*. Princeton, NJ: Princeton University Press.

Cooper, George, and Gavan Daws (1985). *Land and Power in Hawaii: The Democratic Years*. Honolulu: Benchmark Press.

Council on Language Planning and Policy (c. 1996). "Statement of Goals." Honolulu: mimeo, Council on Language Planning and Policy.

Crane, Jeffrey L., and Alton M. Okinaka (1992). "Social Dynamics of the Aloha State: The Population of Hawai'i." In *Politics and Public Policy in Hawai'i*, eds. Zachary A. Smith and Richard C. Pratt, chap. 3. Albany: State University of New York Press.

Dahl, Robert A. (1961). *Who Governs? Democracy and Power in an American City*. New Haven, CT: Yale University Press.

Damon, Francis W. (1907). "Hawai'i's Example to California," *Independent*, 62 (February 14), 363–68.

Dannemiller, James E. (1973). "Ethnicity at the University of Hawaii." Honolulu: unpublished manuscript, Survey Research Office, Social Science Research Institute, University of Hawai'i at Manoa.

Daws, Gavan (1968). *Shoal of Time*. New York: Macmillan.

Day, A. Grove, and Carl Stroven, eds. (1959). *A Hawaiian Reader*. New York: Appleton-Century-Crofts.

Day, Richard R. (1985). "The Ultimate Inequality: Linguistic Genocide." In *Language of Inequality*, eds. Nessa Wolfson and Joan Manes, 163–81. New York: Mouton.

Digman, John, and Daniel W. Tuttle (1959). "An Analysis of Oahu's 1956 City-County Election." Honolulu: Center for Research on Ethnic Relations, Social Science Research Institute, University of Hawai'i at Manoa, *Working Paper* #6 [reprint].

Digman, John, and Daniel W. Tuttle (1961). "An Interpretation of an Election by Means of Obverse Factor Analysis," *Journal of Social Psychology*, 53 (April), 183–94.

Dollard, John (1949). *Caste and Class in a Southern Town*. New York: Harper.

Donnelly, Christine (1996). "Report Flunks Hawai'i on School Funding," *Honolulu Star-Bulletin*, April 4, A1.

du Puy, William Atherton (1932). *Hawaii and Its Race Problem*. Washington, DC: Government Printing Office.

Dudley, Michael Kioni, and Keoni Kealoha Agard (1990). *A Call for Hawaiian Sovereignty*. Honolulu: Na Kane o Ka Malo Press.

Durkheim, Émile (1893). *The Division of Labor in Society*. New York: Free Press, 1949.

Eisenstein, James, and Herbert Jacob (1977). *Felony Justice: An Organizational Analysis of Criminal Courts.* Boston: Little, Brown.

Endicott, George (1979). "An Outside View of Hawaii Politics," *Star-Bulletin & Advertiser,* July 22, B1, B4.

Epstein, Henry (1975). "Interview." In *History of the United Public Workers Union in Hawai'i.* Honolulu: microfiche, Hamilton Library, University of Hawai'i at Manoa.

Etzioni, Amitai (1993). *The Spirit of Community: Rights, Responsibilities, and the Communitarian Agenda.* New York: Crown Publishers.

Faludi, Susan C. (1991a). "Homeland History: Plan of a Prince Is Co-opted," *Star-Bulletin & Advertiser,* September 15, B3 [reprinted from *Wall Street Journal,* September 9, A1, A4].

Faludi, Susan C. (1991b). "How Everyone Got Hawaii Homelands Except Hawaiians: Federal Mandate Is Abused as Natives Wait Decades for Small Plots of Land; State Gives VIPs Huge Tracts," *Star-Bulletin & Advertiser,* September 15, B1, B3 [reprinted from *Wall Street Journal,* September 9, A1, A4].

Fanon, Franz (1961). *The Wretched of the Earth.* New York: Grove, 1968.

Farrington, Wallace R. (1904). "The Honolulu Newsboy," *Paradise of the Pacific* (December), 41–43.

Feagin, Joe R., and Clairece Booher Feagin (1996). *Racial and Ethnic Relations.* 5th ed. Upper Saddle River, NJ: Prentice-Hall.

Fernandez, Yvette (1993). "KIKI Exec Apologizes to Hawaiians," *Honolulu Advertiser,* June 19, A5.

Fishman, Joshua A., et al. (1982). *Language Resources in the United States.* Roselyn, VA: Inter-American Research Association.

Forbes, David W. (1991). "Look the Rock Whence Ye Are Hewn: A Reappraisal of Punahou's Early History." In *Punahou: The History and Promise of a School of the Islands,* ed. Nelson Foster, 119–49. Honolulu: Punahou.

Forer, Lois G. (1987). *A Chilling Effect: The Growing Threat of Libel and Invasion of Privacy Actions to the First Amendment.* New York: Norton.

Forman, Sheila M. (1991). "Filipino Participation in Civil Rights Policies and Practices in Hawai'i," *Social Process in Hawai'i,* 33, 1–11.

Fornander, Abraham (1880). *An Account of the Polynesian Race.* London: Trübner, 3 vols.

Friend, The (1887). "Anglo-Saxonizing Machines," *The Friend,* 45 (August), 63–64.

Fuchs, Lawrence H. (1961). *Hawaii Pono: A Social History.* New York: Harcourt, Brace & World.

Fujii, Edwin T., and James Mak (1985). "On the Relative Economic Progress of U.S.-Born Filipino Men," *Economic Development and Cultural Change,* 33 (3), 557–73.

Fujikane, Candace (1994). "Between Nationalisms: Hawai'i's Local Nation and Its Troubled Racial Paradise," *Critical Mass,* 1 (2), 23–58.

Fujiyama, Rodney M. (1967). *The Social Backgrounds of Hawaii's Legislators, 1945–1967.* Honolulu: senior honors thesis, University of Hawai'i at Manoa.

Gallimore, Ronald, Joan Whitehorn Boggs, and Cathie Jordan (1974). *Culture, Behavior and Education: A Study of Hawaiian-Americans.* Beverly Hills: Sage.

Geertz, Clifford (1973). *The Interpretation of Cultures.* New York: Basic Books.

Gereben, Janos (1970a). "Request for Racial Survey at UH an Error, HEW Says," *Honolulu Star-Bulletin,* October 19, A20.

Gereben, Janos (1970b). "UH Integrated, U.S. Study Shows," *Honolulu Star-Bulletin,* November 10, D18.

Geschwender, James A. (1978). *Racial Stratification in America.* Dubuque, IA: Brown.

Geschwender, James A. (1980–81). "Lessons from Waiahole-Waikane," *Social Process in Hawaii,* 28, 121–35.

Geschwender, James A. (1982). "The Hawaiian Transformation: Class, Submerged Nation, and National Minorities." In *Ascent and Decline in the World-System,* ed. Edward Friedman, chap. 8. Beverly Hills: Sage.

Geschwender, James A., and Rita Carroll-Seguin (1988). "Asian-American Success in Hawai'i: Myth, Reality or Artifact of Women's Labor?" In *Racism, Sexism and the World-System,* eds. Joan Smith et al., 187–207. New York: Greenwood.

Geschwender, James A., Rita Carroll-Seguin, and Howard Brill (1988). "The Portuguese and Haoles of Hawaii: Implications for the Origin of Ethnicity," *American Sociological Review,* 53 (August), 515–27.

Gladwin, Thomas (1972). "Institutional Racism at the University of Hawaii: The Ethnic Studies Program." Honolulu: Center for Research on Ethnic Relations, University of Hawai'i at Manoa, *Working Paper* #7 [reprint].

Glauberman, Stu (1979). "University Asked to Reconcile 8-Year-Old Dispute on Sex Bias," *Honolulu Star-Bulletin,* December 11, A2.

Glauberman, Stu (1988). "Misconduct at Schools Seems to Be Declining," *Honolulu Advertiser*, May 21, A4.

Glauberman, Stu (1992). "Hawaiian Nation Bill Gets OHA OK: Legislation Now Goes to Congress," *Honolulu Advertiser*, February 6, A1, A2.

Glazer, Nathan (1982). "Politics of a Multiethnic Society." In *Ethnic Relations in America*, ed. Lance Liebman, chap. 5. Englewood Cliffs, NJ: Prentice-Hall.

Glazer, Nathan, and Daniel P. Moynihan (1963). *Beyond the Melting Pot: The Negroes, Puerto Ricans, Jews, Italians, and Irish of New York City.* Cambridge, MA: MIT Press.

Glick, Clarence E. (1980). *Sojourners and Settlers: Chinese Migrants in Hawaii.* Honolulu: University Press of Hawai'i.

Goodale, W.W. (1914). "Brief History of Hawaiian Unskilled Labor," *Thrum's Hawaiian Almanac and Annual*, 170–91.

Goodman, Morris (1985). "Bickerton, Roots of Language," *International Journal of American Linguistics*, 51 (January), 109–37 [book review].

Gordon, Milton M. (1964). *Assimilation in American Life: The Role of Race, Religion, and National Origins.* New York: Oxford University Press.

Gordon, Milton M. (1981). "Models of Pluralism: The New American Dilemma," *Annals of the American Academy of Political and Social Science*, 454 (March), 178–188.

Greeley, Andrew M. (1974). *Ethnicity in the United States.* New York: Wiley.

Griffin, John (1987). "Hawaii's Evolving Elements of Political Power," *Honolulu Advertiser*, November 16, A7.

Griffin, John (1994). "Hawaii Easy Days Are Over: All Goals Will Take More Effort," *Honolulu Advertiser*, November 13, B3.

Gulick, Sidney L. (1937). *Mixing the Races in Hawaii: A Study of the Coming Neo-Hawaiian American Race.* Honolulu: Porter.

Haas, Michael (1976). "Neodarwinism in Race Relations: Ethnocide in Hawaii." Paper presented at the Tenth World Congress of the International Political Science Association, Edinburgh, Scotland, August.

Haas, Michael (1977). "Multiracialism in American Local Politics: The Case of Hawaii." Honolulu: Center for Research on Ethnic Relations, Social Science Research Institute, University of Hawai'i at Manoa, *Working Paper* #11 [reprint].

Haas, Michael (1988). "Violent Schools—Unsafe Schools: The Case of Hawaii," *Journal of Conflict Resolution*, 32 (December), 727–58.

Haas, Michael (1989a). *The Asian Way to Peace: A Story of Regional Cooperation.* New York: Praeger.

Haas, Michael (1989b). *The Pacific Way: Regional Cooperation in the South Pacific*. New York: Praeger.

Haas, Michael (1991). "Discoverers' Day, 1555: Gaetano Beat Capt. Cook by More than 2 Centuries," *Star-Bulletin & Advertiser* (Honolulu), June 16, C3.

Haas, Michael (1992). *Institutional Racism: The Case of Hawai'i*. Westport, CT: Praeger.

Haas, Michael (1994). "Hawaiian Ethnic Diversity." In *Encyclopedia of Multiculturalism*, ed. Susan Auerbach, 811–14. New York: Cavendish.

Haas, Michael (1995a). "The Politics of Displacement: The Case of Hawai'i." Paper presented at the annual convention of the Western Political Science Association, Portland, March 18.

Haas, Michael (1995b). "What Shapes Attitudes in Hawai'i? Class, Ethnicity, or . . . ?" Paper presented at the Ethnic Studies Community Conference, Honolulu, May 20.

Haas, Michael, and Peter P. Resurrection, eds. (1976). *Politics and Prejudice in Contemporary Hawaii*. Honolulu: Coventry.

Hall, Jack (1968). "Speech at Western Jurisdictional Conference of the United Methodist Church, Honolulu, July 25, 1968." San Francisco: ILWU International Library and Archives.

Hamasaka, Richard (1993). "Mountains in the Sea: The Emergency of Contemporary Hawaiian Poetry in English." In *Readings in Pacific Literature,* ed. Paul Sharrad, 190–207. Woolongang: University of Woolongang New Literatures Research Center.

Hammes, David L., Ronald A. Oliveira, and Marcia Sakai (1992). "The State Economy." In *Politics and Public Policy in Hawai'i*, eds. Zachary A. Smith and Richard C. Pratt, chap. 2. Albany: State University of New York Press.

Hanford, George H. (1982). *Minority Programs and Activities of the College Board: An Updated Report*. New York: College Entrance Examination Board.

Hannahs, Neil J. (1983). *Native Hawaiian Educational Assessment Project Final Report*. Honolulu: Native Hawaiian Educational Assessment Project.

Hansen, Marcus L. (1937). *The Problem of the Third Generation Immigrants*. Rock Island, IL: Augustana Historical Society.

Hara, Marie (1994). "Some Thoughts on the Nature of Exclusionary Activity." In *Hawai'i Literature Conference Reader's Guide*, ed. Lorna Hershinow, 48–50. Honolulu: Hawai'i Literary Arts Council.

Harada, Wayne (1996). "Hawaii's Changing Face of Radio," *Honolulu Advertiser*, March 17, D1, D10.

Harpham, Anne (1983). "Lucky They Come Hawaii: We Take It to the Bank," *Honolulu Advertiser*, May 14, A1.

Hartwell, Jay (1987). "Sometimes Waves in 'Melting Pot' Swamp the Aloha," *Star Bulletin & Advertiser*, February 15, A1,4.

Hawai'i (1874). *Palapala Hoike aka Peresidena o Ka Papa Hoonaauao.* Honolulu: Board of Education, Kingdom of Hawai'i.

Hawai'i (1878). *Palapala Hoike aka Peresidena o Ka Papa Hoonaauao.* Honolulu: Board of Education, Kingdom of Hawai'i.

Hawai'i (1888). *Biennial Report of the President of the Board of Education.* Honolulu: Board of Education, Kingdom of Hawai'i.

Hawai'i (1890). *Biennial Report of the President of the Board of Education.* Honolulu: Board of Education, Kingdom of Hawai'i.

Hawai'i (1892). *Biennial Report of the President of the Board of Education.* Honolulu: Board of Education, Kingdom of Hawai'i.

Hawai'i (1894). *Biennial Report of the President of the Board of Education.* Honolulu: Board of Education, Republic of Hawai'i.

Hawai'i (1895). *Report of the Labor Commission on Strikes and Arbitration.* Honolulu: Labor Commission, Republic of Hawai'i.

Hawai'i (1896). *Biennial Report of the President of the Board of Education.* Honolulu: Board of Education, Republic of Hawai'i.

Hawai'i (1897). *Biennial Report of the President of the Board of Education.* Honolulu: Board of Education.

Hawai'i (1898). *Biennial Report of the President of the Board of Education.* Honolulu: Board of Education, Republic of Hawai'i.

Hawai'i (1899). *Report of the Minister of Public Instruction.* Honolulu: Department of Public Instruction.

Hawai'i (1900). *Report of the Superintendent of Public Instruction.* Honolulu: Department of Public Instruction, Territory of Hawai'i.

Hawai'i (1901). *Report of the Governor of Hawaii to the Secretary of the Interior.* Honolulu: Governor of Hawai'i, Territory of Hawai'i.

Hawai'i (1902a). *Report of the Governor of Hawaii to the Secretary of the Interior.* Honolulu: Governor of Hawai'i, Territory of Hawai'i.

Hawai'i (1902b). *Report of the Superintendent of Public Instruction.* Honolulu: Department of Public Instruction, Territory of Hawai'i.

Hawai'i (1904). *Report of the Superintendent of Public Instruction.* Honolulu: Department of Public Instruction, Territory of Hawai'i.

Hawai'i (1905). *Report of the Governor of Hawaii to the Secretary of the Interior.* Honolulu: Governor of Hawai'i.

Hawai'i (1906a). *Report of the Governor of Hawaii to the Secretary of the Interior.* Honolulu: Governor of Hawai'i.

Hawai'i (1906b). *Report of the Superintendent of Public Instruction.* Honolulu: Department of Public Instruction, Territory of Hawai'i.

Hawai'i (1907). *Report of the Governor of Hawaii to the Secretary of the Interior.* Honolulu: Governor of Hawai'i.

Hawai'i (1908a). *Report of the Governor of Hawaii to the Secretary of the Interior.* Honolulu: Governor of Hawai'i, Territory of Hawai'i.

Hawai'i (1908b). *Report of the Superintendent of Public Instruction.* Honolulu: Department of Public Instruction, Territory of Hawai'i.

Hawai'i (1909). *Report of the Governor of Hawaii to the Secretary of the Interior.* Honolulu: Governor of Hawai'i.

Hawai'i (1910a). *Report of the Governor of Hawaii to the Secretary of the Interior.* Honolulu: Governor of Hawai'i.

Hawai'i (1910b). *Report of the Superintendent of Public Instruction.* Honolulu: Department of Public Instruction, Territory of Hawai'i.

Hawai'i (1911). *Report of the Governor of Hawaii to the Secretary of the Interior.* Honolulu: Governor of Hawai'i.

Hawai'i (1912a). *Report of the Governor of Hawaii to the Secretary of the Interior.* Honolulu: Governor of Hawai'i, Territory of Hawai'i.

Hawai'i (1912b). *Report of the Superintendent of Public Instruction.* Honolulu: Department of Public Instruction, Territory of Hawai'i.

Hawai'i (1913). *Report of the Governor of Hawaii to the Secretary of the Interior.* Honolulu: Governor of Hawai'i.

Hawai'i (1914a). *Report of the Governor of Hawaii to the Secretary of the Interior.* Honolulu: Governor of Hawai'i.

Hawai'i (1914b). *Report of the Superintendent of Public Instruction.* Honolulu: Department of Public Instruction, Territory of Hawai'i.

Hawai'i (1915). *Report of the Governor of Hawaii to the Secretary of the Interior.* Honolulu: Governor of Hawai'i.

Hawai'i (1916a). *Report of the Governor of Hawaii to the Secretary of the Interior.* Honolulu: Governor of Hawai'i, Territory of Hawai'i.

Hawai'i (1916b). *Report of the Superintendent of Public Instruction.* Honolulu: Department of Public Instruction, Territory of Hawai'i.

Hawai'i (1917). *Report of the Governor of Hawaii to the Secretary of the Interior.* Honolulu: Governor of Hawai'i.

Hawai'i (1918a). *Report of the Governor of Hawaii to the Secretary of the Interior.* Honolulu: Governor of Hawai'i.

Hawai'i (1918b). *Report of the Superintendent of Public Instruction.* Honolulu: Department of Public Instruction, Territory of Hawai'i.

Hawai'i (1919). *Report of the Governor of Hawaii to the Secretary of the Interior.* Honolulu: Governor of Hawai'i.

Hawai'i (1920a). *Report of the Governor of Hawaii to the Secretary of the Interior.* Honolulu: Governor of Hawai'i, Territory of Hawai'i.

Hawai'i (1920b). *Report of the Superintendent of Public Instruction.* Honolulu: Department of Public Instruction, Territory of Hawai'i.

Hawai'i (1921). *Report of the Governor of Hawaii to the Secretary of the Interior.* Honolulu: Governor of Hawai'i.

Hawai'i (1922a). *Report of the Governor of Hawaii to the Secretary of the Interior.* Honolulu: Governor of Hawai'i.

Hawai'i (1922b). *Statistical Tables for the Biennium Ending Dec. 31, 1922.* Honolulu: Department of Public Instruction, Territory of Hawai'i.

Hawai'i (1923). *Report of the Governor of Hawaii to the Secretary of the Interior.* Honolulu: Governor of Hawai'i, Territory of Hawai'i.

Hawai'i (1924a). *Report of the Governor of Hawaii to the Secretary of the Interior.* Honolulu: Governor of Hawai'i, Territory of Hawai'i.

Hawai'i (1924b). *Biennial Report.* Honolulu: Department of Public Instruction, Territory of Hawai'i.

Hawai'i (1925). *Report of the Governor of Hawaii to the Secretary of the Interior.* Honolulu: Governor of Hawai'i, Territory of Hawai'i.

Hawai'i (1926). *Biennial Report.* Honolulu: Department of Public Instruction, Territory of Hawai'i.

Hawai'i (1927). *Report of the Governor of Hawaii to the Secretary of the Interior.* Honolulu: Governor of Hawai'i, Territory of Hawai'i.

Hawai'i (1928a). *Report of the Governor of Hawaii to the Secretary of the Interior.* Honolulu: Governor of Hawai'i, Territory of Hawai'i.

Hawai'i (1928b). *Biennial Report.* Honolulu: Department of Public Instruction, Territory of Hawai'i.

Hawai'i (1929). *Annual Report of the Governor of Hawaii to the Secretary of the Interior.* Honolulu: Governor of Hawai'i, Territory of Hawai'i.

Hawai'i (1931). *Annual Report of the Governor of Hawaii to the Secretary of the Interior.* Honolulu: Governor of Hawai'i, Territory of Hawai'i.

Hawai'i (1932a). *Annual Report of the Governor of Hawaii to the Secretary of the Interior.* Honolulu: Governor of Hawai'i, Territory of Hawai'i.

Hawai'i (1932b). *Biennial Report of the Department of Public Instruction.* Honolulu: Department of Public Instruction, Territory of Hawai'i.

Hawai'i (1933). *Annual Report of the Governor of Hawaii to the Secretary of the Interior.* Honolulu: Governor of Hawai'i, Territory of Hawai'i.

Hawai'i (1934). *Annual Report of the Governor of Hawaii to the Secretary of the Interior.* Honolulu: Governor of Hawai'i, Territory of Hawai'i.

Hawai'i (1940). *Annual Report of the Governor of Hawaii to the Secretary of the Interior.* Honolulu: Governor of Hawai'i, Territory of Hawai'i.

Hawai'i (1953). *Annual Report.* Honolulu: Department of Public Instruction, Territory of Hawai'i.

Hawai'i (1964). *Annual Report: Statistical Supplement.* Honolulu: Department of Health, State of Hawai'i.

Hawai'i (1965). *Annual Report: Statistical Supplement.* Honolulu: Department of Health, State of Hawai'i.

Hawai'i (1966). *Annual Report: Statistical Supplement.* Honolulu: Department of Health, State of Hawai'i.

Hawai'i (1967). *Annual Report: Statistical Supplement.* Honolulu: Department of Health, State of Hawai'i.

Hawai'i (1968). *Annual Report: Statistical Supplement.* Honolulu: Department of Health, State of Hawai'i.

Hawai'i (1969). *Annual Report: Statistical Supplement.* Honolulu: Department of Health, State of Hawai'i.

Hawai'i (1970a). *Data Book: A Statistical Abstract.* Honolulu: Department of Planning and Economic Development, State of Hawai'i.

Hawai'i (1970b). *Statistical Report.* Honolulu: Department of Health, State of Hawai'i.

Hawai'i (1971). *Statistical Report.* Honolulu: Department of Health, State of Hawai'i.

Hawai'i (1972). *Statistical Report.* Honolulu: Department of Health, State of Hawai'i.

Hawai'i (1973). *Statistical Supplement.* Honolulu: Department of Health, State of Hawai'i.

Hawai'i (1974). *Statistical Supplement.* Honolulu: Department of Health, State of Hawai'i.

Hawai'i (1975). *Statistical Supplement.* Honolulu: Department of Health, State of Hawai'i.

Hawai'i (1976). *Statistical Supplement.* Honolulu: Department of Health, State of Hawai'i.

Hawai'i (1977a). *Crime in Hawaii, 1976.* Honolulu: Hawai'i Criminal Justice Statistical Analysis Center, State of Hawai'i.

Hawai'i (1977b). *Data Book: A Statistical Abstract.* Honolulu: Department of Planning and Economic Development, State of Hawai'i.

Hawai'i (1978). *Statistical Supplement.* Honolulu: Department of Health, State of Hawai'i.

Hawai'i (1979). *Data Book: A Statistical Abstract.* Honolulu: Department of Planning and Economic Development, State of Hawai'i.

Hawai'i (1980). *Legislative Report Relating to the Needs of Students with Limited English Speaking Ability in the Public Schools of Hawaii.* Honolulu: Department of Education, State of Hawai'i.

Hawai'i (1981). *Data Book: A Statistical Abstract.* Honolulu: Department of Planning and Economic Development, State of Hawai'i.

Hawai'i (1982). *Final Report: Socio-Economic and Demographic Characteristics of Offender Population.* Honolulu: Departrnent of the Attorney General.

Hawai'i (1983). *Data Book: A Statistical Abstract.* Honolulu: Department of Planning and Economic Development, State of Hawai'i.

Hawai'i (1985). *Data Book: A Statistical Abstract.* Honolulu: Department of Planning and Economic Development, State of Hawai'i.

Hawai'i (1986). *Data Book: A Statistical Abstract.* Honolulu: Department of Planning and Economic Development, State of Hawai'i.

Hawai'i (1987). *Data Book: A Statistical Abstract.* Honolulu: Department of Planning and Economic Development, State of Hawai'i.

Hawai'i (1988). "Task Force Recommendations." Honolulu: Board of Education, Citizen Task Force on Affirmative Action for Filipinos. Honolulu: Center for Research on Ethnic Relations, Social Science Research Institute, University of Hawai'i at Manoa, *Document Series* #9 [reprint].

Hawai'i (1990). *Data Book: A Statistical Abstract.* Honolulu: Department of Business and Economic Development, State of Hawai'i.

Hawai'i (1992). *State of Hawai'i Data Book: A Statistical Abstract.* Honolulu: Department of Business, Economic Development, and Tourism, State of Hawai'i.

Hawai'i (1993–94). *Data Book: A Statistical Abstract.* Honolulu: Department of Business, Economic Hawai'i, State of Hawai'i.

Hawai'i (1994a). *Crime and Justice in Hawai'i*. Honolulu: Department of the Attorney General, State of Hawai'i.

Hawai'i (1994b). *Native Hawaiian Data Book*. Honolulu: Office of Hawaiian Affairs, State of Hawai'i.

Hawai'i (1995). *Crime in Hawaii, 1994*. Honolulu: Department of the Attorney General, State of Hawai'i.

Hawaii Association for Asian and Pacific Peoples (1974). *A Shared Beginning: An Asian and Pacific Perspective of Social Conditions in Hawaii*. Honolulu: Hawaii Association for Asian and Pacific Peoples.

Hawaii Educational Review (1921). "The New Course of Study," *Hawaii Educational Review*, 10 (September), 1–12.

Hawaii Medical Association (1990). *Directory of Hawaii Physicians*. Honolulu: Hawaii Medical Association.

Hawaii State Bar Association (1991). *Annual Directory*. Honolulu: Hawaii State Bar Association.

Hawaiian Sugar Planters' Association, Bureau of Labor and Statistics (1916). *Report of Montague Lord on the Filipino Contract, July 27, 1916*. Ai'ea: HSPA Archives.

Hawaiian Sugar Planters' Association (1926). *Report on Industrial Relations in the Hawaiian Sugar Industry*. Ai'ea: HSPA Archives.

Hayashi, Chikio (1956). "Theory and Examples of Quantification II," *Proceedings of the Institute of Statistical Mathematics*, 4 (2), 10–30.

Herbig, Paul A., and Hugh E. Kramer (1994). "The Potential for High Tech in Hawai'i," *Social Process in Hawai'i*, 35, 56–70.

Hershinow, Lorna, ed. (1994). *Hawai'i Literature Conference Reader's Guide*. Honolulu: Hawai'i Literary Arts Council.

Hippensteele, Susan K., and Meda Chesney-Lind (1995). "Race and Sex Discrimination in the Academy," *Thought & Action*, 11 (Fall), 43–66.

Hirata, Lucie Cheng (1971). *Immigrant Integration in a Polyethnic Society*. Honolulu: Ph.D. dissertation, University of Hawai'i at Manoa.

Hitch, Thomas (1992). *Islands in Transition: The Past, Present, and Future of Hawaii's Economy*. Honolulu: First Hawaiian Bank.

Hiura, Arnold, Stephen Sumida, and Martha Web, eds. (1979). *Talk Story: Big Island Anthology*. Honolulu: Bamboo Ridge Press.

Hofstadter, Richard (1944). *Social Darwinism in American Thought*. Philadelphia: University of Pennsylvania Press.

Holm, John (1986). "Substrate Diffusion." In *Substrata Versus Universals in Creole Genesis*, eds. Pieter Muysken and Norval Smith, 359–78. Amsterdam: Benjamins.

Holt, John Dominis (1964). *On Being Hawaiian.* Honolulu: Star-Bulletin Printing Company.

Honolulu Advertiser (1957). "Segregated Kam?" *Honolulu Advertiser,* December 20, A4.

Honolulu Advertiser (1972). "Race (Not Racism) Is Factor in Politics," *Honolulu Advertiser,* February 15, II10.

Honolulu Advertiser (1974a). "Cultural Deprivation in Schools Debated," *Honolulu Advertiser,* October 30, A8.

Honolulu Advertiser (1974b). "Pro-Ariyoshi Speech Sparks Controversy," *Honolulu Advertiser,* September 21, A3, A12.

Honolulu Advertiser (1976). "Civil Rights Review OKd," *Honolulu Advertiser,* October 22, E7.

Honolulu Advertiser (1986). "Fasi Says Bunye 'Most Qualified' Candidate," *Honolulu Advertiser,* July 24, A5.

Honolulu Advertiser (1994a). "Assessing the Candidates," *Honolulu Advertiser,* November 4, A2.

Honolulu Advertiser (1994b). "How the Electorate Lines up," *Honolulu Advertiser,* November 6, A2.

Honolulu Advertiser (1996). "Union Impasse: Time for Swift Arbitration, 'The State Is out of Money,'" *Honolulu Advertiser,* January 11, A6 [editorial].

Honolulu Advertiser (1997). "Expert Says Pidgin Classes Support Ebonics Effort," *Honolulu Advertiser,* January 5, A1, A4.

Honolulu Star-Bulletin (1954a). "Democratic Party Platform," *Honolulu Star-Bulletin,* May 3, 7.

Honolulu Star-Bulletin (1954b). "7,000 New Citizens Took Oath under McCarran Act; 2nd Anniversary Today," *Honolulu Star-Bulletin,* December 23, A3.

Honolulu Star-Bulletin (1971). "AJAs Had 45% of State Jobs in '64–67," *Honolulu Star-Bulletin,* December 22, A2.

Honolulu Star-Bulletin (1972). *The Men and Women of Hawaii.* Honolulu: Star-Bulletin.

Honolulu Star-Bulletin (1975). "Filipinos Petition for Probe of DOE," *Honolulu Star-Bulletin,* November 19, A1, A6.

Honolulu Star-Bulletin (1978). "Professor Critiques Newspaper's Poll," *Honolulu Star-Bulletin,* November 3, A4.

Honolulu Star-Bulletin (1993). "Where Will the Jobs Be?" *Honolulu Star-Bulletin,* August 13, C1.

Honolulu Weekly (1995). "Official Guide and Map," *Honolulu Weekly,* December 27.

Hopkins, Jerry (1982). *The Hula.* Hong Kong: Apa.

Hormann, Bernhard (1947). "Speech, Prejudice, and the School in Hawaii," *Social Process in Hawaii,* 11, 74–80.

Hrabe, Joseph (1994). *American Ethnicity.* 2nd ed. Itasca, IL: Peacock.

Ikeda, Kiyoshi, and Linda K. Johnsrud (1991). *Preliminary Faculty Pay Equity Analysis, University of Hawai'i at Manoa.* Honolulu: University of Hawai'i at Manoa.

Ikeda, Kiyoshi, and Linda K. Johnsrud (1993). *Faculty Pay Equity Study: Gender and Ethnicity Pay Analysis.* Honolulu: University of Hawai'i at Manoa.

Ikeda, Kiyoshi, Shuk Han Pun, and Lisa Torro (1984). "The Relationship Between Admission Variables and Academic Performance: A First-Year Analysis of First-Time Freshmen Registered in Fall 1983." Honolulu: unpublished manuscript, University of Hawai'i at Manoa.

Infante, Esme J. (1991a). "HPD Urges Anti-Gang Program: Want Police Talks Required in Every School," *Honolulu Advertiser,* August 31, A2.

Infante, Esme (1991b). "Farrington Opens Health Academy: School-Within-a-School Is a First for Hawaii," *Honolulu Advertiser,* September 4, A1, A4.

Infante, Esme (1991c). "Measuring Hawaii's Progress Toward Bush's Education Goals," *Honolulu Advertiser,* October 1, A4.

Inglis, William (1907). "Hawaii's Lesson to Headstrong California," *Harper's Weekly,* 51 (February 16), 226–28.

Innis, Harold (1951). *The Bias of Communication.* Toronto: University of Toronto Press.

Innis, Harold (1972). *Empire and Communications.* Toronto: University of Toronto Press.

International Longshoremen's Association (1912). "Annual Meeting, Pacific District," *ILA Proceedings,* May.

International Longshoremen's and Warehousemen's Union (1965). *Proceedings, 7th Biennial Convention.* Honolulu: ILWU.

Isaacs, Harold R. (1975). *Idols of the Tribe: Group Identity and Political Change.* New York: Harper & Row.

Jankowski, Gene F., and David C. Fuchs (1995). *Television Today and Tomorrow: It Won't Be Like You Think.* New York: Oxford University Press.

Jarman, Robert (1838). *Journal of a Voyage to the South Seas, in the "Japan" Employed in the Sperm Whale Fishery, under the Command of Capt. John May.* London: Longman.

J.N. (1873). *"Pehea la e Hiki ai ia Kakou e Kamailio Pololei i Ka 'Olelo Hawai'i,"* Nupepa Ku'oko'a, December 6, 7.

Jacobs, Paul, and Saul Landau (1971). *To Serve the Devil: A Documentary Analysis of America's Racial History and Why It Has Been Kept Hidden;* vol. II: *Colonials and Sojourners.* New York: Vintage.

Johannessen, Edward (1956). *The Hawaiian Labor Movement: A Brief History.* Boston: Humphries.

Johnson, Donald D., and Michael F. Miller (1986). *Hawaii's Own: A History of the Hawaii Government Employees Association.* Honolulu: Hawaii Government Employees Association.

Johnsrud, Linda K., and Christine D. Atwater (1991). *Barriers to Retention and Tenure at UH-Manoa: The Experiences of Faculty Cohorts, 1982–1988.* Honolulu: University of Hawai'i at Manoa.

Johnsrud, Linda K., and Christine D. Des Jarlais (1994). "Barriers for Women and Minorities," *Review of Higher Education,* 17 (4), 335–53.

Johnsrud, Linda K., and Kathleen C. Sadao (1993). "Ethnic and Racial Minority Faculty Within a Research University: Their Common Experiences." Paper presented at the annual convention of the Association for the Study of Higher Education, New Orleans, November.

Jokiel, Lucy (1988). "The New Big Five?" *Hawaii Business,* 33 (January), 19–26.

Jones, Larry (1967). "Negroes Here & Discrimination," *Star-Bulletin & Advertiser,* June 11, B2.

Junasa, Bienvenido D. (1982). *A Study of the Relationship Between Selected Variables and Levels of Academic Performance Among Filipino Full-Time Freshmen Students.* Ft. Lauderdale, FL: Ph.D. dissertation, Nova University.

Kajimura, Noboru (1988). *Nihonjin no shinkô.* Tokyo: Iwanami shinsho.

Kakesako, Gregg K. (1974). "No Place for Racism, Fasi Says," *Honolulu Star-Bulletin,* August 20, A1, A4.

Kakesako, Gregg K. (1977). "Ariyoshi: Limit Population," *Honolulu Star-Bulletin,* January 25, A1, A4.

Kallen, Horace (1915). "Democracy Versus the Melting Pot," *The Nation,* 100 (February 18, 25), 190–94, 217–22.

Kallen, Horace (1924). *Culture and Democracy in the United States.* New York: Liveright.

Kamakau, Samuel (1976). *The Works of the People of Old.* Honolulu: Bishop Museum Special Publication # 61.

Kanahele, George S., ed. (1979). *Hawaiian Music and Musicians: An Illustrated History*. Honolulu: University Press of Hawai'i.

Kappeler, Victor E., et al. (1994). *Forces of Deviance: Understanding the Dark Side of Policing*. Prospect Heights, IL: Waveland.

Kaser, Tom (1975a). "Classes in Japanese on Decline," *Honolulu Advertiser*, April 28, A3.

Kaser, Tom (1975b). "U.S. Probing Charges of Hiring Bias in Schools," *Honolulu Advertiser*, October 23, A9.

Kaser, Tom (1990). "UH Will Seek Funds to Add Women, Minority Faculty," *Honolulu Advertiser*, October 6, D6.

Kawaharada, Dennis (1994). "Towards an Authentic Local Literature of Hawai'i." In *Hawai'i Literature Conference Reader's Guide*, ed. Lorna Hershinow, 56–60. Honolulu: Hawai'i Literary Arts Council.

Keir, Gerry (1974a). "In Demo Primary For Governor: It's Still a Tight, Three-Way Race," *Star-Bulletin & Advertiser*, September 29, A1, A4.

Keir, Gerry (1974b). "State Race Doesn't Look Close," *Honolulu Advertiser*, October 29, A1, A4.

Keir, Gerry (1974c). "A Tight Race for Governor," *Honolulu Advertiser*, September 3, A1, A3.

Keir, Gerry (1978a). "Fasi, Ariyoshi in Dead Heat, First Primary Survey Reveals," *Honolulu Advertiser*, August 25, A1, A17.

Keir, Gerry (1978b). "Fasi Surge into Strong Lead; Impact of Kohala Uncertain," *Honolulu Advertiser*, September 30, A1, A4.

Keir, Gerry (1982a). "Ariyoshi Has Sizable Lead; Anderson Gains over Fasi," *Honolulu Advertiser*, October 28, A1, A4.

Keir, Gerry (1982b). "Ariyoshi Maintains Wide Lead over King," *Honolulu Advertiser*, September 12, A1, A3-A4.

Keir, Gerry (1986a). "Cec Heftel Way Ahead in Democratic Governor's Race," *Honolulu Advertiser*, August 4, A1, A3.

Keir, Gerry (1986b). "Governor's Race a Toss-up with 20% Still Undecided," *Honolulu Advertiser*, October 28, A1, A4.

Keller, Mike (1978). "Judges' Decisions Free of Race Bias," *Honolulu Advertiser*, September 13, A3.

Kelly, Marion (1956). *Changes in Land Tenure in Hawai'i, 1778–1850*. Honolulu: M.A. thesis, University of Hawaii.

Kent, Noel J. (1983). *Hawaii: Islands Under the Influence*. New York: Monthly Review Press.

Kent, Noel J. (1994). "The End of the American Age of Abundance: Whither Hawai'i?" *Social Process in Hawaii*, 35, 179–94.

Kent, Noel J. (1996). "Economic, Political and Moral Bankruptcy in Hawai'i: The End of a 'Unique' Experiment in Multiculturalism." Paper presented at the annual convention of the Association for Asian American Studies, Northwest Region, Honolulu, March.

Kerkvliet, Melinda Tria (1991). "Pablo Manlapit's Fight for Justice," *Social Process in Hawaii*, 33, 153–68.

Key, V. O. (1949). *Southern Politics in State and Nation.* New York: Knopf.

Keyes, Charles F., ed. (1981). *Ethnic Change.* Seattle: University of Washington Press.

KHET-TV (1991). *Blackout Baby.* Honolulu: KHET-TV [televised performance].

Kim, Karl (1994). "The Political Economy of Foreign Investment in Hawai'i," *Social Process in Hawaii*, 35, 40–55.

Kimura, Larry L. (1985). "Language." In *Native Hawaiian Study Commission Report: Report on the Culture, Needs and Concerns of Native Hawaiians*, vol. 1. Washington, DC: Government Printing Office.

Kingston, Maxine Hong (1976). *The Woman Warrior: Memoirs of a Girlhood Among Ghosts.* New York: Knopf.

Kirch, Patrick Vinton (1985). *Feathered Gods and Fishhooks: An Introduction to Hawaiian Archaeology and Prehistory.* Honolulu: University of Hawai'i Press.

Knowlton, Edgar (1991). "Sailor Juan Gaetano Was Probably Spanish," *Honolulu Star-Bulletin*, July 29, A14 [letter].

Kobayashi, Ken (1993). "Fired Kauai Police Officer Harry J. Victorino Wins Bias Case: Awarded $80,700," *Honolulu Advertiser*, September 23, A1.

Krauss, Bob (1992). "Our Honolulu," *Star-Bulletin & Advertiser* (Honolulu), February 16, A3.

Kresnak, William (1988). "Isle Politics Is Inextricably Linked with Ethnicity, Forum Panel Concludes," *Honolulu Advertiser*, September 30, B3.

Kresnak, William (1990). "Political Parties Wooing Islands' Filipino Vote," *Star-Bulletin & Advertiser*, September 30, A3.

Kresnak, William (1994). "Lewin Factor Enlivens Race for Governor," *Honolulu Advertiser,* September 11, A4.

Kresnak, William, and Ann Botticelli (1995). "Gov. Makes First Budget Cuts: Two-Year Plan Has More Trims to Come," *Honolulu Advertiser*, February 7, A1-A2.

Kuroda, Yasumasa (1993). "Sociology of Paradise: Hawaii Today and Tomorrow," *Kansai University Review of Law and Politics*, 14 (March), 1–19.

Kuroda, Yasumasa, and Chikio Hayashi (1995). "Rashomonesque Yamazakura." Paper presented at the Conference on Japanese Identity: Cultural Analysis, Teikyô Loretto Heights University, Denver.

Kuroda, Yasumasa, and Tatsuzô Suzuki (1991). "A Comparative Analysis of Arab Culture: Arabic, English and Japanese Languages and Values," *Behaviormetrika*, 30 (1), 35–53.

Kuykendall, Ralph S. (1938). *The Hawaiian Kingdom, 1778–1854*. Honolulu: University of Hawai'i Press.

Kuykendall, Ralph S. (1967). *The Hawaiian Kingdom: The Kalakaua Dynasty*. Honolulu: University of Hawai'i Press.

Lal, Brij, Doug Munro, and Edward Beechert, eds. (1993). *Plantation Workers: Resistance and Accommodation*. Honolulu: University of Hawai'i Press.

Laudan, Lawrence, et al. (1990). "Racism Does Not Belong Here," *Ka Leo O Hawai*, October 26, 4.

Lebart, Ludovic, Alain Morineau, and Kenneth M. Worwick (1984). *Multivariate Descriptive Statistical Analysis*. New York: Wiley.

Levinson, David (1994). *Ethnic Relations: A Cross-Cultural Experience*. Santa Barbara, CA: ABC-CLIO.

Ligot, Cayetano (1926). "Report of the Director of Labor to His Excellency the Governor-General of the Philippine Islands," *Bulletin of the Bureau of Labor*, 7 (March), 1–65.

Lijphart, Arend (1984). *Democracies: Patterns of Majoritarianism and Consensus Government in Twenty-One Countries*. New Haven, CT: Yale University Press.

Lili'uokalani, Lydia (1898). *Hawaii's Story by Hawaii's Queen*. Tokyo: Tuttle, 1964 [reprint].

Lind, Andrew W. (1938). *An Island Community: Ecological Succession in Hawaii*. Chicago: University of Chicago Press.

Lind, Andrew W. (1946). *Hawaii's Japanese: An Experiment in Democracy*. Princeton, NJ: Princeton University Press.

Lind, Andrew W. (1957). "Racial Bloc Voting in Hawaii," *Social Process in Hawaii*, 21, 16–19.

Lind, Andrew W. (1967). *Hawaii's People*. 3rd ed. Honolulu: University of Hawai'i Press.

Lind, Andrew W. (1980). *Hawaii's People*. 4th ed. Honolulu: University of Hawai'i Press.

Lind, Andrew W. (1982). "Immigration to Hawaii," *Social Process in Hawaii*, 29, 9–20.

Lum, Darrell H. Y. (1986a). "Beer Can Hat." In *The Best of Bamboo Ridge: The Hawai'i Writers' Quarterly*, eds. Eric Chock and Darrell H. Y. Lum, 175–83. Honolulu: Bamboo Ridge Press.

Lum, Darrell H. Y. (1986b). "Local Literature and Lunch." In *The Best of Bamboo Ridge: The Hawai'i Writers' Quarterly*, eds. Eric Chock and Darrell H. Y. Lum, 3–5. Honolulu: Bamboo Ridge Press.

Lum, Darrell H. Y. (1986c). "Primo Doesn't Take Back Bottles Anymore." In *The Best of Bamboo Ridge: The Hawai'i Writers' Quarterly*, eds. Eric Chock and Darrell H. Y. Lum, 184–88. Honolulu: Bamboo Ridge Press.

Lum, Darrell H. Y. (1986d). "Paint." In *The Best of Bamboo Ridge: The Hawai'i Writers' Quarterly*, eds. Eric Chock and Darrell H. Y. Lum, 189–94. Honolulu: Bamboo Ridge Press.

Lum, Darrell H. Y. (1994). "Asian American Conference Talk." Paper presented to the annual convention of the Association for Asian American Studies, Ann Arbor, April 7.

Lum, Wing Tek (1986). "Chinese Hot Pot." In *The Best of Bamboo Ridge: The Hawai'i Writers' Quarterly*, eds. Eric Chock and Darrell H. Y. Lum, 63. Honolulu: Bamboo Ridge Press.

Lynch, Russ (1996). "Isle Economy Weakest in Nation," *Honolulu Star-Bulletin*, March 12, D1.

MacDonald, Alexander (1944). *Revolt in Paradise*. New York: Daye.

Maharidge, Dale (1996). *The Coming White Minority: California and America's Immigration Debate*. New York: Random House.

Maier, John (1975). "Yucky-You-Live-Hawaii?" *Impulse* (Summer), 28–29.

Manlapit, Pablo (1933). *Filipinos Fight for Justice; Case of the Filipino Laborers in the Big Strike of 1924, Territory of Hawaii*. Honolulu: Kumalai.

Marable, Manning (1986). *W. E. B. Du Bois: Black Radical Democrat*. Boston: Twayne.

Martin, Lynn J., ed. (1994). *Musics of Hawai'i; "It All Comes from the Heart": An Anthology of Musical Traditions in Hawai'i*. Honolulu: State Foundation on Culture and the Arts.

Martorana, S.V., and Ernest V. Hollis (1962). *The University of Hawaii and Higher Education in Hawaii*. Honolulu: Department of Budget and Finance, State of Hawai'i.

Marumoto, Masaji (1983). "The Ala Moana Case and the Massie-Fortescue Case, Revisited," *University of Hawaii Law Review*, 5 (Winter), 271–87.

Matsunaga, Mark (1987). "Some AJAs Fear a Dimmer Future," *Honolulu Advertiser*, February 16, A1, A4.

Mau, Rosalind Y. (1986). *Sources of Alienation in the Secondary School Setting of Hawaii*. Honolulu: Ph.D. dissertation, University of Hawai'i at Manoa.

Mayberry, John (1979). "Hawaii's Ethnic Media: Adjusting to Changing Community Needs," *Honolulu*, 13 (June), 118–24.

McGregor, Davianna P. (1991). "Providing Redress for *Ka Po'e Hawai'i*: The Hawaiian People." Paper presented at the Spark M. Matsunaga Institute for Peace conference on Restructuring for Peace: Challenges for the 21st Century, Honolulu, June 3.

McLaughlin, Sean (1989). "Cable TV Is Hawaii's Channel to the Future," *Honolulu Star-Bulletin*, February 16, A23.

McLuhan, Marshall (1962). *The Gutenberg Galaxy: The Making of Typographic Man*. Toronto: University of Toronto Press.

McLuhan, Marshall (1964). *Understanding Media: The Extensions of Man*. New York: New American Library.

McNicol, Donald (1974). *Radio's Conquest of Space*. New York: Arno Press.

Melahn, Christopher Lee (1986). *An Application of an Ecological Perspective to the Study of Educational Achievement Among Native American Hawaiians*. Honolulu: Ph.D. dissertation, University of Hawai'i at Manoa.

Meller, Norman (1955). *Hawaii: A Study of Centralization*. Chicago: Ph.D. dissertation, University of Chicago.

Meller, Norman (1958a). "Centralization in Hawaii: Retrospect and Prospect," *American Political Science Review*, 57 (March), 98–107.

Meller, Norman (1958b). "Missionaries to Hawaii: Shapers of the Islands' Government," *Western Political Quarterly*, 11 (December), 788–99.

Meller, Norman (1961/62). "Recent Changes in Composition of Hawaiian Legislatures," *Social Process in Hawaii*, 25, 45–52.

Meredith, Gerald (1965). "Observations on the Acculturation of Sansei Japanese-Americans in Hawaii," *Psychologia*, 8 (June), 41–49.

Michener, James A. (1959). *Hawaii*. New York: Random House.

Midkiff, Frank E. (1935). *The Economic Determinants of Education in Hawaii*. New Haven, CT: Ph.D. dissertation, Yale University.

Miller, Sally M. (1987). *The Ethnic Press in the United States: A Historical Analysis and Handbook*. New York: Greenwood.

Minerbi, Luciano (1994). "Sustainability Versus Growth in Hawai'i," *Social Process in Hawai'i*, 35, 145–61.

Missionary Herald. (1841). "Afflictive Dispensations of Providence," *Missionary Herald*, 37 (April), 149–50.

Moore, Richard A. (1969). *Lanai Management and Development Study.* Honolulu: Richard Moore Associates.

Morgan, Theodore (1948). *Hawaii: A Century of Economic Change, 1778–1876.* Cambridge, MA: Harvard University Press.

Morita, Stirling (1986a). "Isle Voters Cast Ballots Along Cultural Lines," *Honolulu Star-Bulletin*, October 7, A10.

Morita, Stirling (1986b). "Ethnic Factor Plays Role in Isle Voting, but Effect on Election Is Hard to Gauge," *Honolulu Star-Bulletin*, October 6, A1, A3.

Morita, Stirling (1986c). "Young Local Japanese Vote Same Way Their Elders Do," *Honolulu Star-Bulletin*, October 7, A1, A10.

Morris, Aldyth (1955). *Captain James Cook.* Honolulu: University of Hawai'i Press.

Morris, Aldyth (1980). *Damien.* Honolulu: University Press of Hawai'i.

Morton, N.E., W.T. Stout, and C. Fischer (1976). "Academic Performance in Hawaii," *Social Biology*, 23 (Spring), 13–20.

Murayama, Milton (1975). *All I Asking for Is My Body.* San Francisco: Supa Press.

National Center for Higher Education Management Systems (1991). *University of Hawaii System Longitudinal Database Project.* Boulder, CO: NCHEMS.

National Institute of Education (1978). *Violent Schools—Safe Schools: The Safe School Study Report to the Congress.* Washington, DC: Government Printing Office, 3 vols.

Nelligan, Peter J., and Harry V. Ball (1992). "Ethnic Juries in Hawaii: 1865–1900," *Social Process in Hawaii*, 34, 113–62.

Nemo (1888). "Island Notes," *Pacific Commercial Advertiser*, January 16, 2.

New York Times (1971). "Alaskans Accept Land Claims Bill: Nixon Signs Settlement and Calls It a 'Milestone,'" *New York Times*, December 20, 9.

Newman, Katharine (1979). "Hawaiian-American Literature: The Cultivation of Mangoes," *Melus*, 6 (Summer), 44–47.

Newman, William M. (1973). *American Pluralism: A Study of Minority Groups and Social Theory.* New York: Harper & Row.

Newport, Tuck (1991). "What Makes It Tick? The Management of Punahou." In *Punahou: The History and Promise of a School of the Islands*, ed. Nelson Foster, 151–67. Honolulu: Punahou.

Nicol, Donald (1974). *Radio's Conquest of Space.* New York: Arno Press.

Nordyke, Eleanor C. (1989). *Peopling of Hawai'i.* 2nd ed. Honolulu: University of Hawai'i Press.

Novak, Michael (1971). *The Rise of the Unmeltable Ethnics: Politics and Culture in the Seventies.* New York: Macmillan.

O'ahu Filipino Community Council (1975). "Task Force on Education Status Report." Honolulu: Center for Research on Ethnic Relations, University of Hawai'i at Manoa, *Document Series* #9 [reprint].

Odo, Franklin, and Susan Yim (1993). "Ethnicity: Are Race Relations in Hawai'i Getting Better or Worse?" In *The Price of Paradise*, ed. Randall W. Roth, chap. 31. Honolulu: Mutual Publishing.

Ogawa, Dennis M., and Evarts C. Fox, Jr. (1986). "Japanese Internment and Relocation: The Hawaii Experience." In *Japanese Americans: From Relocation to Redress*, eds. Roger Daniels, Sandra C. Taylor, and Harry H. L. Kitano, 135–38. Salt Lake City: University of Utah Press.

Okamura, Jonathan Y. (1982). "Ethnicity and Ethnic Relations in Hawai'i." In *Ethnicity and Interpersonal Interaction: A Cross-Cultural Study*, ed. David H. Wu, 213–35. Singapore: Maruzen.

Okamura, Jonathan Y. (1990). "Ethnicity and Ethnic Relations in Hawai'i," *Operation Manong Resource Papers.* Honolulu: Operation Manong Program, University of Hawai'i at Manoa.

Okamura, Jonathan (1991). "Filipino Educational Status and Achievement at the University of Hawai'i at Manoa," *Social Process in Hawaii*, 33, 107–29.

Okamura, Jonathan (1992). "Filipino Cultural Norms and Values and Higher Education," *Teaching & Learning*, 5 (Spring), 6–8.

Okamura, Jonathan Y. (1994). "Why There Are No Asian Americans in Hawai'i: The Continuing Significance of Local Identity," *Social Process in Hawai'i*, 35, 161–78.

Okamura, Jonathan (1996a). "The Jangling Discourse of Race Relations in Hawai'i." Paper presented at the annual convention of the Association for Asian American Studies, Northwest Region, Honolulu, March.

Okamura, Jonathan (1996b). "Some Have Been Left out," *Honolulu Advertiser*, May 19, B1.

Okamura, Jonathan Y. (in press). "The Illusion of Paradise: Privileging Multiculturalism in Hawai'i." In *Making Majorities: Composing the Nation in Japan, China, Korea, Fiji, Malaysia, Turkey, and the United States*, ed. Dru C. Gladney. Palo Alto, CA: Stanford University Press.

Ola'a Sugar Company manager (1925). "Memo to HSPA, C. Brewer & Co., Hawaiian Agriculture Co.," *HSPA Memos*, January 25. Honolulu, Hamilton Library, University of Hawai'i at Manoa [microfilm].

Oleson, William B. (1886). "The Resultant Language," *The Friend*, 44 (April), 10.

Olzak, Susan (1992). *The Dynamics of Ethnic Competition and Conflict*. Stanford, CA: Stanford University Press.

Omandam, Pat (1994). "Pacific Island Broadcasters Hone Their Skills in Hawaii," *Honolulu Star-Bulletin*, December 27, A3.

Omi, Michael, and Howard Winant (1986). *Racial Formation in the United States: From the 1960s to the 1980s*. New York: Routledge & Kegan Paul.

Ong, Vickie (1980). "State's Educators 'Just Want the Feds off Our Back,'" *Honolulu Advertiser*, November 29, A3.

Oshiro, Sandra (1976). "Filipinos Stand up to Be Counted," *Honolulu Advertiser*, November 1, A3, A10.

Otaguro, Janice (1997). "Islanders of the Year: Alana Dung—and 30,000 Others," *Honolulu*, 31 (January), 34–37ff.

Pacific Commercial Advertiser (1860). "Editorial," *Pacific Commercial Advertiser*, May 3, 2.

Pacific Commercial Advertiser (1911a). "Japanese as Public School Teachers," *Pacific Commercial Advertiser*, January 4, 4 [editorial].

Pacific Commercial Advertiser (1911b). "Japanese on Teaching Staff: Lightfoot Announces He Will Not Stand for 'Outrage'—Will Inform Keefe," *Pacific Commercial Advertiser*, January 4, 1.

Pacific Commercial Advertiser (1919). "Territory Should Control Foreign Language Schools," *Pacific Commercial Advertiser*, March 17, 4.

Pai, Gregory (1986). "The Evolution of the Hawaiian Economy and Its Relationship to the Social and Economic Status of Women in Hawaii." Paper presented to the Honolulu County Committee on the Status of Women, Honolulu.

Pai, Gregory (1989). "Foreign Investment in Hawaii: An Assessment of Future Prospects." Paper presented to the Honolulu Japanese Chamber of Commerce.

Park, Robert Ezra (1928). "The Bases of Racial Prejudice," *Annals of the American Academy of Political and Social Science*, 140 (November), 11–20.

Parsons, Talcott (1969). *Politics and Social Structure*. New York: Free Press.

Peery, Nelson (1993). *Entering an Epoch of Social Revolution*. Chicago: Workers Press.

Pennybacker, Mindy (1991). "The 'Haole Rich Kids' School': An Update." In *Punahou: The History and Promise of a School of the Islands*, ed. Nelson Foster, 119–49. Honolulu: Punahou.

Polynesian, The (1854). "The English Language," *The Polynesian*, 10 (April 15), 2.

Port, Richard J. (1979). "The Relationship Between the Achievement of Students on the Hawaii State Test of Essential Competencies and Specific Student Background and School Related Variables." Honolulu: unpublished manuscript, Department of Education, State of Hawai'i.

Portes, Alejandro, and Robert D. Manning (1986). "The Immigrant Enclave: Theory and Empirical Examples." In *Competitive Ethnic Relations*, eds. Susan Olzak and Joane Nagel, 47–68. Orlando, FL: Academic Press.

Porteus, Stanley D., and Marjorie E. Babcock (1926). *Temperament and Race*. Boston: Badger.

Postman, Neil (1985). *Amusing Ourselves to Death: Public Discourse in the Age of Show Business*. New York: Viking.

Reich, Robert B. (1991). *Work of Nations: Preparing Ourselves for 21st Century Capitalism*. New York: Knopf.

Reilly, Rick (1996). "Heaven Help Marge Schott," *Sports Illustrated*, 84 (May 20), 72–87.

Reinecke, John E. (1935). *Language and Dialect in Hawaii*. Honolulu: M.A. thesis, University of Hawai'i.

Reinecke, John E. (1969). *Language and Dialect in Hawaii*. Honolulu: University of Hawai'i Press.

Reinecke, John E. (1970). A *History of Local 5: Hotel and Restaurant Employees and Bartenders International Union, AFL-CIO, Honolulu*. Honolulu: Industrial Relations Center, University of Hawai'i at Manoa.

Reinecke, John E. (1979). *Feigned Necessity: Hawaii's Attempt to Obtain Chinese Contract Labor, 1921–1923*. San Francisco: Chinese Materials Center.

Reinecke, John E. (1997). *The Tragic Filipino Piecemeal Strike of 1920*. Honolulu: Social Science Research Institute, University of Hawai'i at Manoa.

Research Committee on the Study of Honolulu Residents (1986). *The Third Attitudinal Survey of Honolulu Residents, 1983*. Tokyo: Institute of Statistical Mathematics, Monograph #3 [distributed by the University Press of Hawai'i].

Research Information Services (1977). *ESAA Needs Assessment Study*. Honolulu: Research Information Services.

Reyes, Donna (1987). "Switch to English May Mean Talking Pidgin," *Honolulu Advertiser*, September 28, A1, A4.

Rifkin, Jeremy (1995). *The End of Work: The Decline of the Global Labor Force and the Dawn of the Post-Market Era.* New York: Putnam.

Roberts, Helen H. (1926). *Ancient Hawaiian Music.* New York: Dover, reprinted 1967.

Roberts, Julian M. (1995a). "Pidgin Hawaiian: A Sociohistorical Study," *Journal of Pidgin and Creole Languages,* 10 (1), 1–56.

Roberts, Julian M. (1995b). "A Structural Sketch of Pidgin Hawaiian," *Amsterdam Creole Studies,* 12 (1), 97–126.

Roberts, Julian M. (1997). "The Role of Diffusion in Creole Genesis," *Language,* 72 (in press).

Roosevelt, Theodore (n.d.). "Assimilation." In *American Mix: The Minority Experience in America,* eds. Morris Freedman and Carolyn Banks, 444–49. Philadelphia: Lippincott [reprint].

Rosegg, Peter (1994a). "The—sssshhh!—Ethnic Vote Factor," *Honolulu Advertiser,* September 11, A1, A4.

Rosegg, Peter (1994b). ". . . Because Diversity Overwhelms Ethnic Ties," *Honolulu Advertiser,* October 23, B1, B4.

Ryan, William (1976). *Blaming the Victim.* New York: Vintage.

Sahlins, Marshall D. (1958). *Social Stratification in Polynesia.* Seattle: University of Washington Press.

Saiki, Pat (1994a). "A Pacific Partnership." Honolulu: Saiki for Governor Committee.

Saiki, Pat (1994b). "Pat Saiki Plan for Reform in Hawai'i." Honolulu: Saiki for Governor Committee.

Sananikone, Thanlo (1991). *Project Degree: Report on the Cambodian, Laotian, Vietnamese Students in Hawaii.* Honolulu: Office of Minority Student Affairs & Office of the Chancellor for Community Colleges, University of Hawai'i.

Savard, W.G., and C.T. Araki (1965). *The Relationship of Socioeconomic Background to Student Achievement in the Public High Schools of the State of Hawaii.* Honolulu: Department of Education, State of Hawai'i.

Saxton, Alexander (1971). *The Indispensable Enemy.* Berkeley: University of California Press.

Schlesinger, Arthur M., Jr. (1991). *The Disuniting of America: Reflections on a Multicultural Society.* New York: Norton.

Schmitt, Robert C. (1961). "Characteristics of Voters and Non-Voters in Hawaii." Honolulu: Romanzo Adams Social Research Laboratory, University of Hawai'i, *Report* #31.

Schmitt, Robert C. (1977). *Historical Statistics of Hawaii*. Honolulu: University Press of Hawai'i.

Schmitt, Robert C. (1978). "Some Firsts in Island Leisure," *Hawaiian Journal of History*, 12, 99–107.

Settle, Irving (1983). A *Pictorial History of Television*. 2nd ed. New York: Ungar.

Shaw, R. Paul, and Yuwa Wong (1989). *Genetic Seeds of Warfare: Evolution, Nationalism, and Patriotism*. Boston: Unwin Hyman.

Sherman, Ruth G. (1984). "An Ecological Survey of the College Student Experiences, UHM." Honolulu: unpublished manuscript, University of Hawai'i at Manoa.

Shoemaker, James H. (1946). "Hawaii Emerges from the War," *Pacific Affairs*, 19 (June), 182–92.

Sibley, Gay (1988). "Conversations with a Nesomaniac: An Interview with A. Grove Day," *Literary Arts Hawai'i*, 88/89 (Spring and Summer), 22–26.

Simonson, Douglas (1981). *Pidgin to Da Max*. Honolulu: Peppovision.

Sing, David K. (1986). *Raising the Achievement Level of Native Hawaiians in the College Classroom Through the Matching of Teaching Strategies with Student Characteristics*. Claremont, CA: Ph.D. dissertation, Claremont Graduate School.

Smith, Kit (1995). "Index Shows Hawaii's Economy on Upswing," *Honolulu Advertiser*, April 19, C1.

Smith, Michael G. (1975). "Race and Stratification in the Caribbean." In M.G. Smith (ed.), *Corporations and Society,* 271–345. Chicago: Aldine.

Smyser, A.A. (1992). "Immersion May Fail a Careful Examination," *Honolulu Star-Bulletin*, March 24, A10.

Spear, Rev. William (1856). "The Chinese in the Sandwich Islands," *The Friend*, 13 (August 19), 58–59.

Spohn, Cassia, et al. (1981–82). "The Effect of Race on Sentencing: A Reexamination of an Unsettled Question," *Law and Society Review,* 16, 71–88

Stannard, David E. (1992). *American Holocaust: Columbus and the Conquest of the New World*. New York: Oxford University Press.

Stannard, David E. (1989). *Before the Horror: The Population of Hawai'i on the Eve of Western Contact*. Honolulu: Social Science Research Institute, University of Hawai'i at Manoa.

Star-Bulletin & Advertiser (1991). "OHA: A Primer," *Star-Bulletin & Advertiser* (Honolulu), May 12, B3.

Steinberg, Danny D., Ronald Johnson, and Robert S. Cahill (1975). "Testimony on Renaming of Porteus Hall—Before the Board of Regents on April 23, 1975." Honolulu: Center for Research on Ethnic Relations, Social Science Research Institute, University of Hawai'i at Manoa, *Document Series* #5 [reprint].

Stern, Bernard (1986). *Labor Relations in the Honolulu Transit Industry.* Honolulu: Center for Labor Education and Research, University of Hawai'i at Manoa.

Stern, Bernard (1988). *The Aloha Trade: Labor Relations in Hawaii's Hotel Industry, 1941–1987.* Honolulu: Center for Labor Education and Research, University of Hawai'i at Manoa.

Stevens, Sylvester K. (1945). *American Expansion in Hawaii, 1842–1898.* Harrisburg: Archives Publishing Company of Pennsylvania.

Stueber, Ralph (1964). *Hawaii: A Case Study in Development Education, 1778–1960.* Madison: Ph.D. dissertation, University of Wisconsin.

Sue, Newton (1991). *Review of Equal Employment Opportunity and Affirmative Action at the University of Hawaii.* Honolulu: Legislative Auditor.

Sullam, Brian (1976). *Bishop Estate: The Misused Trust.* Honolulu: Hawai'i Observer.

Sumida, Stephen (1986). "Waiting for the Big Fish: Recent Research in the Asian American Literature of Hawaii." In *The Best of Bamboo Ridge: The Hawai'i Writers' Quarterly*, eds. Eric Chock and Darrell H. Y. Lum, 302–21. Honolulu: Bamboo Ridge Press.

Sumida, Stephen (1991). *And the View from the Shore: Literary Traditions of Hawaii.* Seattle: University of Washington Press.

Takara, Kathryn (1992). *Opele: Report on African Americans at the University of Hawai'i.* Honolulu: Center for Studies of Multicultural Higher Education, University of Hawai'i at Manoa.

Takeuchi, Floyd K. (1986a). "Bunye Charges Job Discrimination in State Government's Hiring Ratio," *Honolulu Advertiser*, August 6, A3.

Takeuchi, Floyd K. (1986b). "Bunye Remark Denounced by Cayetano," *Honolulu Advertiser*, August 7, A3.

Tanahara, Kris M. (1993). "KIKI Radio Station's Manager Made Racist Remarks, OHA Said," *Honolulu Advertiser*, June 15, A3.

Tangonan, Shannon (1991). "A Century of History Is Tied up in Ewa Church," *Honolulu Advertiser*, September 23, A3.

Tatar, Elizabeth (1993). *Hula Pahu, Hawaiian Drum Dances*, vol. 2: *The Pahu-Sounds of Power.* Honolulu: Bishop Museum Press.

Taylor, Charles (1992). *Multiculturalism and the Politics of Recognition.* Princeton, NJ: Princeton University Press.

Taylor, William (1935). *The Hawaiian Sugar Industry.* Berkeley: Ph.D. dissertation, University of California.

Territorial Surveys (1950). "A Political Analysis, 1950." Honolulu: mimeo, Hamilton Library, University of Hawai'i at Manoa.

Thompson, Edgar (1975). *Plantation Societies, Race Relations and the South: The Regimentation of Populations.* Durham, NC: Duke University Press.

Thrum, Thos G. (1893). *Hawaiian Almanac and Annual for 1892.* Honolulu: Press Publishing Company.

Tilly, Charles (1978). *From Mobilization to Revolution.* Reading, MA: Addison-Wesley.

Tinker, Hugh (1974). *A New System of Slavery: The Export of Indian Labour Overseas, 1830–1920.* Oxford: Oxford University Press.

Trask, Haunani-Kay (1990). "Caucasians Are Haoles," *Ka Leo O Hawai'i,* September 19, 5.

Trask, Haunani-Kay (1992). "Racism Against Native Hawaiians at the University of Hawaii: A Personal and Political View," *Amerasia Journal,* 18 (3), 33–50.

Trimillos, Ricardo (1987). *Na Mele Paniolo: The Songs of Hawaiian Cowboys.* Honolulu: State Foundation on Culture and the Arts [booklet and two cassette tapes].

Tsai, Stephen (1992). "UH Lauded for Handling Concerns of Black Athletes," *Honolulu Advertiser,* January 18, C1.

Tsuzaki, Stanley (1971). "Problems in the Study of Hawaiian English." In *Pidginization and Creolization of Languages,* ed. Dell Hymes, 279. Cambridge, England: Cambridge University Press.

United States, Bureau of Education (1920). *A Survey of Education* in *Hawaii.* Washington: Bureau of Education.

United States, Bureau of the Census (1902). *Twelfth Census of the United States: 1900; Population.* Washington, DC: Government Printing Office.

United States, Bureau of the Census (1913). *Thirteenth Census of the United States, Taken in the Year 1910: Abstract of the Census with Supplement for Hawaii.* Washington, DC: Government Printing Office.

United States, Bureau of the Census (1922). *Fourteenth Census of the United States, Taken in the Year 1920;* vol 3., *Population: Occupations.* Washington, DC: Government Printing Office.

United States, Bureau of the Census (1923). *Fourteenth Census of the United States, Taken in the Year 1920;* vol. 4, *Population: Occupations.* Washington, DC: Government Printing Office.

United States, Bureau of the Census (1932). *Fifteenth Census of the United States, Taken in the Year 1930; Population: Outlying Territories and Possessions.* Washington, DC: Government Printing Office.

United States, Bureau of the Census (1942*). 16th Census of the United States, 1940; Manufactures, 1939.* Washington, DC: Government Printing Office.

United States, Bureau of the Census (1943). *16th Census of the United States, 1940; Census of Business, 1939: Alaska, Hawaii and Puerto Rico.* Washington, DC: Government Printing Office.

United States, Bureau of the Census (1952). *United States Census of Population; Detailed Characteristics: Hawaii.* Washington, DC: Government Printing Office.

United States, Bureau of the Census (1962). *Census of Population, 1960; Characteristics of the Population: Hawaii.* Washington, DC: Government Printing Office.

United States, Bureau of the Census (1972). *1970 Census of Population; Detailed Characteristics: Hawaii.* Washington, DC: Government Printing Office.

United States, Bureau of the Census (1972b). *1970 Census of Populahon; Detailed Characteristics: Hawaii.* Washington: Bureau of the Census.

United States, Bureau of the Census (1973). *1970 Census of Population; Subject Reports: Japanese, Chinese, and Filipinos in the United States.* Washington, DC: Government Printing Office.

United States, Bureau of the Census (1983). *1980 Census of Population: Characteristics of the Population; General Social and Economic Characteristics: Hawaii.* Washington, DC: Government Printing Office.

United States, Bureau of the Census (1993). *1990 Census of Population: Social and Economic Characteristics, Hawaii.* Washington, DC: Government Printing Office.

United States, Bureau of Education (1920). *A Survey of Education in Hawaii.* Washington: Bureau of Education.

United States, Commission on Civil Rights, Hawai'i Advisory Committee (1980). *Breach of Trust? Native Hawaiian Homelands.* Washington, DC: Government Printing Office.

United States, Commission on Civil Rights, Hawai'i Advisory Committee (1983). *Policy vs. Results: Affirmative Action in the Hawaii Department of Education.* Washington, DC: Government Printing Office.

United States, Commission on Civil Rights, Hawai'i Advisory Committee (1991). A *Broken Trust: The Hawaiian Homelands Program; Seventy Years of Failure of the Federal and State Governments to Protect the Civil Rights of Native Hawaiians.* Washington, DC: Government Printing Office.

United States, Congress (1946). *Statehood for Hawaii.* Washington, DC: Subcommittee on the Territories, House of Representatives.

United States, Congress (1983). *Native Hawaiians Study Commission: Report on the Culture, Needs and Concerns of Native Hawaiians.* Washington, DC: Government Printing Office.

United States, Congress (1993). *Kahoolawe Island: Restoring a Cultural Treasure; Final Report.* Washington, DC: Government Printing Office.

United States, Department of the Interior, Bureau of Education (1920). *A Survey of Education in Hawaii.* Washington, DC: Government Printing Office.

United States, Department of Labor (1948). *The Economy of Hawaii in 1947.* Washington, DC: Government Printing Office [*Bulletin #926*].

University of Hawai'i (1985). *1985 Survey of Hawai'i's Newsrooms.* Honolulu: Department of Journalism, University of Hawai'i at Manoa.

University of Hawai'i (1986a). *Ka'u: University of Hawai'i Hawaiian Studies Task Force Report.* Honolulu: Hawaiian Studies Task Force, University of Hawai'i.

University of Hawai'i (1986b). *A Study to Improve Access to Public Higher Education Programs and Support Services for Minority Students: Report to the 1987 Legislature.* Honolulu: University of Hawai'i.

University of Hawai'i (1988). *Pamantasan: Report of the University of Hawai'i Task Force on Filipinos.* Honolulu: Task Force on Filipinos, University of Hawai'i.

University of Hawai'i (c.1995). *Hawaiian Studies Program Guide.* Honolulu: Center for Hawaiian Studies, University of Hawai'i at Manoa.

Van Den Berghe, Pierre (1967). *Race and Racism: A Comparative Perspective.* New York: Wiley.

Van Den Berghe, Pierre (1975). *Man in Society: A Biosocial View.* New York: Elsevier.

Van Zile, Judy, and William Feltz (1992). *Asian Dance in Hawai'i.* Honolulu: East-West Center and Department of Theatre and Dance, University of Hawai'i at Manoa.

Verploegen, Hildegaard (1974). "Students Will Discuss Violence," *Honolulu Star-Bulletin*, October 12, A1.

Verploegen, Hildegaard (1976). "2.5 Million DOE Fund in Jeopardy," *Honolulu Star-Bulletin*, June 25, A2.

Verploegen, Hildegaard (1986). "Low Scores of Hawaiians, Part-Hawaiians Analyzed," *Honolulu Star-Bulletin*, August 27, A3.

Verploegen, Hildegaard (1988). "Critical Study No Surprise to Toguchi: A Survey Pinpointed Some Old Problems," *Honolulu Star-Bulletin*, December 21, A3.

Verploegen, Hildegaard (1989a). "Study: Muscle Needed in Curbing School Violence; A Task Force Says Very Little Has Been Done in 13 Years to Correct the Problems," *Honolulu Star-Bulletin*, September 8, A3.

Verploegen, Hildegaard (1989b). "10 Schools on Waianae Coast to Get Extra Aid: Toguchi Says the Troubled Schools Should Get an Extra $4.2 Million," *Honolulu Star-Bulletin*, May 19, A1, A8.

Viotti, Vicki (1989). "ACLU Asked to Sue State over Quality of Education Offered on Waianae Coast," *Honolulu Advertiser*, February 15, A4.

Wakukawa, Ernest K. (1938). A *History of the Japanese People in Hawaii*. Honolulu: Toyo Shoin.

Wegner, Eldon L. (1976). "A Comparison of School Climates and Student Outcomes in Four Public High Schools in Hawaii." Honolulu: unpublished report to the Hawai'i Department of Education.

Wegner, Eldon L. (1977). "Misinterpreting the Policy Implications of Social Science Research and Suggestions for a New Direction: The Case of School Effects," paper presented at the annual convention of the Society for the Study of Social Problems, Chicago, August.

Wegner, Eldon L. (1978). "A New Look at Research on School Environments," *integratededucation*, 16 (March-April), 36–39.

Wegner, Eldon Lowell, Gary Kazuo Sakihara, and David Takeo Takeuchi (1976). *The Social Climates of Public High Schools in Hawaii: An Exploration of the Needs and Dissatisfactions of High School Seniors*. Honolulu: Legislative Reference Bureau.

Wendt, Albert (1977). "Towards a New Oceania." Paper presented to the International Colloquium on the Cross-Cultural Encounter in Literature, Honolulu.

Werner, Emmy E., Jessie M. Bierman, and Fern E. French (1971). *The Children of Kauai*. Honolulu: University Press of Hawai'i.

Werner, Emmy E., and Ruth S. Smith (1977). *Kauai's Children Come of Age*. Honolulu: University Press of Hawai'i.

Western Association of Schools and Colleges (1991). *Visiting Team Report*. Oakland, CA: Western Association of Schools and Colleges.

Wilcox, Leslie (1974a). "Fuchs Fears Two-Class System: 'Nightmare' Would Heighten Tensions," *Honolulu Star-Bulletin*, August 8, A15.

Wilcox, Leslie (1974b). "Mink Says DOE Lost Millions," *Honolulu Star-Bulletin*, April 9, D20.

Wiles, Greg, and Esme Infante (1994). "One Shot as Gangs Clash," *Honolulu Advertiser*, October 14, A1.

Willis, Arnold L. (1955). *Labor-Management Relations in Hawaii*. Honolulu: Industrial Relations Center, University of Hawai'i.

Wist, Benjamin O. (1940). *A Century of Public Education in Hawaii*. Honolulu: Hawai'i Educational Review.

Witeck, John (1995). "Working Poor in Hawai'i: The Myth of Hawai'i's Anti-Business Climate and Largesse to Workers." Paper presented to the Ethnic Studies Community Conference, Honolulu, May 20–21.

Wolfinger, Raymond E. (1965). "The Development and Persistence of Ethnic Voting," *American Political Science Review,* 59, December, 896–908.

Wong, Norma (1975). "The Educated Hawaiian." Honolulu: Center for Research on Ethnic Relations, Social Science Research Institute, University of Hawai'i at Manoa, *Working Paper* #4 [reprint].

Woo, Douglas (1976). "School Bias Review Sought," *Honolulu Advertiser*, October 21, A3.

Wright, Theon (1966). *Rape in Paradise*. New York: Hawthorn.

Wright, Theon (1972). *The Disenchanted Isles: The Story of the Second Revolution in Hawaii*. New York: Dial.

Wyllie, Robert (1848). *Answers to Questions Proposed by His Excellency, R.C. Wyllie, His Hawaiian Majesty's Minister of Foreign Relations, and Addressed to All the Missionaries in the Hawaiian Islands, May 1846*. Honolulu: Kingdom of Hawai'i [filed with *Annual Reports*].

Wyllie, Robert (1858). "Mr. Wyllie's Address," *The Polynesian*, 15 (November 13), 1, 4.

Yamanaka, Lois-Ann (1993). *Saturday Night at the Pahala Theater*. Honolulu: Bamboo Ridge Press.

Yamanaka, Lois-Ann (1996). *Wild Meat and the Bully Burgers*. New York: Farrar Straus Giroux.

Yaple, Peter, and Felipe Korzenny (1989). "Electronic Media Effects Across Cultures." In *Handbook of International and Intercultural Communication*, eds. Molefi Kete Asanti and William B. Gudykynst, 195–317. Newbury Park, CA: Sage.

Yoneyama, John, and Susan Hooper (1990). "The Japaning of Hawaii," *Hawaii Business*, 35 (January), 14–16, 19–20.

Young, Crawford (1993). "The Dialectics of Cultural Pluralism: Concept and Reality." In *The Rising Tide of Cultural Pluralism: The Nation-State at Bay?*, ed. Crawford Young, chap. 1. Madison: University of Wisconsin Press.

Yount, David (1996). *Who Runs the University? The Politics of Higher Education in Hawaii, 1985–1992.* Honolulu: University of Hawai'i Press.

Yuen, Mike (1993). "Poll: Saiki Favorite in Governor's Race," *Honolulu Star-Bulletin*, November 4, A1, A8.

Yuen, Mike (1994a). "Candidates Must Court the Ethnic Vote," *Honolulu Star-Bulletin*, June 6, A3.

Yuen, Mike (1994b). "Saiki's Ahead; Cayetano, Fasi Tangled Second," *Honolulu Star-Bulletin*, A1, A6.

Yuen, Mike (1994c). "Poll: Cayetano Edges by Saiki, Fasi Is Far Back,"*Honolulu Star-Bulletin*, A1, A8.

Zangwill, Israel (1914). *The Melting Pot: Drama in Four Acts.* New York: Macmillan.

About the Contributors

Ibrahim G. Aoudé, (Ph.D., University of Hawai'i, 1984), a native of Lebanon, chairs the Department of Ethnic Studies at the University of Hawai'i at Manoa. He is the author of *The Battle of Lebanon: A Study of Revolutionary Development* (1980) and *The Political Economy of Hawai'i, 1980–1994; The State of Research: 1994*. The latter appears as *Working Paper* #5 in the *Working Paper Series* of the Center for Research on Ethnic Relations, Social Science Research Institute, University of Hawai'i at Manoa.

Edward D. Beechert (Ph.D., University of California at Berkeley, 1957) is Professor Emeritus of History, University of Hawai'i at Manoa. A labor historian, he has written extensively on organized labor, particularly in the Pacific, and his publications include *Honolulu: Crossroads of the Pacific* (1991) and *Working in Hawai'i: A Labor History* (1985).

Derek Bickerton (Ph.D., Cambridge University, 1976) is Professor Emeritus of Linguistics, University of Hawai'i at Manoa. A specialist in language evolution, pidgins, and creoles, his recent publications include *Language and Species* (1990) and *Language and Human Behavior* (1995).

A. Didrick Castberg (Ph.D., Northwestern University, 1968) is professor of political science, University of Hawai'i at Hilo. He is the author of *The Ethnic Factor in Criminal Sentencing* (1966), *Cases on Constitutional Law* (1973), and *Japanese Criminal Justice* (1990).

Helen Geracimos Chapin (Ph.D., Ohio State University) is vice president and dean of Hawai'i Pacific University. She is the author of *Shaping History: The Role of the Newspapers in Hawai'i* (1996), which analyzes the ethnic and Native Hawaiian newspapers as well as the English language press of Hawai'i.

Michael Haas (Ph.D., Stanford, 1964) is professor of political science and co-director of the Center for Research on Ethnic Relations, Social Science Research Institute, University of Hawai'i at Manoa. His most recent publications are *Institutional Racism: The Case of Hawai'i* (1992) and *Improving Human Rights* (1994).

Yasumasa Kuroda (Ph.D., University of Oregon, 1962) is professor of political science and co-director of the Center for Research on Ethnic Relations, Social Science Research Institute, University of Hawai'i at Manoa. He has written extensively on the comparative politics and international relations of Japan and the Middle East. Among his publications are *Palestinians Without Palestine* (1978), *Political Socialization in the Arab States* (1987), and *Japan in a New World Order* (1994). He has coauthored four monographs and several articles on attitudes of Honolulu voters based on a longitudinal sample survey conducted every five years from 1971.

Rodney Morales is an assistant professor in the Department of English, University of Hawai'i at Manoa. He is the editor of *Ho'i Ho'i Hou: A Tribute to George Helm and Kimo Mitchell* (1984), and the author of a collection of short stories entitled *The Speed of Darkness* (1988).

Jonathan Okamura (Ph.D., University of London, 1982) is assistant specialist, Center for Student Equity, Excellence, and Diversity, University of Hawai'i at Manoa. A sociologist, he is the author of *Immigrant Filipino Ethnicity in Honolulu, Hawai'i* (1982), *Ethnographic Research* (1985), and *Participatory Approaches to Development: Experiences in the Philippines* (1986).

Anthony J. Palmer (Ph.D., University of California at Los Angeles, 1975) is associate professor of music, University of Hawai'i at Manoa. He specializes in music education and is the author of *World Musics in Elementary and Secondary Music Education* (1975).

Index

Cayetano, Benjamin, 50–51, 154,
157, 160, 250, 280–83
Cazimero brothers, 92
Center for Hawaiian Studies, 241
Center for Research on Ethnic
Relations, 238–39
Center for Studies of Multicultural
Higher Education, 238, 241
Central Labor Council, 175, 179
Chaminade College, 229
Chaminade University, 229–30
Chang, Ernie, 97
Chief's Children's School, 206
Children, the development of a
universal language by, 58–59
Chillingsworth, Sonny, 91
Chinen, Joyce, 185, 187
Chinese
adjudication of, 262–64
arrests of, 258–61
as college administrators, 242
as college professors, 244–50
in craft unions, 175–76
in the criminal justice system,
255–57
educational attainments, 198–200
higher education for, 230–33
income levels, 196–97
as laborers, 28, 29, 168–69
music, 102–3
newspapers, 73
occupational status, 188–96
performance at University of
Hawaii (Manoa), 239–40
political party preference of, 149
population statistics, 25, 36–38
private school enrollment, 210
public school enrollment, 216
as teachers, 212

as victims of crime, 257–58
as voters, 148
in youth gangs, 255
Chinese Communication
Broadcasting Co., 79
Chinese Exclusion Act (1886), 34,
170
"Chinese Hot Pot" (W.T. Lum), 113
Chock, Eric, 111, 117, 123
*Chung Hua Hsin Pao (United
Chinese Press),* 73
Church College of Hawaii, 230
Citizens' Task Force on Affirmative
Action for Filipinos, 224
Civil Rights Act (1867), 35
Civil Rights Act (1964), Title VI,
217, 221, 233
Clark, Charles, 221, 222
Cleveland, Grover, 31, 170
Cleveland, Harlan, 237, 246
Clinton, Bill, 49, 271
Cohen, Walter, 277
Coleman, Lee, 77–78
College of Agriculture and Mechanic
Arts, 229
College of Hawaii, 229
College Opportunities Program
(COP), 233, 241
Colleges
formation of, 229–30
See also Education, higher;
under name of
Colonialism, model of ethnic
diversity, 9
Committee of Safety, 31
Community colleges, 229
Congress of the Hawaiian People
(1971), 48–49
Contois, David, 237